DIVIDED
HIGHWAYS

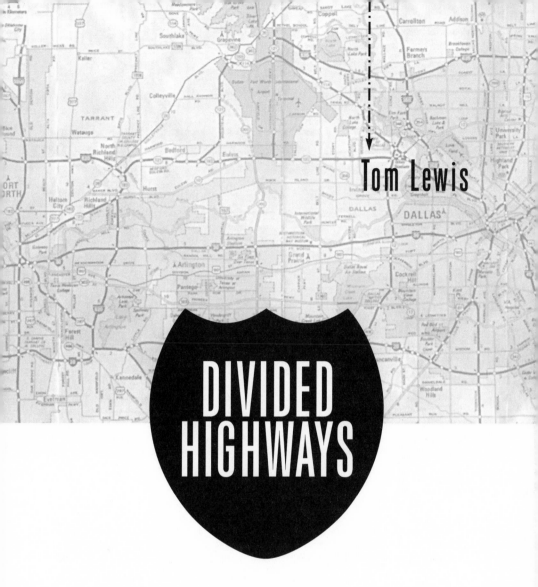

Tom Lewis

DIVIDED HIGHWAYS

Building the Interstate Highways,
Transforming American Life

VIKING

VIKING

Published by the Penguin Group

Penguin Putnam Inc., 375 Hudson Street, New York, New York 10014, U.S.A.

Penguin Books Ltd, 27 Wrights Lane, London W8 5TZ, England

Penguin Books Australia Ltd, Ringwood, Victoria, Australia

Penguin Books Canada Ltd, 10 Alcorn Avenue, Toronto, Ontario, Canada M4V 3B2

Penguin Books (N.Z.) Ltd, 182–190 Wairau Road, Auckland 10, New Zealand

Penguin Books Ltd, Registered Offices:
Harmondsworth, Middlesex, England

First published in 1997 by Viking Penguin,
a member of Penguin Putnam Inc.

10   9   8   7   6   5   4   3   2   1

Grateful acknowledgment is made for permission to reprint the following copyrighted works:
    "Song of the Open Road" from *Verses From 1929 On* by Ogden Nash.
Copyright 1932 by Ogden Nash. First appeared in *The New Yorker*. By permission of Little, Brown and Company.
    Excerpt from "Desert" by Barbara M. Smith. By permission of the author.

The following images are reproduced by permission of the American Association of State Highway and Transportation Officials (AASHTO): insert, page one (below): photo by Thomas J. Mcdonald; page 125: from *American Highways*, January 1957, Copyright 1957 by the American Association of State Highway and Transportation Officials, Washington, D.C.; and page 211: from *American Highways*, March 1970, Copyright 1970 by the American Association of State Highway and Transportation Officials, Washington, D.C.

LIBRARY OF CONGRESS CATALOGING IN PUBLICATION DATA
Lewis, Tom, date.
    Divided highways : building the interstate highways, transforming American life / Tom Lewis.
        p.   cm.
    Includes bibliographical references and index.
    ISBN 0-670-86627-X
    1. Roads—Social aspects—United States—History.   2. Transportation. Automotive—
Social aspects—United States—History.   I. Title.
HE355.L484   1997
388.1'22'0973—dc21   97-17452

This book is printed on acid-free paper.
∞

Printed in the United States of America
Set in Perpetua
Designed by Pei Koay

Contents

Preface: A Space Filled with Moving

◄━ ▪━ ▪━ ▪━ ▪━ ▪━ ▪━ ▪━ ▪━ ▪━ ▪━ ▪━ ▪━

Think of anything, of cowboys, of movies, of detective stories, of anybody who goes anywhere or stays at home and is an American and you will realize that it is something strictly American to conceive a space that is filled with moving, a space of time that is filled always filled with moving.

GERTRUDE STEIN

This is the story of the creation and consequences of the greatest and the longest engineered structure ever built, the Interstate Highway System. Imagine the state of Connecticut knee deep in earth; that's how much was moved for the Interstates. Or a wide sidewalk extending from the earth to a point in space five times beyond the distance to the moon; that's how much concrete was poured for the Interstates. Or a land mass the size of the state of Delaware; that's how much property highway authorities acquired in order to site the Interstates. Or enough drainage culverts to handle all the needs of a city six times the size of Chicago; that's how much was laid beneath the Interstates. The Great Wall of China and the Interstate Highway System are among the only human creations that can be seen by astronauts from an orbiting spacecraft.

But statistics are the least interesting chapter in the story. The highways became a stage on which we have played out a great drama of contradictions that accounts for so much of the history of this century. On this stage we see all our fantasies and fears, our social ideals and racial divisions, our middle-class aspirations and underclass realities.

The system connects American cities and people in a vast web of roads that carry the life of the nation; yet to build it, tens of thousands of Americans were dispossessed of their land and saw their homes and neighborhoods destroyed. It gave Americans almost complete mobility and yet endless congestion. It ranks as the greatest public works project in the history of the nation, though its plan was set in motion by a Republican president who disliked the excessive authority of big government. It was first conceived of by highway planners in the thirties when Americans considered the automobile one of the blessings of the modern age; in the eighties, when it was nearly complete, many considered the automobile a blight. It made many people wealthy, dispossessed others and left them in poverty. In 1956, when the U.S. Congress enacted the legislation to create it, politicians and writers celebrated the goal of "man's triumph over nature"; by 1991, when the last section of Interstate 90 was opened, connecting Boston to Seattle with a three-thousand-mile strip of concrete, some regarded that "triumph" as a tragedy. It enabled us to speed across the land into vast stretches of wilderness; yet it distanced us from the very land we sought. It added new words to our vocabulary, like "beltway" and "drive time," and it lent new meaning to old ones like "smog" and "pollution," "ecology" and "environment," "traffic jam" and "pileup."

While the Interstate Highway System was envisioned and designed by white men, its impact has been felt by everyone. Most people in the 1950s and early 1960s regarded the highways as a technological and social triumph. The roads afforded those who once had to live in a city and walk to work at a factory the chance to have a home in the relative safety, privacy, quiet, and cleanliness of the suburban countryside. Beginning in the mid-sixties, however, many people began to blame the highways for a new spate of problems in American society. Often, city neighborhoods were chopped up and destroyed, downtown centers abandoned for the easy-access malls that sprang up at exit ramps. The Interstate made long-distance commuting possible, thereby contributing to the "white flight" that separated races and classes from each other. More often than not, urban planners laid down the roadways in the neighborhoods of African-Americans, Hispanics, and other minorities, people who did not possess the political power to challenge them. In the ensuing years, planners and residents alike found that new highways had the power to divide rather than unite us, and that they could transform a once vibrant neighborhood into a cold, alien landscape.

The small towns not on the main thoroughfares have dwindled, some have disappeared completely. The highway engineers chose time and again to put the roadways hard upon the banks of the country's rivers, severing city dwellers from the waterways that had once been the most significant natural features in their landscape.

For the most part we take the Interstates for granted. Most books about the 1950s or the Eisenhower presidency devote but a few sentences—if that—to one of the most significant pieces of legislation of this century. Yet we depend upon these Interstates daily, as roadways, of course, but also as a mainstay of American commerce and middle-class life. These are the highways that bring grapes to Maine in the middle of winter, and relief workers to Florida in the aftermath of a hurricane. They allow many of us to live where we want and to go where we wish. For all of their virtues and despite their faults, the Interstates bind us together.

Some of the new roads meant an end to a familiar past: Route 30, known to many as the Lincoln Highway, and Route 40, the National Road, merged in many places with Interstate 80; while much of old Route 66, the road from Chicago to Los Angeles, made famous by John Steinbeck in *The Grapes of Wrath,* and more recently by a popular song, would now be succeeded by a new road, Interstate 40. The Interstates would bypass hundreds of small towns with names like Hackberry, Arizona; Deeth, Nevada; Walker, Kansas; and New Russia, New York, and turn them into ghostly derelicts.

The new roads meant unparalleled windfalls for thousands of civil engineers. In the first four years of the Interstate program the Colorado highway budget jumped from $15 million to $60 million. For many years Kansas added twenty engineers to its department annually. In Mississippi, where many of the roads were gravel, clay, and dirt, which became a thick mud every spring that the locals called "gumbo," the highway department had to learn the ways of constructing multilane, limited-access roads, something the state had never known. Yet few among those who planned the new highways realized that in addition to reordering our landscape, they were reordering our lives.

It took forty years—not thirteen as specified by the legislation President Eisenhower signed in 1956—to build the Interstate Highway System. In that period the Soviet Union launched the first artificial satellite and humans walked on the moon; the federal government extended civil rights to all Americans and a civil rights leader who held the Nobel Prize for peace was slain; one president was assassinated and another resigned in disgrace; two new states, Alaska and Hawaii, entered the Union; the population of the nation rose from 165 million to 250 million; the United States fought in two wars and university students took to the streets to protest another; scientists virtually eliminated polio, while a new disease, Aquired Immune Deficiency Syndrome, began; and the number of professional baseball teams increased from sixteen to twenty-six, most playing in new ballparks accessible only by car and Interstate.

This is also the story of the American desire for freedom and movement, our desire to resolve our destiny in our vast landscape. Sometimes exploring and migrating, always roaming and circulating, we have shaped

Preface

our lives by moving across and about three time zones, twenty-five degrees of latitude, and forty-five degrees of longitude. Always prizing freedom of movement, we have realized it by taking new jobs in distant places, moving to new houses and apartments, and driving hundreds of millions of miles each year in automobiles. Moving. Always moving.

Like citizens of other civilizations, we profess to cherish stability—or at least an *illusion* of stability—while relentlessly celebrating our mobility. Our nineteenth-century heroes sang of the open road or piloted a fugitive raft down the Mississippi; our twentieth-century anti-heros celebrate being "on the road" or acting out a Bonnie and Clyde outlaw fantasy across the broad landscape. "Tonight the night's bustin open," sang Bruce Springsteen, "these two lanes will take us anywhere."

Refugees, failures, religious zealots, wanderers, colonizers, criminals on the lam, visionaries, romantic idealists: America's European fore-bears came to invent and reinvent themselves in unfamiliar spaces. Eight decades after they formed a union, they took care to manumit those whom they had brought in chains and, in limited ways, granted the newly emancipated the freedom to go forth and invent themselves also.

Contrast this with the sense of time and space of native Americans. Above all it was *land,* not property, theirs to inhabit, not to own, and never to conquer. The transplanted newcomers labeled such people "savages," inhabiting a savage land. Painters went west and sent back portraits of the new land, a wilderness that must be overcome and exploited. Even if they did not wish it, the natives would be moved— and oftentimes moved again. In the minds of many, movement and civilization became one. "How beautiful to think of lean tough Yankee settlers," Thomas Carlyle in London wrote to Ralph Waldo Emerson in Boston in 1848, "tough as guttapercha, with a most occult unsubduable fire in their belly, steering over the Western mountains to annihilate the jungle, and bring bacon and corn out of it for the Posterity of Adam."

Across the landscape of the continent, Americans have left the imprint of their movement: paths, roads, turnpikes, and canals in the eighteenth century; railroad tracks in the nineteenth; and an ever increasing number of wide roads and streamlined highways in the twentieth. These signa-tures of civilization spell out America's notions of progress and above all speed. The conventional wisdom that automobiles changed America in the twentieth century is true only because of the extraordinary road system that the nation developed to carry them. But the notion of auto-mobiles without roads is rather like having computers without software.

Preface

Without high-speed roads automobiles would never be able to fulfill our desire to conquer the vast spaces of our landscape. The Interstates concretely testify to the ultimate expression of our desire.

Ironically, while the Interstates have done much to diminish distance and travel time, they have also increased both. Most of us take about a half hour to get to our jobs each day—that time hasn't changed much over the decades—but we now live farther from where we work than ever before. The communities we live in have changed, too. Few of us know a place we consider to be the center of town, because there is no center. Instead, convenience stores, post offices, and banks, each accessible only by automobile, cluster at the exits of our Interstates, or line the service roads like so many beads on a string. We drive faster and cover more of the landscape but have the disturbing thought that we are seeing and feeling less of what we pass. Few of us consider walking anywhere, as the great, wide roads obstruct our path.

Today, forty years after the great building program began, we can see how it has changed our landscape and our lives. If you go west across America on Interstate 40 from Wilmington, North Carolina, you will pass through the tobacco country of Greensboro and Winston-Salem; the Great Smoky Mountains; the city of Nashville, home to country music; Memphis, the city of W. C. Handy and Elvis; fireworks shacks in Arkansas; oil derricks in Oklahoma, the remnants of old Route 66; the parched, dusty towns of the Texas Panhandle; the Continental Divide in New Mexico; the banded purple, scarlet, and pink tints of the Painted Desert in Arizona; and the desolate, desert blur of California before reaching the end of the road at Barstow. Along the way there will be ghostly signs to places like Clinch River, Crab Orchard, and Bon Aqua; Palestine, Beulah, and Lonoke; Canute, Clinton, and Elk City. And you will pass thirty-six KOA campgrounds and thirty-seven Holiday Inns; forty-six Burger Kings and eighty-two McDonald's—a Whopper or Big Mac for every thirty-one miles of Interstate.

Although many deplore what the Interstate Highway System has done to the nation, few would desire, or could even imagine, an America without it. When the Century Freeway—one of the last significant sections of the Interstate Highway System—opened in Los Angeles in October 1993, the governor of California spoke to a very different group than Eisenhower might have imagined. Those who came to celebrate—native Americans, blacks, Latinos, and Asians among them—heard the governor tell them it was their freeway to use and enjoy. A black minister prayed for the structure that "links us and binds us together." As it has always been, our highways hold the promise of connection.

In building the Interstate Highway System, we displayed ourselves in all our glory and our meanness; all our vision and our shortsightedness. We showed democracy's virtues and not a few of its vices. The highways represent the height of American technological achievement; but no one, not the engineers, the planners, the builders, not even the naysayers—those who opposed the highways—understood how the roads would ripple through the culture.

What follows is a story of the land itself—and our desires to control it; how we committed our treasure to support those desires; how we achieved great engineering feats; and how at times we fell because of great engineering hubris. Finally, this is a story of consequences, how for better and worse the Interstates have changed our lives.

In the Interstate Highway System we have done nothing less than express our vision of ourselves. In the fifties we thought there was nothing beyond us. We could do everything and we could do it to excess. The fins on our cars couldn't be too high, the chrome on our bumpers couldn't be too great, and the fewer miles we got to the gallon the better. In the sixties we began to have second thoughts about what the roads were doing to our society, especially the ways in which they could divide our neighborhoods and destroy vital parts of our older cities. In the seventies, about the time we experienced gasoline shortages, we wondered what harm the highways and the automobiles and trucks that rode upon them were causing to our environment. Some began to ask if we weren't slaves to our automobiles and our highways. In the eighties, we seemed almost embarrassed at times by the presence of the Interstates and were angry about the ways they had changed the way we live. Today, as we head toward the millennium, we debate the place of the automobile and the highway in our future; we ask just what the vision of ourselves should be.

Ultimately, the Interstates have become a physical expression of the part of the American character that desires to resolve our destiny in this seemingly limitless land. "From this hour I ordain myself loos'd of limits and imaginary lines," Walt Whitman wrote in his "Song of the Open Road." The Interstate Highway System allows us to be—or at least gives us the illusion that we can be—our own masters, as Whitman said, "total and absolute," to "inhale great draughts of space." And as we do so, we are moving. Always moving.

PART 1

THE CHIEF

The Lord put roads for travelling: why He laid them down flat on the earth. When he aims for something to be always a-moving, He makes it long ways, like a road or a horse or a Wagon, but when He aims for something to stay put, He makes it up-and-down ways, like a tree or a man.

WILLIAM FAULKNER

The National Road in the Allegheny Mountains west of Cumberland, Maryland, on a spring day in the early 1920s. Leo J. Beachy, a self-taught photographer crippled by multiple sclerosis, has been transported to the site on Negro Mountain by his sister. She has helped him to set up his camera and record scenes of the road and its travelers. Beachy flags down a touring car as it crests the hill. The seven passengers—two families, perhaps—get out, stretch, and pose. The women are dressed in coats and hats, which help to keep off the dust. The men appear to take a proprietary interest in the car. One leans his left foot on the running board, cocking his right arm on his hip, while the other rests his hand on the roof support. The shutter opens and closes; in an instant a glass plate preserves the moment.

More than merely capturing a party of travelers, perhaps on a Sunday outing through the Alleghenies, Beachy's camera has recorded a moment in America's landscape and culture. The automobile is shiny, with just a few traces of mud at the tips of the fenders. Its split windshield is

Tom Lewis

open slightly to let in the breeze. There is no danger that any sharp rocks on the road will cause the solid rubber tires to go flat.

Beachy seems to have been as interested in the road as he was in those who traveled upon it. The photographer preferred to call the National Road the "ocean to ocean highway," and he visited it often. At this point on Negro Mountain, the road seems to stretch into an endless series of hills and dips beyond. Its surface is compacted stone that at the shoulders has broken into mud. The grades of the roadway are short and steep, enough to tax a team and a wagon or an early automobile. Telephone and electric poles encroach from the sides, and the very woods themselves seem to threaten safe passage. Nevertheless, the road points the way through the wilderness and represents a first step in taming it. In time, as the speed and traffic of automobiles increase, work crews will widen it and level some of the hills and dips.

By the 1920s, parties like this one were a common sight. Their dress tells us that they are neither migrants nor settlers, but are traveling for the pleasure of making an afternoon social call, or just to see the countryside—as much as they could through the dense woods—or for the pure enjoyment of moving. There were nearly eight million automobiles across the United States in 1920, about one for every four families. They had access to about 369,000 miles of roads, most with surfaces in worse condition than the National Road. More than a horse and wagon or a railroad car of the nineteenth century, the road and the automobile best suited what Alexis de Tocqueville called the "restless temper" of Americans. "O to realize space!" Walt Whitman wrote in the nineteenth century. Roads and cars were enabling Americans of the twentieth century to realize the full import of Whitman's thought: "The plenteousness of all—that there are no bounds."

The growth of the automobile brought another important change to the National Road. In 1926, it officially became part of U.S. Route 40, a federally supported road and major east-west thoroughfare. The route began at Atlantic City in New Jersey and crossed the Atlantic states of Delaware, Maryland, and Pennsylvania; touched the tip of West Virginia at Wheeling; passed into the midwestern states of Ohio, Indiana, Illinois, Missouri, and Kansas; and traversed the western states of Colorado, Utah, and Nevada before stopping at the corner of Harrison and Tenth streets in downtown San Francisco, California. The change of the National Road into a federal highway was a simple but profound one. Though the road followed the same route, it was now part of a larger

4

web of federal "interstate" routes. The narrow passage through the Alleghenies in Maryland was now linked to the nation.

The man who created the interstate routes did as much as Henry Ford or Alfred Sloan to put America on wheels. He funneled billions of federal dollars to the forty-eight states to build roads. His momentous decisions transformed the American landscape and affected the daily lives and movements of almost every citizen. Yet few in America in 1926 knew his name or even his office; today, almost no one does. He was Thomas Harris MacDonald, chief of the Federal Bureau of Public Roads.

Small wonder that Thomas Harris MacDonald was unknown, for he rarely courted publicity. Photographs of him show a man of complete formality and propriety. His five-foot-seven-inch thickset frame always appears perfectly erect. His dark suit jacket—usually single-breasted—is buttoned neatly over a vest and dark tie. His hands always hang tensely at his side, while his eyes stare directly and intensely into the lens. His round face, marked by taut lips, a high forehead, and thinning hair, looks imposing and cold.

The actual man was little different. Thomas Harris MacDonald wore a coat and tie even when fishing or horseback riding on vacation in Nebraska. Colleagues and subordinates described him as reserved, austere, dignified, and cool, and often spoke of the severe stare of his cobalt-blue eyes. "When you were in Mr. MacDonald's presence you were quiet. You spoke only if he asked you to," one subordinate remembered. "He came as close . . . to characterize what I would call royalty." Subordinates, colleagues, and his closest associates always addressed him as "Mr. MacDonald" or "Chief"—never "Thomas" or "Tom." To his wife, even in the private intimacy of their home, he was always "Mr. MacDonald." In accordance with a demand he had made in his youth, his brother and sisters called him "Sir."

Little of the place where MacDonald spent his childhood suggested romance, despite its exotic labeling. Pioneers had enthusiastically named the spot about fifty miles east of Des Moines, Iowa, after Montezuma, a place of victory in the recent war with Mexico and, originally, a fabled sixteenth-century Aztec emperor. The soil—far richer than could be found in New England or the Northwest Territory—lured the first settlers to the south-central part of what became Poweshiek County with the promise of great harvests, much as Cortés had been drawn to the

Aztecs by the promise of gold. After the Civil War, the Rock Island and Missouri and St. Louis railroads established branch lines to the town, the first reliable connections its twelve hundred citizens had with the rest of the state.

For up to a third of the year Montezuma was isolated by mud. The same thick soil that yielded the abundant harvest of crops became a giant quagmire whenever it rained. Iowa natives regarded their state's mud with the same respect and dread one might accord some uncontrollable primeval force. It swallowed horses up to their knees and wagon wheels up to their hubs. "It had the consistency of thick and sticky horse glue," MacDonald's daughter remembered. "When it rained, you were stuck, your wagons, your feet, you just stayed in your house until it dried. That could be two, three weeks, a month." Though twenty-seven railway companies with nearly ten thousand miles of track crisscrossed the state, and few farms were more than six or eight miles from a depot, rain made travel to the station impossible. As a boy living with his brother and two sisters in Montezuma and working in his father's lumber and grain store, MacDonald saw firsthand how farmers struggled with the roads and how the town's commerce came to a standstill whenever it rained.

In 1900, when he turned nineteen, MacDonald announced that he would attend the Iowa State College of Agriculture and Mechanic Arts in Ames. He intended, he said, to become a civil engineer. There was little doubt about his commitment. Years later the family remembered his expression was assured; his will was implacable.

The foresight of a conservative Republican congressman who had quit school at age fifteen enabled Thomas MacDonald and thousands like him to attend college. In 1862, Representative Justin Smith Morrill of Vermont introduced a bill granting public lands in each state for the "endowment, support, and maintenance of at least one college . . . to teach such branches of learning as are related to agriculture and the mechanic arts." The Senate approved the measure, and President Lincoln signed the Morrill Land Grant Act into law. In 1890, Congress passed a second Morrill Act (the octogenarian Vermonter, now serving in the Senate, knew nothing of term limits). It provided money to colleges and universities, the first federal aid for education.

As a result of Morrill's act, western American states in the closing years of the nineteenth century blossomed with agricultural and technical colleges. They were past due. Prior to 1862, there were just six schools of engineering in the United States—including those at the military academy at West Point, Rensselaer Polytechnic Institute, Harvard, Yale, and MIT. By 1872, there were seventy, most in land-grant colleges, opening opportunities for people like Thomas MacDonald, who likely would not have ever considered attending a traditional college or university. Armed with a practical degree, many went on to careers in American industry, producing petroleum, steel, and of course automobiles. Still others built modern America's great civil engineering works—its bridges, skyscrapers, subways, tunnels, and roads.

The Iowa State College of Agriculture and Mechanic Arts at Ames, established in 1868, testified to Justin Smith Morrill's vision. While the college stressed the mechanic arts, it also took care to include the "other scientific and classical studies," as stipulated by the Land Grant Act. In addition to physics, chemistry, mathematics, and civil engineering, (twenty-nine courses), the curriculum also demanded four terms of English and two each of Latin, military science, and library. MacDonald's grades hovered about 3.85 on a 4-point scale, more than enough to qualify him for honors.

At Iowa State, MacDonald fell under the tutelage of the school's dean, Anson Marston, who taught courses in road building and was an early and important advocate of the "good roads" movement. At the turn of the century the term "good roads" was a prevailing theme among travelers. It had been popularized by a manufacturer of shoe forms and Union veteran of the Civil War, Colonel Albert Augustus Pope, who introduced a "safety bicycle" in 1878. Pope's machine made bicycling the rage. Sedentary town men, and later women, joined together to tour the countryside on weekend afternoons. By 1900, more than three hundred companies were producing over a million bicycles a year.

Pope did not stop with manufacturing but turned his attention to the road conditions bicyclists had to endure. "American roads are among the worst in the civilized world, and always have been," he wrote in a pamphlet entitled *Highway Improvement*. "I hope to live to see the time when all over our land, our cities, towns, and villages shall be connected by as good roads as can be found." Pope organized riders into an early lobbying group, the League of American Wheelmen, financed courses in road engineering at MIT, and built a short stretch of macadam road in Boston to show people how wonderful a smooth pavement could be. He helped persuade the Commonwealth of Massachusetts to create a highway commission. By the turn of the century, the "good roads" movement was sweeping the country.

The League of American Wheelmen became the first highway lobby group that served as a model for others to follow. Through its own publication, *Good Roads*, the league supported "good roads" associations across the country; it held "good roads" conventions and argued ceaselessly before state legislatures for road improvements. In New Jersey in 1891, it lobbied the legislature to pass the first state aid bill for road construction in the nation. In the next quarter century all other states followed New Jersey's progressive thinking.

The League of American Wheelmen joined with Pope to persuade J. Sterling Morton, President Cleveland's Secretary of Agriculture, to create in 1893 an Office of Road Inquiry to "furnish information" about road building. The office began modestly by publishing pamphlets on road building, but within four years it furnished information in the form of "object lesson roads," short sections of well-constructed pavement. After completing a section, the office held a "Good Roads Day" and invited farmers from around the country to see for themselves what travel could be like.

Recognizing his pupil's ability, Dean Marston encouraged MacDonald to write his senior thesis on the highway needs of Iowa farmers and the horsepower necessary to pull heavy loads over highways. MacDonald's graduation in 1904 fortuitously coincided with the state legislature's appropriation of $3,500 to Iowa State College for a highway commission to study the state's roads. It fell to Anson Marston to hire a chief engineer at $1,000 a year. Though he toured eastern engineering schools in search of a likely candidate, Marston turned to MacDonald as the only person who understood Iowa's conditions, especially its mud.

Thomas Harris MacDonald regarded road building as something more than a mere livelihood; it was a calling of higher moral purpose. "Next to the education of the child," he wrote, road building ranked as "the greatest public responsibility." It contributed to the common good and did more to increase the "possibilities of enjoyment and happiness of life than any other public undertaking." Good roads could improve the living standards of all, but especially rural Americans. For decades, agrarian life had been on the decline as young men and women on farms, unable to tolerate their isolation, abandoned their parents' land and succumbed to the lure of the city. It was only a matter of time before people living in cities would outnumber those living on farms. Surely, MacDonald and others believed naively, roads connecting the country with the city could reverse this decline. Not only would he pull farmers out of the mud, but with good roads he would connect those farms with the county seat, the state capital, and ultimately with other states and cities. Greater mobility would make rural life more attractive and help keep Iowa's sons and daughters on the farm. Automobiles were beginning to appear in the state, and they, too, needed good roads if they were to travel beyond the limits of large cities. Isolated no longer, rural life would prosper.

MacDonald's high ideals were sorely tested: Many of the men building roads in Iowa in 1904 were either fraudulent or ignorant. Throughout the state's ninety-nine counties, private companies—often with the knowledge of county officials—conspired to rig their construction bids so that each would be guaranteed a portion of the contracts. While their collusion was merely unethical, their construction was dangerously incompetent: wooden bridges too weak to carry an automobile or a horse and wagon; bridge decking that left no room for expansion and contraction; wooden culverts without any reinforcement. Within a few months of completion, the structures invariably collapsed or broke apart and county officials and construction companies repeated the process.

Shortly after his appointment, MacDonald challenged the cozy relationship that bridge contractors and cement producers enjoyed with county officials. Traveling the state on horseback and by train, he demonstrated to county officials how to build culverts with concrete and bridges with steel, as well as the principles of road maintenance. He checked construction projects personally; often he uncovered serious structural flaws, and sometimes fraud. Many farmers and local officials did not know quite what to make of this formal and dispassionate young man who brought efficient management, scientific detachment, and an unassailable integrity to what they regarded as simply an easy and benign way to spread a little extra money about the state. But word spread quietly and quickly: Unlike others concerned with road building, Mac-Donald could not be bought. He exposed bid rigging in Clinton and Polk counties. County officials went to jail and companies had to reimburse counties for shoddy work. "There has never been a straighter man any place," a writer for the Montezuma newspaper said in a fulsome tribute, "he has always stood to the fore . . . for protection of the taxpayer and that they get the worth of their money."

More important than exposing fraud, MacDonald actually improved the roads in his state. Highway crews now graded the six thousand miles of road regularly. They stabilized the soil and spread gravel and stone on about two thousand miles, and they paved about five hundred miles with brick or portland concrete. Instead of rebuilding the same faulty wooden bridges and culverts again and again, engineers designed new structures of reinforced concrete. Modest though those improvements were by today's standards, they represented a quantum leap for the time. Seeing the ways that better roads ended isolation, Iowans were happy to pay for them. As roads improved, state residents began to buy automobiles. By 1914, Iowans owned more automobiles per capita—one for every 5.5 persons—than citizens of any other state in the Union. Just a decade after MacDonald began, Iowa boasted a full-fledged highway commission with a staff of sixty-one and an annual budget of $15 million.

MacDonald was ready for a bigger challenge. It came in the spring of 1919, when David Houston, the Secretary of Agriculture under Woodrow Wilson, invited him to become chief of the Federal Bureau of Public Roads, successor to the Office of Road Inquiry, in Washington. MacDonald accepted after he held out for a salary of $6,000—$1,500 more than his predecessor received. That March, after the appointment was announced, the Des Moines *Capital* published an editorial about the commissioner. "Mr. MacDonald is a steady going man," the writer said, who had to endure "all the unhappy features of Iowa road work." Iowans had known he would be offered the job, "but hoped that he might not accept." Still, the editorial continued, "in the larger field, he may accomplish more."

The "larger field" was the United States of America—over three million miles of roads, of which just three hundred fifty thousand could be described as "surfaced." As more and more people across the United States purchased automobiles, pressure mounted to increase the federal government's role in road building. By 1916, people were relying on them for their work as well as for pleasure. Farmers began to buy small trucks. Congress and the American people were beginning to realize that transportation was essential to the nation's economy. Farmers needed roads as never before. One study commissioned by Congress found that poor roads forced an American farmer to pay 21 cents in labor and time to haul a ton of produce over a U.S. road, while a French farmer paid the equivalent of just 8 cents. Another study reported that it cost more for a Georgia farmer to ship a bushel of peaches twenty miles by road to Atlanta than it did for a California farmer to ship a bushel by rail across the country. On July 16, 1916, Woodrow Wilson signed the first Federal-Aid Road Act into law. The act gave the new federal Bureau of Public Roads $75 million to distribute over the next five years and allowed for the federal government to pay half of a state's costs for road improvement and construction. At the time, there were over twenty-one million horses, three and a half million automobiles, and a quarter million trucks.

World War I, however, foiled Congress's plan. Shortages forced an end to roadwork, and civil engineers were drafted from their state highway agencies and the Bureau of Public Roads to serve in Europe. Even more harmful was the destruction brought by military traffic. The army had decided to drive the trucks and materials it was producing in the Midwest to eastern ports and ships bound for Europe. Though the roads were dreadful—the first convoy that left Toledo, Ohio, in mid-December 1917 took three weeks to get to Baltimore—more than thirty thousand trucks made the journey. Following the army's lead, private companies, which had previously used trucks only for local deliveries, now sent them on interstate trips from places like New York, Philadelphia, and Cleveland. Recognizing that trucks could provide a more convenient service at a comparable cost, businesses began to ship goods interstate over roads rather than by rail.

As trucks took to the roads, the roads took a pounding. Many tons heavier than automobiles, trucks also rode on unforgiving, hard rubber wheels rather than pneumatic tires. Whatever thin layers of concrete or asphalt there might be quickly crumbled under their destructive weight. One engineer likened the punishment to "the shells a big gun hurls into a fortress."

When Thomas MacDonald arrived in Washington in 1919, he found confusion and discouragement in the Bureau of Public Roads and impatience in Congress. The Bureau of Public Roads had spent only about $500,000 of the $75 million Congress had voted it in 1916 and had built just twelve and a half miles of road. The little money it had spent brought controversy. States complained of restrictive federal regulations, needless delays, and arrogant federal engineers, all of which hindered construction. Since the 1916 bill did not demand that federal aid roads in one county or state connect with those in another, maps often charted short isolated squiggles of improved pavement stranded in the midst of unimproved territory. So frustrated was Congress by the lack of progress that some representatives and senators, along with a number of powerful road and automobile associations, had proposed replacing the Bureau of Public Roads with a national highway commission that would bypass local planning entirely and construct three or four new federally owned roads across the length and breadth of the country.

To all the disorder and confusion MacDonald applied two central principles, which he had worked out in the Iowa soil for the past fifteen years: cooperation and technical expertise. They lay at the core of every decision he would make for the next three decades.

At the heart of cooperation lay federalism, an active partnership of state and national government. To MacDonald, highway building put into practice the concept of federalism as outlined by Hamilton, Madison, and Jay. The proper federalist attitude would, he believed, enable states to maintain their sovereignty as to the placement of roads and at the same time promote a policy of road building to federal standards that would best serve the nation's needs. The previous head of the bureau, an imperious man whose style and directives only served to anger state highway departments, had no ability to compromise. Now consultation and cooperation replaced arbitrary edicts from Washington. "Those who do not have the qualities of manliness, square dealing, good temper, and ability to get along with people must go," MacDonald wrote to one engineer. "So long as I am in this office, the door will be open."

The Chief always linked technical expertise to what he called the "gigantic business" of highway building. Roads served four different but interrelated components of American life, each of which contributed to the economic welfare of the nation: *agriculture,* farm-to-town or farm-to-city traffic—as well as "social, educational, and religious activities which produce traffic from farms to the schools, to the churches, and to the community centers"; *recreation,* the practice of combining business with pleasure travel, as well as the increasingly popular motor tour; *commerce,* the transport of goods between towns and cities about a hundred miles apart; and *defense,* the use of roads for military vehicles. What was good for American life was good for America's defense, too. Building should proceed along "sane and sound economic lines," and only after a thorough study of road use, MacDonald reported in the bureau's monthly publication, *Public Roads: A Journal of Highway Research.*

Through his openness and willingness to find common ground, Mac-

Donald was creating a large network of interrelated groups, each with an interest in building good roads, which functioned like well-oiled parts in a giant machine. Never mind that some of them had favored abolishing the Bureau of Public Roads a few months earlier; each part was now vital to the machine. The Portland Cement Association, the American Automobile Association, the American Road Builders Association, the Association of Highway Officials of the North Atlantic States, the Rubber Association of America, the Mississippi Valley Association of State Highway Officials, the National Paving Brick Manufacturer's Association, the National Automobile Chamber of Commerce, and scores of others each had a place. MacDonald incorporated any group into his machine as long as it supported the cause of building federal-aid roads on the basis of sound economic and engineering principles. "This is an All-American job," he said, stressing cooperation. "We must recognize the important part that the states have in the work."

The Chief even added parts of his own invention to his machine. One was the Highway Education Board. The board would overcome resistance to highway building by teaching Americans the value and importance of good roads. Facts generated by the Bureau of Public Roads flowed into Highway Education Board booklets and, later, films disseminated to schools around the country. Speakers from the board fanned out from the Washington headquarters to address school assemblies, Rotary clubs, and local chambers of commerce. With the help of other individuals running MacDonald's highway machine—men like the rubber baron Harvey Firestone—the bureau sponsored essay contests for high school students and awarded college scholarships for engineering.

Surely the most important part of MacDonald's giant machine, the component essential for its operation, was a seemingly innocuous and stodgy-sounding group, the American Association of State Highway Officials, known by its acronym AASHO. In fact, AASHO ranked with the most powerful lobbying groups in Washington. As chief engineer of Iowa's highway department, MacDonald had been present at the group's formation in 1914. Now he used the association to strengthen the ties between federal and state governments. He realized that through AASHO, each state highway official could cultivate a close liaison with members of Congress, senators, and their staffs. While the state officials might not be allowed to lobby formally for votes on legislative matters, their opinions would carry great weight—so great that in 1923, AASHO installed its executive secretary in a Washington office to advise members of Congress about highway matters and sometimes even to help them draft legislation.

Along with his belief in federalism MacDonald brought a belief in the superiority of technical expertise. For the Chief, road building was a scientific enterprise. Henceforth all decisions about matters like proper building materials and methods as well as the size and location of the roads themselves would be made with detached scientific objectivity.

MacDonald led a new governmental class just then emerging in Washington—the technocrats. The word was a modern invention, a combination of *techno,* the Greek word for "art" or "craft," with *cratos,* the Greek word for "ruler." World War I had taught many Americans that democracy would prosper in the twentieth century only with the help of technocrats' mastery of the scientific and the physical world. Technocratic experts would ameliorate living conditions in America. Americans believed experts in the Public Health Service would control, if not eradicate, diseases like diphtheria, polio, and tuberculosis. They relied upon experts in the Forest Service and Parks Service to manage the land to the best advantage of the country. They looked to experts with the Department of Agriculture to help them get the greatest yield from each acre of farmland and each dairy cow.

As the leader of the technocrats in the Bureau of Public Roads, Mac-Donald always kept the larger vision of what America's road system should be. It was never a single road he was building, but a federally financed network of roads that would span the country. The network would not only serve a commercial purpose of enabling goods to be moved from one place to another, but respond to defense and cultural needs as well.

The technocratic spirit that extended throughout the Bureau of Public Roads was most visible in the area of research. From its inception the bureau had conducted research and published its findings in a series of pamphlets. After the wartime truck convoys pulverized road pavements, the bureau redoubled its research efforts. What was the optimum sand to use with cement when making concrete, and in what ratio? The optimum mixing time and pouring conditions, and curing time? The optimum reinforcing steel and its placement? The optimum joint fillers? The questions were far more complex than they might at first appear. On the bureau's test farm in Arlington, Virginia (at the site of the present Washington National Airport), engineers laid control sections of pavement and tested each with a variety of pounding machines.

Away from the test farm, the bureau conducted research on various heavily traveled roads. On the Benjamin Franklin Bridge in Philadelphia, it investigated the strength of different pavement compositions. Bureau economists toiling in the Washington office analyzed the effect of gasoline taxes on highway building, and income that communities and states derived from motor vehicles. Working with the National Bureau of Standards and AASHO, the bureau determined the best shapes, colors, lettering, and placement of road signs. In conjunction with the National Academy of Sciences, MacDonald established and helped finance the Highway Research Board in 1920 to study matters such as the economics of highways, traffic analysis, maintenance, and materials. The results appeared regularly in *Public Roads*, which highway builders and officials across the country read avidly.

Wrapped as they were in the mantle of technical expertise, and using information generated by state highway departments and the National Board on Highway Research, MacDonald and the highly skilled professionals he marshaled at the Bureau of Public Roads earned the respect of Congress and presidents for the quality of their arguments, their attention to facts and details, and the thorough analysis that went into their decisions.

Americans' faith in technocracy soon extended to road building. Prior to this time rural communities held weekend road repair parties in which farmers could have a portion of their county taxes forgiven if they graded the section of road that ran in front of their farm. It was a chance for neighbors to get together and swap stories, but do little other than spread gravel. Sometimes officials left road building and heavier repairs to an unskilled prison chain gang working under the sharp eye of a shotgun-toting sheriff. But farmers and criminals could not do the job of building and maintaining a "modern" road. County officials knew they must yield to road-building technocrats who operated on scientific principles. MacDonald quickly capitalized on this new faith, realizing that it, too, would help to keep his highway machine well oiled. Technical knowledge would enable the government to build stronger and safer roads wherever they were needed. The knowledge would save the government money and help to increase commerce. State highway departments followed the Chief's lead. They established their own research laboratories, which often conducted tests of conditions particular to their region of the country.

In his first months in office, MacDonald seemed to be everywhere. He spoke to dozens of organizations and met frequently with senators and representatives. He got results. Within a few days of his arrival, he arranged for the government to transfer $130 million worth of surplus military trucks and equipment to state highway departments. He cemented the ties between good roads and defense by charting with General Pershing the routes across the country essential for military operations. Known as the "Pershing Map," the document is a prototype of an interstate system. No detail seemed too small for MacDonald. When a shortage of railway cars threatened the supply of cement and stone for road building, the Chief smoothed the way with the Interstate Commerce Commission to secure thousands of extra cars. Most important, with the end of the war MacDonald was able to release federal funds for highway building. By the end of 1921, the bureau could cite five thousand miles of completed highway and another seventeen thousand miles under way. Congress knew it could rely on the Chief as someone who would get things done. It dropped the idea of a national highway commission, and in 1921 passed a new federal-aid highway bill that gave MacDonald everything he wanted. In his first two years in Washington, Chief MacDonald had taken complete control of the federal-aid highway program.

The high-minded seriousness of the sort that possessed Thomas Harris MacDonald and the cadre of highway engineers he assembled at the Bureau of Public Roads does not square with the conventional picture of the 1920s. No raccoon coat and social whirlwind for the Chief. His world was neither one of roof gardens and jazz, nor hip flasks and prohibition alcohol, nor the scandal and corruption of the Teapot Dome. This was all the more reason for members of Congress and the succession of Republican administrations that followed Woodrow Wilson to respect the square-built man from Iowa.

The conventional picture of the 1920s also suggests that the progressive thinking of social reformers and presidents Roosevelt and Wilson was being eclipsed in Washington. Indeed, it was true that the Harding, Coolidge, and Hoover administrations had less interest in the issues that had motivated progressives—unbridled corporate wealth, child protection laws, and rights for workers. The administrations were more inclined to return the role of leadership to the business community. Yet in the case of the Bureau of Public Roads, where serious and resolute men of quiet regularity and reserved formality worked with the states for the public good, life went on just as it had under Wilson. Presidential administrations came and went, from Democrat to Republican and, with Franklin Roosevelt, to Democrat again. By the time Herbert Hoover left the White House in 1933, six agriculture secretaries had come and gone, too. But Thomas Harris MacDonald remained, doling out millions.

The machines that MacDonald and his highway builders were using to create new roads were bigger and more sophisticated than ever. Until the end of the nineteenth century, road builders relied on teams of horses and wagons to move earth and rock. In 1887, at the St. Leandro Plow Works in California, Daniel Best, a forty-nine-year-old farmer and inventor, had the idea that a steam engine attached to wheels could be used for logging, plowing, and earth moving. Steam on the farm was not new, nor were steam engines on wheels. Best himself had built some, and would build a colossal combine with wheels fifteen feet wide and nine feet in diameter that could do little more than go in a straight line. His new steam-driven machine of 1887 was different. He reduced its size and gave it large wheels to go through the deep earth of farmers' fields. Best called his creation a "traction engine." Others called it a tractor.

Best's tractor quickly gained in popularity, but soon he had a formidable rival. In 1890, in nearby Stockton, California, Benjamin Holt, a forty-one-year-old builder of farm machines and compulsive tinkerer, created his own steam traction engine. Over the next twenty-four years he turned out 130 more, including a miniature model for the king of Spain. But the large, wide wheels of Best's and Holt's tractors proved their greatest liability. Farmers found that no matter how great the width of the wheels, the machines sank in the rich California soil. Holt set to tinkering. In 1904 he replaced the wheels on his traction engine with a smaller set that turned an endless steel band of movable self-laying tracks. These, he found, distributed the machine's weight over a broad path and made it far more agile on rough ground, too. "In a tract where a man could not walk without sinking up to his knees," reported *Farm Implement News*, "the new traction engine was operated without a perceptible impression in the ground." Because of the way it moved across the landscape, Holt called his new machine a "caterpillar" tractor.

While Holt was busy developing his caterpillar tractor, Daniel Best was not idle. By 1895 he had developed a gasoline-powered engine for his tractor, thereby lowering the risk of fire and eliminating the need for water, a boiler, and a fireman. In 1908, at age seventy, Best decided to retire and sell his company to his old rival, Benjamin Holt, who moved the new company east to Peoria, Illinois. Just what Clarence Leo Best—Daniel's son, who was a superintendent at his father's company—thought of the sale is unknown, but he did not join Holt in the new company. In 1910 he organized the C. L. Best Gas Traction Company and introduced his own caterpillar-type tractor. For fifteen years the two companies competed for much of the same business. Each had its strengths. The Holt company sold many of its machines in foreign countries, while Best developed a network of dealers in the United States. Finally, in 1925, after Benjamin Holt's death, Clarence Best decided to merge with his former rival's company. Best became chairman of the board of the new venture, the Caterpillar Tractor Company.

The movement from horses to steam, and then to gasoline and diesel, was gradual. Over the years men wielding shovels and pickaxes and driving horse-drawn wagons yielded to power shovels and dump trucks. Engineers began using bulldozers along with large power shovels to make cuts and grades more efficiently. The cost of moving a cubic yard of earth declined from 40 cents in 1922 to 21 cents in 1938.

In its 1916 Federal-Aid Road Act, Congress funded the federal road program with $75 million for five years; in its 1921 Federal-Aid Highway Act, it funded federal roads with an average of $75 million a *year*. By the end of the decade, the Bureau of Public Roads would spend $750 million.

In addition to giving the Chief and his bureau more money to distribute to the states, the 1921 act made real the idea of a national road system. Each state would designate seven percent of its roads to be linked with those in other states. Linking all the county seats in the country, these primary routes would create, MacDonald wrote in his best bureaucratic style, a "complete and economical highway transport service throughout the nation." They were, he said, "interstate."

Armed with the 1921 highway bill, MacDonald and the Bureau of Public Roads coordinated with each state the designation of federal interstate roads so that they would correlate at each state's borders. The bureau and officials reached agreement on the shape of traffic signs. Beginning in 1925, the Chief worked again with AASHO to bring further order to road chaos by changing route designations from names to a uniform system of numbers. Under the Chief's direction the committee designated north-to-south routes with odd numbers beginning with 1 on the East Coast and 101 on the West, and east-to-west routes with even numbers beginning with 2 across the top of the country and 70 across the bottom. By October 1926, the scheme was in place and federal shields emblazoned with route numbers began to appear on federal interstate roads around the country.

As Congress produced the money, MacDonald produced the miles. "Without overstatement," the Chief wrote in his annual report, "it may be said that greater progress has been made in providing the means of highway transportation during the fiscal year 1922, than in any similar period in the history of the country." He was right. With his bureau's assistance, states had added ten thousand miles, "something more than the equivalent of three transcontinental roads," to the federal-aid highway system. State highway departments in the East usually used concrete or asphalt, while in the West, where traffic was light, workers graded the surface, solved drainage problems, and put down gravel or sand-clay. The results were often dramatic. Engineers redesigned the road between Ariton and Clayton, Alabama, two small towns southeast of Montgomery, to eliminate thirteen of fourteen railroad crossings. On the road from Baltimore to Washington they eliminated a curve that over the years had accounted for the loss of thirty-five lives.

Although the initial impact of a road project was always local, it usually fit into a larger scheme binding the nation in a web of interstate highways, a design, MacDonald said, "no less important to the country . . . than that offered by the railroads." At the moment, highway transportation was still intermittent. But the day would come when it was continuous. "My aim is this," MacDonald said in 1924. "We will be able to drive out of any county seat in the United States at thirty-five miles an hour and drive into any other county seat—and never crack a spring."

As the 1920s continued, MacDonald's highway machine operated with superb precision. Speakers from the Highway Education Board continued to tell children at school assemblies about the myriad ways good roads would improve their lives and help America grow. Civic groups showed the latest "good roads" film, often produced by an automobile manufacturer in cooperation with the Bureau of Public Roads. Statisticians in the Highway Research Board ground out reports on traffic flow and "desire lines"—those roads Americans used most frequently. And most important, AASHO officials from each of the forty-eight states connected with their senators and representatives to ensure that they voted more money for highway projects.

By any measure MacDonald's achievement in the twenties was

impressive. In just one year, 1927, the Bureau of Public Roads was responsible for the construction of 10,220 miles of new roads costing $84 million in federal and $105 million in state funds. By the end of the decade, the Chief and his bureau had built or resurfaced over 90,000 miles of federal-aid highways and were expending an average of $78 million each year.

Given the size and efficiency of his highway machine, it was no wonder MacDonald felt it was his destiny to lead America to highway greatness. "There have been just three great programs of highway building within recorded history," he told the annual meeting of the American Association of State Highway Officials in 1926, "that of the Roman Empire, beginning with Julius Caesar and extending to Constantine; that of France under the Emperor Napoleon; that of the United States during the last decade." The first two, he noted, were conducted under the rule of despots. Only the United States had produced a comprehensive system under democratic rule.

In MacDonald's mind the economic well-being and therefore the success of democracy and freedom depended on federal construction of roads that, by a stipulation in the first paragraph of the 1916 Federal-Aid Road Act, would be "free from tolls of all kinds." The power of MacDonald's machine was such that few in state legislatures resisted the logic and the money that flowed from the Bureau of Public Roads. The reins upon the growing trucking industry remained loose. Roadside strip development and billboards grew without control. With the federal government paying fifty percent of construction costs, few states thought of building toll roads. Anyone who suggested regulations or tolls threatened, MacDonald said, "freedom of the road."

The Chief need not have worried. Automobile congestion and its threat gave him additional leverage with the greatest ally in his quest to build a great highway system: the ever-growing number of American motorists. Drivers who had braved dirt roads in the summer but usually abandoned their cars in the winter when it snowed or in the spring when it rained now found that they could use them year-round. In 1921, Americans drove almost nine million automobiles, ninety percent of all automobiles in the world. Buying on credit became the norm. By 1925, just one of every four car buyers paid cash. By the crash of 1929, states had registered 26.5 million automobiles, about one car for every four people, nearly a two hundred percent increase since the start of the decade. The mere threat that road capacity might "limit the production and use of motor cars," as one highway official put it, was enough to goad motorists into pressuring their legislators for more road funds.

Allied with those who drove automobiles were those who built them and those who made the thousands of parts that kept them running. More and more workers in factories, steel mills, rubber plants, oil refineries, repair shops, gasoline stations, showrooms, road and highway departments, insurance companies, construction industries, cement quarries, and state license and tax departments owed their jobs to the automobile. Increasingly, obsolescence became an important part of American car culture. In 1929, manufacturers produced over five million motor vehicles while owners scrapped two and a half million.

Only the railroads suffered. In the late nineteenth and early twentieth centuries, railroads had enthusiastically supported the "good roads" movement in order to get wagons and people to and from their stations. With a quarter million miles of railroad track—more than half the rail in the world—they had little to fear from automobiles. Few people traveled long distance by automobile. After all, in 1903, it had taken Horatio Nelson Jackson, a physician from Vermont, and Sewell K. Crocker, his personal mechanic, sixty-three days to travel from San Francisco to New York in their two-cylinder Winton. The same trip by railroad took about four days. After World War I and the army's successful transport of trucks and matériel from midwestern factories to eastern ports, railroads began to feel automobiles and trucks were challenging both passenger and freight lines. In the 1920s and 1930s, the relationship between railroads and automobile interests—particularly the emerging trucking industry—became acrimonious. Shouldn't truckers, the railroads argued before Congress, be regulated by interstate commerce laws just as they were? As it was, the truckers enjoyed an unfair advantage. Yet Congress did not impose federal regulations on trucking until 1935, when it passed the Motor Carrier Act.

As recently as 1915, railroads carried over one million people and over two million tons of freight each year. There were more than sixty-five thousand locomotives, fifty-five thousand passenger cars, and an astounding two and a quarter million freight cars. One million eight hundred thousand workers—one of every twenty-three in the country—collected a paycheck from a railroad, while millions more worked for companies that supplied the railroads with everything from pencils and paper for offices to silverware and glasses for dining cars. By 1929, track mileage had dropped below a quarter million miles and the number of passengers to seven hundred eighty-six thousand.

Every week, evidence flowed into the offices of the Bureau of Public Roads that railroads were withering like a great and noble but diseased oak tree. The first symptoms had manifested themselves at the tips of the branches, and they were dying back, slowly in some parts, more rapidly in others. The Rock Island and St. Louis and Missouri soon abandoned the lines to Thomas MacDonald's hometown of Montezuma. Eventually the disease spread to the trunk, and it would fall or be left standing as a withered reminder of what once was great. Each time a railroad abandoned a line, it had to tell the bureau of the grade crossings on federal-aid roads that would be eliminated. Notice after notice flowed into the bureau's offices, while bureau secretaries clipped newspaper articles about the demise of rail lines. Typical was an article about the Boston and Maine Railroad in the *New York Times* that MacDonald saved for his personal files: Headlined B. & M. WOULD DROP 1,000 MILES OF ROAD TO SAVE ITS SYSTEM, the story told of the line's plan to abandon forty-five percent of its track because of the "rapidly increasing losses," resulting from "motor traffic." But MacDonald willfully ignored the facts. Intercity trucking on intercity highways, he argued, would help relieve railroad congestion. Not until 1929 did he acknowledge "a loss of passenger business on the steam railroads." But he was quick to note "an increase in the freight business," saying that "as a business enterprise the railways of a country have more to fear from a lack of adequate highway improvement than from any honest and intelligent highway development."

The Depression only increased federal highway funding as politicians came to see the direct connection between highway construction and employment. In 1930, Herbert Hoover raised federal aid from $75 million to $125 million and added an additional $80 million in future federal funds. The amount was paltry compared with that of his successor, Franklin Delano Roosevelt. Almost immediately after FDR took office, governors from all regions of the country flooded the new president with roadwork proposals. As one put it, "There is no form of improvement more necessary and will better serve to relieve the acute unemployment situation than sorely needed highway construction projects on trunk roads in this state." Roosevelt's New Deal programs, including the Works Progress Administration, the the Public Works Administration, and the Reconstruction Finance Administration, worked through the Bureau of Public Roads to funnel hundreds of millions of dollars each year to road-building projects. To the mind of the new head of the Department of Agriculture, Henry Agard Wallace, from MacDonald's home state of Iowa, road building well served the paramount social purpose of the day, putting people to work. Between 1933 and 1940, the New Deal was responsible for more than $1.8 billion in road construction and millions of man-years of employment.

The eastern counties of New Mexico, dusty and hardscrabble places like Hobbs and Melrose, Tucumcari and Clayton, provide a good example of what was taking place across the country. In the fall of 1933 through the spring of 1934, road work provided employment for about thirty-three hundred drought-stricken farmers. They formed crews to build and rebuild three hundred miles of highways. The farmers worked thirty hours a week, earning 50 cents an hour single-handed or 70 cents with a two-horse team. To ensure that as many worked as possible, engineers used hand labor instead of machines. Supervisors of road crews often found both workers and horses so malnourished that they had to give them "proper feed" before issuing shovels or hitching the horses to a wagon.

The Chief rode the crest of this new employment wave. Republican and conservative to the core, he had more in common with Henry C. Wallace, who had directed the Agriculture Department under Warren G. Harding, than he did with his radical and seemingly socialist son who was now directing the department under the revolutionary Franklin D. Roosevelt. The ever-cautious MacDonald, who was a holdover from Woodrow Wilson's administration and had survived the last three Republican administrations, kept his thoughts private while he quietly gathered in the power that naturally accrued to one who helped to dispense hundreds of millions of federal dollars. More federal dollars kept his machine well oiled. Still careful to maintain the partnership he had forged with state highway departments, MacDonald consulted with state officials through AASHO. At times Congress flirted with the idea of bypassing the Chief and his bureau and having one of the New Deal administrations grant road money to the states directly, but whenever it did so the results were less than satisfactory. Speaking quietly, MacDonald would remind his network of senators and congressmen that his bureau had all the expertise; his bureau had always been careful to spread federal money across the country and in their districts; his bureau had a superb administrative record for more than a decade, and no agency could hope to duplicate his bureau's record in a single year.

As power accrued in the Bureau of Public Roads, the Chief became even more energetic than he had been before, conferring with legislators, planning with AASHO officials, speaking at conventions, and writing articles. In 1936, a year the federal government awarded $225 million for highway building, MacDonald held 160 meetings on eighty-three different days with eighty-five members of the House of Representatives and Senate. He spent an additional five days testifying before House and Senate Committees on highway legislation.

In 1936, the Chief spent almost half the year traveling to conferences and road inspection tours, including one trip to Germany to see the Reichsautobahn, the impressive new roads designed and built by the renowned German engineer, the Inspector General for German Highways Dr. Fritz Todt. Like MacDonald, Todt was reticent and single-minded, a technocrat with an obsession for building. In 1936, Todt built great roads for the Reich. Soon he would build great factories for armaments and munitions. Unlike MacDonald, Todt built for the aggrandizement of his government and its Führer, not to fulfill a need. With great pride, Dr. Todt arranged to introduce MacDonald to his Führer. Ever proper and formal, the Chief said that he was pleased to meet "Mr. Hitler."

Though he was impressed by the construction methods, grade separations, and superb engineering, MacDonald saw little justification for Hitler's two thousand miles of Reichsautobahn that Dr. Todt and his laborers were creating. Despite the propaganda that went with the superhighway, he thought it of little practical value. The Chief knew Todt's highways could not possibly challenge the nearly 225 thousand miles of federal-aid roads he had built. Those miles, along with the twelve thousand miles he was adding to the system each year, made Thomas Harris MacDonald the most important highwayman in the world.

MASTERING
NATURE

—·—·—·—·—·—·—·—·—

*A great many things are going to
change. We shall turn out to be masters
rather than servants of Nature.*

                    HENRY FORD

From the perspective of the sky, the scene suggests effort-
less mastery. In the foreground are the distinctive buildings
of the 1939 New York World's Fair. Surrounding them is a
gigantic network of roads, resembling the appendages of an
immense creature a mythic hero might use to tame the sprawl of sea and
rivers and land. At the middle left, one of the creature's arms rises
gracefully toward the center, leaps a wide expanse of water, gently
declines to the right across an island, and spans more water to yet
another island. The arm divides. One aims toward the top of the photograph, crossing estuaries, kills, and small islands, and drifts off into
infinity. The other aims sharply left, leaping yet another river before
coming to rest in a tangle of buildings, narrow streets, and humanity.
Not imaginary, but concrete and steel is this creature. Its many roads
bind Queens and Long Island, land of Walt Whitman's birth, to Manhattan and beyond Manhattan to the continent. The poet had made connection a major theme of his *Leaves of Grass*:

Tom Lewis

Lo, soul, seest thou not God's purpose from the first?
The earth be spann'd, connected by network . . .
The oceans to be cross'd, the distant brought near,
The lands to be welded together.

To the north and west—beyond the scope of the camera's lens—yet more appendages reach out across the landscape. The new Henry Hudson Parkway along Manhattan's west shore runs north from 72nd Street to connect with the George Washington Bridge at 178th Street. Farther north it meets with the Henry Hudson Bridge at the top of the island. If they wished, motorists could continue still farther north to the Saw Mill River Parkway and towns upstate. Or they might choose to drive across the George Washington Bridge to New Jersey and then up the Palisades Interstate Parkway along the west bank of the Hudson. Those New Yorkers who owned automobiles no longer had to rely on rail lines and ferries to leave their island. Parks, playgrounds, beaches, and recreation were but a short distance from their apartments—by car.

To the east, again beyond the camera's view, yet more appendages: The Triborough Bridge connects to the Grand Central Parkway, which proceeds through Queens and crosses Flushing Bay. The road divides. One arm curves north and east on the Whitestone Parkway, crosses the East River over yet another suspension bridge to join with other roads leading to upstate counties and New England. The other arm curves south and east through greenswards and parks, and joins with the Northern State Parkway. It runs halfway along the top of Long Island and past Whitman's birthplace. Arms of the Northern State, the Meadowbrook State, and Wantagh State parkways connect to the Southern State, another parkway across the bottom of the island. Crossing the Southern State, the arms of the Meadowbrook or Wantagh traverse islands and estuaries to rest, finally, in beaches and parks whose names— Fire Island, Gilgo Beach, and most important of all, Jones Beach—had become synonymous with escape from the heat of summer for anyone with a car who lived in New York City's crowded boroughs.

By 1939, the man who created this creature had become an urban mythic hero. To New Yorkers penned in the city's tenements or small, fetid and un-air-conditioned apartments, Robert Moses was the master builder—the progressive who defeated politicians, plutocrats, and entrenched and backward interests to open Long Island and upstate

New York to the people; the visionary who had seen beyond wastelands and slums to verdant parks with swings and seesaws and sandboxes; the planner who would bind communities and peoples with parkways for the efficient and smooth movement of automobiles—Robert Moses the hero. In time, New Yorkers would learn that despite his Old Testament name, Moses, like so many mythic heroes, was flawed. But for now most were content to revere the man and his works.

From his father, a prosperous New Haven department store and real estate owner, Robert Moses received a bankroll sufficient to sustain him; from his mother he received an almost missionary zeal for public service, an indomitable will, a passion for building, and arrogance. Armed with degrees from Yale, Oxford, and Columbia, a mind filled with progressive ideals, his mother's forceful encouragement, and his father's willingness to support his son with an allowance of thousands each year, Moses set forth to reform public service and government. After some early and frustrating defeats, which shook his faith in reform methods, Moses earned the confidence and respect of New York's Governor Al Smith. In 1924, the governor gave the thirty-six-year-old Moses his first break, by appointing him president of the Long Island Park Commission.

With the power of his new position and the strength he acquired by rewriting crucial laws regarding the commission, Moses developed an extraordinary park system for the people of New York City in Suffolk and Nassau counties on Long Island. To do so he had to defeat those landowners on the island who together had so effectively resisted intrusions from the outside. On the north shore lay the "Gold Coast," the huge private estates of the great monied families: Vanderbilt, Phipps, Harkness, Whitney, Winthrop, and Kahn, among others. On the south shore resided the families of the "baymen," those who made their living by fishing in the Great South Bay, insular xenophobes who carefully guarded every foot of shore property. And through the middle of the island lived farmers, some of whose families had grown vegetables and potatoes on the same plots since the American Revolution. But Moses found another large and improbable landowner on the island: the city of New York. Before it joined with Manhattan, Queens, Staten Island, and the Bronx to form the city of New York in 1898, the city of Brooklyn had acquired lakes and large watersheds on Long Island to bring fresh water to its residents. Manhattan's own huge watershed and reservoirs upstate provided more than enough for the rest of the city and made

Brooklyn's system unnecessary. By 1920, most people had forgotten the overgrown tracts. Employing his powers as park commissioner, Moses connected these city properties with other parcels of land he acquired through deals he cut with county politicians (many of whose families would get rich on the construction contracts he would award) and wealthy landholders on the North Shore. The few who refused to sell under any circumstances often found surveyors protected by state police driving stakes in their front yards for a roadway that would pass through their living rooms. If they *still* refused to yield, Moses simply took their tracts by the power of eminent domain. Through this patchwork quilt of properties he threaded the series of parkways that enabled New Yorkers to get to hundreds of acres of beaches and parks. Late in 1924, Moses broke ground for the first road leading to those parks, the Southern State Parkway. In the next decade he would break ground for the Meadowbrook, the Wantagh, the Northern State, and the Cross Island, among others.

Moses' first Long Island parkways were like none other in the world, and none other that he built elsewhere. They anticipated superhighways to come: four-lane, limited-access roads, with grade separations at crossroads and railroad tracks. Flanking the roadway were wide, verdant parks lined with azaleas and dogwoods. The road followed the contours of the landscape. It represented the best in public works: an organic integration of architecture, landscape design, and engineering. No aesthetic detail escaped Moses' eye. He ordered light poles and barrier posts to be hewn from massive logs and stained brown; signs to be mounted on rustic wooden standards; each of the hundred bridges and overpasses to be faced with a different pattern of granite; flowering bushes and dogwoods to be planted along the roadway; and gasoline stations and maintenance buildings to be built of stone and topped with slate and copper roofs. Moses set the speed limit at a stately forty-five miles per hour, though cars of the day were capable of going much faster. A trip to Jones Beach had all the trappings of a leisurely ramble through the English countryside. All in all, Moses' parkway stood as a singular accomplishment for a man who never held a driver's license and never learned to drive a car.

For his inspiration to build parkways, Moses had to look no further than to select roads in Brooklyn, the Bronx, Manhattan, and Long Island. In the nineteenth century, Frederick Law Olmsted and Calvert

Divided Highways

Vaux proposed a series of roadways through New York City, to which they gave a name of their own devising, "parkways." Two of their projects, the Eastern and Ocean parkways, survive today. Olmsted and Vaux also threaded a series of carriage trails through Prospect Park in Brooklyn and Central Park in Manhattan. (They repeated the scheme in the "Emerald Necklace," a series of parks around Boston, including the Fenway.) These often featured grade separations so pedestrians need not cross the carriage path, which inevitably was fouled with horse manure. By the turn of the century, landscape designs for Kansas City, Philadelphia, and Chicago, among other cities, contained parkways.

In 1907, following Olmsted's example, workers removed hundreds of squatters' shacks, shabby commercial establishments, and years of accumulated debris from the banks of the Bronx River north of Manhattan to build a new two-lane parkway. The road followed the contours of the land and the natural bends in the river. It, too, had grade separations at crossroads and bridges over railroad tracks. No doubt the landscaping of the roadway impressed Moses, too, for he hired its architect Gilmore D. Clarke to oversee critical parts of the design of his Long Island parkways, including the bridges. But care took time. While the design for the Bronx River Parkway suited automobile speeds of 1907, it was hopelessly obsolete when workers finally completed the road sixteen years later in 1923.

Surely the most remarkable parkway, and the one that most closely resembled those Moses envisioned, could be found nearby on Long Island. The Long Island Motor Parkway served the fantasies of William Kissam Vanderbilt, Jr., the indolent grandson of the railroad baron Commodore Vanderbilt. In 1899, young Willie K., as he was known, imported a red Mercedes to his summer house at Newport and proceeded to challenge all comers to races around the resort. After the Newport police arrested him for speeding, Vanderbilt decided to try his hand at European racing. In 1902, he set the record for the course from Monte Carlo to Paris. But Europe, too, proved inhospitable to speeders. After several incarcerations for reckless driving and destruction of property with his Mercedes, Willie K. returned to the United States to introduce European-style racing to Long Island. In 1904, he charted a triangular course of local dirt and macadamized roads that passed through Queens, Hicksville, and Hempstead. He hired the Standard Oil Company to spray ninety thousand gallons of crude oil on the roadway to keep the dust down. And he commissioned Tiffany to design the prize to be awarded to the winner: a ten-and-a-half-gallon ornate silver "Vanderbilt Cup."

Racing was good sport, but driving fast every time he was behind the wheel of his Mercedes, which he named the "Red Devil," would be even better. Vanderbilt decided that he and his friends should build their own private road. In 1906 he joined with August Belmont, Harry Payne Whitney, and others to plan a sixty-mile "Motor Parkway," much of it on family-owned property, from Queens to Lake Ronkonkoma in central Long Island. "The day of the automobile has come," Willie K. wrote for remarks at the groundbreaking of the new road. "A highway is about to be constructed . . . free from all grade crossings, dust and police surveillance."

Like no other road in America, the Long Island Motor Parkway would be, said its general manager, "as revolutionary and unusual as was the construction of the first steam railroad." It was "the forerunner" of roads that would one day radiate from cities across the country. Engineers designed it with two inches of compacted igneous, or "trap," rock, a steel mesh reinforcement, and two more inches of smaller compacted stone, topped by five inches of reinforced concrete. They built in smooth straightaways and banked curves. They ordered the pavement to be colored with lamp black so "that [it] not be painful or tiresome to the eye." Most important, they eliminated level grade crossings with roads or railroad tracks by erecting sixty-five reinforced concrete bridges over the intersecting traffic.

At the time Vanderbilt built his parkway, the automobile was a private pleasure reserved for the wealthy, who regarded it as a means of leisure and "healthful recreation." Typical of those who delighted in the pleasures of "automobiling" were the intrepid pair Charles Jasper Glidden and his wife, Lucy. Having made a fortune by investing in early telephone companies, Glidden retired in 1900 at age forty-three, to indulge himself in his twin avocations—flying in hot-air balloons and driving. In 1904, he and Lucy left Boston in a large, English-built Napier touring car for a trip around the world. Nearly eighteen thousand miles later, after visiting such places as Hawaii and Fiji, New Zealand and Sweden, the Gliddens returned home to sponsor "Reliability Tours" that promoted automobiling and good roads.

Divided Highways

The automobile owed its exclusivity to its cost. By 1904, eleven European and twenty-four American manufacturers sold automobiles in the United States. The imports, which proudly imitated the design of Vanderbilt's low-slung Mercedes, averaged $8,000. Domestic models that imitated the Mercedes averaged $3,700, while primitive, high-wheeled motorized carriages averaged $1,400. The arbiter of domestic style and consumption of the day, *Country Life in America*, found it cheaper to maintain a team of horses and two carriages for a year than to drive a "first class American Automobile" four thousand miles. Even running a primitive model twenty-five hundred miles, the magazine declared, cost more than owning a horse and buggy. Given the cost of motor cars and the attitude of those like Vanderbilt who drove them, it is little wonder that the president of Princeton and future president of the United States, Woodrow Wilson, declared in 1906, "Automobilists are a picture of arrogance and wealth, with all its independence and carelessness. . . . Nothing has spread socialist feeling in this country more than the automobile."

Exclusivity did not augur solvency, however. As long as they were able to do so, Willie K. and his partners had kept their motor parkway a private affair, but they could not escape the fiscal realities. The first nine miles cost more than they had projected for the entire parkway, and the final cost of $6 million proved too high a price to pay even for pleasure. The partners learned, too, that maintenance costs could be exorbitant. In 1912, they ordered the guards posted at the entrances and exits to open it to the public and charge a $2 toll.

By 1912, automobile ownership was gradually trickling down to those of modest means. In 1906, when work on the Long Island Motor Parkway began, there were just 108,000 automobiles in the United States; a half dozen years later, when Vanderbilt opened the parkway to the public, the number had grown nearly nine-fold to 944,000. Ten percent of that number were Model T's. The Model T was a democratic machine, or, as its creator, Henry Ford, said without exaggeration, "a car for the great multitude."

Few creations so mirrored the style and idiosyncrasies of its originator as did the Model T. Provincial and populist, anti-elite and anti-intellectual, and at times fiercely anti-Semitic, Ford anchored his sentiments in distrust of monied people from the East. He was an agrarian American, far removed from the likes of Glidden and Vanderbilt. Full-faced and weighing in at something over two hundred pounds, Glidden looked the part of the industrial baron that he was. Spare, angular, almost gaunt, Ford stood five feet nine inches, weighed 135 pounds, a perfect model for a Grant Wood portrait. Raised in New England, Glidden loved to tinker with machinery as a hobby, a pleasant diversion from the work that made him a multimillionaire; raised in the Midwest, Ford employed his love of machinery and his mechanical abilities to escape the drudgery of his father's farm. Vanderbilt had vacated his elegant rooms and dropped his formal education at Harvard after a year; Ford finished his formal education studying from a McGuffey Reader in a sparse, bare schoolroom. Busying himself in a life of relaxed indolence at Newport and at his Long Island house named Idle Hour, Vanderbilt lived for amusement; practicing self-reliance, thrift, and hard work on his parents' farm in Dearborn, Ford regarded all pleasures with deep suspicion.

Ford's Model T was simple, temperamental, and, after some initial difficulties, sturdy. "As a vehicle, it was hard working, commonplace, heroic," wrote E. B. White in an elegiac essay, "Farewell My Lovely," "and it often seemed to transmit those qualities to the persons who rode in it." To White, the driver "was a man enthroned," sitting upon the car's gas tank manipulating its spark and throttle levers on the steering column while controlling its three pedals with his feet. While more sophisticated American manufacturers emulated the sleek, low-slung lines of the Mercedes and other European automobiles, Ford designed his Model T for the rough midwestern American landscape.

While others made cars for pleasure, Ford made his for work. Homely but practical, his Model T seemed able to do almost anything and go almost anywhere. He deliberately gave it high axles and three-and-a-half-inch-wide tires, the better to traverse roads cut deep with ruts made by farm wagons. "Because of their highness, one of the chief attributes of their ugliness, [they] could travel along . . . without hindrance," wrote one person who attempted a cross-country trip in a sleek, fashionable European car, "whereas we discovered to our chagrin that we had far too little clearance, and the first venturing into New Mexico ruts held us fast." The light vanadium alloy steel gave the chassis strength, and made it a relatively easy task to lift the car back onto the road when it veered off. Farmers attached steel wheels to the rear to make it into a crude tractor. Firefighters lengthened the chassis to make it into a hook-and-ladder truck. The post office used it to carry the mail over rural free delivery routes. A Ford dealer in Nashville, Tennessee, drove his Model T up the steps of the state capitol to prove its ruggedness. The only sleek lines on Ford's machine could be found in the flowing script of his name, which appeared prominently on every part. A 1913 Model T advertisement put it best: "Open your eyes and watch the Fords go by."

The Fords went by because their price went down. Ford offered the first Model T for $850—windshield, top, and headlamps extra—when he introduced it in October 1908, but by 1913, more than seven thousand dealers were offering the car for as little as $525. That year, after Ford began building the chassis for his Model T on a moving assembly line, his first significant step toward full mass production, the price began to drop.

Henry Ford's achievements in the production and sales of his Model T soon attracted competitors. By far the most serious was William Crapo Durant of General Motors, who in 1912 began a new automobile line that he named after the Swiss-born French racing car driver Louis Chevrolet. In 1915, Chevrolet introduced the "490." Featuring electric lights and electric starter, the "490" sold for $550, a price, Durant said, that would compete with Henry Ford's Model T. It was an instant success. Competition from General Motors, including the immensely popular Chevrolet, helped as well to hold prices down. By 1924, when Robert Moses began the Southern State Parkway, one could own a Model T for $290. That year American companies produced close to three and a half million automobiles.

Americans began to view the automobile, along with the telephone and electrification, as a necessity. By 1920, thirty-five percent of all households in the country had telephone service and nearly fifty percent of those living in cities had electricity. That year there were nearly nine and a quarter million car and truck registrations. Census takers found that eighty-three thousand people worked full-time manufacturing motor vehicles and equipment, while nearly twenty thousand people worked full-time at service stations and parking lots.

Ford and his chief competitor, William Crapo Durant, had helped to make Americans auto mobile. "Cars, cars, fast, fast!" the French architect and apostle of the mechanized world, Le Corbusier, put it in 1924. "One is seized, filled with enthusiasm, with joy . . . the joy of power.

The simple and naive pleasure of being in the midst of power, of strength. One participates in it. One takes part in this society: it will find a magnificent expression of its power. One believes in it."

Robert S. Lynd and Helen Merrell Lynd confirmed Le Corbusier's sentiments. In 1927, when the Lynds went to Muncie, Indiana, to conduct what would become their classic sociological study *Middletown*, a resident asked, "Why on earth do you need to study what's changing in this country? I can tell you in just four letters A-U-T-O." In Muncie, as everywhere else in the United States, the car had become, the Lynds found, "an accepted essential of normal living." "To George F. Babbitt," wrote another Hoosier, Sinclair Lewis, of the hero of his famous 1922 novel, "as to most prosperous citizens of Zenith, his motor car was poetry and tragedy, love and heroism." Hard-surfaced roads and closed cars had made driving a year-round enterprise. Ministers in Muncie and elsewhere blamed the automobile for the decline in church attendance as parishioners went off on Sunday jaunts. Bankers regretted that it had "unsettled the habit of careful saving for some families." Parents worried that it enabled their teenage children to be alone, unchaperoned, and in the dark. But everyone believed the automobile afforded them greater opportunities for work as well as leisure.

The automobile allowed Americans to engage their passion for movement as never before. Early in the century, automobile clubs began in cities like New York, Philadelphia, and Chicago. In 1902, a number of regional clubs joined together in a federation, the American Automobile Association. The AAA offered its members maps and a yearly publication entitled the *Blue Book*, which described roads, lodging, and auto garages across the country. Begun as a single volume in 1901 by the automobile club in New York, the *Blue Book* grew quickly to five volumes. It relied more on verbal descriptions of routes and a strict mileage count than on cartography:

36.0   Geneva [Illinois] State & 2nd Streets
       Straight thru with trolley (now Lincoln Highway).
       Cross JR. 36.4. Trolley leaves to right just beyond.
36.6   Left-hand road; turn diagonally left, following Lincoln
       Highway signs.
37.7   Diagonal 4-corners; bear right with poles.

38.8   End of road; jog left across RR., and right with poles. Cross
         trolley 49.1

In 1924, Rand McNally, the Chicago cartographer, offered motorists his
national road atlas. Americans were traveling ever farther from their
homes by automobile.

"Auto camping," became a popular pastime in the early twenties as
towns, cities, states, and national parks welcomed the newly mobile
tourists. Auto camping became so popular that in 1924 a group of New
York entrepreneurs began a monthly magazine, *Motor Camper and Tourist*,
with a circulation of fifty thousand. For those families who were tired of
living in a tent, entrepreneurs opened cabin camps, often just primitive
shacks in the woods with communal showers and toilets. Still others built
"motor inns" and "motor courts." Then, in December 1925, James Vail of
San Luis Obispo, California, coined a word that soon became common to
the American highway. He opened a "motel."

Black America also experienced changes that the automobile brought.
By the 1920s, especially in the industrial cities of the north, places like
Detroit, Chicago, Pittsburgh, and Philadelphia, African-Americans began
purchasing cars in numbers significant enough to make advertisers take
note. The Pittsburgh *Courier*, the most influential black newspaper of the
time, carried numerous advertisements and promotional stories that
suggested ways blacks could enjoy their new mobility. Notary publics
announced their services to help blacks secure driver's licenses. The
Auto and Aero Mechanical School of Harrisburg, Pennsylvania, offered a
chance to study automobile repair and "EARN WHILE YOU LEARN."
Car manufacturers, including Studebaker, Dodge, Chevrolet, and Chrysler, ran large advertisements, while local dealers took pains to tell
readers that "race" salespeople were on their staffs. Oil companies,
including Gulf and Standard, ran large advertisements showing black
motorists receiving friendly service at their pumps. Cars were glamorous. The *Courier* reported breathlessly on the sleek automobiles
of stars like Ethel Waters and Aubrey Lyles, including the make, the
model, the cost, even the chauffeur's name.

From across the nation the Associated Negro Press gathered other,
less glamorous news about blacks and automobiles for the *Courier*.
Injuries and deaths captured much of the space. In Chicago, "Aunt
Jemima" of pancake fame was hit by a speeding car while standing on a

street corner; well-known ministers, college presidents, entertainers, and sports figures suffered from mishaps, and less prominent people did as well. Other stories were even more ominous. On April 18, 1929, a black car driver in Brandon, Mississippi, barely escaped lynching after he injured a white man and his daughter in an accident. On September 25, 1925, white motorists near Trenton, New Jersey, refused to help five injured blacks whose car had run off the road.

By the mid-1920s, African-Americans faced the fact that their mobility could provoke hostility. Seeking car repairs, or even trying to buy gas and oil, could pose problems. Finding food and lodging, especially in the segregated South, demanded special planning and perseverance. Established automobile clubs like the American Automobile Association discouraged memberships to people of color. While the association's *Blue Book* could be found in bookstores, the routes and services it described were for white travelers. Late in 1923, Alvin Robinson and a group of black entrepreneurs in Dayton, Ohio, began the Automotive Avocation and Automobile Club, whose purpose was "to render legal, road, and information service to its members and to encourage a better understanding among the colored automobile public."

In 1929, while he was siting the Northern State Parkway across the Gold Coast of Long Island, Robert Moses was approached by the humbled millionaire William K. Vanderbilt. Twenty-three years earlier, Vanderbilt had begun a parkway for the exclusive amusement of himself and his wealthy friends, much of it along the right-of-way of his family-owned railroad line. Now Moses was building a democratic parkway for the pleasure of the people of New York, much of it on land belonging to Vanderbilt's friends. The head of the Long Island Park Commission was seizing the land through eminent domain and sometimes by crude force. For about a decade Vanderbilt's parkway had been slowly falling into disrepair, as fewer motorists were willing to pay the fee he charged to use it. The decline had been even more precipitous after the opening of the Southern State Parkway. Would Mr. Moses like to buy his road? the millionaire asked. Moses said he would be happy to purchase a few miles in the middle, an arrangement that would effectively cut Vanderbilt's parkway into two disconnected sections. Furthermore, Moses said, if Willie K. didn't agree to sell him that section, he just might site his new parkway parallel to Vanderbilt's and match it entrance for entrance. Willie K. protested the terms and the arrogant way Moses delivered them. But Moses did not soften the offer. The millionaire could sell him the section now, he said, or give the entire road away later. Negotiations ceased.

William Kissam Vanderbilt held out another nine years until 1938, when, as Moses had predicted, he gave his Long Island Motor Parkway to the counties of Nassau, Suffolk, and Queens in lieu of $90,000 in back taxes.

Having won his battles with Long Island residents and built or begun his unique parkways and parks by the end of the twenties, Moses set his sights on the greater region. In a speech to a black-tie audience of five hundred at the 1930 annual dinner of the New York Park Association, Moses outlined his plans. On a large map of the metropolitan area he had drawn heavy red lines where future roads would be. They radiated from and encircled Manhattan. They connected with the Long Island parkways and the upstate and Connecticut highways. He had even drawn a bold red line across the narrows between Brooklyn and Staten Island, suggesting the two boroughs would be connected by a bridge. Principal among the red lines was the immense structure of viaducts and bridges that came to be known as the Triborough Bridge. It would become a reality because of a reform-minded mayor of New York and a large purse of money.

The mayor was Fiorello La Guardia. After taking office in 1934, La Guardia appointed Moses head of the Triborough Bridge Authority. Established in 1933 by the previous administration, the Triborough Bridge Authority had served only as a giant engine of fraud for its commissioners, who used it to deflect city money into the pockets of their friends. (When making the appointment, La Guardia said, "These bridges are to be built of steel, not s-t-e-a-l.") The federal government's Public Works Administration provided the purse. With three of every ten nonfarm workers idle, the PWA provided a twenty-year loan of $44.2 million (one-seventh of all its funds that year), with the expectation that the money would help to employ hundreds. To the federal loan, La Guardia added another $5.4 million of city money.

Moses did not stop with roads in New York City and Long Island. Using power given to him by Al Smith and later extending it under the governor's successors, he began parkways north of New York, superbly engineered roads appropriating local mellifluous names like Saw Mill River and Hutchinson River and, most stunningly beautiful of all, a road that followed a ridge of hills in eastern New York, the Taconic State Parkway. The last inspired Lewis Mumford—no champion of Moses' later works—to call it a consummate work of art.

From Washington, engineers in the Bureau of Public Roads watched Moses' parkway projects with envy. As his road designs justly earned much praise, they decided to build parkways of their own. In Virginia in 1928, the Federal Bureau of Public Roads began a parkway from Arlington to George Washington's home at Mr. Vernon. Two years later the bureau started the Skyline Drive through the Shenandoah National Park, which in time would connect with a parkway across the Blue Ridge Mountains. In Connecticut, Congressman Schuyler Merritt championed "a real parkway like the Hutchinson Parkway." On June 29, 1938, Merritt led a procession of automobiles to open the first half of the road named in his honor. In California that year, construction began on the Arroyo Seco Parkway, a six-mile divided roadway that wound its way through a park into the Pasadena section of Los Angeles.

Near Moses' network of Long Island parkways stood the buildings of the 1939 New York World's Fair, which had risen phoenixlike from one of the most unattractive sections of the city, the stinking Corona Dumps of Flushing Meadows—the valley of the ashes in *The Great Gatsby*. Fitzgerald's "fantastic farm where ashes grow like wheat into ridges and hills and grotesque gardens" had been transformed by the fair's backers, including Robert Moses, into a gleaming, if temporary, vision of "the world of tomorrow."

Popularizing the modern as it did, the fair was a watershed in American life. The nation stood on a dividing line between the Depression and prosperity, old and modern thinking, isolationism and internationalism. Though still elusive for many, especially the seventeen percent of the workforce that was unemployed, prosperity seemed closer than at any time in the decade. The average production line worker earned 63 cents an hour, forty-five percent more than in 1933, Franklin Roosevelt's first year in office. Eighty-five percent of American homes had at least one radio. The United States had twenty million telephones, about half of all in the world. At the same time Americans were going to see

Divided Highways

Gone With the Wind at theaters across the country, they were also crowding into the new Museum of Modern Art building on West 53rd Street in New York City. Some Americans were reading in *The Grapes of Wrath* about the trials of the Joad family, who drive from the Oklahoma Dust Bowl to California over Route 66; others were puzzling through Tim Finnegan's fall and resurrection in *Finnegans Wake*. In Racine, Wisconsin, the Johnson Wax Company opened new offices designed by Frank Lloyd Wright. In his State of the Union Address to Congress that year, President Roosevelt had shifted the emphasis from New Deal programs to stimulate the economy to the looming international crisis, warning that democracies across the globe must be prepared. In a Columbia University laboratory on the Upper West Side of Manhattan Island, John Ray Dunning split the atom for the first time in America, and Albert Einstein wrote to President Roosevelt, "Some recent work . . . leads me to expect that the element uranium may be turned into a new and important source of energy."

Aside from a sixty-five-foot high marble statue of President George Washington to commemorate the 150th anniversary of his inauguration, the New York World's Fair of 1939 embraced the future. Sporting knee breeches, waistcoat, a tricornered hat, and a sword, the Gargantuan father of his country gazed from his pedestal across the fair's Constitution Mall at the two-hundred-foot-diameter free-standing sphere ("largest globe ever made by man") and the seven-hundred-foot tetrahedron ("icon of the future")—twin symbols of what soon would be a reality. The architect Wallace Harrison kept the model of his inspiration, a ball of putty and a hairpin, at his drafting table for the rest of his life. Designers of fair souvenirs—teapots and pitchers, chairs and tables, radios and watches, posters and stamps—chose to decorate their wares with Harrison's designs rather than the somber, weighty Washington.

The organizers declared "Building the World of Tomorrow" to be the fair's official theme. They coined new words and streamlined old ones: Harrison's old platonic forms of sphere and tetrahedron became the "Perisphere" and "Trylon"; Aristotelian and Roman ideals combined to form the name of the theme exhibit, "Democracity." The pavilions echoed the theme as well. In the Radio Corporation of America's pavilion, which from the air looked like a giant radio tube, the first commercial television flickered to life. Each day thousands of entranced visitors looked on in wonder at the magical black and white images emanating from a modern Plexiglas cabinet in which gleamed a wondrous collection of colored wires, glowing tubes, and electronic wizardry. Over the entrance to the Johns-Manville pavilion the figure of an asbestos-clad man stepped from flames above the bold inscription ASBESTOS THE MAGIC MINERAL. Inside, visitors saw evidence of the way the magic mineral heralded a bright future of products that included insulation and clothing. At the "Electrified Farm" off Rainbow Avenue, new machines replaced farmhands to serve the needs of an assortment of cattle, chickens, and horses.

More than anything else at the fair, however, the automobile pointed the way to the future. No exposition in history had planned so thoroughly for the car. The city of New York installed thousands of amber lights on its streets to guide motorists to Flushing Meadows, while drivers traveling from New England and upstate New York could approach the fair by crossing the new Bronx-Whitestone suspension bridge. Designed by Othmar Ammann and built by Moses with $39 million in bonds issued by the Triborough Bridge Authority, the structure stood as a consummate work of art. Most parked at the 215-acre Roosevelt Field, the largest parking lot in history, which could accommodate forty-three thousand cars. Many of the exhibitors—the petroleum pavilion, Firestone, and B. F. Goodrich, among others—displayed their products for the car. In the "Town of Tomorrow," across from the "Electrified Farm," architects had designed fifteen houses with the latest materials like plywood, glass brick, and steel windows. All but the four least expensive models featured garages; one, promoted as the "Motor Home," placed its main entrance off a two-car "motor room."

Nowhere were fairgoers more assured of the importance of the automobile than in the transportation zone, which lay across the "Bridge of Wheels" that spanned the newly constructed extension of Robert Moses' Grand Central Parkway. Though the "Court of Railways," exhibit equaled the size of the Metropolitan Museum and included a musical review by Kurt Weill, and aviation and shipping had their own distinctive structures, the exhibits of the automobile manufacturers, especially Ford and General Motors, proved to be the most popular.

Albert Kahn, the creator of the Ford pavilion (and designer of many Ford factories), anchored one corner of his building with a graceful half-mile, two-lane, helical ramp that spiraled heavenward. Ford called it the "Road of Tomorrow." Visitors rode in automated Fords, Lincoln-Zephyrs, or Mercuries, past murals illustrating modern highway construction. At the building's crown, above a rounded wall of glass brick,

Divided Highways

Kahn placed a gigantic stainless steel sculpture of the messenger to the gods, patron of travelers, and overseer of highways, Mercury. Even more arresting were exhibits installed by one of the leading apostles of streamlined design, Walter Dorwin Teague. A pragmatist who took pride in combining aesthetics with sound engineering, Teague believed that good design could improve the human condition, "raising," as he put it, "the standard of living for all people."

For the Ford exhibit Teague created a vast entrance hall, which held a thirty-foot-high animated mural of a V8 engine, its pistons, valves, and gears moving in perfect harmony. In an adjacent room, visitors saw Teague's triumph, a thirty-foot-high stepped conical display of enterprising animated figures busy turning raw materials into sleek new Fords. Teague called it the "Ford Cycle of Production." FROM THE EARTH COME THE MATERIALS, read the huge letters Teague inscribed on the wall behind the display, TO BE TRANSFORMED FOR HUMAN SERVICE BY FORD MEN, MANAGEMENT AND MACHINES.

Teague's display was a marvel of compactness. He had replicated in miniature the process of Albert Kahn's great River Rouge Ford plant in Dearborn, Michigan, a mile-long structure where iron ore literally went in at one end and new Fords came out at the other. The Ford Motor Company had brought the factory tour to Flushing Meadows; but with the "Futurama," at the intersection of the Street of Wheels and the Avenue of Transportation close by, General Motors had brought a new way of life to America.

According to a poll conducted by Dr. George Gallup's American Institute of Public Opinion, the seven-acre General Motors exhibit "far outranked all others in popularity." General Motors' specially confected name, "Futurama," suggested the wondrous scene. More than half a century later, men and women in their sixties and seventies remembered with awe waiting patiently with their parents in queues numbering as many as fifteen thousand to see the exhibit. Like the Ford pavilion, the Futurama had been designed by Albert Kahn. Similar to traffic lanes for automobiles, Kahn's ramps organized the crush into a steady flow of people, which one reporter likened to pilgrims "bound for some magic shrine." The ramps vanished into a narrow break in the building's metallic, silver-gray wall, flanked on either side by a colossal, stylized G and M. Once inside, the visitors descended still more ramps that encircled a huge map of the United States floating in the gray-blue dawn of the future. A quiet voice explained that the bands of red lights on the map showed the highways of 1939. New clusters of lights glowed to show, so the voice said, traffic congestion in 1960. Then lights of a different color glowed to reveal the solution to the congestion: "Magic Motorways."

It was the fifteen-minute ride on an upholstered, high-backed love seat into the world of 1960 that visitors remember best. From their seats they gazed upon a thirty-six-thousand-square-foot diorama that suggested the American landscape. It included farms, an amusement park, "a prosperous and thriving steel town," mountains, a climate-controlled apple orchard covered by glass, a giant hydroelectric dam, and a Le Corbusier–like city. Running across the landscape and tying the civilization together were Magic Motorways, one fourteen lanes wide, on which moved model cars, trucks, and buses. From high towers technicians monitored the traffic flow so that traffic moved at one hundred, seventy, and fifty miles per hour across the landscape to the city of tomorrow. At night, lights on the highway itself made headlamps unnecessary. From speakers in the back of each seat, visitors heard, "The world of tomorrow is a world of beauty":

Looming ahead is a 1960 Motorway intersection. . . . By means of ramped loops, cars may make right and left turns at rates of speed up to fifty miles per hour. The turning-off lanes are elevated and depressed. There is no interference from the straight ahead traffic in the higher speed lanes. . . .

Now we are traveling high above the mountains and valleys below—a bird's-eye view of a paradise for vacationers. With the fast highways of 1960, the slogan "See America First" has taken on new meaning and importance. . . .

Contrast the straight, unobstructed path of the Motorway at the right with that of the twisting, winding, ordinary road to the left of the quiet and peaceful monastery. One marvels at the complete accord of this man-made highway with the breath-taking scenic beauty of its route. . . .

At the end of the ride across America, the moving love seats brought visitors to "an important intersection in the great metropolis of 1960," with an apartment house, department store (crammed with Frigidaire appliances), auditorium, and "automobile display salon" (exhibiting the latest Chevrolets, Buicks, Oldsmobiles, LaSalles, and Cadillacs). It was all the result of "modern and efficient city planning—breath taking architecture," that produced "space, sunshine, light, and air." While pedestrians walked above on carefully planned elevated walkways in the "World of Tomorrow," traffic—General Motors cars, trucks, and buses—sped by on the motorway below. At the exit, an attendant handed each visitor a white lapel pin on which bold blue letters proclaimed: I HAVE SEEN THE FUTURE.

"We enter a new era. Are we ready for the changes that are coming?" asked Norman Bel Geddes, creator of the General Motors exhibit. In his writings and designs, Bel Geddes saw himself as one who would usher in the future. A curious mixture of flamboyance, vision, and reality, his extravagant plans often emphasized effect. For a production of *The Miracle*, a dramatization of the Madonna coming to life, he transformed the theater into a cathedral, complete with pews, stained-glass windows, groined Gothic arches supporting the ceiling, and a thirty-foot-high altar. Some of the 470 costumes he designed for the production were so heavy that stagehands had to lower them on to the actors' shoulders by means of ropes and pulleys. He once designed a new stadium for the Brooklyn Dodgers that would dispense hot dogs, peanuts, beer, and soda through the arms of the individual seats.

In 1927, Bel Geddes brought the world of theater to the enterprise of industrial design. "Just as surely as the artists of the fourteenth century are remembered by their cathedrals," he pronounced windily a half decade later, "so will those of the twentieth be remembered for their factories and the products of those factories." In Bel Geddes's world, ships, buses, trains, and cars would all be "streamlined" to resemble teardrops. In 1932, at the depth of the Depression, he published his prophesies in a lavishly illustrated book entitled *Horizons*. So influenced by Bel Geddes's words were the engineers at Chrysler that they designed a car around the aerodynamic theme, which they named the "Airflow."

Not everyone bought the Bel Geddes vision. Robert Moses termed the idea of a national highway system "bunk" and pressed for more local parkways; Lewis Mumford found Bel Geddes's design ideas so out of date that he likened them to one who "discovered" America in 1592. Others pointed out that Le Corbusier had anticipated his design of cities. Still others remarked that his motorways seemed to avoid the cities altogether. But the designer took little notice. In *Magic Motorways*, another lavishly illustrated book, he proposed his "national motorway system" in great detail. "A modern highway system would extend a city's commuting radius 6 times," he insisted. By 1960, Bel Geddes prophesied, cars would travel from New York to Los Angeles in just twenty-four hours. "Every highway intersection is obsolete," he maintained. Only "roads originally designed for wagons" prevented his vision from becoming a reality.

"All eyes to the future," proclaimed the voice from the speaker in the love seat at the Futurama as it glided to a halt. The connection had been made: roads were not merely concrete, but "highways to new horizons of a country's welfare and happiness." Highways—especially those filled with General Motors cars and trucks on them—held the key to the nation's future.

Few bothered to think through what the designer and automaker were actually proposing: If Americans wanted to enjoy their cars and all the benefits they could bring to the modern world, they would have to rebuild their highways and move beyond the limits of their cities. In its seductive Futurama, General Motors had created a terrible temptation combining speed, mobility, and freedom that Americans would find irresistible.

In General Motors' and Bel Geddes's vision, replanning and rebuilding the city would take place simultaneously with highway building. The profession of urban planning had developed in the twenties largely in response to the chaotic conditions of American cities. By 1939, New Deal planners had begun to focus on solutions to the problem of urban "blight." Many of those who had stood in line at the Futurama had taken the subway to the fair from crowded apartments in Manhattan, Brooklyn, or the Bronx. They were dazzled by the idea of a city of the sort Bel Geddes had created. In the Futurama there were three separate units, "residential, commercial and industrial." Instead of walking to work or the store, Americans in 1960 would depend on "a highly developed modern traffic system" of "wide open thoroughfares" that displaced "outmoded business sections and undesirable slum areas." Workers would live in new suburbs, accessible only by automobile, with better homes, parks, schools, and healthful surroundings. The connection was complete: Automobiles—and a modern highway system on which they traveled—would solve urban problems.

. . .

Divided Highways

The influence of Robert Moses' road construction projects and Norman Bel Geddes's transcontinental diorama extended far beyond Long Island and Flushing Meadows. Their work signaled a far different future for America that few at the time envisioned.

Moses built his highways principally to enable eight hundred thousand middle-class New Yorkers who owned automobiles to escape the city to the Long Island beaches. As brilliantly engineered and designed as his roads were, Moses made them the exclusive preserve of automobiles. He excluded trucks and all commercial traffic. Nor did he allow buses; indeed, the clearance of the striking, granite-faced parkway bridges was too low to accommodate them. In later years some critics would charge Moses as being racially motivated, as his decision kept African-Americans, most of whom did not have cars, off Long Island. He refused to allow train or subway cars to cross the Bronx-Whitestone Bridge.

Despite Moses' contemptuous dismissal of Bel Geddes's vision of a national highway system as "bunk," the theatrical designer's ideas often eclipsed the master builder's. Like Moses' roads, Bel Geddes's helped to decentralize the city. The designer's highways accommodated trucks and buses (his de Medici patron, General Motors, made both) as well as cars; were engineered for speeds of one hundred miles per hour; and allowed cars to travel down exit ramps at fifty. It was Bel Geddes's and General Motors' vision, not Moses', that became the reality of the Inter-state Highway System.

By 1939, automobile driving had long since passed from an amusing activity for the enjoyment of the indolent and wealthy to become an essential part of American life. Even the Joads in Steinbeck's *Grapes of Wrath* drove to California in their own truck. When Robert and Helen Lynd returned to Muncie, Indiana, in 1935 to see how residents were enduring the economic crisis that gripped the nation, they found car ownership to be "one of the most depression-proof elements of the city's life." The average person in Muncie, they declared, "owns some kind of an auto instead of riding other people's streetcars and buses."

The pattern that the Lynds saw in Muncie held for the rest of America, too. While the Depression, which had crippled so many of the nation's industries, curbed the number of automobile registrations briefly, there were still 3 million more cars on the road in 1939 than a decade earlier. By 1939, the 130 million people of the United States were driving more than ever before. Thirty-one million automobiles, trucks, and buses in the United States traveled 285 billion miles over 3.25 million miles of streets, roads, and highways.

By 1939, Americans fully embraced that expression of power, though international and national events would not enable them to realize it fully for nearly two decades. Nevertheless, Robert Moses and Norman Bel Geddes had shown them the future and they trusted it with an avidity rarely matched in American history.

THE DREAMWAY

Every Valley shall be exalted, and every mountain and hill shall be made low: and the crooked shall be made straight and the rough places plain.

ISAIAH, 40:3–4

It is exactly 12:01 A.M. on the morning of Tuesday, October 1, 1940. Men and youths, nearly all wearing ties and many in suits and jackets, pose around a truck. The mood is festive as they swarm around the cab and the front hood. The driver smiles as he stands on the running board, his left hand gripping the open door. The arms of many wave high in celebration. There is a sense among them that they are a part of a significant moment. One man wearing a sweater beneath his suit jacket leaps into the camera's view and lands on his right leg with his arm outstretched. A broad smile crosses his face as though he were relieved to be included in the camera's frame just as the shutter clicks. The camera has recorded revelry. The truck is the first vehicle to pass through the Irwin tollbooth of the Pennsylvania Turnpike. Though its builders have chosen to call it a "turnpike"—an honorable word of French and Anglo-Saxon ancestry little used in America since the last century—it is the nation's newest and best engineered highway, and it ranks with the finest in the world. "It is," says Walter Adelbert Jones, the chairman of the Turnpike Commission, "the cynosure of all eyes, a Dreamway."

The Pennsylvania Turnpike is a triumph of engineering. One hundred and sixty miles of reinforced four-lane concrete pavement extending from the western side of Harrisburg to the eastern side of Pittsburgh, the road tunnels under the Allegheny Mountains and cuts about five hours off the journey between the cities. It is like no other road in America: a maximum rise at any point of just three feet in every hundred; a minimum sight distance of six hundred feet; bridges and underpasses to do away with cross traffic; and wide, banked curves that eliminate the need to slow down. Cars and trucks enter and exit the highway at one of the places turnpike officials call "interchanges." Those returning from a visit to the New York World's Fair, which closed in October 1940, found 160 miles of the future just as Norman Bel Geddes and General Motors had presented it.

For Franklin Delano Roosevelt the Pennsylvania Turnpike represented a triumph of the New Deal programs that had paid for it. It would help strengthen national defense, which increasingly was relying on efficient motor transportation to move men and matériel. And the jobs the highway created might help FDR to win the state in that fall's presidential election over his Republican rival, Wendell Wilkie.

For Thomas Harris MacDonald the highway marked the first significant and successful challenge to the authority of the Bureau of Public Roads in two decades.

Certainly no American president before him took such an intense delight in driving and in roads as did Franklin Delano Roosevelt. While living in a cottage on the New Jersey shore in the summer of 1908, he commuted to his Wall Street law office each day in his new Ford. When campaigning for a seat in the New York State Senate, he canvassed for votes in a two-cylinder Maxwell touring car. In Warm Springs, the town in southeastern Georgia where Roosevelt took hydrotherapy for his paralyzed legs, he had a local blacksmith equip a Model T with hand controls of his own design. The series of levers, attached through the dashboard to each of the pedals, enabled him to drive the car about the Georgia countryside and restored some of the freedom he had lost with his paralysis. After he became president, he often drove a similarly equipped Packard on the country roads of Dutchess County near his family home at Hyde Park. Never mind that

FDR's friends and family considered him a terrible and dangerous driver, so dangerous that his wife, Eleanor, refused to ride if he was at the wheel. Others, like Winston Churchill on a visit to Hyde Park, were willing to venture out on a drive with the president, even if they felt their lives were in great peril.

Franklin Roosevelt's letters, memoranda, and actions make it clear that he took almost as much enjoyment in planning the construction of roads as he did in driving on them. As president of the Taconic State Park Commission in New York in 1924, he had overseen the planning for the spectacularly beautiful 125-mile parkway that would open to motorists the upstate counties and the Hudson River valley. As governor of New York, he worked to improve farm roads and moved to have the state shift the responsibility for construction and maintenance from the counties to the state, thereby ensuring that roads through poorer counties would equal those in wealthier areas.

As president, Franklin Roosevelt took immense delight in not merely supporting the financing of roads but tinkering with the details of their construction. In May 1936, when Mussolini's Legions were overrunning Ethiopia, Hitler's Army of the Third Reich was reoccupying the Rhineland, Spain was drifting toward civil war, and Roosevelt himself was preparing for his reelection campaign, he still found time to dictate a two-page memorandum to Harold Ickes, his Secretary of the Interior, approving a loan to build an "overseas road and bridge" to Miami. "But," he said, "the total cost of the construction is too high." It should be reduced by $784,000. "About 4,334 feet of trusses can be made single. This would give a saving of $75.00 a foot or $325,050. . . . The draw spans can be made single— 302 feet—at a saving of $200.00 per foot or $60,400. . . . A saving of about 27,000 feet at $15.00 per foot on the plate girder spans, and on about 36,000 feet, at a saving of $11.00 on the arch spans, would save $399,000."

The president's friends described his knowledge of American geography, the contours of the landscape, its coastline and rivers, its mountains and plains, as "uncanny." In another 1936 memorandum to Harold Ickes, Roosevelt spoke of a parkway that would make it possible for motorists to drive from the Shenandoah National Park in Virginia to Worcester, Massachusetts. He favored a "mountain route" over "the so-called metropolitan route":

Tom Lewis

If you remember, the route I suggested ran on high ground following roughly the eastern slope of the Blue Ridge, through Virginia, Maryland and Pennsylvania; thence through northern New Jersey connecting with the Bear Mountain Park road through Sterling, New York; thence through Bear Mountain Park over existing roads across Bear Mountain Bridge; thence Fahnstock Park, Putnam County, New York; thence following the existing Eastern Parkway a few miles and then east through Southern Duchess County to Pawling; thence working gradually east through the Berkshires and Northern Connecticut to Worcester.

Given his interest in road building, it is little wonder that early in 1937 Roosevelt called Thomas MacDonald, chief of the Bureau of Public Roads, to the White House. On a map of the United States, the president had drawn three lines north and south and three lines east and west. These would be the routes for a new transcontinental system of interstate toll highways, he explained.

From the time of the first automobile, Americans had been fixated on the idea of crossing the continent by road. After Horatio Nelson Jackson and his personal mechanic made the trip from San Francisco to New York in the spring of 1903, other intrepid drivers followed. Six years later, Alice Huyler Ramsey, a twenty-one-year-old graduate of Vassar, became the first woman to drive across the country. Ramsey piloted her forest-green Maxwell and three female companions from New York City to San Francisco in forty-one days. In 1913, Carl Graham Fisher, an aggressive entrepreneur from Indianapolis who had recently built a motor speedway on the edge of town, proposed the transcontinental road that came to be called the Lincoln Highway. "The highways of America are built chiefly of politics," Fisher said, alluding to those who determined the amount of money to be spent on road building, "whereas the proper material is crushed rock or concrete." A natural salesman who sported yellow polo coats, stickpins for his ties, and a pince-nez on the bridge of his nose, Fisher pitched his idea to a party of automobile barons he assembled in Indianapolis. The "coast-to-coast rock highway" would begin at New York City's Times Square and end in San Francisco's Golden Gate Park.

Fisher wanted his Lincoln Highway ready in time for San Francisco's 1915 Panama-Pacific Exposition. "Let's build it," he told the barons, "before we're too old to enjoy it." Many, including Henry Bourne Joy, president of Packard, and Frank Sieberling, president of the Sieberling Tire Company and known to all as the "Rubber King," opened their wallets; but others, like Henry Ford, would have nothing of the scheme. As Willie K. Vanderbilt and his friends had already learned on Long Island, the task of highway building went beyond the means of any group of wealthy individuals. Fisher and his friends had to settle for designating the route and creating "seedling miles," one mile of—for the time—superb concrete pavement. The miles would, the boosters hoped, prompt citizens to campaign among local and state governments for improvements along the Lincoln Highway.

Other transcontinental highways followed, including the Roosevelt (named in honor of the president's uncle, Theodore), between Washington and Los Angeles; the Jefferson, from Winnipeg to New Orleans; and the Dixie, from Duluth and Chicago to a new resort Carl Graham Fisher was building on the south Florida coast, Miami Beach. And, of course, on Mac-Donald's federal-aid highway system, motorists could choose from a network of roads that would take them across the continent.

Proposals for superhighways had been in the air since the beginning of the New Deal. In an address on national planning, Harold Ickes had spun out his vision of a "high speed highway from the Atlantic to the Pacific." Local heads of chambers of commerce were inspired to write about the ways in which the new highway would benefit their communities. "Imagine this Super-Highway," wrote an official of the Greater Pittsburgh Chamber of Commerce who allowed his enthusiasm to overtake his logic. "Since there is no reason for speed limits . . . travel is expedited to the point where it combines the speed of the aeroplane with the safety of the railroad." Futuristic artists delighted in showing an endless highway fading straight into the horizon, with trucks and cars hurtling along, thin lines denoting great speed trailing in their wake. Clouds appeared to lift and become lighter over the highway. The entire scene suggested the dawn of a new day.

Some planners believed super transcontinental highways would also help counter the continuing decline in rural life. The 1920 census showed more people lived in urban areas than on farms; ten years later, the trend continued. Five cities now counted more than a million inhabitants, up from three a decade before. The number of cities with 25,000 to 50,000 and 50,000 to 100,000 inhabitants increased by thirty percent. Surely, so the thinking went, transcontinental highways would help distribute the population more evenly across the landscape. As early as 1934, Henry Wallace, the Secretary of Agriculture, had discussed the idea with Roosevelt. "Undoubtedly, decentralization properly worked out in connection with concrete roads and electricity will have a lot to do with providing a more satisfactory life for the next generation," Wallace wrote after a conversation in early October. But he added, "The effect on real estate values in the large cities may not, of course, be altogether happy." By February 1935, word of superhighway discussions reached the *Washington Post*. The president, the newspaper reported, had "discussed with congressional advisers the possibility of using a substantial portion of the works fund" for the project.

At one point Roosevelt and his staff considered the possibility of "excess land taking," using the government's power of eminent domain to take a broad tract of land—a thousand feet or even half a mile—for superhighways and then lease the land back to businesses, including factories and hotels. The president was intrigued by the idea, which he sketched out on a sheet of paper. As the roads increased in popularity, the land would increase in value, making the entire project "self-liquidating." If, as some around Roosevelt suggested, the government sold gasoline at stations along the way, the roads would pay for themselves even faster.

As he sat in the White House two years later watching Roosevelt trace the six lines across the continent, MacDonald faced an unprecedented challenge. The new superhighways were going to be toll roads, a method of financing construction and maintenance that he believed unsound and impractical and, most important, threatened his control of road building. In the past, he had endured other New Deal highway schemes that bypassed the Bureau of Public Roads by pointing out their inefficiencies. His allies in Congress worked to insure that money flowed through the bureau.

No doubt the president presented his plan with enthusiasm. It was the sort of pet project that appealed to his flair for boldness. No doubt the Chief balanced Roosevelt's enthusiasm with caution. His quiet circumspection had enabled him to survive four presidents and six Secretaries of Agriculture, any one of whom might have dismissed him in an instant. MacDonald was never known to allow a casual word or phrase to slip through the fence of his teeth. He was far too wise to do so at this moment. He would study the proposal—the study would take time—and deliver a report.

Divided Highways

. . .

In April 1938, the Chief delivered *Toll Roads and Free Roads* to the White House, at about the same time Congress was taking up the question of a superhighway system. *Toll Roads* was vintage MacDonald: charts, maps, economic statistics, data on transcontinental travel, construction costs, enough dust to fill the eyes of even the most ardent bureaucrat. A plate showed the six roads, 14,336 miles, crisscrossing the country in almost the same fashion as Roosevelt had drawn them a year earlier. Yes, the Chief reported, it would be possible to construct toll, four-lane, divided superhighways. But, he said, it would be economically impractical.

MacDonald backed his prediction with "facts" generated by his highway machine. Forecasters at General Motors estimated that by 1960 motor vehicle use would increase by fifty percent. The Department of Commerce found that less than half of the families owning automobiles earned over $1,500 a year. This fact suggested most drivers would not be willing (or able) to pay a toll. The bureau's own enumerators found actual transcontinental highway travel was extremely light and that the length of most trips fell far short of thirty miles, the average distance between access points on a toll highway. Only a toll road on the 172 miles between Philadelphia and New Haven, MacDonald concluded, would earn "slightly more than its estimated cost" by 1960. If Congress wanted to fund a road with a "reasonable prospect of the recovery of costs through tolls," it should vote to build one between Washington and Boston.

While MacDonald marshaled his facts with conviction, he did not consider all the information at his disposal. To find a convincing argument for a toll road he need have looked no further than Robert Moses' experiences in New York City. Each day motorists crammed the approaches to the tollbooths at his Triborough Bridge, where they gladly paid 25 cents to cross. The Triborough was netting a cool $1.3 million a year. Bankers had thought Moses' predictions for traffic on the Henry Hudson Bridge far-fetched. They refused to buy the bonds to finance it until he had scaled the bridge down from two decks to one. Yet after its first year of operation, the Henry Hudson brought in $600,000 above expenses, and engineers were busy preparing designs for the second deck. Every month since the opening of the two bridges, the number of cars—and the amount of revenue—had increased. Motorists traveling Moses' parkways which fed his bridges now complained of frequent traffic jams. The master builder responded with plans for more bridges and parkways to accommodate more cars. In a short time, these, too, would fill with cars—and fill Moses' coffers as well.

The Chief chose to disregard such facts. New York, after all, was an exception to the rule, and he and others in the Bureau of Public Roads were not happy about it. "The real question is the very simple one of whether it is sound public policy to grant the right to collect a private profit from the user of the highway," he wrote. "The answer ought to be a vigorous and authoritative 'No.' There is no place on the highway today for the privately-owned toll bridge."

Still, MacDonald realized that the nation's roads were becoming increasingly crowded, especially in large cities like Chicago and Los Angeles. Despite the Depression, Americans were buying automobiles. Production had climbed from a Depression low of 1.1 million cars in 1932 to nearly four times that in 1937. That year seven states registered over a million motor vehicles, and two of them—New York and California—counted about 2.5 million.

Understanding that the bureau's rejection of toll roads did nothing to address the growing problem of highway congestion, MacDonald proposed a "master plan for highway development." It called for a series of interregional roads. Older thoroughfares were to be upgraded: Curves were to be lengthened, sight lines were to be increased, and near cities the thoroughfares were to be widened to four lanes. Only in the cities that were choking on traffic did the plan call for radical changes. By-passes to convey traffic around the congestion would not suffice, for the bureau's origin and destination studies had found that ninety percent of the traffic on main roads near cities was bound for the city itself. Express highways cutting "into and through the center of big cities" would have to be built. Whenever possible, the report suggested, highway builders should take the right-of-way for the new roads in the areas of slum clearance where the land would be cheap.

In *Toll Roads and Free Roads* MacDonald and his engineers in the Bureau of Public Roads had hit upon a central question of modern life: what to do with the automobile in the city. The Chief had begun his professional life when "better roads" groups repeated the slogan "To get the farmer out of the mud" almost as though it were a mantra. Now officials in cities like Philadelphia, Boston, and New Orleans called upon MacDonald's engineers and Robert Moses to help them relieve their traffic-congested streets. Moses drew up plans that eradicated slums, less desirable neighborhoods, and parks, which would, he said, help the automobile to move freely and thus help cities to survive. The solution, so Moses and many other engineers believed, was to drive highways farther into the cities.

For the moment MacDonald's strategy had worked: FDR's six roads remained simply lines on paper. By 1939, Roosevelt had become increasingly preoccupied with world events. That spring General Francisco Franco's Junta of National Defense captured Madrid to end the Spanish Civil War. Prime Minister Benito Mussolini's fascist forces invaded Albania. Adolf Hitler's Army of the Third Reich invaded Czechoslovakia to effectively annihilate the Czech state. Roosevelt grew concerned, too, about the United States' military force, whose strength ranked eighteenth in the world, behind even Sweden and Switzerland. Prior to 1939, the Roosevelt administration had always regarded massive public works projects like road building as a way of providing employment. Now defense contracts of more than a billion dollars would enable American industries to hire thousands of new workers. But there was still federal money for the Pennsylvania Turnpike. The project would give Franklin Delano Roosevelt a small portion of his national system of superhighways, and it proved much of what Thomas MacDonald presented in his report *Toll Roads and Free Roads* to have been wrong.

To a traveler crossing the state, Pennsylvania presents a series of stark topographic contrasts. At Philadelphia on the Delaware River, where most seventeenth- and eighteenth-century travelers arrived, the land is nearly flat, an extension of the Atlantic coastal plain. Westward, the rolling hills of Chester and Lancaster turn into the three divisions of the Appalachian range: the Piedmont, the Appalachian ridges and valleys, and the Allegheny Plateau. Like fingers, the mountains stretch diagonally from the southwest to the northeast across the center of the state. One after another they appear: Blue Mountain, Kittatinny, Tuscarora, Jacks Mountain, the Allegheny Mountains, and Laurel Hill. Beyond Laurel Hill lies the Allegheny Plateau and Pittsburgh, about 800 feet above the sea. Though the height of each mountain (between 1,775 feet at Kittatinny and 2,800 feet at Laurel Hill) is not particularly demanding, in the aggregate the 160-mile climb over six mountains challenges even the heartiest traveler.

From the beginning of European settlement in the region, the mountains have proven a formidable obstacle. In 1758, during the French and Indian Wars, British General Edward Braddock found them so. Braddock set out with twenty-two hundred British and colonial troops and 150 Conestoga wagons from Fort Cumberland at the head of the Potomac River to drive the French from Fort Duquesne on the Monongahela River near Pittsburgh. To get there, Braddock ordered two hundred woodsmen to widen a narrow Indian trace into a twelve-foot-wide road across dozens of creeks and swamps and over eight major mountains. The first long major road on the continent, it straddled the Pennsylvania-Maryland border until it crossed the Laurel Ridge, where it swung north toward Fort Duquesne. But eight miles from his destination, Fort Duquesne, the general was ambushed and killed by a party of the Ottawa and Potawatomi tribes. It fell to a young colonel from Virginia, George Washington, to bury the general's remains.

Thirty-six years after Braddock's death, President George Washington ventured into the mountains once again, this time to put down the Whiskey Insurrection of 1794. Angry over the federal government's new tax on distilled liquor, a group of rebellious Scotch-Irish farmers were roaming the frontier counties of the state burning official buildings, robbing the U.S. mails, and insulting government officers. After one officer was tarred and feathered, Washington decided to muster a militia of fifteen thousand at Bedford in the middle of the state to quell the rebellion. The road west proved to be a formidable obstacle to the force. Even Washington took fifteen days to travel 210 miles from the capital at Philadelphia to Bedford.

The nation's third president, Thomas Jefferson, built a "National Road" through the mountains to link the young nation with the new territory in Ohio. When engineers built the Pennsylvania Canal in the nineteenth century, they had to use railroad links and long inclined planes to haul canal boats over the Alleghenies. (It was there that a young engineer from Germany, John Augustus Roebling, got the idea of replacing the hemp ropes used to pull the canal boats up the incline with ropes made of twisted strands of iron, thus starting him in the wire rope and cable business. Roebling went on to design suspension aqueducts and bridges that employed cables of iron and steel.)

With the nation's industrial expansion after the Civil War and the lure of great profits to be made transporting goods, railroad competition often turned savage. When the Pennsylvania Railroad built a line parallel to William Henry Vanderbilt's New York Central Railroad tracks up the Hudson River, Vanderbilt retaliated by starting construction on a line of his own parallel to the Pennsylvania's across the western part of the Keystone state. In two years, between September 1883, and September 1885, engineers directed thousands of Hungarian, Italian, and black laborers as they furiously cleared the right-of-way, graded the roadbed, built bridges, and blasted nine tunnels into the mountains for the new South Penn Railroad. They were nearing completion when J. P. Morgan stepped into the fray. Fearing that a battle of the two rail titans might lead to the mortal wounding of each, Morgan brokered a deal whereby the Pennsylvania resigned all interest on the Hudson and Vanderbilt abandoned the South Penn. On September 12, 1885, two years and $10 million after he had begun the work, Vanderbilt ordered it stopped. Along the track beds, inside the tunnels, and at half-built bridges, workers dropped their tools and, bitter at their firing, wandered off into the mountains, some to use their skills working underground in Pennsylvania's coal mines. For half a century, "Vanderbilt's Folly," as locals called the old railroad bed, would lie abandoned and derelict.

By 1935, Pennsylvania had 2.2 miles of road for every square mile in the state, two and half times the national average. But as the commonwealth also boasted seven percent of all motor vehicles in the nation— sixteen vehicles for every mile—Pennsylvania's main roads were hopelessly inadequate. The principal federal east-west route, 30 (the former Lincoln Highway), was narrow, steep, icy in winter, and often clogged with interstate truck traffic. The accumulated vertical climb over the mountains amounted to nearly fourteen thousand feet, the equivalent of a trip to the summit of Mt. Wilson in California. On a good day the three-hundred-mile trip over Route 30 from Pittsburgh to Philadelphia, through Greensburg, Bedford, Chambersburg, Gettysburg, York, and Lancaster, could take ten hours. But if one happened to get behind a truck pulling a heavy load up the steep, narrow road over, say, Tuscarora Mountain; if a factory in York changed shifts; if school let out in Chambersburg; or if the road was slick with rain or ice, the trip became an even longer and more arduous ordeal of twelve, thirteen, fourteen hours.

For relief, Henry Van Dyke, the commonwealth's farsighted state highway commissioner, looked to Vanderbilt's South Penn route.

Perhaps it might serve as a new road. Works Progress Administration funds, the first of many federal grants for what became the Pennsylvania Turnpike, enabled Van Dyke to have the route surveyed to see if a highway was possible. A year later the state legislature voted to create a five-person Turnpike Commission to be appointed by the governor, but did not vote a single dollar of the $70 million engineers had estimated it would take to build the road. Skeptical Pennsylvanians doubted the turnpike would ever become a reality.

Nor were people reassured when Pennsylvania's Democratic governor, George H. Earle, appointed Walter Adelbert Jones of Pittsburgh to be the commission's chairman. The son of an Ohio window glass manufacturer, Jones had grown up in Toledo and received a bachelor's degree from Ohio Wesleyan University. After graduation, he made many millions in glass manufacturing, banking, and oil refining in Ohio and Pennsylvania. But Jones knew nothing about road building or highways; indeed, he preferred to travel by train. Critics alleged that Earle had appointed the millionaire only to repay him for his generous financial support in the 1934 gubernatorial election.

Whatever thoughts of repayment might have been in the governor's mind, he had made a wise appointment nonetheless. Jones was one of those shadowy figures in the American political scene: a person of considerable wealth and power who, though never at center stage and sometimes never onstage at all, influenced all the action. Beginning with his friend Warren G. Harding, Jones enjoyed easy access to the White House. In 1924, he was a Republican elector for Harding's successor, Calvin Coolidge. But with the coming of the New Deal, Jones switched to the Democratic Party, and in 1936 contributed $150,000 to help re-elect Franklin Delano Roosevelt. That contribution and his friendship with Marvin McIntyre, one of the president's chief advisers, gave him a quiet influence in the New Deal. He maintained apartments at the Duquesne Club in Pittsburgh, the Penn Harris Hotel in Harrisburg, the Waldorf-Astoria in New York, and the Mayflower in Washington, each city a place where Jones knew politicians who might be of use to him in his numerous business ventures. Now Jones divided his time between the Penn Harris and the Mayflower.

Jones believed he had to raise about $60 million to build the road. Finding bankers skeptical about purchasing bonds, he turned to the New Deal's Reconstruction Finance Corporation. It agreed to buy nearly $35 million (later increased to $41 million) in bonds at three and a half percent. After securing Roosevelt's approval, Harold Ickes, head of the Public Works Administration, added an additional $25 million grant to cover the costs of labor.

To the Roosevelt administration, building the road was a practical and political imperative. Figures of the federal government's first "Unemployment Census," conducted between November 16 and November 30, 1937, found 566,437 Pennsylvanians unemployed and in want of work and 300,809 partly employed and in need of more work. Should the president decide to run for an unprecedented third term, it would be useful to have helped fund a superhighway in the middle of a state with thirty-eight electoral votes, a highway that would give employment to thousands of men at the site and thousands more in factories across the Northeast.

Now, with federal government backing, building could begin. On October 10, 1938, the PWA gave its formal notice of the grant. Seventeen days later, Walter Adelbert Jones led the commissioners of the Pennsylvania Turnpike Authority to the hamlet of Newburgh in Cumberland County, about fifty miles from Harrisburg. There, at a place locals called the Eberley Farm, which would become the eastern end of the turnpike, Jones turned the ceremonial spade of earth to break ground for his "dreamway."

As Jones walked to the spot in the field that would soon be a four-lane highway, Mrs. Eberley told her nine-year-old daughter, Edna, to shake the commissioner's hand. "It might be," she told the girl, "the only time you'll hold on to a million dollars."

Federal requirements called for engineers to complete the entire Pennsylvania Turnpike by the end of May 1940—160 miles in twenty months, an average of about a quarter mile of four-lane highway a day. No one could remember ever having built a road of this length over such rugged terrain in so short a time, and no one had ever built a road with such demanding specifications as the Pennsylvania Turnpike. But the Roosevelt administration wanted the road completed in time to influence the outcome of the state's upcoming race for governor. Later the administration would extend the deadline another thirty days. But, given the reality of the two winters and two springs in the construction period, and the fact that this highway was different from any that had gone before, even with an extra month the task seemed impossible.

The job of building the turnpike fell upon the shoulders of Samuel Marshall, who had worked with Henry Van Dyke on the initial survey for the road. By all accounts, the forty-seven-year-old Marshall was a first-rate civil engineer. A native of Philadelphia, a graduate of Central High—the city's premier public school—and the University of Pennsylvania's School of Engineering, he had served as an infantry captain in France during World War I. After the war he became chief engineer of Pennsylvania's Highway Department. In 1938, he resigned to direct construction of the turnpike. Many of the practices and standards Marshall developed when building the superhighway served as a model others would emulate when building the Interstate Highway System.

Marshall brought the organizational precision of a major general to his job. From a central command post at Harrisburg the chief engineer directed the work of five divisions—highway, tunnels, bridges, architectural, and electrical. A field commander whom Marshall appointed to head each division reported directly to him. The construction was far too large for one company to complete, so Marshall decided to divide the job into parts and award a series of smaller contracts. In the end the Turnpike Commission awarded 155 contracts to 118 different companies. To meet the deadline, work would have to proceed in sequence, on a timely schedule, and around the clock. Over eleven hundred men and women of his professional engineering staff would oversee the progress and maintain the quality of the construction.

"It was, in my opinion, the fastest moving, hardest hitting engineering organization with which I have ever been associated," Marshall later wrote. Engineers, equipment manufacturers, and contractors approached the chief engineer to tell him "in great confidence that the thing could not be done," that equipment could not operate twenty-four hours a day, laborers could not be found, the commission could not oversee the construction. Marshall ignored them and went forward.

"You were there when something was to be done," remembered Jesse Aycock, who worked as an inspector overseeing the contractors as they mixed cement and poured concrete. "Frequently there were maybe two or three days that you didn't leave the site. You had to see it through."

Even before he got the final word of approval from Washington for the loans and grants, Henry Van Dyke loaned Jones money from the state's highway department to hire a Baltimore engineering firm to design the turnpike. Jones also awarded an additional contract to drain the water and muck from the tunnels. Plans called for the turnpike to use thirty-four miles of railroad property, including seven tunnels, for which Jones paid $1 million. The remaining right-of-way for the road would come from 750 properties in its path. Jones was fortunate to have the power of a unique clause in Pennsylvania's eminent domain law behind him. Owners who refused to agree on a price for their land learned that the Turnpike Commission had the right to take their property *before* reaching terms for a final settlement.

The first contracts Marshall awarded were for grading of the roadway, building bridges at overpasses, and laying drainage culverts. Contract No. 29, for example, called for grading and the construction of nineteen bridges on what would become nine and a half miles of Turnpike near the Fort Littleton interchange. The work had to be completed in 120 calendar days, 2,880 hours of around-the-clock work. Highway builders completed the job on time at a cost of nearly three quarters of a million dollars.

Contracts demanded that construction companies equip all earth-moving equipment with headlamps. Special portable generator plants provided electric lighting for night work. Nearly all the grading equipment was diesel-powered. Of the more than two hundred power shovels that contractors brought to the site, just two were steam. To avoid costly delays, the commission required contractors to have an ample reserve of spare parts to fix their machines. No breakdowns were going to stop this road-building machine.

A highway like U.S. Route 30 customarily followed the contour of the terrain, including many of the narrow twists and turns in the landscape, while climbing over mountains and descending into valleys. Builders used graders to spread earth and level the roadbed. But the new turnpike leveled the landscape and straightened the curves in ways rarely done before. Workers employed dynamite, power shovels, and graders to make enormous cuts through ridges, and used much of the earth they removed to fill valleys in between.

Blasting operations showed best the organization that Marshall imposed on the job. At one end of a cut, a team of workers drilled holes fifteen to twenty-five feet into the rocks, loaded them with dynamite, and detonated them, moved their operation to the other end of the cut, and repeated their drilling and loading. Meanwhile, a second team of workers moved in with power shovels, bulldozers, and heavy hauling equipment to remove the loose rock and earth. At the half-mile-long, 150-foot-deep Clear Ridge Cut east of Everett, workers removed over a million cubic yards of material—mostly rock—enough to fill Yankee Stadium to the upper deck.

The culverts and bridges for overpasses proved to be relatively easy for the contractors, though most had never built such structures before. Turnpike engineers called for rigid-frame concrete bridges, usually seventy-eight feet in length and always reinforced with steel. Carpenters erected a false structure of local wood under the span and built the forms of heavy plywood. At nearby railroad sidings the Turnpike Commission built temporary cement plants to supply the concrete. Commission inspectors, testing engineers, geologists, and bridge engineers moved from site to site overseeing the construction. After the concrete cured, carpenters removed the forms and scantling work to reveal a gracefully curved span of concrete suspended between two massive vertical concrete piers. Flanking the pillars were concrete buttresses that added to the bridge's stability.

It took turnpike contractors only 160 days to build the longest bridge, the 600-foot New Stanton Viaduct. Designers called for a 170-foot-long main span flanked at each end by three rigid-frame concrete spans. Rather than follow the usual practice of completing one span and then moving the false work to the next, a small army of carpenters working night and day erected all the false work at once. They completed the viaduct within the allotted time. That the bridge is on a grade and contains a super-elevated curve makes the feat all the more remarkable.

By the end of 1939, all the grading work and nearly all of the 307 bridges and culverts were ready.

While laborers were bringing dramatic changes to the contours of the landscape, the most dramatic work took place hundreds of feet beneath the mountains in the seven tunnels. Although the partially completed tunnels of the South Penn Railroad determined the path of the road, each had to be enlarged to accommodate two lanes of traffic, one in each direction, twenty-three feet wide and fourteen feet high. Again, builders broke the construction into teams to work from each end toward the center simultaneously. One team of about twelve drillers and twelve helpers called "chukkers," working from a large steel scaffold that workers called a "jumbo," drilled as many as a hundred holes deep into the rock face. Toward the end of an eight-hour shift the men packed the holes with explosives and left the site. A bulldozer pulled the jumbo, which moved on railroad tracks, away from the wall. After detonating the charges, a second team followed to muck out rock and rubble. Progress from each side of the tunnels averaged seventeen feet a day. The drillers and excavators were followed by a third team that shored up the excavation with steel and concrete. To keep a ready supply of concrete, contractors erected cement mixing plants close to the tunnel openings. So isolated was the Laurel Hill tunnel site that the contractor had to open a quarry to supply the coarse aggregate that was mixed with the cement. As the digging proceeded, yet another team of engineers working outside the tunnel installed huge, specially designed ventilating fans to supply the passageway with air. Again, construction proceeded at a three-shift, twenty-four-hour pace.

Many of the companies that held contracts to bore the tunnels drew from an experienced labor pool of Pennsylvania coal miners who had been idled by the Depression or by coal strikes. But the work also drew men from outside the region. Some stayed at hotels for a dollar a night, while others boarded at local farms. Drinking among the men was heavy. Often local girls, daughters of farmers, some in their early teens, became easy victims. Stories of sexual escapades, romance, and pregnancy were whispered through the valleys before the men bored the last tunnel and moved on.

Stories of racial anger and violence were occasionally whispered, too. The Chicago company that won the bid to bore the Blue Mountain tunnel hired southern blacks with no drilling experience to do the job. Lacking expertise, the men fell behind the pace required. The company quickly demoted the blacks to chukkers, replacing them with experienced whites. Soon racial fights erupted. The violence escalated. Blacks and whites packed guns on the job, and many used them. The company suppressed all stories of the incidents.

What could not be suppressed were the construction-related deaths. Many of the nearly two dozen who died lost their lives in tunnel cave-ins. Such construction, which is always dangerous, was made even more so because of the condition of the abandoned tunnels of the South Penn Railroad. The walls had never been properly shured up before Vanderbilt ordered the work on them halted, and they had deteriorated significantly over the next half century.

In mid-1939, Marshall ordered twenty-eight contracts for the four-lane concrete pavement to be awarded. The pavement was to be nine inches of concrete reinforced with welded steel fabric. Using dual mixers, contractors would be able to lay about 228 feet of a single lane. Once masons poured and tamped the concrete, they gave it a final finish by dragging a burlap strip parallel to the long axis of the roadway. The result was an unusually smooth surface. The amount of concrete, sand, and aggregate required the daily shipment of over one thousand 40-ton freight car loads each day, so contractors would need the winter to stockpile the materials. In all, the pavement would take 1,225,000 cubic yards of concrete, enough to build four pyramids the size of Cheops. That November before winter set in, contractors paved a thirteen-mile stretch of turnpike in Cumberland County. If all went well, they would resume paving in the spring at a rate of three and a half miles a day.

From his office at the Bureau of Public Roads in Washington, Thomas Harris MacDonald kept a wary eye on the events in Pennsylvania. MacDonald still clung to his position that toll roads were a pernicious idea. True, privately owned turnpikes had flourished in the eighteenth century, especially in Pennsylvania. But to be attractive to travelers, the roads had to be maintained, something most private companies could not afford to do. When those companies went bankrupt, as they often did, the government had been forced to take over a derelict road, usually at considerable expense. Such had been the case when William K. Vanderbilt had given his Long Island Motor Parkway to local governments in lieu of unpaid back taxes. Now, in the wilderness of western Pennsylvania, a group of wrongheaded entrepreneurs had devised a new turnpike scheme on a roadbed built by Vanderbilt's grandfather. Even worse, the federal government, for reasons that had more to do with good politics than good roads, had given the entrepreneurs the money to proceed.

MacDonald might have been opposed to toll roads, but he was a professional engineer above all. Respect for the turnpike's chief engineer, Samuel Marshall, and the staff he assembled to complete the project far outweighed the differences MacDonald had with Walter Adelbert Jones about the efficacy of a toll road. The Chief and his staff cooperated fully with Samuel Marshall. For his part, Marshall consulted frequently with the bureau about the details of construction, seeking advice from federal engineers about design matters like drainage, width of the median strip, composition of the roadbed, and thickness of the concrete.

As the plans for the turnpike crystallized in 1938, secretaries in the Bureau of Public Roads clipped newspaper stories about the progress. Field engineers working for the bureau sent in articles from papers around the country as well. When press reports on a collapse in the Laurel Hill Tunnel and the subsequent gruesome deaths of five workers in 1939 drifted into Washington, Bureau of Public Roads secretaries filed them carefully along with all the numerous press releases and public relations brochures that Jones's staff sent from Harrisburg. Often, when the chairman delivered a speech about his dreamway to a Rotary Club or civic organization, a bureau employee attended and sent a report on Jones's remarks to the ever-growing file in Washington.

With only the pavement, landscaping, and other relatively minor tasks remaining, Marshall and his staff believed they would meet the June 30 deadline for opening. The paving companies had stockpiled all the materials and equipment to lay the roadway. But spring 1940 proved one of the coldest and wettest on record. Week after week, torrents of rain poured on the mountains of Pennsylvania, halting all construction. So frequent were the storms that the roadbed could not properly dry to permit paving. Electrical, hail-, and windstorms seemed more the norm than the exception, and on June 20, it even snowed in the higher elevations. At the end of June, when the road should have been opened, a severe electrical storm at Johnstown, a few miles north of the turnpike, took two lives. Marshall and his crews could only wait.

In late June, after the weather moderated, as many as thirty thousand workers converged on the turnpike site, five times as many as had worked during the construction of the great Boulder (Hoover) Dam on the Colorado River. Workers in the tunnels completed reinforcement and paving. Engineers rushed to complete the air-handling equipment. Electricians installed lighting in the tunnels and at the eleven interchanges. Hundreds of men armed with shovels and rakes hurried to complete the landscaping and planting. Others erected the new tollbooths. Even in its toll collection, the turnpike would differ from all that had gone before. Rather than collecting tolls at intervals along the roadway—the practice on some parkways—the turnpike devised a system of issuing tickets to drivers as they entered the highway at one of the eleven interchanges and collecting the tickets as they left. Drivers would pay only for the exact number of miles they traveled, and would not be delayed by traffic jams at tollbooths along the way.

By August the completed miles of highway became a testing ground of sorts. General Motors shipped a fleet of its cars to the site to see how well they performed at high speeds. The U.S. National Guard put its cars and trucks to the same test, but they failed. Though publicity photographs showed the convoy passing beneath one of the turnpike's new concrete bridges while local farm families who had gathered at the railing waved and cheered the trucks, the reality was different. The turnpike maneuvers proved to the War Department just how ill-equipped it was for high-speed transportation and a modern mechanized war. Boiling-over radiators and mechanical breakdowns forced many trucks to the side of the highway. Some trucks still rode on wheels with solid rubber tires, the same type of unforgiving wheels that had so damaged the roads during World War I. This time it was the vehicles that failed, not the road.

With the end of construction finally in sight by late August, the turnpike commissioners and Samuel Marshall led 150 members of Congress, military experts, automobile manufacturers, highway officials, and a number of newspaper reporters on an inspection tour of the highway. A fifty-car motorcade stretching for a mile entered at the Middlesex interchange near Carlisle and zoomed the entire 160 miles to Irwin at speeds as high as a hundred miles per hour. Even the morning fog and steady rain did not daunt the party cruising what publicity proclaimed to be the "all-weather highway." At Midway the group stopped for gas at the Esso station and had lunch at the Howard Johnson's restaurant. That evening Walter Jones gave a large dinner for his guests at the Duquesne Club in Pittsburgh. Jones, who was ill in Washington, read a message to his guests over the telephone. "Imagine a great road stretching from New Orleans to Boston and by-passing all small towns," he said. "This is a super-defense highway for troops to move rapidly from populous areas. Pennsylvania has shown the way with this great road."

That night the reporters filed their stories. "I never thought I could drive at 75 miles an hour around mountain curves in heavy rain and live to write about it," began the story in the Washington *News*. "This road is absolutely extraordinary," said Wilburn Cartwright, the enthusiastic chairman of the House Roads Committee to a reporter for the *New York Times*. "I think we should have roads leading to and from other eastern cities." The turnpike, he added was "the mother of them all."

A delegation from the Bureau of Public Roads headed by the Chief made the trip. Even Thomas MacDonald could not fail to be impressed by Jones's and Marshall's highway. The Chief generously called it "a magnificent accomplishment that will be a monument to the foresight of its builders."

Every feature of modern road design contributing to a strong, durable roadway and safe, smooth, uninterrupted flow of traffic has been incorporated in the design. . . .

This highway represents the best in American practice based on a long experience in road building. . . . Such work could have been done only by a highly competent engineering staff, working under able administrative direction.

MacDonald also recognized the turnpike's value as a "strategic military route" and suggested it was "imperative" to extend the turnpike to Philadelphia.

The Pennsylvania Turnpike's opening to paying motorists was a quiet affair. In the spring rumors circulated that Franklin Delano Roosevelt, whose New Deal programs had freed millions of dollars to fund the project, might attend a ceremony. But the Pennsylvania voters had elected a Republican governor, Arthur James, to succeed George Earle. By October, FDR was preoccupied with his Republican presidential challenger Wendell Wilkie; the three-power pact that Germany, Italy, and Japan recently pledged; and the Battle of Britain—that vast German air offensive against England that began on August 8. On October 1, the day the turnpike opened, the president stayed in the White House, where he held a press conference in the Oval Office and later met with General George Marshall, chief of staff of the army, and a large delegation of military men from other republics of the Western Hemisphere. As was so often the case that year, the subject of both meetings was war.

There would be no ribbon-cutting ceremony, no parade, no windy speeches. At 12:01 A.M. on October 1, the toll road simply opened for business, an event recorded by the triumphal photograph at the beginning of this chapter. That opening weekend there were traffic jams at every interchange as thousands of motorists wanted to try the new superhighway for themselves.

Even during the war, a time of rationing and a national speed limit of thirty-five miles per hour, the highway remained popular. "I expect you are wondering how the tire rationing and gasoline rationing have affected the Turnpike," Walter Jones wrote the head of the Reconstruction Finance Corporation in September 1942. "Our passenger car traffic has decreased, naturally, but the truck traffic is increasing. . . . People will use super-highways if they have them."

Robert Moses never made the journey to Pennsylvania to celebrate the turnpike's opening. From his office at the Triborough Bridge, he sent a letter to the Turnpike Commission belittling the achievement: "Jones says that he felt that he was at a disadvantage in building the Pa. Turnpike because no one else in this country had ever built a super-highway. . . . He goes on to say that he went to Germany to get his ideas. This is sheer rubbish." The parkways and arterial roads in New York were evidence enough for Moses that he alone had led the way to high-speed superhighways.

The Pennsylvania Turnpike's success challenged many of Thomas Mac-Donald's assumptions about highway building. The Chief had always built highways in response to need. But new state highway planners built them on a hunch that the roads would pay for themselves. Eastern states where congestion was greatest were the first to follow Pennsylvania's lead.

Believing that the federal coastal highway, Route 1, could never be updated to handle the twenty thousand vehicles that daily clogged the road in the summer months even before the war, Maine legislators authorized a state turnpike authority. After engineers completed their study of the route in 1945, the authority quickly sold bonds for its construction. After its opening in 1947, the Maine Turnpike, too, generated revenue far in excess of expectations.

In 1942, New York decided to build its own toll road, which it called the "Thruway." Delayed by the war, it was not until July 1946 that Governor Thomas E. Dewey broke ground near the city of Syracuse for the first section of his state's superhighway.

A study in New Hampshire found that just one of every ten cars traveling Route 1 belonged to a state resident; the other nine were tourists. A fifteen-mile turnpike would serve motorists well and add millions to the state's treasury. The New Hampshire Turnpike opened in 1948.

New Jersey created a turnpike authority in 1949 and—what must have been particularly bitter to MacDonald—decided to build a road just where Franklin Roosevelt and the Bureau of Public Roads' own *Toll Roads and Free Roads* had suggested. In 1952, its first year of operation, the New Jersey Turnpike took in $16 million in tolls, an amount far beyond anyone's wildest expectations.

Quickly, Indiana, Ohio, Kansas, and West Virginia decided to cash in. Each state created a turnpike authority and announced plans to build toll roads. They would connect, too: Ohio to Pennsylvania; Indiana to Ohio. By 1955, a driver could travel from New York to Chicago over superhighways without ever encountering a stoplight.

Officials found that turnpikes were far safer than other roads. This was a matter of no small concern to highway engineers and automobile manufacturers, who each year recorded more and more fatalities: 9,103 in 1920; 29,080 in 1930; and 32,245 in 1940. In 1941, the last year of carefree driving before the war, 37,512 people lost their lives in automobile accidents. Many collided with a train, truck, streetcar, or another automobile at grade crossings. The number of deaths declined dramatically when the federal government began to ration gas, but with peace it was rising once again. Statisticians reported, however, that for every hundred million miles of travel on two-lane, unimproved U.S. roads, 22.8 people lost their lives, while on the Maine Turnpike the number was just 2.8. Other turnpikes also showed dramatic increases in safety.

Quietly forgotten by the Pennsylvania Turnpike Commission was its oft-repeated pledge to make the road free once it had paid off the bonds needed to build it. Jones realized early on that the money generated at the tollbooths could be used to build more and more miles of superhighway. In September 1940, before the turnpike opened, he and Roosevelt, who was increasingly concerned with preparation for war, discussed the need to push the highway to the Philadelphia Navy Yard, and "by present and future main arteries to the Brooklyn Navy Yard."

While the Pennsylvania Turnpike and the toll roads across other states that followed after World War II represented a victory for the limited-access highways, they also represented a bellwether of future challenges to MacDonald and the Bureau of Public Roads. No longer would the Chief's word on highway construction be taken at face value. Across a relatively desolate mountainous stretch of Pennsylvania that throughout the Depression had been caught in the snare of poverty, a private entity employing vast sums of federal money had built a road that not only paid for itself, but helped to bring prosperity to those along its path.

THE GI AND
THE GENERAL

*The motor car . . . separated work and
the domicile, as never before. It
exploded each city into a dozen suburbs, and then extended many of the
forms of urban life along the highway
till the open road seemed to become
non-stop cities.*

MARSHALL MCLUHAN

Moving day; Lakewood, Los Angeles County, California;
summer 1953. A *Life* photographer captures the moment
the trucks unload the contents of dozens of homes. At
dawn, houses and streets had been quiet and empty; by
dusk, they would teem with children on bicycles, husbands and wives,
babies in strollers, and, always, cars in driveways.

On the fringes of the nation's great metropolitan areas—Philadelphia,
New York, Boston, Chicago, and Los Angeles—moving day repeats
itself continually. A land of farms and cities is fast transforming into a
nation of cities and suburbs. Los Angeles leads the way—400 people
arrive in the county every day; 2,800 new faces a week; 146,000 a year.
By 1960, more Americans would live in suburbs than cities. By 1980,
eighteen of the nation's twenty-five largest cities would decline in population, while the suburbs would swell by 60 million people, eighty-three
percent of the nation's growth.

Every month in the 1950s developers across the land devour thousands of acres of farmers' fields, timbered lands, former estates, and

new-growth forests to build subdivisions to which they give pleasant and bland names like Maple Glen, Cherry Hill, Green Acres, and White-marsh Village. They break ground for 122,000 new homes a month. They divide their land into an endless pattern of streets and plots: six plots—each about sixty by one hundred feet—to the acre. Those with no imagination impose a right-angled street grid across the landscape; those with a spark of inspiration plot their streets with curves and cir-cles. On every plot they erect a single-family dwelling, each with its own living room, kitchen, bath, and two or three bedrooms, and, always, a place for the family car.

The year 1953 marked a turning point in America's history. The flush of victory over Germany and Japan had been short-lived. Americans now had to reconcile themselves to a new world order of stalemate. Dwight Eisenhower took the presidential oath on January 20, the first Repub-lican to do so in two decades. The new president brokered an armistice in Korea, thus enabling the United States to return to full peacetime production. After more than two decades marked by a Great Depression and two wars, Americans were ready to become consumers and en-joy life. Each month that year they installed 145,000 new telephones and bought 600,000 new television sets and half a million new auto-mobiles. Americans played more than ever before: when not watching TV, they amused themselves around a Scrabble board, a game intro-duced a year earlier that quickly became a rival of the old Depression standby Monopoly. More than two and a quarter million Americans bowled regularly; more than three and a quarter million (including the new president and vice president) played golf. The number of fishing and hunting licenses issued rose to an all-time high.

An air of great promise swept the land. Americans made more money in 1953, an average of $1,788 per person—and the Internal Revenue Service collected more taxes, $68 billion, than at any time in history. Jonas Salk announced he had developed a vaccine that promised to wipe out polio, the scourge of children, particularly those children still unfor-tunate enough to live in a city. Scientists and engineers sought ways to harness the power of the atom for benign purposes, leading President Eisenhower to present a bold plan to the United Nations that he called "Atoms for Peace." At the Brookhaven laboratory on Long Island, scien-tists investigated the ways radiation might produce larger vegetables in new shapes. Some saw a day when nuclear power companies would give electricity away.

The only danger Americans could perceive on their relentless march to a better life was the Soviet Union and its Communist agents around the globe. Some Americans were ensnared by fear. In January, the New York City Housing Authority demanded that those living in its projects sign an oath declaring that they were not members of a subversive organization. In March, Joseph Stalin died, raising apprehensions in the West of who might preside over life behind the Iron Curtain; in June, authorities at Sing Sing Prison north of New York City executed Julius and Ethel Rosenberg for divulging atomic secrets to Soviet scientists; and in October, the saturnine and alcoholic junior senator from Wisconsin, Joseph McCarthy, proclaimed on national television that the Truman administration had been "crawling with Communists."

The suburban houses from which many Americans followed these events were hardly a new phenomenon on the landscape. For more than a century there had been places outside the city center where, as Walt Whitman said, "men of moderate means may find homes at a moderate rent." In the closing years of the nineteenth century, upper-class Americans in the large cities chose to escape the rising tide of immigrants by moving to the fringes of the city: Chestnut Hill and the Main Line on the outskirts of Philadelphia, Yonkers north of New York, and Oak Park west of Chicago. By 1920, more Americans were living in urban than rural areas, but the number of square miles in cities, especially in younger western ones, had increased dramatically. In 1910, Houston counted just 16 square miles; by 1930, it had grown to 72. In the same period, Los Angeles quintupled itself to 440 square miles. Developers and speculators divided those miles into lots and erected houses.

After World War II, however, the nature of suburbs and suburban life changed dramatically, principally because of three interrelated changes in American life: the passage of the GI Bill of Rights, developments in building materials and methods, and the new mobility provided by the automobile and the highway.

The first, the GI Bill—or the Serviceman's Readjustment Act, as it was formally known—ranks among Franklin Roosevelt's greatest legacies. Roosevelt and the Congress that passed the act unanimously thought of it as a way to thank the nearly ten million men and women who would be discharged from military service at the end of the war—

proof, Roosevelt said, "that the American people do not intend to let them down." But the implications of the GI Bill went far deeper than mere gratitude, for it enabled veterans to attend college or a trade school virtually free of charge, and it guaranteed them loans to buy houses. With the stroke of the ten ceremonial pens he used to sign the legislation, the president significantly changed the future course of the nation, for ten million people could acquire two of the most important attributes of those with means: education and a house.

Suddenly, young men and women whose parents were Irish and Italian and Jewish immigrants, and those whose parents had migrated from farms in the South to factories and mills in the North, people who had a grade school education and had grown up in city apartments and played in city streets—suddenly they could realize the American dream: a plot of land, a house, privacy, independence.

To be sure, when the veterans first returned, there was a severe housing shortage. Several million GIs, many with young families of their own, had to return to their parents' apartments; still others lived in barns, trailers, even chicken coops. But as new housing became available, the shortage eased. Changes in the Federal Housing Act of 1949 offered builders profit incentives to construct large developments, usually single-family homes in suburban areas. Armed with mortgage guarantees, veterans purchased government-approved houses with no money down. Many communities followed the government's lead by discounting property taxes for veteran owners, often by fifty percent. Like the automobile, which had begun as a toy of the rich before trickling down to the rest of America, the single-family suburban house, once exclusive to those of means, now became available to any veteran who held a job. Just as it had participated in and stimulated the construction of roads earlier in the century, the federal government now believed it fitting to participate in and stimulate the construction of homes for its veterans. With Washington's help, five million veterans became homeowners.

For many of those who bought a house on the GI Bill, the suburb offered the best opportunity. It was a small opportunity, to be sure, but nevertheless it was a chance that many had not dared dream about when they were growing up in the Depression. They could raise a family in the clean countryside, far from polio and the other diseases that they had to survive while growing up in the city. They could add to their houses, and build up equity. If they were prudent and lucky, they could even trade up to a new house with more bedrooms, a den, more land, even a two-car garage.

New and standardized building materials, along with the streamlining of construction techniques—by-products of the war—helped bring down the cost of constructing a new house. Airplane manufacturers made propellers of laminated wood and used plywood in some airplane hulls, while builders found plywood panels were excellent for sheathing and flooring military housing. Plywood, gypsum board, and copper tubing replaced older building materials—tongue-and-groove lumber, plaster, and galvanized iron pipe—that had been in general use before the war. Helped by the federal Bureau of Standards, builders and manufacturers brought uniformity to the dimensions of many house components: plywood and gypsum board in sheets in multiples of four feet; bricks and concrete blocks in multiples of four inches; and windows and doors sized in similar multiples. Builders found new materials easier to handle, usually lighter, and faster to install.

Contractors changed their practices, too. Prior to the war, housing had been an almost exclusive province of small builders who purchased land from a speculator and erected a small development of perhaps a dozen single-family houses. After 1945, however, housing in the United States became a large-scale industry dominated by streamlining and standardization.

It is often the case that one person in an industry rises above the rest, accrues fabulous wealth, and so dominates the public imagination to become synonymous with the enterprise itself: Rockefeller in oil; Carnegie in steel; Ford in automobiles. In the newly emerging housing industry of the 1950s it was Levitt.

William Jaird Levitt brought the house to the masses. In 1947, his bulldozers sculpted the earth of a Long Island potato field into two thousand house plots. On each he erected a simple four-room Cape Cod bungalow designed by his architect brother—780 square feet of living space and an unfinished attic in which to expand as the owner's family grew. Though Levitt first planned to rent the homes to veterans at $60 a month, he found that the Serviceman's Readjustment Act and full government financing enabled veterans to purchase a home for $6,990, or a combined mortgage and tax payment of $52 a month. For Levitt, his development was the best assurance of the power of democracy. "No man who owns his own house and lot can be a Communist," the builder was fond of saying. "He has too much to do."

Levitt established himself as the Henry Ford of home builders, for he brought to housing what the man from Dearborn had brought to the automobile: mass production and economy of scale. Like Ford's Model T, every Levitt house was almost exactly the same.

There was a difference, however, between Ford's and Levitt's production lines. In the builder's case, the product remained stationary and the workers moved from one site to the next. Preassembled and precut components were dropped off at each lot, where masons had already poured a concrete pad over radiant heat coils. Teams of workers followed: framers, then carport builders, floor and tile layers, electricians, kitchen and bathroom installers, painters (one group of workers for each color), and so on. A crew of siding installers put up shingles made of that magic mineral, asbestos. Finally, teams of landscapers completed the job with shrubs, grass, and fruit trees. In all, twenty-seven different crews moved from lot to lot. Never one to tolerate union workers, the builder paid his men a standard wage based on a normal production rate and gave bonuses to those who exceeded it. "The same man does the same thing every day, despite the psychologists," said Levitt. "It is boring; it is bad; but the reward of the green stuff seems to alleviate the boredom of the work." Levitt organized the houses in multiples of four feet to take advantage of standardized building materials, bought a forest in Oregon to produce the lumber on his schedule and at his price, bought machines to make his own nails, and even bought a company to supply the appliances he built into each house. At peak production, those workers doing repetitive tasks completed forty new homes a day, twenty each morning and twenty each afternoon.

Curiously, the person whose name became synonymous with postwar suburbia lived not in the suburbs, or even on Long Island. Each day William Jaird Levitt commuted to his Long Island office in his flashy Cadillac convertible from his twelve-room apartment in Manhattan.

Levitt was careful to add amenities to his new community: seven "village greens" for shops, land for churches and schools, swimming pools (one for every thousand families), recreation centers, playgrounds, athletic fields, and handball courts. He gave the streets idyllic names like "Mistletoe," "Quiet," "Meander," "Meadow," and "Shelter." And Levitt avoided the word "street" altogether, choosing to call them "lane" or "road" instead. Initially, Levitt called his development "Island Trees," but upon reflecting that his bulldozers had eradicated almost every tree from the face of the land, he changed the name to "Levittown." From the initial 2,000 houses in 1947—"the most perfectly planned community in America," as the builder called it—Levittown grew to 10,000 by 1950 and topped out at 17,447 by 1953. Levittowns in Pennsylvania and New Jersey followed.

Like automobiles, Levitt's houses had model years, and each year he equipped them with special features oriented toward hungry consumers—stoves and refrigerators, fireplaces and washing machines. He placed a television in a specially built niche in the living room wall. As the federal government considered these features—even the television—to be "built-ins" and part of the house, they became part of the mortgage. The federal government subsidized not only new housing but a new way of living. When the United States was planning for Nikita Khrushchev's visit to America in 1959, the White House press corps asked President Eisenhower what he would like the Soviet dictator to see. "Levittown," Ike replied, for the suburb was "universally and exclusively inhabited by workmen."

"The entire concept of the Island Trees development," said an editorial in an early edition of Levitt's newspaper, the *Island Trees Tribune*, "is a tribute to our American way of life." The residents agreed. In the evenings, many Levittown families gathered in their living rooms around the Levitt-supplied TV to watch Jackie Gleason and Audrey Meadows play Ralph and Alice Cramden, the *Honeymooners*. Some had come from meager apartments like the one at 328 Chauncy Street, Bushwick, Brooklyn, where the Cramdens lived. Its hand-me-down dresser, wooden table, icebox, sink, and single window looking onto a fire escape were familiar, as were Ralph's farcical schemes to get rich and move with his wife to a better life. Levittowners laughed in part because they had moved on to something of which the Cramdens could only dream. In flickering shadows they also saw Ozzie and Harriet Nelson, who lived at 822 Sycamore Road in Hillsdale, or Robert Young and Jane Wyatt, the Andersons of *Father Knows Best* at 607 South Maple Street, Springfield. These families showed the Levittowners what they might still achieve. Ozzie disappeared to an unidentified white-collar job in the city; Robert Young, paper in hand, seemed to be perpetually crossing the threshold of his gracious house after a hard day at the office. The

Nelson and Anderson houses were large, their living rooms and kitchens capacious. They represented an upper-middle-class suburbia just within sight, perhaps, of those residing in Levittown.

Another television family, William Bendix and Gloria Blondell, Chester and Peggy Riley of *The Life of Riley*, more closely mirrored their present experience. Lunch pail in hand, Riley trotted off each morning to his blue-collar job as a riveter for the Stevenson Aircraft Company, and he returned each evening to his tract house at 1313 Blue View Terrace. Though he was none too bright, his house modest, and his aspirations limited, Riley was decent and kind in a way that always triumphed by the show's end. Therein lay a lesson for many of the Levittown viewers. The new world of suburbia, a small plot of land for all, was a possibility not only for well-educated white-collar folks, but for everyone.

Everyone, but not all. William Levitt's progressive thinking in the area of home building was matched only by his regressive attitudes in race relations. His parents, Jewish immigrants from Russia, had fled to Manhasset on Long Island from Bedford-Stuyvesant in Brooklyn when the first black family moved into the neighborhood. No matter that the father was a district attorney. When a black moves into a neighborhood, Abraham Levitt believed, others will soon follow, and then the value of all the white-owned properties will plummet. "The longer we wait," said the early pioneer in white flight as his sons packed for the Island, "the more the price will go down." Adopting his father's ideas, William Levitt barred blacks from his new town, stating in a sales prospectus, "No dwelling shall be used or occupied except by members of the Caucasian race, but the employment and maintenance of other than Caucasian domestic servants shall be permitted." The title to each of his houses contained a covenant forbidding its resale to any but a Caucasian. "I have come to know that if we sell one house to a Negro family, then 90 or 95 percent of our white customers will not buy into the community," Levitt said in his defense, adding, "We can solve a housing problem, or we can try to solve a racial problem but we cannot combine the two."

The National Association for the Advancement of Colored People and other groups thought otherwise and tried to break the covenant. Early in 1949, James Mayweathers, a black man who operated a floor-polishing service in East Williston, Long Island, stood in line overnight at the Levitt office, waiting with hundreds of fellow veterans for a chance to buy a new house. The next morning, when the builder arrived, he personally told Mayweathers that he would not sell a Levittown house to a black, and that he might as well go away.

Curiously, the Federal Housing Administration appeared to condone Levitt's race discrimination. It chose to ignore a 1948 Supreme Court ruling that outlawed such covenants as Levittown included in its deeds. The FHA concerned itself only with the plans, materials, and financial backing of houses, said the agency's state director. It could not intrude in the area of "social values." Though eventually forced to lift the clause, Levitt found other more subtle and informal ways to keep his community almost uniformly white. Other builders across the land followed Levittown's lead. This particular American dream remained a fantasy for African-Americans.

Other clauses in a Levitt contract underscored uniformity, too: Owners could erect no fences or walls. They had to maintain neat yards and mow their lawns regularly. They could not string clotheslines across their yards, but would use Levitt-approved clothes-trees instead. When Levitt produced the "Country Clubber," an upscale version of the basic Levittown house (and costing about seventy percent more), he separated the new houses from the old by a wide street. Rumors traveled through the Pennsylvania Levittown that the builder even separated Democrats from Republicans.

Critics decried the uniformity, street upon street of sameness. But often those same critics had fled the city before the war and were living comfortable lives in older suburbs or the country. To Lewis Mumford, who in 1929 abandoned his apartment in Sunnyside Gardens, Queens, for a farmhouse in upstate Amenia, the suburb had become "almost as much of a nightmare, humanly speaking, as a universal megapolis; yet it is towards this proliferating nonentity that our present random or misdirected urban growth has been steadily tending."

But the critics missed the point. Suburbs like Levittown offered those with lesser means the opportunity to participate in the exodus from the city that wealthier Americans had begun before the war. An entirely new class of men and women backed by a federally guaranteed long-term, low-interest mortgage could delight in the amenities of country life—the quiet, the space, the privacy, and the safety—that wealthier suburbanites had enjoyed for decades. They were freed of the civic obligations—especially the responsibility of caring for the poor and the underclasses—and the higher taxes that city dwellers had to shoulder.

Yet the sophistication, variety, culture, and stimulation that cities offer were only a short drive away.

Along with hundreds of other developers, Levitt had started a mass migration from the nation's cities to the new, mass suburbs, and the cities were left in chaos. It seemed almost axiomatic—the older the city, the greater the chaos. Los Angeles, a relatively young urban area, had been developing horizontally almost since its inception and, pollution aside, adapted relatively well to its new suburbs. But on the East Coast, older and honorable places like New York, Philadelphia, Trenton, and Boston suffered acutely. Each city found itself locked into an all too familiar pattern: Those who were white and who could afford to fled, thereby eviscerating the tax base and leaving the funding of older streets, schools, and civic amenities to the black and white poor. With no money or tax base, houses, streets, and entire neighborhoods deteriorated; businesses and corporate headquarters followed the suburban money, eroding the tax base even more. To break the pattern, to stop the flow of people and money and the consequent gaping holes in the urban physical and social structure, well-intentioned planners would propose new hotels, low-income housing, renaissance centers, and the like. In the coming years federal highway planners, too, would participate in schemes to assist the rebirth of the cities. But of course their highways had made the exodus more attractive than ever.

Without the new mobility of the automobile and the highway, the suburban housing boom never would have spread so wide. Earlier suburban developments stretched out upper-middle-class housing along railroad lines. The builder always made the number of minutes it took to walk from home to the station one of the house's principal selling points. The men who lived in such a house generally commuted to a white-collar job, usually in a large office building in "center city." Their wives, who stayed home, often called for services—food, dry cleaning, and the like—to be delivered. The postwar, automobile-centered society made it possible for blue-collar workers to commute from their suburban houses to factories or perhaps construction sites that had never been stops on commuter railroad lines.

The automobile became the passport to the postwar American dream. It was no accident on William Levitt's part that the potato fields he chose for his great development lay in the middle of a triangle formed by three of Robert Moses' parkways—the Southern State, Northern State, and Wantagh State. Because of Levittown, these roads would now carry more traffic than even Moses had believed possible. Before the war, trolley lines and railroads had carried wealthy commuters from their suburban homes to the city centers, and builders located their houses near stops and stations. But now those affluent enough to own a house could afford an automobile to carry them there. No longer concerned about locating their suburban house near a stop on a railroad line, developers thought more about the location of the driveway, carport, or garage.

In relative terms, cars and accessories were cheaper and better in 1953 than ever before. That year the federal government lifted the production restrictions it had imposed in order to manufacture hardware for the Korean War. The models were sleek, if a little heavy on the chrome. Studebaker introduced all-new, low-slung bodies designed by Raymond Lowey. A new Ford Mainline, a six-cylinder, two-door coupe, sold for $1,734, heater, power steering, automatic transmission, and directional signals extra. New Plymouths went for as little as $1,598; new Chevrolets for $1,523. Henry J. Kaiser, the wartime shipbuilder turned automaker, offered his eponymous "Henry J." for $1,399. More expensive lines such as Buick, Oldsmobile, Pontiac, Mercury, and DeSoto offered models well below $2,500. One could even purchase a mighty finned Cadillac Coupe DeVille two-door hardtop for $3,995, complete with "Hydra-Matic Drive" and a self-winding clock. Air-conditioning, a feature that Cadillac introduced in 1953, was an additional $620. Statistics for the decade between 1950 and 1960 revealed the increase in suburban living: the number of families owning automobiles rose from sixty to seventy-seven percent; station wagon sales from 142,000 to 1,059,000 vehicles; the number of families owning two or more automobiles from four to twelve percent. In the same decade the number of railway passenger cars declined from 37,359 to 25,746.

Because Americans were enjoying their auto-mobility and choosing to drive cars rather than ride on trains or trolleys, they soon choked streets and highways of cities and suburbs with traffic. Before the war, most county highway superintendents had maintained the few miles of paved and numerous miles of unpaved roads with ease. Traffic was light, increasing only gradually each year. In the winter they kept the roads plowed, while in the summers they attended to grading, resurfacing, and sometimes adding new pavement. During the war they had made do with limited resources of workers and equipment. Now the pace was quickening, often to an alarming degree. Farmers in suburban counties across the country were selling their corn and grain fields to developers, who each month produced fresh crops of houses, streets, schools, shopping centers, and churches. Residents and builders besieged township, county, and state officials with demands for better roads to give them access to their new communities.

Farms and rural life were fast disappearing. "The county now has all the characteristics of a metropolitan area," complained Harvey Bronson, who had been the highway engineer for Ramsey County, Minnesota, since 1935. Though the county seat was the sizable city of St. Paul, Ramsey still thought of itself as agricultural before the war. In the 1950s, builders changed that. Now most of the "breadwinners," as Bronson called them, drove to work in Minneapolis or St. Paul. In 1953, Ramsey County spent $1,284 a mile to maintain its roads. But the roads were inadequate, and there was no money to build more.

When would the demand for more roads ease? County highway superintendents across the country complained that they could not keep up with the traffic. Highways built before the war were now crumbling under the unprecedented automobile traffic as well as the weight of heavy trucks. In 1954, Pennsylvania could boast about forty-one thousand miles of roads, more roads than all of New England and the states of New York, New Jersey, Maryland, and Delaware combined, yet traffic jams in the suburbs around Philadelphia and Pittsburgh became the stuff of lore. Highway engineers knew how to build the roads, said E. L. Schmidt, Pennsylvania's Secretary of Highways, but "we are not keeping step with needs and cannot hope to meet the required goal without additional funds."

While the new suburbs presented one problem of access, older cities presented quite another. They were often congested by the automobiles and trucks destined for the suburbs or country. The traffic, so planners concluded, was hastening the demise of older cities. The future vitality of a city lay in enabling people to commute to its businesses easily, planners said, or to enable drivers to pass *through* or *around* it quickly. More highways would solve the problem. But the solution had more to do with automobiles and businesses than it did with residents. Indeed, the highways would just exacerbate the problem, as they would encourage those people with the means to do so to live in a suburb and abandon the cities to residents without the means or mobility to move.

Foremost among the urban planners was Robert Moses. In the 1950s, Moses was still regarded by most in the popular press as a great builder, the one who could return the city to greatness. Part of Moses' key to success, aside from a well-oiled public relations machine that ranked second to none, was his ability to sell transportation as the solution to a myriad of urban problems that arose in part because of the exodus from the cities. Moses connected public housing to the automobile. Replace slums with highways and move slum dwellers to high-rise housing projects, so his thinking went. Failing to recognize that his solution merely substituted a vertical ghetto for a horizontal one, Moses believed he was solving two problems. In the future the twin problems of housing and highways would converge repeatedly.

The successes with four-lane roads were regional, not national in scale. On the federal level, the progress of Thomas MacDonald's Bureau of Public Roads—renamed the Public Roads Administration in a New Deal government reorganization plan—seemed to be as bumpy as the highways themselves.

As it had in the past, MacDonald's organization reacted to meet the nation's traffic and defense needs, which meant that it was always playing catch-up. The two needs were not always compatible, nor were they necessarily within the United States: MacDonald's engineers supervised construction of highways across the Isthmus of Panama (in case the canal should be bombed), which connected with another PRA road from Mexico to the Canal Zone. Another group of PRA engineers went north to build an all-weather road from Dawson Creek, British Columbia, to Big Delta, Alaska. During the war, the Chief used funds from the Defense Highway Act of 1941 to build a huge network of roads around the Pentagon in Arlington, Virginia, and in Michigan to begin an expressway from Detroit to Ford Motor Company's industrial plant at River Rouge. But, as in World War I, trucks carrying military matériel pounded the highways. States like Colorado compounded the problem by allowing truckers to carry overloads. Steel became scarce soon after Pearl

Harbor, forcing highway engineers to remove reinforcements from concrete pavements and to rely on wood for bridges. Few local engineers had money, materials, or workers enough to think of maintenance.

After the war, the catching up continued. In 1944, Congress had looked forward to the end of the conflict by passing a federal-aid highway act that ordered the Bureau of Public Roads to create a master plan for an interstate highway system. Though other highway bills had been passed since then, they seemed to go nowhere.

By 1953, a phalanx of organizations was warning of the dire consequences that would befall the United States if it did not improve its roads. In some ways the nation was falling victim to its own progress and improving economy. By 1953, the population exceeded 157 million, an increase of twenty percent since the start of World War II. Wages increased; the standard of living rose; people had more time for relaxation and recreation than at any time in history. That year visits to national parks topped seventeen million; the number of golfers and bowlers increased. Only attendance at motion pictures and some spectator sports declined, no doubt because people were watching TV. Clearly, people were enjoying greater prosperity than at any time since the 1920s, and they knew it. Many chose to spend their new wealth on an automobile. In 1953 alone, the low-priced automakers Chevrolet, Ford, and Plymouth sold over 3.3 million cars. As more Americans became mobile, they increased the traffic; that year they logged nearly 550 billion miles on inferior roads.

The railroads, especially passenger railroads, weren't going anywhere either. At the turn of the century, the railroad "was an institution," as the historian Jacques Barzun put it, "a source of poetry." But by the 1950s there was little inspiring about rail passenger service. Railroad companies were moving in a swift downward spiral toward bankruptcy. Since 1936, their passenger operations had made a net profit only during the war, when the government had curtailed automobile travel. The Long Island Rail Road, the line that shuttled passengers between Manhattan and communities like Levittown, already faced insolvency and was surviving only through tax exemptions granted by the state and local governments. In the twenty years between 1953 and 1955, the number of freight cars, passenger cars, locomotives, and miles of track had all declined. Those who did travel by train found little poetry in the shabby cars that often were unheated in winter and overheated in summer, or the frequent delays caused by antiquated and neglected equipment.

Nor was there poetry in the well-publicized train crashes. Though the accidents were often caused by reckless drivers of automobiles or trucks trying to beat trains to grade crossings, the deaths redounded upon the railroads, as newspapers published the horrifying statistics—the accident on the Long Island Rail Road in 1950 that killed seventy-nine passengers, the one on the Pennsylvania Railroad in 1951 that killed eighty-four. A driver might be at fault, but the railroads suffered the consequences of bad publicity.

Critics then and now debated the cause of the railroads' demise: excessive government regulation; a cabal of highway builders; the conspiracy of the automobile makers, oil interests, and the construction industry. In fact, the Interstate Commerce Commission did impose strict regulations on railroads. Ample evidence demonstrates that highway builders joined with users and automakers to lobby for better roads. But it is also true that railroads invested little in improving their service. With the single exception of a run on the Baltimore and Ohio between Washington, D.C., and Chicago in 1955, previous speed records for trains had stood since 1937. Confronted with dreadful conditions and relatively slow speeds, Americans chose to abandon their antiquated railroad system for overcrowded highways. The railroads set about to abandon the few passengers who remained.

Even if the railroads had maintained their service for passengers, even if they had updated the amenities of their cars, it is doubtful that they would have succeeded against the longing most Americans had to indulge their desire for space, land, and their own house—all the features of suburban living. With their fixed tracks, fixed timetables, and fixed points of arrival and departure, railroads were more adapted to the apartment and the city than to the house and the country. They simply could not compete with the flexibility and mobility that the automobile offered.

Much to the consternation of some in his party, Dwight David Eisenhower fancied himself as "liberal on human issues, conservative on economic ones." In his first presidential term he annoyed conservative Republicans by expanding the federal government's role in education ("the most important thing in our society") and housing projects. He increased Social Security benefits and brought an additional ten million people into the system. At the same time he practiced thrift, and here, too, he annoyed many. In the interest of balancing the budget, he opposed Republican plans to cut taxes, and he worked to postpone the elimination of taxes the previous administration and Congress had levied to pay for the Korean War. Eisenhower even vetoed a Republican-sponsored bill to eliminate the twenty percent tax the federal government placed on the price of tickets for motion pictures, plays, and musicals.

The president also quickly learned, as his Democratic predecessors had before him, that human and economic issues were not mutually exclusive and in fact were inextricably intertwined. Overcoming resistance of the old guard of his party and other reactionaries—"who," he complained, "want to eliminate everything that the federal government has ever done that represents social advance"—Eisenhower asserted that fiscally sound social programs could benefit the economy. Haunted by the fact that the Republican Party, and particularly Herbert Hoover, still wore the mantle of shame for the Crash of 1929, Eisenhower had an almost pathological fear of a depression. He was anxious to demonstrate that a Republican president leading the federal government could help to strengthen the economy. When a mild recession pushed unemployment over 5 percent (it had been as low as 2.9 percent at the height of the Korean War), he looked to public works and defense procurement as a way to prevent another depression. At his direction the undersecretary of commerce for transportation submitted a report in December 1953 entitled "The Potential Use of Toll Road Development in a Business Depression." He wanted a real public works program, the president told his cabinet in February 1954, ready to use in the event of an economic setback. "If we don't move rapidly, we could be in terrible trouble." Highway construction would be the keystone of public works.

Simply put, the president knew he could not fail with highways. Highway building would be popular with the electorate, fiscally sound, and above all would give people jobs. Each federal dollar, so his Commission on Public Roads reported, generated close to a half hour of employment, not only in construction but in steel mills, cement plants, and mines, and among various manufacturers. Like a stone cast into a pond, each mile of modern, four-lane, limited-access highway would produce ripples that would be felt throughout the economy.

For that new mile of road, surveyors would have to site its two-hundred-foot-wide right-of-way across the landscape. Property would receive compensation for twenty-four and a quarter acres of land; bulldozer operators would have to level and prepare the road's surface; gravel contractors would have to haul in truckloads of rubble and fill; compactor operators would have to compress the materials and smooth them. The mile would consume fifty tons of cement to make up the concrete pavement, and twenty tons of steel for reinforcing screens and rods embedded in the concrete. The mile would give jobs to welders to secure the steel, and masons to spread the concrete. Each bridge or overpass, culvert or drainage line meant still more construction and more materials.

That mile of road would ripple through other parts of the economy, too. Literally dozens of industries would grow by producing goods for the construction: Powder manufacturers like Hercules would profit from the sale of explosives. Lumber mills like Georgia-Pacific would produce plywood and wood for construction forms. Great companies like Allis-Chalmers, General Motors, Westinghouse, Caterpillar, and Ingersoll-Rand would get new orders to produce heavy equipment, gargantuan bulldozers, and jumbo trucks and rollers. Rubber plants like Goodyear and Firestone would produce strips of expansion buffers between the sections of concrete pavement. And to keep all the equipment operating, companies like Standard Oil and Texaco, Phillips and Sinclair would supply a steady stream of fuel and grease.

The ripples continued to spread outward through the economy. Paint manufacturers like Pittsburgh and Sherwin Williams would receive orders for yellow and white traffic paint. The Minnesota Mining and Manufacturing—3M—produced a unique reflecting material sign makers used for the huge letters of the traffic signs a high-speed road demanded. Lighting companies like Sylvania and General Electric would receive contracts to produce high-intensity mercury vapor lamps at interchanges. Still other steel companies would have to produce lampposts, dividing barriers, and signposts, each of which required a contractor to install it. Landscapers would provide trees and ground cover. Materials laboratories would get contracts to test core samples of new concrete pavement. As construction workers often traveled a considerable distance to the job site, sometimes even from another state, hotels and motels as well as restaurants and diners would benefit. Still other vendors followed along with the workers, like Mother Courage behind the army, to sell coffee, sandwiches, and snacks.

The new mile of highway depended on the services of an average of eight engineers. State highway departments would increase their staffs. Behind all the engineers were colleges and universities across the nation that would benefit from the construction boom as they enlarged their faculties to teach the growing number of students.

Nor would the rippling cease when local politicians cut the ribbons and the automobiles cruised down the pavement. Drivers of that mile would have to purchase cars and trucks—and then gasoline, tires, and insurance—to ride on it. If that mile was in the Northeast, say New Hampshire or New York, road crews would have to spend many dollars to maintain it, including money for salt and sand and plows to keep it open in the winter. Police would have to patrol it night and day. If the mile happened to be near an exit or entrance, businesses and small companies might locate there.

Plans for many such miles were not hard to come by in 1954; indeed, each of the forty-eight states had just such proposals before them. With wartime shortages of steel, concrete, and labor behind him, Eisenhower proposed a highway bill whose ripples would continue for many months, even years. On May 6, the president signed into law the nearly $2 billion Federal Aid Highway Act—money to employ about seven hundred thousand people building highways for the next two years. Using a fistful of pens for the ceremony in the Oval Office, the president handed them out to eager senators as souvenirs. "That's about all the pens I can use," Eisenhower quipped, giving the last one away, "unless I use one for a period." Then he added: "That gets us started, but we must do more."

What if that mile of highway became a part of the federal Interstate Highway System that Thomas MacDonald and the Bureau of Public Roads had had created on paper. Then that single mile would be but one of more than forty thousand. Why stop at $2 billion a year in federal aid? Why not propose a highway bill costing $7 billion, $10 billion, even more? Indeed, if Sinclair Weeks, Secretary of Commerce, used the money properly, these billions of dollars in federal highway funds could save the economy from falling into a recession by assisting a myriad of industries in the employment of hundreds of thousands. No mere ripple or even a splash, a highway program could become a great tidal wave of federal money breaking over every sector of the American economy and influencing every aspect of American life.

Beyond the economic benefits of highways, which any president might have understood, Eisenhower appreciated the idea of what roads meant to communications and defense of the nation. In each case, events on the Kansas plains and his experiences in the army had led him to recognize the importance of roads.

The president had been raised in a small frame house on the wrong side of the Union Pacific and Santa Fe tracks that ran through Abilene, Kansas. "Large crops of wheat and other grains are raised there," were the kindest words Baedeker could summon to describe Abilene at the turn of the century. "It was definitely a small town," Eisenhower himself remembered. When he arrived as a child in 1891, "paving was unknown. . . . Crossings of scattered stone were provided at each corner, but after a heavy summer rain the streets became almost impassable because of the mud. Rubber boots were standard equipment for almost everyone." The railroad had made Abilene. Shortly after the Civil War a livestock shipper picked the hamlet of about a dozen log huts to be the stockyard for cattle he would send by rail to the Chicago markets. Soon ranchers from Texas packed hundreds of thousands of cattle in pens by the railroad line, and packed Abilene's saloons with prostitutes and gunfire. But about a decade before the Eisenhower family arrived, the railroad had pushed into the southwest to Dodge City, taking the ranchers and cattle with them. Those who remained closed the saloons and turned to farming for a living. Now they depended on the railroad to bring in goods from the East and take out the grain and, when it was possible or necessary, take them to Kansas City or even north to Chicago. The railroad, built with generous land grants from the federal government, was the town's only link to the outside world.

The Union Pacific and Santa Fe carried the young plebe from Abilene to West Point in 1911, but it was the army that taught Eisenhower the importance of automobiles in war. At 11:15 on the morning of July 7, 1919, at a spot known as the "Zero Milestone" just south of the White House grounds in Washington, he joined the army's first transcontinental trip by car and truck. After numerous speeches from senators and the Secretary of War, a three-mile caravan of army motorcycles, cars, and trucks, along with 260 enlisted men, 35 officers, and a 15-piece band provided by the Goodyear Tire & Rubber Company, set out for Union Square in San Francisco, three thousand miles away. Red, white, and blue bunting draped the trucks and cars. Banners on the sides of the trucks proclaimed MOTOR TRANSPORT CORPS MOVES THE ARMY and

WE'RE OFF FOR FRISCO. Eisenhower, who had volunteered "partly for a lark and partly to learn," carried the lessons from the journey with him to the White House.

As the caravan traveled westward through cities like Bedford, Pennsylvania; Canton, Ohio; South Bend, Indiana; Chicago, Illinois; and Cedar Rapids, Iowa, people came out in force to greet them with receptions and long-winded speeches. At the estate of tire magnate Harvey Firestone, a covey of young ladies dressed in gay frocks treated the men with a magnificent feast. In the Rockies of Wyoming and Utah and across Nevada, they went where few automobiles had gone before. At Carson City, Nevada, they bivouacked on the statehouse lawn. And when the convoy reached California, the governor met it at the state line and rode in triumph with it to San Francisco.

It took sixty-two days for the soldiers to cross the country; they had averaged but five miles an hour. Some days they covered as few as three miles. Breakdowns and accidents were frequent; one truck rolled into a steep ravine in the Sierras. Eisenhower described the trip as a journey "through darkest America with truck and tank." Road conditions, he said, ranged "from average to non-existent." Like the other officers en route he recommended getting Americans "interested in producing better roads."

While the "old convoy" started Eisenhower "thinking about good, two-lane highways," the autobahns of Germany made him "see the wisdom of broader ribbons across the land." "Adolf Hitler's roads are roads to peace," declared the Führer's engineer Dr. Fritz Todt, but by 1939, the beautifully sculpted broad concrete ribbons led to war. "We have enjoyed the blessings of the Reich Autobahn on the march to liberate Vienna and then on the march to the Sudetenland," General Heinz Guderian, a commander of Hitler's panzer force, boasted as wave after wave of tanks cruised into Austria.

In World War II the Allied Forces found it was easier to destroy the mobility and might of a country that relied principally upon railroads, as Germany did. For six days in February 1945, the Allies showered thousands of bombs upon rail lines and roads. Removing just one section of track could disrupt trains for days, but the autobahn proved a harder target. A convoy could still get through, even over a road pocked with bomb craters. After V-E Day, when he traveled the autobahn, Eisenhower learned firsthand the value of modern highways to defense. Now that he was president, the United States faced the threat of nuclear attack. What better way to evacuate cities than by superhighway? "I decided . . . to put an emphasis upon this kind of road building," Eisenhower wrote in his memoirs. But he had yet to figure out a way to pay for it.

The federal government would build a modern highway system with thousands of miles of high-speed, limited-access roads, but Thomas Harris MacDonald would not direct its construction. President Woodrow Wilson had appointed him chief of the Bureau of Public Roads in 1919, just a few months before Dwight David Eisenhower had embarked from Washington on his cross-country trip with the army. MacDonald had survived a succession of Democratic and Republican presidents—Wilson, Harding, Coolidge, Hoover, Roosevelt, and Truman—over thirty-four years. In thirty-four years he had seen the name of the bureau change from the Bureau of Public Roads to the Office of Public Roads and back again. He had seen it move from the Agriculture Department to the Federal Works Agency, and then to the Commerce Department. He had seen the organization chart grow from a single $8^1/_2$-by-11-inch page to an inch-thick book measuring 11 by 17 inches. His Bureau of Public Roads now had a central office in Washington and nine regional divisions across the United States, one for the territory of Alaska, and one for the national forests and parks. He had established additional BPR offices abroad in countries like the Philippines, Ethiopia, Turkey, Liberia, Puerto Rico, Guatemala, El Salvador, Honduras, and Costa Rica. In 1952, more people worked for the Bureau of Public Roads in the Philippines than had worked in the *entire* Bureau of Public Roads in 1919.

All the while, the Chief alone controlled the entire operation with an iron hand and a stiff formality. After he was widowed in 1935, the bureau seemed his single passion. Thomas MacDonald knew every aspect of its operation because he had created it. There was little coordination between the few high-level deputies in the Bureau of Public Roads. They reported to him and that was enough. Years after other federal agencies had created personnel offices, he resisted. Why waste money on a personnel office? MacDonald argued. After all, he knew every civil engineer worth knowing. Since many were over the mandatory retirement age of seventy, he engineered special exceptions to keep them employed. Within the bureau his formality had become legendary. Woe to the poor new employee who happened to step into an elevator car in which the Chief was riding. No one, save his secretary, Miss Fuller, could enjoy that privilege.

But World War II and the Korean War had hurt the highway program, while more and better cars and heavier trucks, capable of traveling faster, were tearing up pavements at an alarming rate. The only solution, MacDonald said to the annual meeting of the American Association of State Highway Officials in December 1952, was to consider alternate routes and to "activate coordinated efforts" by legislators and road builders. In this way they would be able to create "informed public opinion." The Chief did not realize that crumbling, congested roads had already mobilized public opinion for change.

MacDonald always regarded his job as meeting road needs. He failed to see that roads might attract cars and trucks, businesses and population, that road building could actually lead the economy rather than follow it. The Chief's vision had served the nation well in the twenties and thirties, and even the forties, but he was now in the sixth decade of the twentieth century. Eisenhower did not want to play catch-up; he wanted to create a more fundamental change in the economy.

When MacDonald turned seventy in 1951, President Truman had extended his appointment on a yearly basis. But on Thursday afternoon, March 26, 1953, Sinclair Weeks, Secretary of Commerce, told MacDonald that President Eisenhower did not wish to continue the appointment. He was being dismissed. After learning the news, MacDonald returned to his office and told Miss Fuller, "I've just been fired, so we might as well get married." They would start a new life in College Station, Texas, where for many years the chancellor of Texas A&M had wanted him to head a highway research center. Less than a month after being dismissed, the newly wedded couple left Washington for College Station. By train.

PART 2

POINT FORTHE
MEASUREMENT
OF DISTANCES
FROM WASHING-
TON ON HIGH-
WAYS OF THE
UNITED STATES

© E. L. Crandall

A GRAND PLAN

All government—indeed, every human bene-fit and enjoyment, every virtue and every prudent act—is founded on compromise and barter.

EDMUND BURKE

Though much altered from his original conception, the city of Washington still bears the bold signature of its visionary designer, Pierre Charles L'Enfant. L'Enfant believed the city's landscape should reflect the mind of the new republic. Congress had decided to build its "Capitol City" on ten square miles beside the Potomac River, at the symbolic center of the nation. It is to L'Enfant's credit that he could see any greatness at all in the site, which was largely marsh and swamp. The population of America stood around four million; its largest city, New York, had about 33,000 people. Nevertheless, L'Enfant envisioned a city of eight hundred thousand people— about its population in 1954—and a nation of five hundred million. Atop the highest elevation, Jenkins Hill, at the city's center, L'Enfant located the home of the people's representatives, the Capitol. He chose another commanding promontory a mile and half away for the president's house. Extending at right angles from the Capitol is the grid of streets that aligns in both longitude and latitude with the system that Thomas Jefferson later used to organize the landscape of the new federal territories.

Overlying the grid is the topographical hallmark of L'Enfant's plan: broad diagonal avenues that radiate from the Capitol and the president's house. As they intersect about the city, the avenues form circles or squares—du Pont, Logan, Mt. Vernon, and Lafayette, among others—which would afford viewers, so L'Enfant said, "a reciprocity of view." One of the diagonal avenues, Pennsylvania, would pass from the Capitol and the White House to provide a visual connection between the two branches of government. The streets and avenues would overshadow almost everything else. Of the 6,111 acres in Washington, public buildings and grounds would use 541, private building lots 1,964. L'Enfant reserved the remaining 3,606 acres, for streets as wide as 110 feet and avenues as broad as 160. They would make the city "magnificent enough to grace a great nation."

Before volunteering in the American Revolutionary Army in 1777, L'Enfant had studied painting and sculpture in Paris at the French Royal Academy. Much captivated by the flamboyance of the Baroque, L'Enfant looked back to Paris—its boulevards, vistas, open spaces, fountains, and monumentality—when drawing up his plans for Washington. His plan could only be executed by a despotic and wealthy force, one that would seize land from private parties ruthlessly and lavish in a short time huge amounts of money to erect great monumental structures as well as to clear, pave, and plant the broad avenues. Such could never be the case for an impecunious nation whose pride was rooted in its having overthrown an oppressive authority. The federal government took little land by eminent domain and erected few buildings. Private parties built a hodgepodge of buildings about the city's core with little attention to order. On his visit to Washington in the mid-nineteenth century, the British novelist Charles Dickens saw "spacious avenues that begin in nothing and lead nowhere; streets, mile long that only want houses, roads, and inhabitants; public buildings that need only a public to be complete; and ornaments of great thoroughfares, which only lack great thoroughfares to ornament."

L'Enfant never got the chance to execute his plan in the fashion he desired. His arrogance and inability to compromise proved his undoing. The house of Daniel Carroll, the largest private landowner, protruded seven feet into the path of L'Enfant's contemplated New Jersey Avenue. Though George Washington cautioned "it will always be found sound policy to conciliate the good-will rather than provoke the enmity of any man," and though the new city's commissioners had ordered him not to do so, the planner had already torn the house down. It was a portentous act, and hardly the last: a road builder—the nation's first—had torn down a house in a city to make way for a four-lane avenue that was as wide as a modern highway. Next, L'Enfant defied the president by refusing to publish his plan for the city and declared to the commissioners that he would not submit to their requests in any way. Washington had no choice but to dismiss him. It was a blow from which L'Enfant would never recover. He lived in Maryland in his later years, broken and penniless, claiming that he had been deprived of just payment for his work. He would travel to the city he had planned when Congress was in session and could be seen daily, a lone figure pacing the rotunda of the Capitol, clutching the papers that he believed proved his case.

Pierre Charles L'Enfant's Washington has served as a vast stage for countless actors to play in innumerable dramas about the proper course for the nation to take. Unlike L'Enfant, whose will proved intractable, later protagonists have known enough to bend their seemingly unalterable wills at a crucial moment in their drama. Their actions have enabled the business of the nation to proceed. At those times when the principal actors have forgotten Burke's dictum that "all government . . . is founded on compromise and barter," the nation has become caught in stasis, or worse, civil war.

The drama that ended with the creation of the Interstate Highway System in 1956 marks a culmination of just such a process of compromise and barter. In the end the cast would include engineers, a retired general, corporate leaders, congressmen and senators, and a president who knew how to get his way. And no one in the drama understood fully the implications of his actions.

However, this drama was different from most that took place on the capital stage, if only because every one of the players realized that the subplots turned on power, prestige, and money. Senators and representatives from each of the forty-eight states had very different interests to protect. What was all right for the senators from New York or California might be wrong for the senators from Arkansas or New Mexico. What representatives of Boston or Chicago might regard as a benefit for their areas, the representatives of Meddybemps, Maine, or Spotsylvania Courthouse, Virginia, might regard as harmful for theirs. The drama was related to the interests of major industries—such as automobile, trucking, railroad, and petroleum—as well as those of hundreds of minor industries. The amounts of money involved were, for the time, staggering, some said as much as $50 billion, an amount greater than the cost of the recently ended war in Korea. And, perhaps most important, the outcome affected each of the millions of people who owned a car, and the millions more who wanted one.

It took over two years of bartering, from April 1954 to July 1956, before Dwight David Eisenhower, some of the most powerful members of Congress, and a collection of people representing automobile, trucking, and highway interests could fashion a compromise that would guide the way Americans would conduct their lives for the rest of the century. At times the odds that they might reach an agreement seemed slim at best, and few thought it possible.

To most, the impediments in the way of compromise seemed too great to overcome, and they seemed to increase rather than diminish as Eisenhower's first term in the presidency progressed. Chief among those obstacles were the president's health and a reluctant Congress. Between April 1954 and July 1956, Eisenhower suffered a heart attack that disabled him for six weeks and underwent an operation for ileitis that weakened him for four more. In November 1954, the Republican Party lost control of both houses of Congress. Indeed, given Eisenhower's own fiscal prudence and the country's preoccupation with military preparedness, few thought the president would be interested in undertaking a massive program to improve America's highways. Nevertheless, as Eisenhower believed that an immense highway program was essential to the nation's future prosperity, he decided to take the initiative.

Like so many of the president's undertakings, the creation of a super-highway network would be a team effort. The value of teamwork had been inculcated in him from playing football and baseball in Abilene and was nurtured later at West Point. As commander of the Allied Expeditionary Forces, he had relied on teamwork among his generals to bring about the defeat of Germany. As president of Columbia, Eisenhower even exhorted the faculty to make the university "a more effective and productive member of the American national team." Teamwork meant unity, agreement, and cooperation for a greater good, a victory on the playing field or battlefield. Now that he was captain of the American national team, Eisenhower relied upon teamwork to solve the growing problem of transportation.

While the president believed in teamwork, he cared little for details. Franklin Delano Roosevelt had drawn lines across a map of the United States to show Thomas MacDonald where he thought his highways should go. Dwight David Eisenhower would leave subordinates with this task. Others would have to determine the relationship between a federal highway building program and the states and how the country could afford new road construction and avoid a budget deficit. Eisenhower would let others worry about the relationship between the proposed new highways and older cities, and how to compensate those whose land was taken for construction. These were details and questions the president never appeared to have considered even casually. As he had done throughout his military career, Eisenhower issued orders to his assistants and they carried them out. The first orders came on April 12, when the president told key members of his administration, Francis du Pont, Sherman Adams, and John Stewart Bragdon, to devise a "dramatic plan to get 50 billion dollars worth of self-liquidating highways under construction."

Francis Victor du Pont had replaced Thomas Harris MacDonald as commissioner of the Bureau of Public Roads. Du Pont came from a family that appreciated good roads. Not only did the company that bore his name manufacture the explosives so necessary for road construction, but it also owned a substantial portion of General Motors. Family members had long regarded good roads as a sure way to advance civilization. His father, Thomas Coleman du Pont, had been a great proponent of automobiles and an ardent crusader for their adoption. At the beginning of the century he had founded the National Highways Association, whose goal was "a paved United States of America in our day." The road builder, Thomas Coleman du Pont declared in an advertisement for his organization, was the "soldier of civilization . . . the maker of national prosperity . . . which means national unity." The National Highways Association had joined with the American Automobile Association and the Society of American Military Engineers to propose a network of highways across the nation. "Highways will bind the states together in a common brotherhood and thus perpetuate and preserve the union," read the lofty caption on a map outlining the proposed roads.

Thomas Coleman du Pont had the money to make his proposals into a reality. In 1908, he began a corporation to build a hundred-mile-long highway from Wilmington, Delaware, south to Selbyville at the Maryland state line. "I will build a monument a hundred miles high and lay it on the ground," du Pont boasted. All citizens would benefit if a roadway ran the length of the state. Trained in engineering at MIT, du Pont designed some of the road himself. With extraordinary prescience for problems that the automobile would bring, he decided to site the road through the rural landscape, connecting the towns and cities he bypassed with trunk roads. Preceding some of the New Deal thinking of the Roosevelt administration by about a quarter century, du Pont proposed taking a two-hundred-foot right-of-way for his road and leasing back the excess land to utilities and farmers. Political opposition and du Pont's own ambitions to be a U.S. senator forced him to abandon his lease-back scheme and to make an outright gift of the road to the citizens of Delaware. When workers at last finished the highway in 1923, fifteen years after he had first proposed it, the cost to Senator Thomas Coleman du Pont had been nearly $4 million.

Francis du Pont possessed an altogether different personality from his father. The elder du Pont could be brash and voluble, and sought publicity to further his political ambitions; the younger was quiet, self-effacing, and after a much-publicized divorce in the 1930s had eschewed almost all publicity. His appointment to the Bureau of Public Roads had been buried deep inside the *New York Times* in a story measuring just two inches. But Francis du Pont did share his father's interest in highways and had helped make some of the preliminary surveys for the new road in Delaware. Highways, Francis du Pont believed, were linked to the prosperity of the country. Trained in engineering at MIT, he worked briefly for his family's company as a research engineer until he resigned in 1922 to manage his father's affairs. Many of those affairs concerned highways, of course, and he chaired the Delaware Highway Commission for twenty-three years without pay. By the time Eisenhower chose him to head the Bureau of Public Roads, Francis Victor du Pont enjoyed the reputation of being one of the ablest highway administrators in the nation.

Du Pont had other qualities that attracted Eisenhower's attention. Politically astute, he had headed Delaware's Republican Party for many years. When combined with his engineering experience, his political savvy would enable him to succeed. With no thought of personal gain, du Pont refused to take a salary or even to charge his travel expenses to the government. Unlike so many conservatives in his party, du Pont believed the federal government could stimulate economic growth through judicious spending on programs that would benefit all of society. Early on, du Pont presented Eisenhower with statistics that showed the positive impact federal spending on highway construction would have on the entire economy. In this du Pont departed from the conventional conservative wisdom of many in the administration, including Secretary of Commerce Sinclair Weeks, which held that the federal government should not embark on large-scale public works projects. It was du Pont's rationale about highway construction that helped serve as a cornerstone for the 1954 Federal-Aid Highway Act.

The other key members of the team, Sherman Adams and John Stewart Bragdon, quickly divided into factions. Sherman Adams, the aloof former governor of New Hampshire and Eisenhower's Chief of Staff, had all the warmth of a slab of his state's granite. Humorless and taciturn, Adams made abruptness his hallmark. He had no time for casual chatter. "He doesn't even talk much at dinner," remarked his wife. As Chief of Staff he was also extremely powerful. Adams believed in continuing the federal and state cooperation that Thomas MacDonald had established in the Bureau of Public Roads many years before. It had worked well when he was governor of New Hampshire, and if the federal government increased the funding, it would work even better. After consulting with Robert Moses and Bertram Tallamy, head of New York's Thruway Authority, he proposed a "Continental Highway Finance Corporation" under the direction of the Secretaries of Defense and Commerce and himself. The new corporation would see to the financing of the highway system and leave the planning and construction of the roads to the Bureau of Public Roads and state highway departments.

In the Executive Office Building next door to the White House, another faction headed by Major General John Stewart Bragdon was coming to some very different conclusions on the best way to proceed. Bragdon had known Eisenhower since their days in the Class of 1915 at West Point. In World War II, he had supervised all war construction for the army and air force in the South Atlantic as well as all airfield construction in Central and South America. After his election in 1952, Eisenhower appointed his old classmate to head the Public Works Planning Unit of his Council of Economic Advisers. There Bragdon soon established a reputation as a bull who brought his own china shop with him. His single-minded opinions in a world of teamwork often caused outrage, while his rank inexperience in the world of seasoned political veterans like Sherman Adams caused consternation. For his part, Bragdon seemed almost oblivious to the difficulties he was causing. He was a major general, after all. He would leave teamwork for others beneath him.

Such naïveté led Bragdon to propose a "National Highway Authority" endowed with sweeping powers to be headed by the Secretaries of Commerce, Defense, and Treasury. In a plan remarkably similar to the one Franklin Roosevelt had sketched for Thomas MacDonald seventeen years earlier, Bragdon proposed three roads running east and west, and five running north and south. Ignoring all political realities, Bragdon recommended that his National Highway Authority possess extraordinary powers. The authority would abolish state highway agencies and the Bureau of Public Roads, and take for itself complete control over financing *and* construction of the highway system. In essence Bragdon was proposing that Congress and the states yield all their control over highways to a centralized body within the federal government. Gone would be the pride that individual senators and representatives took when a road construction project went through their district. Gone would be the cooperative alliance between the federal and state governments that had characterized road building since the Federal-Aid Road Act of 1916.

Nor could the president's team agree on a financing plan for road construction. Taken with the success of turnpikes in states like Pennsylvania, New Jersey, and Maine, Bragdon's side argued for a toll system throughout the country. Some in the Commerce Department, which contributed ideas to Adams's team, urged a continuation of the old policy of the federal and state governments each sharing fifty percent of the costs, while others wanted a hundred percent state-financed system. Meanwhile, at the Bureau of Public Roads, Francis du Pont (who provided information to both the Adams and Bragdon factions) proposed that the federal government should pay for the entire system. Whenever pressed on the matter, Eisenhower suggested a self-liquidating program that would impose tolls on the roads until they were paid for. The president remained adamant that whatever highway program the nation adopted, it would not increase the national debt.

Unwittingly, it seemed, Eisenhower had reopened the fundamental and deep fissures—as old as the country—between those who championed states' rights and those who wanted complete federal control. Like other presidents before him, Eisenhower had to face the fact that no clause in the Constitution authorizes the federal government to build or maintain any roads, much less interstate routes.

"I experience great satisfaction at seeing my country proceed to facilitate the intercommunications of its several parts by opening rivers, canals, and roads," Thomas Jefferson wrote to a friend in 1786. "How much more rational is this disposal of public money than that of waging war." Yet as president, Jefferson could not find justification in the Constitution for building the roads he so approved of. He allowed the National Road to be built because it would be paid for by the revenues from land sales in the new territories, but he believed a constitutional amendment would be necessary before the federal government could pay to build a road within a state or states. Even the purchase of the Louisiana Territory in 1803, which doubled the size of the young nation and which surely would benefit from construction of canals and roads, could not move him.

Other presidents shared Jefferson's quandary. In 1822, James Monroe vetoed legislation to repair and establish toll gates on the National Road, arguing in a twenty-five-thousand-word essay—surely one of the longest veto messages ever written—that Congress did not have the right of jurisdiction and construction. Eight years later Andrew Jackson faced a similar dilemma when Congress approved legislation to construct a sixty-mile road from Maysville to Lexington in Kentucky. Though he understood the need for federal support, he believed "the Federal Constitution must be obeyed, State-rights preserved, our national debt *must be paid,* direct taxes and loans *avoided* and the Federal Union preserved." Old Hickory vetoed the bill.

States had accepted the creation of the Bureau of Public Roads in 1893 and, though reluctantly at times, had accepted the cooperative arrangements between the federal and state governments that Thomas Mac-Donald had nurtured throughout his tenure as chief of the bureau. Now, however, Eisenhower found even that relationship under attack. A number of governors wanted their states to have more control over road planning and building. Led by John Fine of Pennsylvania who was about to leave office with a $50 million deficit, a group of governors proposed that the federal government eliminate its gasoline tax of 2 cents a gallon so that each state could raise its own taxes for road building.

By July 1954, when he could see that his team was far from reaching an accord on the best way to proceed, Eisenhower decided to outline his own plan for an accelerated highway construction program at the annual meeting of the nation's governors. Unfortunately, on the day he was scheduled to deliver what his assistant called an "informal" speech, Eisenhower's sister-in-law died, and he had to send Richard Nixon in his place. Speaking from the president's notes, Nixon recalled the transcontinental trip Eisenhower had made as an army lieutenant thirty-five years earlier, which had taken "sixty days and 6000 breakdowns." Today, the vice president said, the country's transportation system was the best in the world in many respects, but it was "far from the best that America could fashion." Now, when America was enjoying unprecedented defensive and productive strength, the nation "requires the absolute best [highway system] that we can have." Continuing from the notes Eisenhower had left him, Nixon said that experts projected the population would be about two hundred million in 1970. If so, the nation would need:

> [a] grand plan for a properly articulated system that solves the problems of speedy, safe, transcontinental travel—intercity communication—access highways—and farm-to-farm movement—metropolitan area congestion—bottlenecks—and parking.

It would require spending $5 billion a year for ten years, figured the president, using a number he probably got from Francis du Pont and the Bureau of Public Roads. He proposed a "cooperative alliance" between the federal and state governments so that "local governments would have charge of their own highways." As he envisioned a collective venture, Eisenhower urged the governors to study the question themselves and make recommendations to submit to the next session of Congress.

Fifty billion dollars. To some, Eisenhower's ideas had provided an "electrifying effect," as one observer noted, for the usually mundane matter of highway building. The governors were unaccustomed to thinking in such broad, nationwide terms. The speech produced a "ferment," such as had not been seen since the 1920s. To be sure, some were suspicious of any federal intrusion into highway building. Governor John Fine used the occasion to demand that "the federal government . . . get out of the gasoline and fuel oil tax for once and for all," but on balance most of the comment was positive.

Clearly something had to be done. Americans were continuing to buy automobiles at an extraordinary pace—nearly sixteen thousand a day since Eisenhower's inauguration, so many that Charles C. Freed, president of the National Automobile Dealers Association, quipped, "We have not built as many miles of highway since World War II as we have built miles of passenger cars." By 1955 there were 62.5 million motor vehicles registered in the United States, and seven of every ten American families owned a car. When Mamie Eisenhower presided over a White House reception for the wives of the nation's automobile dealers (whose husbands were in Washington for their association's annual convention), she was dazzled by the furs and diamonds the women wore. "That is one crowd that is prospering," remarked the president in his diary.

Since his first team had failed to reach any substantive agreement, Eisenhower decided in August 1954 to appoint two more. One he called the Interagency Committee. Composed of representatives from the Departments of Defense, Treasury, and Commerce, the Council of Economic Advisers, and the Budget Bureau and headed by Francis du Pont of the Bureau of Public Roads, it would consider ways to fund the new interstates.

The other group Eisenhower called the President's Advisory Committee on a National Highway Program. It would hold public hearings and produce a report that would cite the need for highways and propose a plan for creating them. If successful, the advisory committee would generate support across America for new highways. Clearly, the president had in mind that this committee would have more public prestige and, since its mandate was broader, would have greater influence.

When Sherman Adams asked who might head such a committee, the president replied, "Call General Clay." Lucius diBignon Clay was an able engineer and administrator whom the president had known from his days at West Point. Clay had overseen the army's construction of airports before the United States entered World War II and later worked with consummate skill to supply the Allied troops in Germany. After the war, he had served as Eisenhower's deputy during the occupation of Germany, deftly and quietly handling all the logistical, financial, and political issues that came before him. In the summer and fall of 1948, Clay had overseen the massive airlift of food and fuel to West Berlin that thwarted the Soviet blockade of the beleaguered city. It was Clay, too, who worked tirelessly to secure the Republican presidential nomination for Eisenhower. After Ike's victory in 1952, Clay and Sherman Adams made most of his cabinet selections.

Now president of the Continental Can Company, Clay disliked Washington politics and had no desire to return to government service. But Clay was just the sort of person Eisenhower liked: soldier, businessman, and Republican. As an old soldier, Clay still regarded Eisenhower as his general, so he agreed to his commander's request. The advisory committee would work with the governors and the Interagency Committee to produce a proposal for highways. Surely the president could trust Clay to use his firm hand to control the squabbling and bring about results. Clay's name and stature would go a long way toward selling the plan to Congress and the nation.

Eisenhower gave Clay full control over the appointments to the advisory committee. He chose just four men. Stephen D. Bechtel, chairman of the board of the company that bore his name, the largest civil engineering firm in the world, had overseen huge construction projects. ("Bechtel had more experience in the construction field than anyone in America," Clay once said. "He wasn't involved in road building, but had a comprehensive knowledge of the construction industry.") S. Sloan Colt, head of Banker's Trust, could use his expertise to fashion a plan for financing the new highways. William A. Roberts headed Allis-Chalmers, a manufacturer of giant earth-moving machinery. The fourth was David Beck, the powerful and, as was later revealed, corrupt head of the International Brotherhood of Teamsters, the union that controlled so many of the nation's truckers.

In years to come, long after du Pont's and Clay's committees had completed their work, many would accuse them of being part of a larger conspiracy of motor vehicle and petroleum companies to make the automobile the only option for American transportation. Eisenhower was awed by wealth and surrounded himself with millionaires, so conspiracy theorists maintain. One need look no further than his first cabinet: All the positions save that of Secretary of Labor, which went to the head of the American Federation of Labor Plumbers Union, were held by milionaires. As one wag commented, the president had chosen "eight millionaires and a plumber." The man from the small town of Abilene had been corrupted. He was a puppet of big business.

Such theorists usually make Lucius Clay into the archdemon of the highway conspiracy. A member of the board of directors of General Motors, Clay served on the corporation's financial committee. Recently he had voted with the rest of the board to buy the Euclid Company, manufacturer of large road-building equipment. When it came time to pick the cabinet, Clay chose GM's president Charles Wilson to be Secretary of

Defense. "Engine Charlie" is best remembered today as the man who said, "What's good for General Motors is good for the nation." In cities across America, General Motors had purchased and systematically destroyed trolley systems, replacing the tracks and cars with GM buses. To one conspiracy believer, Clay had picked a "General Motors Cabinet."

Certainly Clay and each of the men he chose for the President's Advisory Committee on a National Highway Program understood the potential of a massive construction program to benefit their businesses as well as the nation. True, General Motors *did* acquire and replace many of the trolley systems across America. But many trolley systems were going broke because of financial mismanagement and the fact that a changing economy and living patterns enabled people to purchase automobiles and move to the suburbs, to places where the trolleys did not go. Once they bought their automobiles and moved, Americans chose to drive instead of ride. Indeed, there was a plot to build a new system of superhighways, and most Americans of the 1950s were willing co-conspirators.

Eisenhower's appointment of a general to head the advisory committee made plain the connection between highways, national defense, and the fear Americans had about their security. An overwhelming proportion of Americans believed they lived under the shadow of a nuclear attack and were poised for World War III. In August 1953, the Gallup poll reported that seventy-nine percent of Americans believed Russia wanted to "rule the world." Cities appointed civil defense coordinators who found spaces in public buildings that citizens might use in an atomic attack, while each day at noon they tested their air raid sirens. The case for defense could help to sell highways to Congress and the nation.

The Russians had exploded "the Bomb" in 1949, and the news had stunned the nation. Many felt it was only a matter of time until the Russians dropped it on U.S. cities. Experts estimated the number who would die—ten million, fifteen million, twenty million in a single day. Soon after, Edward Teller and a group of atomic scientists built and tested a super hydrogen bomb that generated heat five times as great as the interior of the sun and obliterated an entire island in the South Pacific. Yet in less than a year Russian Premier Georgi Malenkov announced tersely, "The Soviet government deems it necessary to report that the United States has no monopoly in the production of the hydrogen bomb."

Across the land in cities large and small citizens prepared for the inevitable. Families stocked their basements or a closet under the stairs with canned goods and water to help them survive the nuclear strike. Private companies installed concrete bomb shelters in the backyards of suburban houses, while in New York, the city's Civil Defense Bomb Shelter Committee proposed standards for building and equipping shelters in the basements of private homes ("Fire extinguisher, Pails of water, Battery-operated radio, First-Aid kit"). Radio manufacturers inscribed the tuning dials of their sets with a little triangle about the letters CD, better to show citizens where to tune for help when the bombs began to fall. Teachers drilled anxious children in "duck and cover" exercises, huddling them under classroom desks or herding them into school basements. In schoolyards children, no doubt parroting their parents' dinner table conversations, discussed the reasons why their city or town was a top target on the Russians' list of bombing sites. Pittsburgh, Pennsylvania, was first because of its steel, Omaha, Nebraska, because of its railroads and grain production; Portsmouth, New Hampshire, because of its naval base. Almost everyone thought their city or town would be first, even Philadelphians. In fact, the government had compiled a list of 185 "target areas."

The best solution of all, of course, would be to escape to the country before the Russians attacked. Paul Yount, chief of transportation for the army, estimated that at least seventy million people might have to be evacuated in a war. Clearly, so the popular thinking went, the new roads would enable a mass evacuation. Given enough warning, citizens would be able to pack the family in the car and head out of town on one of the new superhighways. Military planners wanted interstate highways around the perimeter of urban areas, because the roads would enable them to bypass cities "on a route that had suffered a direct A-bomb hit." Already federal civil defense agencies across the nation consulted with local highway engineers when formulating their plans to evacuate the 185 target areas, and the Bureau of Public Roads had published an assessment of the highway needs in the event of an attack.

From the time of the Clay committee, members of the Eisenhower administration, highway lobby groups, senators and representatives, and the general public began to consider the nation's defense in relation to its need for highways. Clay would mention it in his final report to the president, and Congress would assume its importance whenever debating a federal-aid highway bill.

As the committee took shape, Clay asked Francis du Pont and his deputy at the Bureau of Public Roads, Francis Cutler Turner, to provide it with information. The committee got more than mere highway statistics, too, as Turner and du Pont were able to convey the rationale and history of federal aid to highways. Turner proved especially valuable, so valuable in fact that Clay named him executive secretary and installed him in the committee's office at the Executive Office Building. The son of a railroad man, Turner had been born and raised near Dallas, Texas. There he had worked on "road drags," the name locals gave to the road repair days the county organized for those who could not or would not pay the local highway tax. After graduating from North Texas State Agricultural College and Texas Agricultural and Mechanical College, Turner took a job with the Bureau of Public Roads as a junior highway engineer. He had designed and supervised highway building in locations as diverse as Arkansas, the Philippines, and Alaska. In Arkansas he had supervised federal-aid highway projects. For three years he supervised building the permanent highway in Alaska. After the war he had helped repair the roads in the Philippines before joining the Washington office of the Bureau of Public Roads as assistant to Thomas MacDonald and later Francis du Pont.

A quiet man with an encyclopedic knowledge of engineering and the history of the federal government's role in highway building—and able to get jobs done in a businesslike and efficient manner—Turner was just the sort of person whose judgment Clay could trust. In the highly charged political atmosphere of Washington, Turner stood apart. As a professional engineer he stuck to the facts, and he conveyed them with the same technocratic aura that had characterized every Bureau of Public Roads pronouncement for thirty-five years. Enjoying Lucius Clay's respect, Frank Turner—and of course the view of the Bureau of Public Roads that he espoused—exerted a considerable influence.

Clay's committee acted with dispatch. It convened its first public hearing on October 7, heard from members of federal agencies in November, considered a study made by a highway committee of the governors in early December, and—about three months after it began—submitted its final report to the president in January. Clay himself spent as little time in Washington as possible—so little, in fact, that his bill at the White House Mess for December, the month the committee did much of its work, was just 65 cents.

Part of the reason Clay stayed out of Washington was his dislike of politics. Though he had helped Eisenhower choose his cabinet in 1952, and though the president-elect offered him a position in that cabinet, Clay would have nothing of the political life. His report to the president showed just how unsophisticated he was when it came to dealing with Congress and the highway lobbyists.

The words "lobbyist" and "to lobby" have been a part of American speech since the middle of the last century. The lobbyist grew out of the system of congressional and senatorial committees that are so much a part of American government. It was about 1850 when men began to frequent the lobbies of the Congress to have a word with members who were bringing legislation through a committee to the floor. A century later the lobbyists were everywhere. Washington had become a city of associations, federations, and institutes—lobbying groups pressuring Congress to act in their favor.

By 1954, the various highway, automobile, trucking, and petroleum groups, many of which had been operating since the turn of the century, had woven a complicated web of many intersecting strands. There were large groups, like the Association of General Contractors, which spoke for the American Public Works Association; the National Asphalt Pavement Association; the National Ready Mixed Concrete Association; the American Concrete Paving Association; and the American Road Builders Association, which represented road builders associations from each state. Other groups, like the National Automobile Dealers Association, the American Automobile Association, the Rubber Manufacturers Association, and the American Truckers Association, had more limited interests. At the center of the web, the American Association of State Highway Officials served the interests of each state highway department through its membership to the various state and local chapters of the national association. Though it had no formal authority to lobby members of Congress for highway funds as industry associations did, its power came from the expertise of its members. The association meetings gave federal and state highway officials a means of meeting with representatives of private industry to determine their common interests.

Everyone seemed connected and interconnected. More often than not, the head of one association served on the board or steering committee of another. At this time it was not unusual for a member of the Bureau of Public Roads to sit on the American Association of State Highway Officials, without any concern about a possible conflict of interest. Yet interconnection did not necessarily mean unanimity of opinion.

Certainly everyone agreed that the United States needed better roads and an interstate highway system, but the lobbyists disagreed as sharply as the president's advisers about how to achieve their goal.

From the outset Clay recognized and tried to get beyond the divisions. "The question really is not whether or not we need highway improvements," he said on the first day of the hearings, but "how to get them quickly, economically, and how they may be financed sensibly and within reason." The spokesmen for each of the twenty-two lobbying groups invited to testify before the committee did little to clarify matters. The American Automobile Association wanted more urban routes to relieve "the strangulation of traffic," while the American Association of Township Officials favored rural roads and opposed urban highways. Meanwhile, the American Trucking Association lobbied hard for better roads and fewer taxes. Only a committee that the governors formed after the president's speech seemed to modify its position. The governors no longer demanded a repeal of the federal gasoline tax.

In addition to the testimony from lobbying organizations, many individuals sent suggestions of their own to Washington. From Elkins, West Virginia, D. D. Brown of the "Crozet Super Highway Commission" proposed a highway from Boston to San Diego that, incidentally, would pass through Elkins. Engineers offered their services. "We are in a position to supply aerial and field control surveys for large projects. . . . We would appreciate your suggestions and assistance in making contacts with reliable clients," wrote one. A secretary in the committee's office filed each suggestion and proposal.

After the hearings, Clay's group wrestled with the matter of finances. No one on the committee or Congress listened very carefully to the argument of the American Automobile Association and the American Petroleum Institute that since an interstate highway system would be so important to defense, general tax revenues should pay for it. Nor did the Department of Defense accept the suggestion that it should absorb some of the construction costs in its budget. From his desk at the Council of Economic Advisers, the great disciple of toll roads, Major General John Stewart Bragdon, furiously sent memoranda to Clay urging adoption of his position for a limited toll road system. But Clay had also heard from du Pont, Turner, and the Bureau of Public Roads on the matter and would have nothing of it. "Dear Stuart," wrote Clay in November, misspelling General Bragdon's name, "I am afraid that our Committee does not believe toll roads to be the answer, nor do we think a national network of toll roads desirable." Rebuffed, Bragdon lapsed for a time into sullen silence.

Disregarding these various proposals from the White House and Bureau of Public Roads, Clay decided instead to consult the chief executives of the nation's leading banking and brokerage houses, including Smith Barney, Drexel, Chase, and National City Bank of New York, for their "views on financing a highway program." It is likely that he took direction from Sloan Colt, the head of Banker's Trust. After hearing from the bankers and brokers, the committee decided upon a radically different plan. A new national corporation created by Congress would sell thirty-year bonds to finance road construction. The federal government would pay ninety percent of the construction costs, while the states would share the rest. As in the past, states and the Bureau of Public Roads would be expected to cooperate in construction. Money received from the federal tax on gasoline and diesel fuel would pay off the bonds. Since the new roads would increase traffic and consequently revenues, Clay figured there would be no need to raise the gas tax.

Clay's move was a bold and clever attempt to find a way through the financing labyrinth that had so eluded others. Roads are "a capital asset," the committee argued, therefore they should be financed by bonds. The program would incur no new taxes, and the indebtedness would rest outside the federal budget on the books of an ambiguous federal corporation. Selling bonds would make the money available immediately. The public would like the plan because it would pump an enormous amount of money into highway construction in a short time; economists would like it because it would create jobs; and the president would approve because it would raise neither taxes nor the debt.

The Clay committee's final report of January 11, 1955, recommended spending $101 billion over ten years for primary, secondary, urban, and rural highways and an Interstate Highway System. The interstate system, the centerpiece of Clay's proposal which he called "the top national economic and defense priority," would be a network of controlled-access highways. Masterful in conception, Clay's proposal—like Bragdon's—was foolish in its basic comprehension of political realities. It was destined to fail.

Three days after the Clay committee sent its report to the White

Divided Highways

House, Francis du Pont resigned his position as head of the Bureau of Public Roads to become special assistant to the Secretary of Commerce for road policy. At the height of his power, Chief MacDonald had been able to get just what he wanted for the Bureau of Public Roads through his lobbying efforts, but those days had passed. Du Pont found he could not run the bureau and lobby for highways effectively at the same time. "There has never been a more opportune time" to get a bill through Congress, du Pont said with urgency to the American Association of State Highway Officials at the time of his resignation. But he wondered, "Are we going to muff the ball?"

The Clay committee report surprised many in Washington, but none more than those gathered around the president. Clay's proposal had divided them deeply. They had to use the administration's preoccupation with a threat from the Communist Chinese to invade Formosa as an excuse to delay transmitting a highway bill to Congress. "There was much discussion as to how to handle the Clay report," Bragdon wrote in a memorandum, "whether it should be forwarded as representing the President's views; forwarded merely as informative; not forwarded at all. . . ." At times the matter was "very warmly discussed." Whenever he spoke of financing arrangements for his highways, Eisenhower became murky, using words like "self-liquidating," which suggested that he favored toll roads. He was clear only in professing his horror of deficit financing. As the president's advisers argued the best course, the delay continued. When he finally outlined his National Highway Program in a special message to Congress on Washington's birthday in 1955, Eisenhower said weakly, "I am inclined to the view that it is sounder to finance this program by special bond issues . . . than by an increase in general revenue obligations." With such a tepid endorsement, the administration's highway bill was in trouble even before it arrived at the Capitol. Before Congress could pass a highway bill, there would be an eighteen-month period of torturous and sometimes tangled barter and compromise about the best way to fund it.

The 84th Congress that convened in January 1955 was very different from the 83rd that swept into office with the president in November 1952. In the midterm elections of November 1954, the Democrats regained a slim margin of control over the Senate and a firm thirty-one-seat lead in the House. Since the House and Senate committees were in the hands of the Democrats, Eisenhower's highway legislation would face the chairman of the Senate Finance Committee, the archconservative Democrat from Berryville, Virginia, Harry Flood Byrd.

Nothing in Harry Byrd's background suggested that a proposal to sell bonds to build highways would ever pass through his Senate Finance Committee unscathed. By 1955, the legend of the man people called "Mr. Economy" was well known to almost everyone in the Capitol: the Shenandoah Valley boy, a direct descendant of a first family of Virginia, who dropped out of high school to return the family's nearly bankrupt newspaper to solvency; the state senator who, in 1923, successfully fought a $50 million bond issue to build highways in favor of a "pay-as-you-go" tax plan; the four-term governor of Virginia who inherited a state with a deficit and left it with a healthy surplus; the senator who from the time of the New Deal had voted against most fiscally progressive programs, including federal aid to education, the Marshall plan, the St. Lawrence Seaway project, and additional money for the Tennessee Valley Authority, among others; the man who steadfastly refused to discuss any additional federal spending until there was a balanced budget.

Three decades earlier, Harry Byrd had opposed a bond sale for highway construction in his home state. Now he faced an even more pernicious plan: to create a nearly autonomous government corporation that would sell $20 billion worth of construction bonds, pay $11.5 billion in interest over thirty years, and pretend that the transaction did not increase the nation's debt. "Nothing has been proposed during my 22 years in the United States Senate," the stentorian senator declared, "that would do more to wreck our fiscal budget system" than the administration's bill. "The result," he said, "would be the end of honest bookkeeping."

Editorial writers across the nation echoed Byrd. To the Nashville *Tennessean* Clay's plan was a "sham." The Columbus, Ohio, *Citizen* termed it "a gold-brick scheme . . . which would hike the debt without acknowledging it." The *Cleveland Plain Dealer* worried whether "one session of Congress would obligate succeeding sessions to continue any appropriation." The administration's bill never got beyond the Senate Public Works Committee. By the end of February it was dead.

The White House watched helplessly as Harry F. Byrd crushed the Clay committee's proposal. General John Stewart Bragdon once again proposed toll highways. "Provide sufficient funds *by appropriation* to cover . . . construction," he told the Council of Economic Advisers. "Collect tolls until the *full costs* are amortized." Bragdon had allies in the executive branch, including Secretary of the Treasury George Humphrey and Arthur Burns of the Council of Economic Advisers. But when Humphrey tried to sell Byrd on the virtues of toll roads, the senator would not be swayed. Building toll roads demanded an initial outlay of money that would increase the national debt. Instead, "Mr. Economy" stuck to a position that he had held since 1923, "pay-as-you-go." Better to store up the federal gasoline tax receipts until there was enough money to build roads than go into debt to build them.

Still, the sentiment with Congress, the administration, and the American people was for a superhighway system. Only the compromise to achieve it seemed elusive. Between the intransigent Harry Byrd and the Eisenhower administration stepped the junior senator from Carthage, Tennessee, Albert Arnold Gore, who produced a plan of his own even before the Clay proposal reached the Senate. A dirt farmer's son, who taught school by day and studied for his law degree at the Nashville YMCA by night, Gore was atypical of the southern senators who populated the Congress. He had gotten to the U.S. Senate because of his ambition, intensity, self-confidence, and silver tongue. First elected to the House of Representatives at the age of thirty-one and reelected five times, he had advanced to the Senate and was now midway through his first term. In an age when conservative southerners like Harry Byrd were preaching against the evils of school desegregation and almost all progressive social legislation, Gore held a liberal outlook on international affairs, supported massive public works programs, and took moderate positions on civil rights. He affirmed the role of the Tennessee Valley Authority, supported dam and highway construction, advocated tax reform, and, in 1956, would refuse to sign the "Manifesto" his fellow southern senators had drafted, which vowed to oppose all efforts at desegregation. Gore believed his was the voice of a progressive, new South, and he hoped it would carry him to the vice presidency, perhaps, or even the White House.

Using information gleaned from the hearings of the Senate Public Works Committee, Gore crafted a highway bill of his own greater than any legislation (other than that dealing with war) ever to come before the Congress. As approved by the Senate, the bill called for the Bureau of Public Roads to spend $10 billion on an interstate system through

1961, with the federal share to be seventy-five percent. But Gore's proposal also kept a tight congressional rein on highway construction, so tight that it funded only about a third of the entire program and demanded that the Bureau of Public Roads return to Congress for annual appropriations. The entire program would last five years instead of Clay's ten. Reminding his colleagues that all taxation bills begin in the House of Representatives, Gore was silent about just how his legislation would be funded. In late May, the Senate passed Gore's bill.

While the senators were debating Gore's bill, on the other side of the Capitol George Hyde Fallon, a fifty-three-year-old, six-foot-two congressman known as the "Big Man from Baltimore," was drafting a comparable highway bill that he hoped would be practical enough to satisfy both Democrats and Republicans in the Congress and the Republican in the White House. A businessman who worked in his family's advertising sign company, Fallon had risen through the ranks of Baltimore's Democratic political machine the old-fashioned way: first as ward heeler in northeast Baltimore; then as member of the Democratic State Central Committee; then Baltimore City Councilman; and finally, in 1944, as member of Congress from Maryland's solidly Democratic fourth district. A man of good sense, good humor, and modest aspirations, Fallon rarely thought of rising further. He had little desire to occupy a seat in the Senate or the Maryland governor's mansion, much less the White House. He was content to rise quietly in seniority in Congress while the Baltimore Democratic machine saw to his reelection term after term. Since he entered Congress, Fallon had served on the Public Works Committee, and now chaired its subcommittee on roads. He thought of little other than highways. Public works were not especially flashy, but then the colorless and unassuming, owl-like and almost shy George Fallon was not flashy, either. "The business of Congress is tedious beyond expression," John Adams had observed while the first Continental Congress was meeting in 1774. Things had not changed much over the following eighteen decades. But George Fallon's blandness endowed him with a capacity to endure tedium and enabled him to have a successful career. Rarely did Fallon speak on the floor of the House except to support a highway bill that his Public Works Committee had written. So myopic and single-minded did George H. Fallon's vision seem that his colleagues in Congress came to say that his middle initial stood for "Highways."

Fallon's fervor for highway construction was rooted in his twin desire to improve the nation—"to help people," as he put it frequently—and to shovel the pork from Congress's ever-increasing barrel of political largesse. Highway projects were popular with voters, members of Congress knew, and therefore they lobbied their colleagues on the Public Works Committee hard in support of road money for their districts. As Fallon's tenure on the committee lengthened and as he rose in seniority, he became more and more popular with his colleagues. Others might abuse their power to punish their enemies, but Fallon never did. "He made sure no congressman or district was slighted," said an editorial in the *Baltimore Sun*. As a result, everyone liked George Fallon.

Realizing that Eisenhower would never sign Senator Gore's highway bill because it raised (by implication, at least) the public debt, and that the Senate would never pass the administration's bill because it called for $11.5 billion to be paid in interest over thirty years, Fallon decided on a third option. With generous help from Frank Turner, Fallon and his fellow Democrats on the House Public Works subcommittee on roads drafted a proposal that kept the general provisions of Gore's bill for interstate construction, while extending them for thirteen years, through 1968, and created a highway trust fund supported by revenues from the federal gasoline and oil taxes. Under Fallon's bill the gasoline tax would rise from 2 to 3 cents; diesel fuel from 2 to 4. Taxes on trucks, trailers, buses, tires, inner tubes, and recapped tires would also rise. In a bow to Harry Byrd (and to make the additional taxes more palatable), Fallon called the funding plan "pay-as-you-go."

The various highway lobbies wanted an interstate highway system but were not ready to accept any new taxes to pay for it. The American Trucking Association objected to the increase in diesel fuel tax that was greater than the tax increase on gasoline. The American Petroleum Institute lobbied against increases in taxes on their products. Trucking and bus companies together fought any increase in excise taxes on equipment or tires. ("We are unalterably opposed to the bill," wrote the president of Southwestern Greyhound to his Texas representative.) The American Automobile Association opposed the bill because the taxes on buses and trucks were not high enough. The Association of General Contractors and heads of chambers of commerce meanwhile criticized the bill's inclusion of the Davis Bacon Act, which required the payment of prevailing wages to workers as determined by the Secretary of Labor.

And urban transit companies took exception to paying increased federal taxes on diesel fuel and gasoline to pay for roads their vehicles would never travel.

The representatives had more than enough reasons to peck Fallon's bill to death. They were for more highways, of course, but they were against increased taxes. In the meantime, members of various highway associations flooded their representatives with letters and telegrams, more than had been received at any time since President Truman fired General MacArthur. One representative received fifty-two telegrams just before he voted. The end came decisively on July 27, 1955, in non-partisan vote of 292 to 123. Just 94 Democrats favored the legislation; 128 voted against it.

An interstate highway program was dead for 1955, and, in the opinion of Sam Rayburn, the Texas Democrat, "probably for next year too." It was the opinion also of the "Road Gang," an informal group of about 250 federal and state highway officials and lobbyists that met in Washington once a month to discuss the progress of highway legislation and what they might do to advance it. At its November luncheon meeting, the Road Gang convened a panel of eight members to discuss the prospects for any highway legislation. Typical of the views were those of John King of the Automobile Manufacturers Association, who thought it unrealistic to expect that a Democratic Congress would send a highway bill to a Republican president in an election year. However, none of the principal actors in the drama—Eisenhower, Gore, Fallon, or the Bureau of Public Roads—was ready to give up. Eisenhower even suggested at a news conference in August 1955 that he was willing to compromise on the matter of financing.

The next significant event took place not in the White House or Congress but in a hospital room in Denver, Colorado. That September, while staying with friends in Denver, Eisenhower suffered a serious heart attack. During his recuperation, which lasted well into 1956, he spent a good deal of time reflecting upon the long-range future of the country. Eisenhower came to consider himself the nation's indispensable steward. His Abilene farming boyhood led him to worry about the consequences of a nation with depleted soil. What of drainage and flood control? What of America's need for more schoolrooms? What would be the consequences for America without the network of superhighways he envisioned? The nation had to have highways and he would compromise to get them.

"Legislation to provide a modern, interstate highway system is even more urgent this year than last," Eisenhower said in his annual message to Congress,

for 12 months have now passed in which we have fallen behind in road construction needed for the personal safety, the general prosperity, the national security of the American people.

The legislation Eisenhower sent to Congress was identical to the previous year's, and destined to fail for the same reasons it had the year before.

In the House of Representatives George Hyde Fallon introduced the Federal-Aid Highway Act of 1956, which provided for the construction of the Interstate Highway System. This time, however, he left the financing of the bill to the House Ways and Means Committee and Representative Hale Boggs of New Orleans. To ensure that the House did not vote to build an interstate system without a means to pay for it, Speaker Rayburn declared that when the bills reached the floor they would be voted on together.

Boggs introduced a separate Highway Revenue Act to pay for the system, though the measure was substantially the same as the one Fallon had included in his bill of the previous year, a tax on gasoline, diesel, and lubricating oils, tires, and heavy trucks, which would flow into a Highway Trust Fund. Separate from the rest of the federal budget, the Highway Trust Fund satisfied opponents of highway bonds like Harry Byrd and put construction funding on a "pay-as-you-go" basis.

This time Fallon vowed that he would not allow the bill to be pecked to death. He need not have worried. By 1956, almost everyone—road-building and civic associations, truckers, and most especially the highway construction industry—realized that the taxes proposed were insignificant in comparison with the benefits that would be reaped. Tire makers realized that an excise tax on tires would not be especially detrimental to an industry that would sell more tires as cars and trucks traveled more miles.

When asked at a press conference on April 25 to comment on the legislation before the House of Representatives, President Eisenhower seemed vague. "We need highways badly, very badly, and I am in favor of any forward, constructive step in this field." His words signaled that the administration had at long last abandoned its proposal for highway bonds. The bill could go through as written. Two days later the House passed the Fallon and Boggs bills by an overwhelming margin of 388 to 19.

Following the House vote, the Senate took up the measure. Gore proposed essentially the same bill as he had the year before, which was in substantial agreement with the legislation passed by the House. On May 29, after a lengthy debate on minor provisions in the bill, the Senate passed on a voice vote the Federal-Aid Highway Act of 1956. "I confidently expect when we go to conference, we can merge my bill and the Fallon bill into a highway measure that will be on the President's desk well before July 1," said Gore when the bill went to conference. On June 25, both houses of Congress approved the conference bill.

Though the provisions of Gore's and Fallon's highway bills remained the same, the tone of the debate between the first and second sessions of the 84th Congress changed dramatically. In 1955, sentiment had been divided over the taxing provisions of the bill, with many Republicans still favoring the administration's proposal to sell bonds through a federal corporation. In 1956, few made mention of the bonding proposal, and instead spoke with conciliation. George A. Dondero, for example, a Republican representative from Detroit, had lobbied long and hard for the administration's bonding plan in the first session, going so far as to introduce it as a substitute motion for Fallon's bill. By the second session, Dondero said simply, "While there may be some portions of this bill I do not like, nevertheless I am supporting the measure and hope it will become the law for the benefit of the American people."

"I am proud to say that political considerations were completely put aside," said one senator about the 1956 Interstate highway bill. Not exactly. One significant change took place between the first and second sessions of Congress that made the road bill more palatable to almost all the members, and especially to those representatives whose districts encompassed major metropolitan areas. The Bureau of Public Roads still had to designate 2,175 miles of Interstate highways and it decided to place them in cities. That September every member of Congress received a one-hundred-page book from the bureau entitled *General Location of National System of Interstate Highways Including All Additional Routes at Urban Areas.* Owing to the color of its cover, everyone came to call it the "Yellow Book." Unlike most documents of that length produced in Washington, the Yellow Book contained just three sentences. The rest of its pages were maps that showed how Interstate highways would cross and circumscribe the major metropolitan areas of forty-three states and the District of Columbia.

The bureau's designation of additional miles of Interstate for cities had been shrewd. Suddenly scores of representatives had dramatic pictures of just how the new Interstates would benefit voters from their district. Thus Harold R. Lovre, the Republican congressman whose district included Minnehaha County in South Dakota, could see that Sioux Falls would be connected to the black lines representing Interstates 90 and 29 at the north and west edges of the city, and also a new bold black line—Interstate 229—that diverged from Interstate 29 south of the city, crossed the Big Sioux River, and curved north to connect at the northeast corner with Interstate 90. Sioux Falls, a city that numbered 52,696 men, women, and children in 1950, had its own beltway. Lovre had voted against the Fallon bill in 1955. Now that Sioux Falls would be surrounded by construction jobs and concrete, how could he resist? The Yellow Book had given Lovre a reason to justify his vote to increase federal taxes on fuel, tires, and trucks. The congressman changed his vote. So did Hugh Scott from Philadelphia, Charles B. Brownson from Indianapolis, John M. Vorys from Columbus, and dozens of other representatives. In the end, only one representative whose city appeared in the Yellow Book voted against the 1956 highway bill. He failed to be reelected to the 85th Congress.

The Federal-Aid Highway Act of 1956 reached Eisenhower on June 29 in Walter Reed Army Medical Center, where he was recovering from surgery for ileitis. The bill was just one of twenty-seven he signed that day. Worried that he might appear physically weak just before his party was to renominate him as its candidate for president, Eisenhower barred all photographers and dispensed with all ceremony when signing the bills. No one other than his press secretary, who reported that the president "was highly pleased," was with him when he signed the legislation. He did, however, set two pens aside that he used in the signing. One went to Albert Gore, and the other to the American Association of State Highway Officials.

Just what had the president signed? The bill authorized $25 billion for twelve years to accelerate construction of a National System of Interstate and Defense Highways; created a Highway Trust Fund supported by increasing the federal tax on gas and diesel fuel from 2 to 3 cents; increased the federal portion of construction costs for Interstate highways to ninety percent; provided for advance acquisition of right-of-way; required that the Interstate highways be built to the highest standards and with the capability of handling traffic projected for 1972; and pledged to complete the Interstate Highway System by 1972.

In its conception, the Federal-Aid Highway Act of 1956 represented a triumph for all: $25 billion issuing in a steady stream from the deep well of the dedicated Highway Trust Fund, and all without a significant increase in gasoline taxes. Motorists were happy because the legislation promised to increase their mobility over safer and better roads. Truckers approved because it provided for superhighways that allowed them to carry increased weights without paying significantly higher taxes. Mayors and managers of large cities applauded the money and jobs the urban portions of the Interstate Highway System would bring to them. Highway contractors were ecstatic because the bill demanded the best and most expensive roads imaginable. They would not want for work for at least a dozen years.

No doubt the happiest groups of all were the manufacturers of automobiles and trucks and the refiners of gasoline. More and better roads promised a steady increase in the number of miles motor vehicles traveled. Seventy-two percent of American families owned an automobile in 1956. By 1970, the number had risen to eighty-two percent; and twenty-eight percent owned two or more automobiles. In the same period, personal purchases of gasoline and automobiles more than doubled. Congress had voted to enact nothing less than a fundamental change in American life. Nearly all acclaimed the decision.

American citizens in 1956 were happy, too. Across the country, editorials complained not that the highways were being built, but that they were not being built fast enough. Americans have always valued their mobility. Traditionally they have been people on the move. As Tocqueville observed of Americans when he visited the young nation in 1831, "Once they migrate, they circulate." The automobile and the new Interstate highways would allow them to circulate as never before.

But did the American people in 1956 foresee the price they would have to pay for their mobility? No. Only one critic, Lewis Mumford, had the prescience to recognize how little Americans understood what the true costs would be.

Divided Highways

When the American people, through their Congress, voted a little while ago . . . for a twenty-six billion dollar highway program, the most charitable thing to assume about this action is that they hadn't the faintest notion of what they were doing. Within the next fifteen years they will doubtless find out; by that time it will be too late to correct all the damage to our cities and our countryside, not least to the efficient organization of industry and transportation, that this ill conceived and preposterously unbalanced program will have wrought.

In the Yellow Book the Bureau of Public Roads and Congress had created the future urban battlegrounds in cities across the land. At first glance the lines looked benign. The map of Boston showed a highway that cut a circular path through the center of the city as well as some adjacent districts like Somerville and Cambridge. The map of Washington showed an outer circle of highways—what became the Beltway—and a much smaller inner circle as well. On the San Francisco map a broad black line appeared along the harborfront. As two-dimensional abstractions the lines looked harmless, but as three-dimensional structures of concrete and steel they became great creatures that threatened the life of the city. That small circle at the center of Washington and Boston would become a concrete noose that promised to strangle the life from people and neighborhoods; that line along the shore in San Francisco would actually become a twin-decked barrier of steel and concrete, moving automobiles and trucks, cutting off citizens from their waterfront.

The concern about what Congress had wrought was for the future, however. For the moment everyone was flushed with excitement about the prospect of new high-speed highways. In the fall of 1956 the Ford Motor Company published a collection of articles about highways, traffic, and safety, *Freedom of the American Road*. In its introduction, Henry Ford II wrote that the title was chosen "simply because we Americans always like plenty of elbow room—freedom to come and go as we please in this big country of ours." The historian and chronicler of the West Bernard De Voto wrote prophetically of the future: "We have seen what was grandfather's pasture when we were boys become a shopping center or an industrial plant. . . . But in 1961 grandfather's pasture may also be the center of a suburban city with schools, movie houses, and acre upon acre of houses." And De Voto concluded with a short exhortation: "We must now solve the problem of giving our culture the highways that its abundance demands."

THE GREAT
PUZZLE

American streets are not sober little walks closed in between houses, but national highways. The moment you set foot on one of them, you understand that it has to go on to Boston or Chicago.

JEAN-PAUL SARTRE

At one-thirty on the afternoon of Wednesday, November 14, 1956, a line of thirteen men stands shoulder to shoulder on a fresh twenty-four-foot wide, nine-inch-thick slab of portland concrete that stretches from Valencia, at the western edge of Topeka, Kansas, eight miles to Maple Hill Corner on the Wabaunsee County line. As they face the camera, each rests a hand on the wide ribbon that stretches before them. At the center, holding a ceremonial pair of scissors, Governor Fred Hall presides over the occasion. Flanking him are the director of the Kansas State Highway Department, Frank Harwi, Jr., the state's junior U.S. senator, Frank Carlson, contractors, engineers, the heads of the chambers of commerce of Topeka and Junction City, and several minor highway officials. The men are gathered to dedicate the first eight miles of the more than forty thousand that will comprise the Interstate Highway System. No longer will people think of the word "interstate" as an adjective. An act of Congress has transformed the word into a proper noun.

Six weeks earlier, at another brief ceremony, the state highway commissioner for the district had scratched "9-26-56" in the wet concrete to mark the first paving of the new Interstate. The total cost for grading, bridges, and paving the eight miles was $1,511,571—about $190,000 a mile.

In truth, the eight miles were just two lanes of Interstate 70, a long snake of highway that would eventually extend from the city of Baltimore on the Atlantic coast; climb through the passes in the Allegheny Mountains of Pennsylvania; cross the Ohio River at Wheeling, West Virginia; cut through the broad midwestern cities of Columbus, Ohio, and Indianapolis, Indiana; head south across southern Illinois; traverse the Mississippi at St. Louis; and proceed straight across Missouri and Kansas, before climbing to Denver and through the Continental Divide in the Rockies and coming to a rest at an intersection with Interstate 15 in the Fishlake National Forest of Utah. Probably by accident the Interstate Highway System had opened at a symbolic point in America. Kansas stands at the geographic center of the United States and the geodetic center of the North American continent. Seventy miles to the west in Dickinson County lies Abilene, the boyhood home of the man who signed the Interstate highway bill into law.

Few paid much attention to the ribbon cutting in Kansas that November afternoon in 1956. No major metropolitan newspaper picked up the story. The Topeka *State Journal* devoted just six column inches to the dedication, noting that it would provide a "straight shot" between Topeka and Junction city. Even *American Highways*, the magazine of the American Association of State Highway Officials, printed only a picture and an eight-line caption identifying the participants at the ceremony. That day Americans had turned their attention to other events. In Washington President Eisenhower, speaking at his first press conference since his landslide victory over Adlai Stevenson, said he regarded the election as a mandate for his programs, including the Interstates, but he devoted much of the press conference to warning the Soviets that the United States would oppose any military intervention in the Middle East. From Budapest came reports that the Communist-led regime had cleaned out the last pockets of resistance to its rule. In New York, the Baseball Writers Association unanimously elected Mickey Mantle as Most Valuable Player for 1956. In New York City, police reported automobile thefts were up eleven percent in the first nine months of 1956 to more than six thousand. And in St. Louis, those attending the annual convention of the Association of Real Estate

Brokers learned that traffic congestion was now threatening metropolitan suburban areas as well as cities.

The quiet ribbon-cutting event signaled the start of the largest public works project in history. Unwittingly, highway planners and builders had become agents of a monumental social and economic revolution of which they had little understanding.

Two weeks after the ceremony on the outskirts of Topeka, representatives from state highway departments traveled to Atlantic City, New Jersey, for the annual convention of the American Association of State Highway Officials. The excitement was palpable, for the highway bill Eisenhower had signed gave the officials all they wanted. With its liberal provision that the federal share of construction costs would be ninety percent, the bill helped ease the pressure on the states to sell bond issues, raise taxes, or create other financing schemes. Nor did they feel they had to justify the need for roads to their public, since the American citizens, through their representatives in Congress, had given their overwhelming support in the form of a never-ceasing supply of cash from the Highway Trust Fund. It was a virtual Möbius strip of money: The more cars traveled, the more gas they consumed; more gas meant more money for the fund; more money in the fund meant more money to build more miles of highways; which allowed more cars to travel more miles and consume more gas. Surely, lopsided victories for highway legislation in both the House and the Senate gave the engineers the mandate to do the job they had been trained to do. Surely the American people, who were buying new cars at a furious pace, were behind the efforts to build highways. Surely everyone would celebrate their work as a great triumph for the nation. They were the men who would create not just a highway but a *system,* the great spine of all the nation's motor transportation. They could rest secure knowing that they were engaged in an enterprise that would benefit everyone.

The task the highway officials faced was Herculean: Build forty-one thousand miles of divided, limited-access highways to rigorous specifications in just thirteen years. In the past, engineers might have taken on individual jobs that were as demanding, jobs that went a few miles, or even jobs on toll superhighways like the Pennsylvania Turnpike or the New York Thruway. But few actually had worked for a sustained period on a project that was in any way comparable to the Interstate Highway

System. Now they would have to build the equivalent of 410 Pennsylvania Turnpikes, 16,000 exits and entrances, nearly 55,000 bridges and overpasses, and scores of tunnels. They were to build these Interstates in sparsely populated places where the citizens had little or no experience with limited-access highways. Since seventy-five percent of the Interstates would be constructed on new right-of-way, they would have to take more land by eminent domain than had been taken in the entire history of road building in the United States. Plans called for them to build through many miles in hostile and rugged territory, places where engineers before them had found it difficult to blaze a dirt trail, much less a four-lane superhighway. "I don't say it scared them," said Charles Shumate, head of Colorado's Department of Highways of his engineering staff, "but it was kind of mind-boggling, the potential size of it." At the same time, engineers knew the highway deficiencies within their own states and viewed the federal legislation as an opportunity to at last catch up with the traffic. Though some pessimists expected states would have a hard time getting the program started, the promise of $25 billion in federal dollars enticed almost all to move ahead swiftly.

The short highway outside Topeka was the first piece of a jigsaw puzzle the size of the United States. When all the pieces were in place, Americans would have a giant web of roads that would bind the nation together. Some of the pieces—those where the land was flat and stable—would be relatively easy to place. Others—those that went high into the Rockies or had to cross lakes and swamps—would prove more challenging. Still other pieces—especially those through congested older areas in the nation—would be difficult if not impossible to place, and rather than bind people together would drive them apart.

Long speeches, formal dinners, and endless photographs characterized meetings of the American Association of State Highway Officials during the 1950s. In two days at the convention, the group heard from no less than seven speakers, including two senators, a congressman, the outgoing president of the association, and three federal administrators whose job it would be to oversee the construction of the Interstate Highway System. Many of the speakers reflected on the awesome nature of the task. One senator, Dennis Chavez from New Mexico, warned the engineers to keep compromise and politics from undermining the system that compromise and politics had created; another senator, Joseph Martin from Pennsylvania, worried about the effect the Interstates would have on business; while the representative from Ohio cautioned against inefficiency, graft, and fraud.

The delegates were especially interested in the speech of John Anthony Volpe. Volpe was serving, temporarily, as federal highway administrator, a new post Congress created in the summer of 1956, at the request of the president, to supervise the commissioner of public roads and set federal policy on Interstate highway construction. Though this was just a subcabinet position, Eisenhower thought it so important that he personally held the Bible for Volpe as a White House executive officer administered the oath of office.

A second-generation Italian-American, John Volpe always held clear and simple values about America's strengths and opportunities, how it valued hard work and afforded people who wanted it a chance to do well. Construction was a noble enterprise that enriched the nation and enabled people like himself to succeed. His family followed a familiar pattern of Italian-Americans in the early twentieth century. His father worked as a plasterer in Wakefield, Massachusetts, until he had saved enough money to establish his own business. His sacrifices, he believed, would enable his sons to receive a better education than he had. But the plastering business failed in 1926, and John Volpe was forced to forgo studying civil engineering at MIT to take a job as a journeyman plasterer. Nevertheless, Volpe's enormous self-confidence, self-discipline, intelligence, and energy assured that he would not remain long in his father's trade. If MIT was no longer an option, he would take courses in his spare time at Wentworth Institute, the local technical trade school. Graduating after seven years, Volpe gathered $300 in capital to begin his own contracting company. Only three years' service in the navy's Civil Engineering Corps during World War II interrupted the John A. Volpe Construction Company's steady growth. Up and down the East Coast the company built shopping centers and university offices, schools and hospitals, and state and military buildings. After the war, it even opened a construction office in Rome. (Volpe said the Italian office was his way of reconnecting with his family's native land.) Volpe himself branched into other areas, too. He became president of two town newspapers, the Malden *News* and Medford *Daily Mercury*, and served on the boards of a score of banks, trust companies, civic organizations, and, proudly, as grand financial secretary of the Massachusetts Grand Lodge of the Order of the Sons of Italy. Everything he did brought him prominence or wealth, and usually both. By the 1950s, John Anthony Volpe, who had begun work at the age of twelve carrying a plaster-filled hod for his father, could count himself a millionaire several times over.

By the 1950s, too, John Volpe had begun to have political ambitions. He served first as deputy of the Republican State Committee, and in 1953, Christian Herter, the patrician governor of the commonwealth, appointed him commissioner of public works. As commissioner, Volpe undertook the greatest highway expansion in the state's history, successfully promoted a $200 million highway bond issue, and developed a highway master plan for the state. Highways, Volpe proclaimed from the Berkshires to Boston, held the key to Massachusetts's economic future.

For Volpe the evidence lay in Route 128, the remarkable semicircular limited-access highway that skirted the congestion of downtown Boston. Possessing the characteristics of the roads that planners envisioned would one day ring America's major cities, Route 128 served as a grandparent to the Interstate Highway System. Originally chartered by the legislature to "provide ready access to the North and South Shore recreational and residential areas," the road did that and a great deal more. Skeptics derided the first twenty-seven miles that opened in 1951 as "the road to nowhere," a route that merely swept through farm fields. By the time of Volpe's appointment, however, entrepreneurs had proved the critics wrong. Real estate values along 128 surged as industries consumed acre after acre of farmland for new corporate headquarters. After just four years, forty companies had built or were building their headquarters along the route, most near the exits.

John Volpe possessed a quality that was often at a premium in Massachusetts political life in the 1950s: honesty. From the time he joined the Republican State Committee, Volpe refused to bid on any state construction projects, and, as he was quick to point out, the John A. Volpe Construction Company never built a highway.

The position of *interim* federal highway administrator might appear as something of a comedown for Volpe, since he was clearly just a utility infielder filling in until Bertram Tallamy, the Secretary of Commerce's first choice, completed the New York Thruway. But a few months in Washington before returning to his construction business suited Volpe well. By 1956 he had begun to entertain thoughts of elective office. In the 1956 Massachusetts elections, however, a Democrat named Foster Furcolo was making a strong bid to take the governorship from the

Republicans. Sensing a Furcolo victory was imminent and that he would soon be out of a job anyway, Volpe left the commissioner's office in October for the post in Washington. It would give him a chance to see highway building at the national level and at a crucial time for the nation.

Volpe cut a commanding figure as he addressed the state officials, the very model of a successful and civic-minded former contractor in control of $25 billion: piercing dark eyes, dark hair parted at the left and slicked back conservatively, white shirt, dark suit. "We must think big. We must act big," he said, challenging the officials to be equal to their task. They should concentrate on the urban sections of the system, he said, since cities had the greatest traffic congestion. At the same time, Volpe continued, the officials must take great care in locating the highways, lest they "impair or even prevent desirable growth and community life." Already, he said, the Bureau of Public Roads was approving an average of $20 million a week in construction contracts for this, the greatest cooperative venture between the states and the federal government. It was only the beginning.

For the most part, those whom Volpe implored to think and act big were male, white, Christian, rural, and almost entirely absorbed in highways. They had neither the experience nor the training for the job of planning, design, and construction that lay before them. At the beginning even some highway officials from rural and sparsely populated states without any divided highways did not understand the concept of the Interstates and limited access as well as they might have. Yet they would have to explain why there would be so few crossroads, and why people who lived beside an Interstate might have to go miles to get on it. Nor were they prepared for the changes that they were to bring to the nation through the Interstates.

In 1956, twenty-two thousand men and sixty-two women earned engineering degrees. Though the war had brought a tenfold increase in the number of practicing female civil engineers by 1944, their ranks decreased dramatically throughout the 1950s. Civil engineering programs were not especially welcoming to female students. Rensselaer Polytechnic Institute in Troy, New York, for example, admitted women to engineering school if they applied, but as one official wrote in 1958,

"We don't stress the fact because we don't want too many gals around." Between 1950 and 1960 Rensselaer graduated no female civil engineers. By 1960, the number of females in the profession had declined to fewer than nine hundred. In fact, few of these women had any part in either the design or the construction of the Interstate system. The American Association of State Highway Officials had no women members, and the Bureau of Public Roads did not employ a female engineer until 1962.

Nor were there many black civil engineers. Census enumerators did not report the race of those in professions, but the evidence and memories of veterans of state highway departments and the Bureau of Public Roads confirms this was the case. The official photograph taken at the annual dinner of the American Association of State Highway Officials in 1956 shows no faces of African-Americans. Indeed, the official photograph remained all white until the 1960s. The case of Walter T. Daniels, the first African-American to earn a Ph.D. in engineering, illustrates the point. In 1925, Daniels attended Prairie View A&M in Prairie View, Texas, the black cousin to Texas A&M in College Station, before transferring to the engineering program at the University of Arizona. Arizona regulations segregated Daniels from his fellow white students and excluded him from laboratory courses because he could not have a white lab partner. Nonetheless, Daniels persevered as the solitary black and received a bachelor of science degree in civil engineering. Since no jobs were available at state highway departments, he become a college instructor, rising by 1956 to the head of Howard University's Department of Engineering.

In 1956, the Bureau of Public Roads employed few African-Americans in any capacity. Though the bureau did not keep such statistics at this time, almost no African-Americans appear in archival photographs before the 1960s. The single exception was William A. Grant, who began work at the bureau in July 1904 as a nineteen-year-old assistant, testing cement and aggregates for concrete. Over the years he studied with the Office of the United States Geological Survey, learning how to polish and mount thin rock sections for petrographic studies. In 1955, Grant retired at the mandatory age of seventy after more than a half century of service.

For the most part, the engineers were Catholics, Methodists, or Baptists. Many grew up on farms and few came from a city with a population greater than twenty-five thousand. "The man we honor today," said the executive secretary of the American Association of State Highway

Officials at an award ceremony, "is an able highway administrator, a skilled highway engineer and he is, above all, a Christian gentleman."

Of greater importance than the gender, race, religion, or background of the engineers was their training. The curriculum at engineering schools was extremely specialized and profoundly limited in its attention to the humanities and social sciences. Though they were charged with executing the largest civil engineering project in the history of the world, the students learned next to nothing about the effect their actions would have upon millions of citizens.

"Anything that wasn't engineering or science was a gut course, and most took the easiest course that would meet the requirement," remembered Frank Griggs, a civil engineer who trained at Rensselaer Polytechnic Institute in the 1950s. (The oldest technical school in the country, Rensselaer trained many who worked in the Interstate program, including Bertram Tallamy.) The nontechnical subjects included writing, history, and economics, or, rarely, public speaking, art, and music appreciation. "I always wanted to take music appreciation because I love music, but I could never get that course because it was filled up early—a capital 'G' Gut we called it." Civil engineering students had no classes in architecture other than one in building construction that overlapped with students in the School of Architecture.

Such narrowness of specialization had not always been the case with engineers. George Shattuck Morison, the august engineer who convinced Theodore Roosevelt to build the Panama Canal, had majored in classics at Harvard College and then taken a degree at Harvard Law before he decided to become an engineer. Engineering, Morison said, would enable him to "lead a good and useful life." At the Polytechnic Institute in Berlin, John Roebling, the designer of the Brooklyn Bridge, studied philosophy under Georg Friedrich Hegel as well as the usual subjects like architecture, hydraulics, mathematics, engineering, and bridge construction. He read voraciously and was an accomplished violinist. Roebling's son, Washington, who built the Brooklyn Bridge, was an accomplished linguist, mineralogist, and violinist, read Greek and Latin with ease, and enjoyed history and literature.

Teaching methods in engineering schools—as well as other disciplines—encouraged passivity and discouraged independent thinking. Professors expected to see their students taking copious notes, but rarely did they expect to hear them speak. "We almost never talked in class," said Griggs. "The teacher taught; you listened. The teacher gave you questions;

you answered in writing usually, but not orally." Teachers never encouraged "thinking on your feet—none of that. Our writing was minimal, and professors didn't evaluate it. Was the idea right?—good enough."

Such civil engineering training as prevailed at this time produced a corps of technical savants, men who could piece together the parts of a structure—the puzzle—but who only rarely considered the structure in its totality or its impact on society. "We were good as technicians," said Griggs. "Ask us to design a beam. Give us the load, we could do it. Ask us to design a highway. Give us the route, we could do it." Tell those engineers to connect two points on a map with a highway between them, and they would know best how to fit the road to the topography. But engineers had little understanding of, nor did they care about, socioeconomic and environmental considerations that should also be factors in the decision of where to place a highway. The Interstates planned for the center of Boston, across Manhattan, into the center of Chicago posed a series of technical problems of soils and land contours, entrances and exits, and the like; but never the very real human problems of lives disrupted, neighborhoods destroyed, and livelihoods lost.

John H. Shafer was typical of the people who worked in a state highway department after the Interstate program began. As a boy, Shafer helped his father with the chores on his family's farm west of Canandaigua, New York. After high school and a two-year pre-engineering course at St. John Fisher College in Rochester, he enrolled in the civil engineering program at the University of Detroit. Classes included "steel design, concrete design," Shafer remembered, "some planning and some traffic forecasting." Graduating in 1958, Shafer took a job with the New York State Department of Transportation, designing the Interstate routes 490 and 590 that ring the city of Rochester. From a technical standpoint, Shafer thought his education was solid. "You learned about traffic studies and you learned about cost-benefit ratios and you learned about incremental costs and diversion of traffic and all those things," Shafer reflected. But he received no training in community participation, "how to hold public hearings; how to deal with the public. . . . That, certainly . . . was the one point that was . . . the weakest in anybody's curriculum at the time." Shafer and thousands of other engineers would learn those lessons firsthand in public meetings, city council chambers, state legislatures, and federal courts across the country.

The training of Ellis L. Armstrong, commissioner of highways for the state of Utah and later commissioner of the Bureau of Public Roads, was not very different from John Shafer's. It was typical of those who headed state highway departments and whose job it was to translate the mandates of the federal-aid highway program into action on the state level. Born in 1914, Armstrong grew up on a farm in Utah. When it was time to go to college, he entered the engineering program at Utah State in Logan. The courses were unexceptional. "I had surveying, which was primarily concerned with highways," Armstrong remembered after he had retired,

> and then I had three courses in highways . . . these involved location studies and economics, from the standpoint of traffic, the standpoint of land use, and the whole array of problems that are connected with highway location . . . then one quarter was on the materials in highways, soils, pavements, the geometry of design, and so on.

What was absent from his education at Utah State is more telling. Armstrong never had a class in public speaking or sociology, much less courses in philosophy or history or environmental science. Fortunately for Armstrong, his mother had told him repeatedly, "You'll never get anywhere if people can't understand what you're trying to say." When he arrived in Logan, he joined Utah State's intercollegiate debating team.

While the teaching methods of civil engineering education had changed very little over the years, the quality of the students had. In the nineteenth century a student in a technical school chose between civil and mechanical engineering. In the twentieth century, however, technical schools adopted a host of new programs in electrical, aeronautical, and chemical engineering that siphoned off many of the best students. In the 1950s, aeronautical and electrical engineering, with their developments in jet propulsion and the transistor, captured the imaginations of many. Civil engineering had no exciting developments to offer. "Civils were building it the way we had built it the last thirty or forty years," Frank Griggs remarked. "When I took surveying they were using instruments that had not changed very much in the last fifty or sixty years, the same basic tools applied to the same basic projects in the same basic way."

Even within civil engineering, highway construction fell in the shadow of more attractive pursuits like dam building or reclamation projects. Though Thomas MacDonald had endeavored to put road building on a scientific footing, engineering students tended to believe that almost anyone with basic civil training could site a highway, clear the land, and lay down a strip of asphalt. The best civil engineering students decided highway building lacked the glamour of spanning a river or gorge with a bridge or building a dam, especially as, since the time of the Roosevelt administration, the federal government had emphasized great dams or reclamation projects. "We tended to consider highways of secondary importance as a career," said Ellis Armstrong of his student days at Utah. "If you couldn't do anything else you could always get a job with the highway department. . . . Compared to engineering dams or water systems or sewage treatment facilities . . . we generally felt that these took more knowledge and understanding of more areas of technical engineering than highways." After graduation, Armstrong worked in reclamation.

As it was paying ninety percent of the construction costs, the federal government did get to set highway construction and safety standards. Shortly after Eisenhower signed the Interstate highway legislation, the Bureau of Public Roads announced construction standards that it had worked out with the American Association of State Highway Officials. This seemingly simple step brought about much-needed uniformity. Some states had no design standards for superhighways; indeed, some lacked even a basic highway design manual. Standardization would give the Interstates "all known" safety features, Sinclair Weeks assured the press, as well as a "pleasing appearance."

The association's Route Numbering Committee debated for close to a year on a standard sign to make the system's routes, considering nearly a hundred shapes—circles, triangles, squares, and an outline of the border of the United States—before deciding in August 1957 on the three-color federal "shield." A sleeker variation of the federal shield that the association had chosen to mark the federal-aid highways in 1926, this sign would proclaim INTERSTATE in white letters across a red background at its top. Beneath that the route number would appear in white numerals on a blue background. At the same time the committee announced its decision on the shape and color of the Interstate sign, it also declared that the numbers of the Interstate routes would be the exact opposite of those a similar association committee had chosen for the federal-aid highways in 1926. Then the association had decided that north-south roads would ascend numerically in odd numbers from route 1 on the East Coast and 101 on the West. East-west roads would ascend numerically in even numbers from Route 2 in the North to Route 90 in the South. Interstate numbers would reverse the system. Now Interstate 5 would follow the West Coast and 95 the East; Interstate 10 would cross the bottom of the nation and 90 the top. By the fall of 1957, the new Interstate markers began to appear on the twenty-one hundred miles of state toll roads that had become a part of the system. The New York Thruway became Interstate 87 from New York to Albany and Interstate 90 from Albany to Buffalo.

Deciding on the Interstate shield and numbering system was relatively easy, but settling on the colors for the large exit signs noting towns and routes along the Interstates was another matter. A committee of the American Association of State Highway Officials working with the Bureau of Public Roads recommended a uniform system of green signs with white letters that would be legible to the average motorist from at least eight hundred feet; however, Bertram Tallamy, the new federal highway administrator, objected. He had personally chosen dark blue signs with white letters for his New York Thruway, and he knew this to be the better choice. The association's committee held its ground. To resolve the dispute, the Bureau of Public Roads built a special, three-mile test road off an expressway near Greenbelt, Maryland, and selected hundreds of motorists to drive over it at sixty-five miles per hour. Along the way they passed three signs—blue, black, and green—that led prophetically to:

> Metropolis
> Utopia
> EXIT 2 MILES

Fifty-eight percent of the drivers favored signs with green backgrounds, twenty-seven percent blue, and fifteen percent black. Faced with the results of this survey, Tallamy reluctantly conceded. Only a few members of the association and the Bureau of Public Roads knew that the federal highway administrator was suffering from severe vision problems, including acute color blindness. For Bertram Tallamy, the green background of the Interstate exit signs was a pale yellow.

If it seemed excessive to build three miles of highway pointing to a nowhere Utopia in order to decide upon the background color for the exit signs, the experiment paled in comparison with the $22 million test road the American Association of State Highway Officials built south of the projected Interstate 80 between Ottawa and LaSalle, Illinois. Money to build the large oval road came from each of the states and territorial possessions, the Bureau of Public Roads, the Automobile Manufacturers Association, the American Petroleum Institute, and the Defense Department. After the association built different roadbeds and mixtures of concrete and asphalt paving, a corps of drivers recruited from the military drove trucks and automobiles thousands of miles around the track to stimulate traffic conditions. From these experiments came the critical design standards for concrete and asphalt pavements.

While the federal government and the engineers were setting standards for highways, automobile manufacturers in Detroit were changing their cars to make them equal to the new stresses of high-speed travel. Consider the gross excess of fins and chrome that characterized every Detroit car at this time. Inspired by the tail of the Lockheed P-38 fighter plane, the famous General Motors stylist Harley Earl placed two small, nubbinlike protrusions on the rear fenders of a 1948 Cadillac. A former customizer of automobiles for Hollywood stars, Earl set the pace for rival stylists at Ford and Chrysler. They followed Earl's lead, raising the rear fins on their models to positively stegosaurian heights around 1959 and 1960, the year when the Cadillac Eldorado convertible took on the appearance of the Batmobile. Not content with fins, Earl added hundreds of pounds of chrome protuberances to Cadillac bumpers, including round front guards named "Dagmars" after the bras favored by the Hollywood starlet. As always, the other stylists at Ford and Chrysler quickly followed Earl's lead. The results were steel and chrome extravagances that the critic John Keats aptly named "Insolent Chariots."

Yet other, more progressive changes than chrome and fins took place. Since automobiles now went faster and over long distances, they had to be safer and better built. Outside mirrors and turn signal lamps became standard equipment. About 1950, the older two-piece windshields gave way to a single curved sheet of glass that afforded drivers greater visibility and safety. In 1953, General Motors created a larger "wraparound" windshield that enhanced drivers' ability to see. For greater visibility at night, General Motors added separate high- and low-beam headlamps to its models beginning in 1956. To make cars more visible to other drivers, manufacturers enlarged taillights and increased the intensity of the brake lamps. Starting in 1956, Ford offered an extra safety package that included a padded dashboard and sun visors, and front seat belts. Few chose the option.

Divided Highways

· · ·

From his office in the MacDonald Highway Transportation Center at Texas A&M University in College Station, Thomas Harris MacDonald followed the progress of the Interstate Highway System with great interest. The Chief could count his last four years as productive. He and his new wife had purchased a house close to the university, and each day he repaired to his office. As "distinguished research engineer," he received all the bulletins of the Bureau of Public Roads, and old friends and colleagues in the bureau kept him up to date. What he heard about the change in the bureau's philosophy must have been astonishing. Though he and his officers had mapped out an interstate highway system in 1941, he had never envisioned its execution on such a grand scale, and indeed had difficulty finding justification for building roads over land that was seldom traveled. The new highways would be four lanes, limited access. The state of Texas alone would have three major east-west Interstates—10, 20, and 40—a major north-south route—Interstate 35—and a host of shorter sections: over three thousand miles in all. As for the traffic, engineers were working on far different assumptions than they had just a few years earlier. These younger planners believed in laying down concrete ribbons through the wilderness, places with few people and a small economy. "If we build the highway, the people and the economy will follow," they seemed to be saying. When MacDonald began in 1919, he had wanted to build roads to carry people from county seat to county seat "without breaking a spring." Now they were building roads to stimulate the economy.

On April 7, 1957, Thomas Harris MacDonald ate a pleasant and leisurely dinner with his wife and some of their highway engineering friends at a local restaurant in College Station. After dinner, the Chief strolled to the front of the restaurant, bought a cigar from the cashier, and, as a friend recalled, "sat down on a comfortable divan and passed away." He was seventy-six years old. Those who knew MacDonald's career spoke reverently of how he "profoundly affected the course of modern life." The *New York Times* and the *Washington Post* reported his death in obligatory short obituaries. To most who glanced at them, his passing meant little.

Many state highway departments quickly found that the new Interstate program sorely taxed their resources. Part of the difficulty states faced, particularly those that had no toll roads or freeways, was explaining just how an Interstate highway differs from a regular road. The state of Utah had almost no experience with a limited-access divided highway, yet it had three cities with populations over fifty thousand—Salt Lake City, Ogden, and Provo—that would be connected to the system. In 1956, engineers had planned for two of the main Interstates to cross Utah: 15, which begins in Los Angeles and ends north of Great Falls, Montana, at the Canadian border; and 80, which crosses the country from New York City to San Francisco. Other Interstates—215 and 84—would also help to move traffic around Salt Lake City and Ogden.

In 1956, Ellis Armstrong was hired by the governor of Utah to replace a highway commissioner who had done little to prepare his department for the new roads. The highway department was under-staffed and scattered in primitive offices around the capital. Utah's salaries for professional engineers ranked with Mississippi's at the bottom of the forty-eight states. Road maintenance was haphazard, and repair crews worked in traffic without even the benefit of reflective safety vests. With the influx of Interstate funds, however, Utah's highway budget jumped tenfold in one year, from $6 million to $60 million. Keeping with John Volpe's advice, Armstrong set up a policy of addressing the heaviest traffic needs first, which meant building Interstate 15 from Provo through Salt Lake to Ogden. "It was rather surprising," said Armstrong. "We expected a lot of trouble in getting the program started. But it was remarkable how fast the states were able to gear up and move ahead."

The standards for the Interstate highways far exceeded any roads in the state: Highways would have to meet the traffic projected for 1975. Traffic lanes would be at least twelve feet wide and shoulders would be ten feet. In rural areas the median strips dividing the oncoming traffic would be at least thirty-six feet, while in urban areas the strips might be reduced to as little as sixteen. The roads would be engineered for speeds of seventy miles per hour and have grades no greater than three percent. No railroad crossings or grade-level intersections would interfere with the traffic, and overpasses would be at least fourteen feet above the roadway. Finally, access to the new Interstates would be strictly limited to entrances and exits.

As early as 1939, engineers in the Bureau of Public Roads had planned for Interstate 15 to run parallel to U.S. 89. It entered Utah from Arizona at St. George, wended its way north through Cedar City and Beaver, skirted the Fishlake National Forest and the San Pitch Mountains, passed through the Juab Valley, Spanish Fork, Provo, Salt Lake, Ogden, and Trementon, before entering Idaho and continuing to Pocatello. But the line was only a vague one. It fell to Armstrong to make the line into concrete. No sooner was the road announced than uncertainty and worry set in, especially among those who lived in small towns along its route. In the 1950 census, Utah's population of not quite seven hundred thousand—less than ten people per square mile—ranked fortieth in the nation. True, there were about 350,000 cars, trucks, and buses in the state, a number that had grown significantly in the last decade, but the present roads seemed adequate to many if not most residents. Few thought superhighways necessary except perhaps in cities like Salt Lake and its satellites, Ogden and Provo. Why was the road to be four lanes? Why did there need to be overpasses for crossroads that were seldom traveled? What about farm and ranch properties that were split in two? Why was the right-of-way so great?

Those living along the path of 15 found the question of limited access most vexing of all. Smaller towns in sparsely populated areas looked to their local highway that served as their main street to bring them commerce and connect them with the world, and in the past, highway departments had worked to improve those roads to bring those towns more automobiles, trucks, and commerce. Now planners were telling them that the new Interstate would bypass their highway and their businesses—the filling stations, grocery stores, restaurants, and drugstores that lined it. They packed public hearings to complain long and hard that the Interstate would take away their livelihoods. Armstrong's job was to convince these residents that their towns would not wither. "Most of them after the Interstate was in operation, fared quite well," said Armstrong. "They were happy with not having that traffic right down the main street." Happy though some were, others most definitely were not. Being bypassed by the Interstate had the same effect on some towns and cities in the 1950s and 1960s as being bypassed by a railroad line did in an earlier age. Commerce suffered, businesses shut down, the tax base eroded, and people moved away.

Though the Bureau of Public Roads did not mandate the practice at the time, Armstrong decided to hold neighborhood meetings in the towns along the route before the state held an official hearing to take the property. "We would explain the problems, discuss the various alternative routes considered, the one that we thought preferable and why."

Local newspapers and radio stations usually appreciated the attention Armstrong was paying, and sometimes lent editorial support. Often Armstrong was able to dissipate any opposition that had built up against the proposed highway.

Sometimes homeowners suffered seriously. In one area where the Interstate cut through, Armstrong recalled, it "took out half a block of old houses that were in the $12,000 to $20,000 class." The replacement cost for houses of comparable size and quality was far greater, yet the law held that those homeowners must be compensated at the market rather than the replacement value. In this case the Utah's Department of Highways and the federal government forced those in the Interstate's path to accept less than what they had had before.

Though others whose property lay within the path of the new highways were often angry, Armstrong himself remained philosophical about the idea of losing property through eminent domain. For him it was the commonweal that mattered most, and what he often called "the risk":

> *Most people recognized that they were not going to get everything they wanted and the highway isn't going to be a half a mile away from everybody. Of course you always have three or four percent . . . no matter what you do that are going to give you a rough time. Somebody is going to be closer to it, and that's the way the ball bounces sometimes. Risk is part of being a member of a free society.*

Others had more luck stopping or at least delaying the highway. A leader of the state legislature, Virginia Peterson, opposed the path of Interstate 215 around the southeast quadrant of Salt Lake City on the grounds that it would take the land and house of a constituent who happened to be a famous local artist. The artist, Ms. Peterson claimed, depended on the particular light on the property for his painting. She was able to delay construction for a decade.

Some of the protestors who gave Armstrong the roughest time were members of his own family. At Cedar City, plans called for Interstate 15 to cut through the site of his grandfather's old farm, which Armstrong's uncles had recently divided into city building lots. After people learned the path that 15 would take, sales stopped. "I was cut off of the family tree," said Armstrong. South of Cedar City, the route cut through a farm belonging to his great-aunt, a former Republican national committeewoman.

Divided Highways

When the decision was made after the public hearing, she came galloping up to Salt Lake and came in to see me, and she said, "Ellis, you can't make a decision on that. The people that provide the funds, they are the ones that have to make the decisions, the final decision . . . If I have to I'll go clear to the United States Commissioner of Public Roads." The next month it was announced that I was the new United States Commissioner of Public Roads.

Almost immediately after Eisenhower signed the legislation creating the Interstates, the program faced financial trouble. The original estimate of $27.5 billion to complete the system, a figure the Clay committee produced in great haste in the fall of 1954, had little basis in fact, though no one questioned it at the time. Soon the estimates rose. Sinclair Weeks told Congress in early January 1958 that it could expect to spend about $40 billion to complete the system. By the end of the decade, most conceded even that amount was too low. Bertram Tallamy told Congress the average cost of a mile of road was increasing, as well—to $379,000 a mile in Montana and over $12 million a mile in the District of Columbia.

Tallamy had some other disturbing news for Congress. The Highway Trust Fund would not generate enough money to complete the entire system on time. Under the existing law, and with the existing flow of revenues into the fund, they would finish the system in twenty years rather than thirteen. The senators were suspicious, for even twenty years did not seem enough. One, the sober and conservative Norris Cotton of New Hampshire, said it might take as long as twenty-five years. Albert Gore was shocked. Since the Interstates were designed to meet the nation's highway needs in 1975, Cotton's estimate meant that the roads would be "inadequate and outdated" before they were complete. The senator argued that the administration should supplement the Trust Fund with money from the general revenues, and, Gore announced, he was willing to "wage a relentless battle" to get enough money to complete the system on schedule.

Gore did not have to fight hard. By January 1958, the U.S. economy was experiencing its first full recession since the Korean War. Unemployment rose in major industrial centers, especially those of the Midwest. As corporate profits declined and unemployment rose, the furies of Hoover and economic depression returned to torment Eisenhower's mind. Democrats called for tax cuts, but Eisenhower remained opposed. He called for increased expenditures for existing public works projects, especially for his favorite program, the Interstate Highway System. He had hoped the Interstate program would ensure the country's economic stability in just such a business downturn as it was experiencing. If he had prevailed with the sale of bonds, all the money he needed to create jobs would be available right now, but he had to agree to a "pay-as-you-go" policy in order to get any program. Now that the American people and the highway interests had a taste of what Interstates could do, he knew that he would have bipartisan support to suspend the "pay-as-you-go" provision and supplement money from the Highway Trust Fund with money from the general revenue.

The administration sent out the word that it wanted to increase the money from the trust fund by an additional $2.2 billion from the general revenue for three years, and the wheels of Congress began to turn. Soon Albert Gore's roads committee heard testimony from the usual highway interests. "The present economy, a continuing, expanding future economy, and the national defense all justify putting the program back on its original schedule," said the president of the American Association of State Highway Officials. Representatives of the American Automobile Association, the American Road Builders Association, various state highway commissioners, and an assortment of governors testified on the need to complete the Interstate Highway System by 1969. In March, Gore delivered a Senate bill to increase the amount of federal funds necessary to do so, and the House Public Works Committee offered a similar bill at the same time. In the end, the Senate, House, and administration compromised on a measure that suspended the "pay-as-you-go" provision for two fiscal years and added another $1.8 billion to bring the total highway expenditures to $5.5 billion for the fiscal years 1959 and 1960. The money committed for Interstate construction now far exceeded the revenue capacity of the Highway Trust Fund.

Predictably, Harry Byrd, "Mr. Economy," was outraged by this blatant move of his spendthrift colleagues (and, now, Eisenhower!) to use federal dollars to prime the economy. "No one involved with the suspension of the pay-as-we-go policy or the exploitation of the suspension can escape blame for what was done," he said after the bill passed. "Our great highway programs were never precipitated into such an inexcusable mess." Those who heard the remarks knew they were toothless, however, for in February, Harry Flood Byrd, chairman of the Senate Finance Committee, had announced his intention to retire from the Senate. Though the septuagenarian senator would later retract his decision, it was clear to all that his power was on the wane. More and more,

Byrd's colleagues perceived his fiscal and social judgments to be antiquated and out of touch with mid-twentieth-century America. Having
had a glimpse of superhighways and what they would do for travel, few
in Congress wanted to delay their construction—especially if that construction affected their states and districts. Byrd's successor in the next
Congress would be a millionaire oilman from Oklahoma, Robert Kerr, a
man who did not object to deficit spending, especially if it was for Interstate highways.

As Interstate construction proceeded, it delayed more and more
motorists. At every road the Interstate crossed, builders had to erect
bridges or overpasses. Often work crews had to divert traffic onto
makeshift, one-lane gravel roads while giant earth movers carved out the
new path for the Interstate. The perky sign that read YOUR HIGHWAY
TAXES AT WORK did little to diminish the impatience motorists felt.
In the spring of 1959, Dwight David Eisenhower was stopped in just such
construction traffic on the edge of Washington while he was being driven
from the White House to Camp David, the presidential retreat named for
his grandson near Catoctin Mountain in northwestern Maryland. When
told that he was stopped because of Interstate highway construction,
Eisenhower was surprised. He had understood that the Interstates were
meant to link cities, but he had no idea they would go into them as well.
Just who in his administration, the president demanded of an aide, had
allowed this to happen? The answer Eisenhower received surprised him
even more: In effect, *he* was responsible, as he had signed the Federal-Aid
Highway Act of 1956. Nevertheless, the president decided to take his
concerns to his assistant for Public Works Planning, the man who had
been part of the discussions about the Interstate Highway System from its
inception, General John Stewart Bragdon.

Stewart Bragdon had been waiting for the moment. Since General
Clay had rebuffed his proposal for a National Highway Authority, and
others in the White House had rejected his call to pay for the new roads
with tolls, Bragdon had turned his attention to different matters,
including planning for the use of public works projects in a recession.
At the same time, however, he had quietly followed with interest the
unfolding disputes between Congress and the Bureau of Public Roads
over the progress and cost of the Interstate system. Occasionally, he
made a pointed inquiry of Bertram Tallamy about the expense and scope

of the Interstate construction program and seemed most concerned with cost containment and urban Interstates. What was the authorization for Interstates to go into and through urban areas? What factors did the Bureau of Public roads consider when determining an urban route? Were local planning authorities consulted? Why were there so many exits on urban portions of the Interstate? Why should the federal government pay ninety percent of a highway that served intracity rather than interstate needs? Tallamy always replied carefully, usually restating those sections of the legislation that gave the Bureau of Public Roads the right to pay for urban Interstates.

Tallamy's answers did not satisfy Bragdon, however. After Eisenhower got stuck in traffic outside Washington, Bragdon saw his chance to act. The Bureau of Public Roads should adopt a policy of "routing the Interstate Highway System close by but not through central cities," he told the president in a memorandum on June 17. Furthermore, Eisenhower should appoint a committee of the Secretary of Commerce, Frederick Mueller; the director of the budget, Maurice Stans; and Bragdon to study ways to save money on Interstate construction. Mueller was necessary because the Bureau of Public Roads was in the Department of Commerce and Bragdon would need his support for any changes; Stans would be useful because he understood the budget and highway financing, and he privately shared Bragdon's concern about the federal government having to pay ninety percent of the escalating costs. On July 2, the president sent Bragdon a "highest priority" directive that gave him all he had wanted.

"Reexamine policies, methods, and standards now in effect," said Eisenhower, including, "intra-metropolitan area routing . . . interchanges, grade separations, frontage roads, traffic lanes, utility relocations, and engineering design." Bragdon should delineate between federal responsibility and state and local responsibility for "financing, planning, and supervising the highway program," and determine ways to improve highway planning, "especially urban planning." Finally, Bragdon was to make recommendations "covering legislative and administrative action required to redirect the program"—in other words, consider legislation the administration could send to Congress to change the present policies.

Since John Stewart Bragdon had been gathering information all spring, he was ready to act in the precise, military manner that defined his character. He consulted with Mueller and Stans. He hired three planning consultants. He recruited a full-time staff of nineteen, which formed "study" groups to consider the concept and need for the highways, the criteria and design standards for building them, the planning of the highways in relation to communities, and the finances and administration of the program. Of course, Bragdon, knew in advance what the outcome of these studies and consultations would be, but he regarded the process as a way of marshaling his arguments for his planned full-frontal assault on the entire Interstate highway program.

The consultants found the serious shortcomings that Bragdon expected. "It is a highway program rather than a transportation program," wrote Harold F. Wise, a planning consultant from Palo Alto, California, and was "in danger of becoming a special-purpose, single-shot solution to problems that are much bigger than just highways." Perhaps the government was using highways "to solve problems of the movement of people and goods that might better be solved by other means of transportation—or by a combination of means."

The study groups found all the shortcomings that Bragdon wanted. The Interstates were failing to meet defense needs because the clearance beneath overpasses and bridges was fourteen feet, while weapons and missiles needed seventeen. To correct this basic flaw in planning would entail lowering the roadways or increasing the height of the bridges and overpasses. Either solution would require exorbitant amounts of money. The entire system might have been built at no cost to the federal government if tolls had been charged, as private roads like the New Jersey Turnpike proved. That toll highway was enjoying 233 percent greater revenues than it had expected. Interstates built for future traffic needs were inappropriate, and limited-access roads in rural areas were extravagant. Interstate highways built into and through cities were excessive and destructive. They were unwarranted when highways around cities would serve defense and transportation needs just as well. These urban highways had too many exits, which clearly served intracity rather than interstate traffic. Moreover, federal and state authorities built them with little or no consideration of urban planning or their relation with trains, trolleys, and subways.

That September, while his study groups were busy generating all the information Bragdon wanted, a staff member in the Bureau of the Budget and the Department of Commerce sent him a memorandum outlining the history of the "Legislative Intent with respect to the Location of Interstate Routes in Urban Areas," which he most certainly did not wish to read. "The 1944 interregional Highway report makes it perfectly clear that the Interstate Highway System would penetrate the cities and metropolitan areas, and would introduce both intracity and circumferential routes." Furthermore, the 1956 highway act that President Eisenhower had signed provided for "extensions" of the Interstates "through urban areas." Only the matter of intracity exits was open to question, and the Bureau of Public Roads had interpreted the legislation to mean that it should consider the needs of local traffic and interstate travel equally.

Bragdon would hear nothing of such reports. By its very name the Interstate Highway System was supposed to serve interstate rather than intracity needs. While there might be some local exits, there should never be as many as the Bureau of Public Roads was allowing. The cost overruns were making the system a burden on the federal budget.

On October 7, after meeting with Bragdon and Maurice Stans, Frederick Mueller sent a letter to Bertram Tallamy, the federal highway administrator, demanding that the Bureau of Public Roads revise the criteria for the design and location of urban Interstates, establish a comprehensive urban planning process before building Interstates in cities, and immediately delay approval of all contemplated urban Interstate projects.

Bragdon, Stans, and Mueller were sorely mistaken if they thought Bertram D. Tallamy and the Bureau of Public Roads would capitulate without a fight. The fifty-seven-year-old Tallamy had been planning and building superhighways in New York State since the end of World War II. He had planned the arterial routes to bring cars and trucks into most of New York's major cities with speed and safety, and he had served as the state's superintendent of public works and chairman of its Thruway Authority. It was Tallamy who had overseen the construction of each of the 562 miles of the New York Thruway, commanding a battalion of engineers to accomplish the job in six years. He had served as vice president and president of the American Association of State Highway Officials. Tallamy fervently believed that Congress had issued a mandate to the Bureau of Public Roads to build highways across the nation of the sort he had constructed in New York, and that he had the law to back him up. The people had spoken, and no triumvirate in the White House would be able to stop him.

Perhaps because of the persistent questions Bragdon had asked over the spring and summer, Tallamy knew what to expect, for he was well prepared for the committee's assault. General Bragdon's philosophy and opinions ran contrary to the will of Congress, he replied in a stern letter to Mueller on October 13. The Bureau of Public Roads had no authority to require a city to make a comprehensive planning process. The bureau had clearly outlined urban routes in the Yellow Book of September 1955, which it had disseminated to every member of Congress. Congress fully understood the highway bill it had passed in 1956. To his letter Tallamy attached a twenty-seven-page rebuttal to each of the Bragdon group's concerns and recommendations.

With this letter, communication between Bertram Tallamy and John Stewart Bragdon all but ceased. The federal highway administrator referred all further questions from Bragdon or any member of his staff to Ellis Armstrong, the commissioner of public roads. The questions still poured forth from Bragdon's White House office. His staff members started showing up without warning at the Bureau of Public Roads' regional offices in Kansas City, Atlanta, New York, and Boston. On November 10, Tallamy responded by expressly prohibiting any member of the bureau from giving Bragdon or his staff any information without an official written inquiry sent though the appropriate channels. Soon, Bragdon was pleading with Mueller to order the federal highway administrator and the Bureau of Public Roads staff to comply with his requests. Mueller appears to have ignored Bragdon. The bureau continued to divulge information only upon a written request.

As the two sides in the dispute became even more intractable, Mueller increasingly found himself in the middle. Some of Bragdon's concerns were valid. The costs of Interstate construction were escalating (Stans, too, had called the ninety percent federal share of construction "a horrible thing"); cities did need to produce more comprehensive plans that considered highways in the context of an integrated transportation system. But Tallamy and the Bureau of Public Roads were also right. The bureau was merely implementing the law that Congress had passed; and the president himself had endorsed the concept of the Interstates many times since 1956. Bragdon's assault seemed relentless, intemperate, and artless. He was seeking not only to develop highway policy but to implement it as well. In this regard he was moving well beyond the law. Caught between Bragdon and Tallamy as he was, Mueller became more and more a noncommittal buffer. Though he knew how unsophisticated Bragdon's assault was, he realized, as secretary of a sprawling bureaucracy as great as the Department of Commerce, how little control he exerted over a department as great as the Bureau of Public Roads. The best he could do was muddle on.

On December 30, Bragdon complained to Mueller about the Bureau of Public Road's failure to consider his recommendations seriously. Sweeping changes were needed to bring the Interstate program under control. In all, there were fourteen recommendations of a similar tone: Henceforth, the Secretary of Commerce should be the ultimate authority. The bureau and the Commerce Department, not the American Association of State Highway Officials, should issue standards for construction. Urban Interstates should be built for through traffic rather than rush-hour traffic. There should be no inner loop highways, such as the ones contemplated for Washington and Boston. Naturally, Bertram Tallamy sent the secretary a point-by-point rebuttal of everything Bragdon had said.

At the same time he was countering Bragdon with detailed memoranda, the federal highway administrator was also working the halls of Congress. Through the American Association of State Highway Officials and numerous other highway lobby groups, the word went out that the Interstate program was under attack. Congressmen like George Fallon and senators like Albert Gore and Thomas Kuchel, the Republican whip from California, rallied to the aid of the bureau and its policies. Gordon Sherer, a member of the House Public Works Committee, argued that Bragdon's study group was merely trying to justify decisions it had already made, and would "cut the heart" out of the Interstate Highway System. Dennis Chavez, the chairman of the Senate Public Works Committee, said flatly, "I would oppose any attempt to cut back the program in any way."

By the time Tallamy issued his reply to Bragdon, it was January 1960. If Bragdon was going to make his recommendations, it had to be soon. On January 3, the junior senator from Massachusetts, John Kennedy, announced in Washington that he would be a candidate for president of the United States. Six days later, Vice President Richard Nixon announced his candidacy. After seven contentious years of preoccupation with the Soviet red menace and defense, worries about the economy and budget deficits, and arguments with free-spending Democrats and truculent congressional conservatives, Dwight David Eisenhower was looking forward to raising his prize cattle, writing his memoirs at his Gettysburg farm, and playing endless rounds of golf unencumbered by the weight of national affairs.

Elsewhere in the White House, General John Stewart Bragdon and his staff were writing drafts of an "interim report" to the president. After reading it, the president called a meeting with Bragdon, Stans, Tallamy, and Mueller on April 6. To support his arguments, Bragdon arrived at the Oval Office armed with an easel, seventeen elaborate charts, and an aide to flip them. Tallamy brought only the Yellow Book.

Bragdon began what he assumed would be a long presentation. But as his aide flipped the charts that proved the enormous waste of the Interstate program and how, contrary to the law's intention, the highways were being built in urban areas, the president grew restless. He actually cared little about urban problems, and for almost eight years his administration had followed an aggressive urban policy of benign neglect. It was true, as some knew, the "matter of running Interstate routes through the congested parts of the cities was entirely against his original concept and wishes," but Bragdon was going on entirely too long. "I'd like to hear what Mr. Tallamy has to say," Eisenhower said, interrupting Bragdon's presentation. Holding up his copy of the Yellow Book, the federal highway administrator said quietly, "Mr. President, I would like to show you this book which was on everybody's desk at the time the Interstate legislation was approved." As Tallamy spoke, he showed Eisenhower several of the book's maps with their broad black lines going through and around cities. "Are you sure this was on everybody's desk?" Eisenhower asked. Bragdon allowed that this was the case. "The meeting's over, gentlemen," said the president. "I'll let you know what I decide." However, the president never let anyone know. In this case his silence was most telling. To reverse course on the Interstate Highway System would constitute an admission of failure to attend to detail on his part. It would be better to drop the entire matter. The Bragdon committee and its threat to the Bureau of Public Roads had ended.

Two weeks after the White House meeting, Frederick Mueller wrote an Ohio congressman who had inquired about the rumors surrounding the Bragdon committee, assuring that "the administration has no intention whatever of abandoning any of the routes . . . in urban or rural areas." Shortly after this, President Eisenhower nominated his old West Point classmate General John Stewart Bragdon to fill an unexpired term as a commissioner on the Civil Aeronautics Board. In true bureaucratic fashion, his staff puttered on. On January 17, 1961, three days before Senator John F. Kennedy took the oath of president of the United States, the final report of the committee to review the

Interstate Highway System arrived at the White House. No one took any notice.

At eight-thirty on the evening of January 17, President Dwight David Eisenhower delivered his farewell address, and the most remembered words of his presidency: "In the councils of government, we must guard against the acquisition of unwarranted influence, whether sought or unsought, by the military-industrial complex." Yet the Interstate Highway System was an organic part of the very military-industrial complex of which he spoke. From 1920, when Thomas MacDonald and General Pershing outlined the main military routes on a map of the United States, highways and the military had shared common goals. When he signed the Interstate legislation in 1956, the president had done as much as anyone to extend the power of the military-industrial complex that so worried him in his farewell address.

The president probably never made the connection between highways and the military; if he ever did, he remained silent about it. Indeed, from the time of his meeting with John Stewart Bragdon and Bertram Tallamy, Eisenhower chose to keep whatever misgivings he might have about the highway system he had created to himself. After January 20, 1961, the Interstate and its troubling questions of funding and impact on the landscape would be someone else's to deal with. Like some latter-day Cincinnatus, Eisenhower wanted to leave the national stage for his farm. Years earlier the boy from Abilene had chosen his agrarian retreat adjacent to the great battlefield at Gettysburg, Pennsylvania; about two miles south of Route 30, the old Lincoln Highway, and about twenty-five miles east of the—still to be built—Interstate 81.

Armed with the Yellow Book, Bertram Tallamy had won the day for the Bureau of Public Roads, but the nation was losing the larger war. For nearly eight years the Eisenhower administration had stalled urban renewal, killed low-rent public housing, and neglected mass transportation. Moreover, it had failed to coordinate and integrate federal urban programs that would encourage cities to develop local solutions that met their particular needs and problems. The president and his team had ignored the cities and their plight. Mayors from the largest cities were forced to strike a Faustian bargain with federal and state highway planners, often splitting neighborhoods in two, or separating them from the city center, or sometimes destroying the neighborhoods altogether.

Divided Highways

Urban highway policies often hastened the deterioration of downtown centers and quickened the development of suburbs.

Desperate for any federal help, the mayors had chosen to sell the souls of their cities for the jobs and the temporary boost to the economy that Interstate highway construction brought. But the price federal and state highway planners exacted for those jobs was enormous. Each mile of freeway took twenty-four acres of land; each interchange, eighty acres—acres that might otherwise have contributed to the tax structure of a city. All the while the mayors knew their greatest need was for an integrated system of roads and mass transportation, not just Interstate highways tearing through their cities; yet the fear of losing the ninety percent federal share of the financing—the only substantial help the Eisenhower administration had given them—was so great that they chose to deal with the devil.

Tallamy and his Bureau of Public Roads had an easy time facing down a flailing opponent like Bragdon, but in many cities angry citizens whose land and houses and lives were being ravaged by Interstate construction were stirring. In San Francisco, they had taken their opposition to the mayor and city council, which decided to refuse any more money to build Interstate 280, the Embarcadero Freeway. San Francisco, second largest city in the state that had more automobiles per capita than any other city in the country, had refused to build a highway! Citizens in other cities were beginning to organize against highway construction, and soon the Bureau of Public Roads would be fighting much larger battles at city halls, community halls, and construction sites across the nation. Congress was stirring, too.

LINES OF DESIRE

Anyone who travels is aware that in building a new national highway system we are re-working the face of the country.

BERTRAM D. TALLAMY

Interstate 80, near North Platte, Nebraska. Situated about twenty-eight hundred feet above sea level in the Platte River Valley, the city of North Platte cleaves to a long narrow delta where the north fork of the Platte River from Wyoming merges with the south fork of the Platte from Colorado. The community of North Platte has long served travelers, a place people pass through on their way to someplace else. Those who traveled the Oregon Trail from Independence, Missouri, usually stopped in North Platte on their way to the Pacific Northwest. In 1846, the Vermont native Brigham Young led the great migration of Mormons through North Platte to their destination on the shore of the placid Great Salt Lake in Utah. Twenty years later, chief engineer Grenville M. Dodge and his force of three thousand men brought the tracks of the Union Pacific Railroad to North Platte. In 1867, the year Nebraska became the thirty-seventh state in the Union, Dodge and his railroad men pushed farther west, but they left a station, railyard, and ten-stall roundhouse in the town, thereby ensuring its future growth. The Union Pacific's railyard grew to become one of the largest in the nation. Trunk line railroads from across the middle of the country sent their freight cars to North Platte, where trainmen joined them with others to create freight trains as long as a mile and a half. From North Platte the freights slowly snaked their way across the nation.

In 1913, Karl Graham Fisher's Lincoln Highway Association determined that the first transcontinental highway would pass through the city of North Platte. Two years later, Emily Post, the prominent New York socialite, divorcée, and future arbiter of America's etiquette, spent a night in North Platte on a cross-country trip over the Lincoln Highway. Many friends had warned her to trust neither the highway beyond the Mississippi ("the roads are trails of mud and sand") nor the people ("outlaws and bad men who would think nothing of killing you"). So many told her to stay far away from North Platte that Post took to calling it the "City of Ishmael." To her surprise, however, she found it to be a "serious railroad thoroughfare, self-respecting and above reproach," and the Union Pacific Hotel there to be "a model of delectability!"

In the summer of 1919, Major Dwight David Eisenhower and his fellow soldiers in the army's Motor Transport Corps went through the city on their way to San Francisco. Just west of the town, the highway was so bad that twenty-five trucks skidded off the road into deep mud and the convoy lost two days. "At one spot," an officer reported, "seven hours were required for the passage of 200 feet." In 1926, the Bureau of Public Roads designated this part of the Lincoln Highway as Route 30, making North Platte a stop on one of the nation's main transcontinental roads. The bureau also designated a north-south highway that extends from Brownsville in the southern tip of Texas to Westhope, on the Canadian Border of North Dakota, to be federal Route 83. In 1956, President Eisenhower's Bureau of Public Roads and the state of Nebraska determined that Interstate 80, the four-lane superhighway that would run parallel to old Route 30, would bypass North Platte.

Stretching from the approach to the George Washington Bridge in northern New Jersey to the San Francisco Oakland Bay Bridge in northern California, Interstate 80 was intended to be one of the nation's main transcontinental highways. Its 2,904 miles would cross eleven states. From New Jersey it would sweep through Pennsylvania, Ohio, Indiana, Illinois, Iowa, Nebraska, Wyoming, Utah, and Nevada, before crossing the Sierras into California. Along the way it would connect with every major north-south Interstate—95 at Teaneck, New Jersey; 75 at

Toledo, Ohio; 35 at Des Moines, Iowa; 25 at Cheyenne, Wyoming; 15 at Salt Lake City, Utah; and 5 at Sacramento—and seventeen other Interstates as well. There would be twenty spur highways into cities, routes like 180 to Lincoln, Nebraska; 180 to Hennepin, Illinois; and 380 to Scranton, Pennsylvania. In time the highway would invite metaphors. To some it would be America's main traffic artery; to others, "America's aorta"; and to still others, resorting to an incongruous vertical image, a vast spinal column across the middle of the nation, through which all the nerve system of the nation travels.

Many residents of North Platte, long accustomed to the presence of the railroad and the visitors who arrived on Route 30, regarded the announcement of the "fancy highway" as not particularly significant. Geography had determined North Platte's location. The railroad had assured the city's life in the late nineteenth century; the automobile and the Lincoln Highway continued that life in the twentieth. Interstate 80 seemed like more of the same.

By 1963, however, the citizens of North Platte began to realize that the new Interstate was not just another highway. It would connect the plains of Nebraska with the Rocky and Sierra mountains to the west and the Great Lakes and Appalachian Mountains in the east. It would take them where they wanted and at speeds they had never known. In time the citizens of North Platte would be able to drive to cities like Reno, Salt Lake, Omaha, Chicago, and Cleveland, as well as smaller places like Little America, Wyoming; Snow Shoe, Pennsylvania; and Brooklyn, Iowa. The Interstate would add a new dimension to their freedom.

On October 1, 1963—in an installment of the "Platte Valley Platter," a regular column that appeared in the city's *Telegraph-Bulletin*—"A Farm Wife," as she called herself, reported on several trips she and "the Boss" had taken through Nebraska and Iowa on the new Interstate. A few months earlier, confessed the Farm Wife, she had "burned with resentment" over the subject of the highway. The state had taken 58 of her family's 108 acres of farmland for the right-of-way, though she believed they "could have gotten by with half of that."

The trip with the Boss, however, the Farm Wife reported, "made a new woman out of me." She had lived a mile from Route 30 all of her married life. The Lincoln Highway had connected her to the outside world. Route 30 brought her family's groceries and coal, and company. She and her family had traveled it to get to "our churches and entertainment." Everyone agreed that the highway was ugly, crowded, and dangerous. Each year since 1951, her children had driven "15 worrisome miles" to and from school on "the most murderous highway in United States." Interstate 80 gave her welcome relief: "No dehy dust, no junkyards, no small town clutter; no sign boards to interfere with the close-up view of Mother Nature at work." Her encomium continued: "no cars coming toward you, fewer bright lights to blind one, no worry about signals or cross traffic." And, the Farm Wife concluded, the seventy-five-mile-per-hour speed limit "shortens the trip."

The Farm Wife was simply putting into words what others in Nebraska and much of the rest of the nation were thinking about their new roads. By 1963, about seventy-five percent of the planned Interstate system had been opened, was under construction, or had been designed. Before their Department of Roads began building Interstate 80, Nebraskans had no experience with superhighways and were suspicious of what they would do to their ways of living. Adding to the citizens' uncertainty was the question of just where engineers would locate the highway. Interstate 80 would follow the Platte River through central Nebraska, but no one had decided if it would run north or south of the river, or if it might take over sections of Route 30. "Those were real contentious days," remembered one Nebraska highway engineer, "I think we held several hundred location hearings." But as sections of Interstate 80 began to open, drivers saw immediately all that it would do to change their lives, and they welcomed it with enthusiasm.

While drivers loved the new roads, citizens and townspeople had other ideas. A fundamental fact distinguished Exit 179 at North Platte from the Union Pacific station, the Lincoln Highway, or Route 30: It did not go through North Platte but passed two miles south of the city's center. Across the 455 miles of Interstate 80 in Nebraska, places like Cozad, Lexington, Overton, Elm Creek, Odessa, Kearney, Wood River, and Grand Island—all towns and cities on the old Lincoln Highway—were bypassed by the Interstate.

Shortly after his election to the presidency in November 1960, John Kennedy appointed Rex Marion Whitton, a career engineer from Missouri, to replace Bertram Tallamy as federal highway administrator. Tallamy was a Republican who had worked for Governor Thomas Dewey in New York and Dwight Eisenhower in Washington. Beginning with Eisenhower's firing of Thomas MacDonald in 1953, the Bureau of Public

Roads and the federal highway administrator's posts had become appointed political positions. This was only natural, given the fact that presidents wanted some say over the billions of dollars the bureau was handling every year. It was natural, then, for John Kennedy to want to replace Bertram Tallamy. Besides, Tallamy's eyesight had deteriorated significantly, and he was ready to retire to upstate New York.

Whitton came right from the heart of middle America and—like his predecessors at the Bureau of Public Roads—the heart of the highway lobby. In a profession marked by deliberate and methodical minds, Whitton's ranked with the *most* deliberate and methodical. At age sixty-two, he seemed the antithesis of the typical New Frontiersmen the youthful president was appointing to federal posts. To outsiders he seemed neither the best nor the brightest, nor did he seem to have much energy. "Whitton moves and acts like a man with low metabolism," remarked a reporter who interviewed him for the *St. Louis Post-Dispatch* in 1961, adding, "He moves slowly, speaks softly, smiles rarely." Yet beneath his laconic speech and quiet, almost sluggish demeanor, Whitton possessed a steel will that reflected his agrarian past.

Marion Rex Whitton—he would reverse his first and middle names when he entered high school—was born in 1898 on a farm his father rented in the isolated southeastern corner of Jackson County, Missouri. At the age of eighteen he was able to escape his farm chores—milking ten cows each day, plowing fields in the spring, hoeing corn in the summer, and putting up hay in the fall—for Columbia, where he worked his way through the University of Missouri. In April 1920, eleven days after graduating with a civil engineering degree, Whitton began his career as a surveyor with the state highway department. Whitton always considered work, hard work, to be a series of steps through successively more difficult tasks that would lead him to bigger and better positions. As he passed through the ranks, the earnest young man recorded his progress on a long role of drafting paper, "1922, Plans Designer, $2,040 a year; 1923, Assistant Project Engineer, $2,220 a year." Quiet and sober-minded, Whitton earned a reputation for unassuming efficiency in all that he did. Once, when he felt he had not gained enough experience at one job, Whitton refused a promotion. It simply was not time to move on to the next level, he said. But openings at the next level came in time, and ones after that, too. In 1951, Rex Marion Whitton reached the top rank, chief engineer of the Missouri Highway Commission. Over the next nine years of Whitton's leadership,

Missouri could boast one of the best highway departments of any state. In testimony before the state legislature, Whitton always stressed sound planning and safe roads built to demanding standards. He embraced the Interstate program with enthusiasm, and in August 1956, made certain that Missouri awarded the first construction contract for the new highway system.

At first Whitton resisted the request from Luther Hodges, Kennedy's nominee for Secretary of Commerce, to become federal highway administrator. Married in 1925, he and his wife had endured a series of boardinghouses and furnished apartments around the state as he went from post to post in the highway department. In their first eleven years of marriage they moved thirteen times. Since becoming chief engineer in 1951, Whitton and his wife had lived in Missouri's capital, Jefferson City. There he enjoyed participating fully in civic affairs: the Rotary Club, the Masons, the Shriners, president of the local Boy Scouts, and a member of the board of deacons of the First Baptist Church of Jefferson City. Like others in his profession, including Tallamy and Volpe, Whitton approached all highway building and especially the construction of the Interstate system as though he were on a mission to serve and even save American civilization. Luther Hodges and others in the New Frontier insisted that he take the post and move to Washington. "They told me it was my duty, so I agreed to accept."

Members of the Road Gang, the informal group of highway builders who met regularly in Washington, knew they could count on Whitton, too. He had once chaired the Highway Research Board and had served on many committees of the American Association of State Highway Officials and had been its president in 1955 and 1956. Over the years he had testified before Congress numerous times on behalf of the Interstate construction program, touching on subjects like finance ("these roads generate vehicular use and therefore highway revenue,") and right-of-way battles ("people do not like to leave their homes, and you cannot blame them, but they are in the way of progress, and so on.") Never had his enthusiasm for the Interstate Highway System wavered in the least. To the executive secretary of the American Association of State Highway Officials, Whitton was the consummate highwayman, "an able highway administrator [and] a skilled highway engineer."

Curiously, the man who built the Interstates and who believed so fervently in them seldom drove on them himself. He and his wife preferred "little back roads, keeping a map of each one we travel," Whitton told a reporter. "That's the finest way to travel unless you're in a hurry to get somewhere."

When he arrived in Washington, Whitton described his job as "simply to build highways quickly, economically, and honestly," a statement that obliquely acknowledged some of the problems that had surfaced recently in the Interstate program—especially in the areas of the construction schedule, financing, and fraud. The new federal highway administrator knew that he would achieve little if he did not encourage cooperation between federal and state officials. Since he had come up through the ranks of the Missouri Highway Department and had served as president of the American Association of State Highway Officials, he knew how little got done unless the state and federal highway builders worked together. The Interstates were a "monument to our system," said Whitton, "[to] the cooperation between local, state, and federal governments in the service of the people for whom these governments serve." Cooperation and service had been the twin hallmarks of the Bureau of Public Roads since the days of Thomas MacDonald, and the new federal highway administrator looked to these ideals to help him solve the problems he faced.

Cooperation was about all Whitton had to bargain with, for Congress had purposely limited the Bureau of Public Roads' role in Interstate construction. Though the federal government paid for ninety percent of the costs of the new highways and could veto expenditures, individual states had the responsibility of initiating construction projects and determining when and where to build particular sections of the Interstate. By 1961, with just eight thousand miles of the system open for traffic, it was clear to all that construction was lagging far behind the scheduled completion date of 1972. Some states, including Arizona, Wyoming, and Mississippi, were completing an average of five miles of Interstate a year. At that rate, their sections of the system would not be ready until the next century—far past the date when the highways would be obsolete. To Whitton this was intolerable. If the states were to finish the Interstates by 1972, the date the Bureau of Public Roads had planned, they would have to complete fifty percent of the miles by the end of 1964.

Whitton took his case to his friends at the American Association of

State Highway Officials. Delay in opening the Interstates frustrated the motoring public, he told them, and he urged the swift completion of "those projects that will link up continuous, long route sections" of the highway as quickly as possible. Such highways, said Whitton, "best demonstrate to the public the benefits of the system—time saving, travel ease, and safety." The strategy worked. He stirred states to increase their construction rate to as many as one hundred miles of new highway per year. By the end of 1964, the halfway mark in the time schedule for completion, Whitton could report that half the miles of Interstate highways were open or nearing completion.

While Whitton was able to get more miles of Interstate built, he did so at a price. For the most part those "long route sections" of which the federal highway administrator spoke went through rural areas where the engineers' plans met with little resistance. The policy reversed the long-standing practice at the bureau, and at state highway departments as well, of building roads where the congestion was greatest. In the 1960s automobiles and trucks were choking many of the major cities, yet federal and local officials decided to proceed slowly with construction of urban sections because of the mounting criticism they were encountering. Once long sections of the Interstate opened, Whitton believed, people would clamor to bring the highways into and through urban areas.

"Problems and challenges are the bedfellows of progress," said Whitton. While he decided for now to avoid some of the challenges that came with building Interstates in the cities in the hope that they would abate with time, he confronted those problems that concerned financing the program. Once again the Highway Trust Fund faced a crisis. In 1959, Congress had legislated a temporary increase from 3.5 to 4 cents in the gasoline tax, but the increase was due to expire in 1962. The increasing number of small cars aggravated the problem. Gas-saving cars accounted for about four percent of sales in 1957 and sixteen percent in 1960. Americans were buying about 500,000 Volkswagen beetles a year, each of which, company advertisements pointed out, got 37.5 miles per gallon. In October 1959, General Motors, whose cars averaged 11 miles on a gallon of gas, introduced the compact, rear-engine Corvair, which it claimed would travel about 27 miles. Ford countered Volkswagen and GM with its own compact, the Falcon, which it claimed was as economical to operate as the Corvair. In its first year, Falcon sales were close to 450,000.

Divided Highways

Americans' infatuation with gasoline savings threatened the very Möbius strip of money on which the Interstate program depended. Without a rising consumption of gasoline, the government could not fund the highways. If Congress and the administration allowed the gas tax to slip back to 3.5 cents, the Bureau of Public Roads would have no other option but to curtail Interstate construction. Whitton devoted his first weeks in Washington to making his case to Luther Hodges, and through him to the president. Kennedy responded. "Our Federal pay-as-you-go Highway Program is in peril," he said in a special message he sent to Congress on the last day of February 1961, asking for continuation of the 4-cent-a-gallon tax. To justify the permanent increase, Kennedy played the defense card as his predecessor had never done. The program made a vital contribution "to our security, our safety, and our economic growth," he said in words Congress had heard many times before. But then, he added: "Timely completion . . . is essential to a National defense that will always depend, regardless of new weapon developments, on quick motor transportation of men and matériel from one site to another." Congress acted with dispatch. Kennedy signed the legislation raising the tax on June 29, 1961—five years to the day after President Eisenhower had signed the bill creating the Interstate Highway System.

When Rex Whitton took over from Bertram Tallamy as federal highway administrator, it was general knowledge in the Bureau of Public Roads as well as Congress that highway builders in some states had yielded their ideals to venality. Service had been subsumed by corruption.

It was logical that the fraud would come to the fore, if only because temptation presented itself in countless ways each day. By 1959, states had awarded sixty thousand contracts to build the Interstates. Every day, thousands of contractors moved twenty million cubic yards of earth and rock to make a path for the new highways; tens of thousands of company representatives and local officials conferred about construction matters; hundreds of local officials met with citizens to consider routing, land taking, and right-of-way; and scores of state and federal inspectors examined completed work for flaws. Every day presented thousands of opportunities for dishonesty.

In truth, road building and maintenance had always been fertile territory for the dishonest, if only because they offered such boundless opportunities for petty fraud. The young chief engineer for roads in

Iowa, Thomas Harris MacDonald, had found bid rigging to be the accepted practice and unearthed enough evidence of malfeasance to send several county officials to jail. Before Robert Moses had taken over the construction of the Triborough Bridge, the project had just served as a scheme to sink large amounts of public money into private hands. In counties across America residents talked from time to time about corrupt road practices, bridges across nonexistent streams, and roads that led to nowhere. Those in charge of road building who were honest could often make a name for themselves merely by acting with integrity. In the 1920s, a Democratic judge named Harry Truman from Rex Whitton's home county of Jackson, Missouri, found widespread abuses in road building. The evidence of corruption had been spread across the county in the form of thin layers of road surface supported by an inferior substrate. So quickly did newly completed roads disintegrate that locals likened them to a crumbling pie crust. Fortunately for the residents of Jackson County, Truman loved driving. He ended the abuses, and he resisted attempts by the grand political sachems in Kansas City who had put him into power, to rig construction bids. He proposed a bond issue to build a 224-mile network of first-class concrete highways, and he delivered the roads ahead of schedule and under budget. He drove over many of those highways when he ran for the U.S. Senate in 1934. Truman likened that campaign to being on a vacation trip. "Fact is, I like roads," said the candidate, "I like to move."

In Jackson County Truman had shown what could be accomplished by those who determined to use public money wisely and honestly. In fact there were far more local officials who acted as Truman had than those who did not. The exceptions to the rule stood out, however, especially in the Interstate Highway System, because the sums were greater than anyone had ever seen before.

By 1959, when Congress heard the first whispers of malfeasance, the House Public Works Committee decided to create a subcommittee to investigate and appropriated $295,000 for its work. Its chair would be a former high school chemistry teacher, school superintendent, and state legislator from northeast Minnesota, John Anton Blatnik. A member of the Democrat-Farm-Labor Party, John Blatnik had also been decorated for his valor in the Army Air Corps before residents of the Eighth Congressional District elected him to Congress in 1946. As the district included Duluth, the mineral-rich Iron Range, and the port at Duluth on

Lake Superior, Blatnik joined the Public Works Committee. From his seat on the committee he campaigned ardently for construction of the Saint Lawrence Seaway—the system of canals, dams, channels, and locks that would allow ships to take minerals from his district to ports around the world.

As the head of the congressional investigating committee, Blatnik had a difficult job, for he had to effect agreement among eleven Democrats and seven Republicans at a time when both parties were positioning themselves for the election of 1960. As luck would have it, allegations of fraud had surfaced in Massachusetts. "We suspicioned that there was some skullduggery going on," Ellis Armstrong, commissioner of the Bureau of Public Roads, recollected. Armstrong's instincts were correct. Examiners from the Bureau of Public Roads, including former agents from the Federal Bureau of Investigation, found numerous instances of malfeasance in the acquisition of right-of-way for a section of Interstate 95 near the Rhode Island border. State officials in the Massachusetts Department of Public Works employed one of several simple schemes to make money. Sometimes an official divulged the location of a proposed Interstate highway to a friend, who then purchased the land for a small sum from an unwitting local resident. Later the friend would be able to sell the land to the state at a greatly appreciated price. The official and his friend would split the profit, which was even greater if the land included an exit for the Interstate. At other times, a state official would collude with a state-hired appraiser to assign a greatly inflated value to a parcel of land. The landowner would then share the profits with the official and the appraiser.

When the bureau's investigators returned with their findings, Armstrong arranged for a meeting with the Secretary of Commerce, Frederick Mueller; Bertram Tallamy; and the bureau's legal counsel. After the investigators reported the fraud, the legal counsel said, "Well, you decision makers have two options. One, you can cut off Federal aid to Massachusetts; or two, one of you is going to go to Sing-Sing." Armstrong turned over the bureau's files to the Justice Department and Blatnik's committee, and stopped over $12 million of federal payments to the state for land acquisition.

Blatnik, however, found himself in something of a quandary. To focus on malfeasance in the state run by the Democratic administration of Governor Foster Furcolo would indirectly embarrass Massachusetts's

Tom Lewis

Democratic Senator John Kennedy, who was running for president. Much to the consternation of the seven Republican members, Blatnik and his eleven Democratic colleagues seemed to be delaying the committee's investigation. True, there was evidence of fraud in other states, especially in Florida, New Mexico, and Oklahoma, but in comparison with the skulduggery in Massachusetts, those instances were "peanuts," said the ranking Republican member. The scandals in the Bay State were "the grand daddy of them all." To stall for time, Blatnik sent two investigators to Boston to ferret out more information. There would be no public hearings until the following year, if ever. That November, while John Kennedy won his home state by half a million votes, Republican John Anthony Volpe won the contest for the governor's office.

Eventually, after the election of 1960, when Whitton had taken over as federal highway administrator, some Massachusetts highway officials, and those in collusion with them, went to prison. Blatnik's committee found that fraud in other states took different forms. In Florida, the Cone Brothers Contracting Company and the Brinson-Allen Construction Company of Tampa had refined the art of petty graft and small payments to midlevel state engineers. "I had a boy in school and had a mortgage on my house," one engineer told the congressmen, justifying "loans" of federal money that Cone Brothers had given him to make favorable inspections. Another engineer working on Interstate 4 between Lakeland and Orlando testified he had received an envelope a week for his consideration. If nothing else the hearings showed just how easy it was to buy an official in Florida's highway department. Julian Lee Cone, Jr., allowed that he had distributed about $42,000—in the form of hunting licenses, whiskey, building supplies, and envelopes containing $25 in cash—to ensure that engineers would "expedite" their inspections. From the millions of dollars in contracts, engineers were willing to settle for a bottle of whiskey, or a ham, or $25. After the revelations, Florida's chief highway engineer dismissed those who admitted receiving payments and forbade Cone Brothers from doing any further highway construction.

Far more onerous for Whitton than the inquiries into corruption were the *allegations* of corruption that many whispered around the country. It was inevitable that journalists would take on the subject of the Interstates. Therefore it came as little surprise when, on Monday, October 1, 1962, David Brinkley hosted a one-hour television exposé on the "swindles, fraud, and thievery" of the Interstate construction program, which he called the "Great Highway Robbery." "The FBI has found evidence of crime in many states," said Brinkley as the National Broadcasting Company cameras focused on crumbling concrete pavements and rotting bridge abutments. Some evidence was even more graphic: Brinkley stood in a swamp appraised by an NBC-hired assessor at $3,000, for which the state of Florida had paid $41,000. One contractor reported giving hams, turkeys, and whiskey to eager engineers. An honest state highway official told of receiving telephone calls threatening the safety of his wife and children if he should testify. In Tulsa, Oklahoma, a newspaper editor accused federal officials of approving roads without ever getting out of their cars to make a proper inspection. As the television screen showed a picture of an overpass and an interchange exit sign for the town of Gary off Interstate 40 in New Mexico, Brinkley told his viewers that the $300,000 exit led to nowhere. "There is no such town and never was," said Brinkley. As the camera focused on the stark landscape, he concluded, "The road goes one hundred feet into the desert and just stops." The camera then cut to John Anton Blatnik, who said his committee had found "millions of dollars lost to fraud." Compounding the damage was Brinkley's depiction of Whitton. In an interview, the federal highway administrator appeared bumbling, inadequately prepared, and unable to answer questions about the allegations.

The facts often differed from what Brinkley's program alleged. The Bureau of Public Roads had refused to approve thirteen miles of Interstate 44 in Tulsa because the pavement did not meet federal standards. The exit off Interstate 40 in New Mexico leads to a railroad siding and pumping station that the locals do indeed call Gary. Despite what the camera showed, a local road does connect with the exit. But the damage had been done. David Brinkley had brought highway fraud and bureaucratic incompetence into American living rooms. From this point onward many viewed the Interstate Highway System as a forty-one-thousand-mile ribbon of dishonesty, and it became a part of America's darker mythology of malfeasance. Everyone, it seemed, had a story to add to the myth—a paving company that made millions by charging for asphalt never delivered to the job; or a friend's uncle who made a timely purchase of land near an Interstate exit after being tipped off about the location of the new highway; or a company that paid off an official to get a job; or a man who built his swimming pool with concrete and steel purloined from the Interstate. Few hard facts supported most of the stories, but no matter. Everyone just knew they had to be right.

In fact, the myths of malfeasance were just that. Since so much money was flowing legitimately, people did not have to resort to illegitimate means to get it. "The Interstate program is not a federal enterprise," wrote Harvard professor and future U.S. Senator Daniel Patrick Moynihan in 1960, "it is only a federal expense." Since the federal government was paying the bill for ninety percent of the expenses, and since the highways were to be the best possible, there was little incentive on the part of the states to curtail expenses. The Bureau of Public Roads felt the pressure from Congress and the Senate to keep the money flowing from the Highway Trust Fund to the states. Through its auditors, the bureau checked for financial irregularities but exercised little real control. As Moynihan said, "It functions rather as a company comptroller who fusses over items on an expense account without ever daring to ask if the trip was necessary."

While there were relatively few instances of outright thievery, there was one way in which both political parties and almost every politician in every state was being indirectly compromised by the federal Interstate program. Across the country, most road contractors gave what Moynihan called an "honest tithe" to the Democratic and Republican parties as part of an unwritten agreement of the price they would have to pay in order to do business with the party that was in power. It was, said Moynihan, " an excellent, if informal means of financing our parties out of tax funds." Such had been the practice for many years, of course, but the billions of dollars that flowed because of the Interstate program increased the level of giving dramatically. The money the contractors gave had its ultimate source in the federal government and the U.S. taxpayer.

With about thirteen thousand miles of Interstates open by the end of 1962, Americans were at last beginning to understand the impact the highways would make on the landscape. Commerce had been quick to understand their potential, too. From the start, the bureau of Public Roads had been the rope in a tug-of-war between commercial interests, who wanted to develop the land alongside the Interstates, and conservationists, who wanted to preserve what they called the "scenic beauty" of the landscape.

Shortly after Interstate construction began in 1957, members of Con-

gress worried that the new highways would look like the old ones—
ribbons of pavement through tunnels of billboards. They had good reason
to fear. Major federal-aid highways like Routes 1, 30, and 101 had become
corridors of advertising that obliterated the natural landscape.

> *I think that I shall never see*
> *A billboard lovely as a tree*

wrote Ogden Nash in a parody of Joyce Kilmer.

> *Perhaps, unless the billboards fall,*
> *I'll never see a tree at all.*

It was time, said many, to write an amendment to the Federal-Aid
Highway Act of 1956, to prevent the Interstate Highway System from
becoming what Robert Moses called "billboard alley." Secretary Weeks
had acknowledged that there was "widespread feeling" among the public
that Congress should take steps to curtail billboards along the Interstates. The advertising lobby, however, objected and mounted strong
opposition. "Billboards are the art gallery of the public," declared Burr L.
Robbins, president of the General Outdoor Advertising Company, in his
argument about this restriction of his freedom of speech. Senators from
automobile- and oil-producing states, including Lyndon Johnson from
Texas, agreed. "I am against those billboards that mar our scenery,"
President Eisenhower lamented, "[but] I don't know what I can do about
it." In the end Congress compromised by voting to give the states a mild
incentive—half of one percent of the cost of highway construction—if
they enacted laws banning billboards alongside the new highways.

By the time Whitton took office in 1961, people were beginning to
realize that it was not merely a question of billboards disfiguring the
landscape, but the very highways themselves. It is a commonplace to say
that the new highways differed from most of their predecessors in the
matters of limited access and geometric alignment that took more land
to enable cars to travel faster, but the Interstates also reflected something deeper about mid-twentieth-century American thinking: engineering
hubris. Engineers knew they had the ability to put a highway anywhere,
including places where automobiles had never been, and many reveled
in the sheer joy of building without attention to the consequences.
Forget following the contours of the natural landscape, just pound the
road through. Should a mountain prove too high, just blast the top off or

tunnel through. Should a ravine prove too deep, just fill it with stone and dirt. No river, lake, or arm of the ocean should be too wide or too deep for a bridge or causeway. For many engineers the structure itself was the goal rather than the structure in relation to the land. Engineers found they were not alone, for many progressive planners regarded the highway, speed, and efficiency to be of primary importance.

There is, perhaps, no greater example of engineering hubris than one that, thankfully, did not take place in the Bristol Mountains about midway between Barstow and Needles, California. In 1963, the Santa Fe Railroad was seeking a way to shorten its route across the Mojave Desert, and the highway department was looking for a route for Interstate 40. Both the railroad and the highway were hindered by the mountains that rise sharply and suddenly about twelve hundred feet from the desert floor. In mid-1963, engineers decided to consider what they delicately called "the nuclear option." The engineers' plan was simple: Bury twenty-two atomic bombs beneath the surface of the mountains and vaporize them. "Our main focus was on whether it was feasible and practical and what savings might be realized in building the Interstate," Robert Austin, the engineer for the project, recalled. Perhaps because the United States had tested nuclear weapons in the desert before—though not in this area—Austin paid little attention to the effects the bombs would have had on the environment.

Since President Kennedy had recently proposed "Operation Plowshare," an extension of Dwight Eisenhower's "Atoms for Peace" program "to harness the atom for the benefit of mankind," the Atomic Energy Commission was looking for ways to use nuclear weapons peacefully. It was enthusiastic about the idea. Yes, the twenty-two bombs with their combined force of 1.73 million tons of TNT (133 times greater than the force of the two bombs that obliterated Hiroshima and Nagasaki) would produce a dust cloud that would take several days to dissipate. But engineers were more taken with the idea of moving sixty-eight million tons of earth and rock with a single blast, almost instantly cutting a channel 325 feet wide and nearly 11,000 feet long. While it would have saved $8 million in construction costs, the explosion also would have contaminated much of the Southwest, especially Kingman, Flagstaff, and Phoenix, Arizona directly east of the site. Knowing that the nuclear explosions would evoke some public interest, Austin scouted out a place for a reviewing stand for the press and VIPs on a ridge about ten miles away from the blast site.

Fortunately, the plan had posed one question that scientists could not answer: How long would it take for the radiation levels at the immediate blast site to return to a safe level for humans? No one could predict how many weeks or months would elapse after the explosion before it would be safe for workers to build the highway. Unable to get an answer, Austin and the California Highway Department finally abandoned the plan in 1965 and decided to build the Bristol Mountains section of Interstate 40 with conventional blasting for about $20 million. The road opened in 1973. "Given what we know today about radiation, it's a good thing we didn't do it," said Robert Ramey, a civil engineer who worked on the project, adding wistfully, "I am kind of disappointed we couldn't have seen how an experiment of this type would have worked."

While the nuclear option in the Bristol Mountains was certainly an extreme example, evidence was growing with every new mile of Interstate that engineers had placed a higher value on the feat of construction than on the aesthetics of the completed structure and its impact on the environment. Supports for bridges and elevated roadways were often ugly. The highways cut through parks and public areas in ways that often denied people access to the land. "Thanks to the miles of superhighways under construction," said one wag about this time, "America will soon be a wonderful place to drive—if you don't want to stop."

In part the new awareness about highway aesthetics came as a result of the Kennedy administration's activist Secretary of the Interior, Stewart L. Udall from Arizona. Up to Udall's tenure, the Secretaries of Interior had mostly confined themselves to treaties with Indian tribes, sale of public lands, the government's mining interests, and the like. Udall, however, took seriously—and even extended—his department's interest in the stewardship of the nation's natural resources and natural environment. "America today stands on a pinnacle of wealth and power," wrote the president in a foreword to Udall's 1963 book *The Quiet Crisis*, "yet we live in a land of vanishing beauty, of increasing ugliness, of shrinking open space and of an overall environment that is diminished daily by pollution and noise and blight."

"I look forward to an America which will not be afraid of grace and beauty," said John Kennedy, to the students and faculty of Amherst College in what was one of his last major addresses, "[an America] which will protect the beauty of our natural environment." As a result of this emphasis, Rex Whitton became more sensitive to the connection between highways and the environment. He stressed to state and federal officials that the Interstates should preserve scenic views and avoid unsightly scars on the landscape. "Make no mistake about it," wrote the federal highway administrator in March 1963 to his regional engineers. "In the final analysis we will be judged by the appearance of our highways as much as any other factor."

> *Fit the highway to the landscape—take advantage of the topography, wherever economically feasible, to have separate one-way alignments and profiles for each one-way roadway—streamline the cross sections—use judicious planting for the prevention of soil erosion, the joining of the slopes with native growth roadsides, and to possibly act as a buffer for noise and sight control—and design structures small and large so that they have architectural excellence.*

Whitton combined his sensitivity with a good measure of pragmatism, too. He understood better than most that if citizens' groups went to court to stop Interstates, they could cause delays and drive up the costs.

The federal highway administrator was enthusiastic when Lady Bird Johnson inveigled her husband to include highway beautification in his Great Society programs. Time and again the road leading to a new Interstate highway turned into a strip of motels and restaurants. Billboards still blighted the landscape along many of the new highways and detracted from the view of passing motorists. The federal highway administrator encouraged officials from regional offices of the Bureau of Public Roads to speak to civic groups about the need for zoning regulations to stop the intrusion of such seedy commerce. It was no good to spend millions of federal dollars on a beautiful Interstate only to have billboards, automobile junkyards, and commercial strips beside it.

There were problems with Lady Bird Johnson's concern for highway beautification. How much power should the federal government wield over states? States already received an incentive of an additional half of one percent of their highway funds if they enacted legislation limiting billboards. Should federal laws go further, or would they intrude on the fundamental rights of the people? The First Lady herself understood the objections that some raised: "How can one best fight ugliness in a nation such as ours—where there is great freedom of action or inaction for every individual and every interest?" she asked at a White House conference she had convened on scenic beauty. Lady Bird's husband was a bit more certain about the matter. "A highway is more than a ribbon of concrete," LBJ told a gathering at the White House. "It is a way for people to travel and it should serve all their human needs. Its purpose is not just to get people from one place to another. Its purpose is to enrich their journey." The solution, Johnson said, was to "eliminate outdoor advertising signs and junkyards from the sight of the Interstate." The president sent a bill to Congress to do just this.

Republicans balked when the bill made it through both committees of Congress. Many voiced concern about the undue influence the president's wife had upon her husband. One conservative congressman from Kansas, Robert Dole, offered an amendment to the legislation to substitute for the term "Secretary of Commerce" (who would have the power to enforce the legislation) the words "Lady Bird." The amendment lost by a voice vote. After other delaying tactics on the part of the Republicans failed, Congress passed the bill. On October 22, 1965, Lady Bird's husband signed the Federal Highway Beautification Act into law. Advertisers had to move billboards six hundred feet from the highway and junkyard owners had to screen their establishments.

Despite the allegations of fraud, the concerns about financing, the misgivings of many about the compatibility of the Interstates with urban areas, and myriad other problems, Whitton pressed forward. The Bureau of Public Roads had to get the message out about the benefits of good roads and win Americans over. The citizens would see all the advantages the Interstate Highway System had to offer and they would support it. As federal highway administrator, he conceived of himself as chief publicity agent. Opening ceremonies were the best way to get the message out. Whenever he could, he arranged to be at a ribbon cutting, and his presence often brought the state's governor to the ceremony. At each ribbon cutting, he would extol the economic and safety benefits the new Interstate would bring, and he would exhort highway builders to move faster. "I look forward eagerly, a few years from now, to the opening of a route clear across the country," Whitton said in a 1962 speech. "What an impact it will have on the public! While we won't drive a gold spike, perhaps we can erect a gold sign—conforming with the Interstate sign manual, of course."

Section after section of Interstate 80, America's aorta, did open over the rest of the decade. In California, builders brought the highway from Sacramento through the Donner Pass. In Nevada, engineers built

Interstate 80 beside the Immigrant Trail across the desert. In Utah, they pushed the highway eastward across the desolate Wendover Desert to the Salt Lake. Wyoming engineers built sections of Interstate through Rock Springs, across the Continental Divide at Table Rock, and past Laramie. Nebraska completed half of its sections of Interstate 80 by 1966. Iowa finished its section of the highway through rich farmland east of Des Moines, and through Poweshiek County, the home of Thomas Harris MacDonald. Illinois's highway department opened all its sections from the Mississippi River to the Indiana line. Most of Indiana's and Ohio's Interstate 80 miles were the states' turnpikes that had opened in the 1950s. In Pennsylvania, where state officials named their section of the highway the "Keystone Shortway," engineers pressed construction in each of the fifteen counties through which it would pass. And in New Jersey, engineers completed the western sections of Interstate 80 and moved closer to the more populated areas in the east.

Across the country, newspapers printed stories extolling the virtues of the highways. INTERSTATES A BOON TO IOWA read the headline in the Des Moines *Register*. "Driving across Iowa is wonderful now," an army sergeant from Detroit commented. The Hackensack, New Jersey, *Record* found that the opening of Interstate 80 "pumped new blood into the housing market, particularly in apartments." The Harrisburg, Pennsylvania, *Evening News* found that the Keystone Shortway had sparked an economic boon. Land values had risen near the highway as industries and homes moved into the region.

However, there were sections of Interstate 80 that did not open during Whitton's tenure. Residents of Reno, Nevada, were angry that the highway would cut the city in half. Residents in Salt Lake City, Utah, worried what the Interstate would do to their lake. Other smaller towns, bypassed by the highway altogether, went into economic decline. "The freeway has just about killed us," said the operator of a service station in Fernley, Nevada. Others across the nation echoed him. Rex Whitton was oblivious to the unhappiness. "Highways are built for people—not vehicles," said the federal highway administrator, ignoring the criticism people were making. "Highway builders have always been aware that the welfare of people underlies the nation's road program, and that program is geared to fulfill people's needs and wants."

For the moment, the consensus was with Rex Whitton and the "Farm Wife" from North Platte. Most believed that the Interstates brought only benefits to the land. The new highways were fast, safe, and efficient. But in many states, engineers had concentrated their efforts on building highways across vast open stretches of country. There they could build with little worry about lawsuits and protests. It was not surprising that Nebraska, which ranked thirty-eighth of the fifty states in population density, should be first among the states to complete its sections of Interstate highway. As the engineers moved their survey crews and bulldozers closer to old and venerable cities filled with houses, parks, and historic sites—places where Congress had mandated them to build four- and six-lane highways—citizens began to ask questions. And the engineers were hard-pressed to answer them.

PART 3

MacDonald as a young man.
(Federal Highway Administration)

The Chief. For Thomas Harris MacDonald, chief of the Bureau of Public Roads, highway building was a "gigantic business." From 1919 to 1953, he funneled billions of federal dollars to the states for road construction. The first to conceive of an "interstate" road system, MacDonald compared the greatness of his road-building program with that of Rome under Caesar and of France under Napoleon.

For thirty-four years, MacDonald served a succession of Democratic and Republican presidents—Wilson, Harding, Coolidge, Hoover, Roosevelt, and Truman—until he was fired by Eisenhower. In his tenure, MacDonald had turned the Bureau of Public Roads into a road-building empire with a central office in Washington, eleven regional divisions, and foreign offices in the Philippines, Ethiopia, Turkey, Liberia, Puerto Rico, Guatemala, El Salvador, Honduras, and Costa Rica, among other countries.

The Chief becomes a chief: MacDonald (left) is named "Father of Great Trails" by the Kiowa tribe, Oklahoma City, 1946.   *(AASHTO)*

A typical rural road in 1919.   *(American Highway Users Alliance)*

Trucks on the Lincoln Highway. The effect of trucks on roads, said a highway official, was similar to "the shells a big gun hurls into a fortress."   *(American Highway Users Alliance)*

Early road construction.   *(American Highway Users Alliance)*

At the 1939 New York World's Fair, the Bureau of Public Roads displayed this artist's rendering of a divided highway of the future. *(Federal Highway Administration)*

In 1941, the Bureau of Public Roads published a sketch of an urban highway of the future—elevated, with few automobiles and no trucks. *(Federal Highway Administration)*

Life goes to The Futurama (continued)

Two 14-lane express highways cross in 1960

Surely the most compelling exhibit at the 1939 New York World's Fair was the seven-acre General Motors Futurama pavilion (pictured below) on the Avenue of Transportation. There the designer Norman Bel Geddes took visitors on a ride over the United States and showed them "Magic Motorways," high-speed, divided highways with sleek interchanges. In 1960, visitors were told, automobiles would cross the country in twenty-four hours. "We enter a new era," said Bel Geddes. "Are we ready for the changes that are coming?" As they left the pavilion, each visitor received a pin that boldly proclaimed, "I have seen the future." *(Both photos courtesy of Alan Wheelock)*

While the Bureau of Public Roads and Norman Bel Geddes were dreaming of high-speed divided highways, the Pennsylvania Turnpike Commission was building one: a smooth four-lane pavement stretching for 160 miles between Harrisburg and Pittsburgh. When the turnpike opened in 1940, Chief MacDonald called it "a magnificent accomplishment," and the federal government recognized its military value.

(All photos: Pennsylvania Turnpike Commission)

After World War II, Americans were often confronted with signposts as confusing as this one.

(American Highway Users Alliance)

Speaking from notes that Eisenhower had prepared for the National Governor's Conference in July 1954, Vice President Nixon outlined the president's "grand plan" for a $50 billion road system. Everyone rushed to get on the bandwagon for a superhighway system, but no one could figure out how to pay for it.

To sort through the conflicting proposals for a national highway system, Eisenhower appointed a committee headed by his old friend General Lucius Clay. Pictured with Eisenhower are (from left) Clay; committee secretary (and later head of the Federal Highway Administration) Frank Turner; Stephen D. Bechtel, head of the largest civil engineering firm in the world; S. Sloan Colt, head of Banker's Trust; William A. Roberts, head of Allis-Chalmers; and David Beck, the powerful and corrupt head of the International Brotherhood of Teamsters. *(American Highway Users Alliance)*

The two members of Congress most responsible for an Interstate highway bill were Albert Arnold Gore (left), the progressive senator from Tennessee who held a liberal outlook on international affairs, took moderate positions on civil rights, and supported massive public works programs; and George Hyde Fallon (right), a congressman with such a single-minded vision that his colleagues in Congress said his middle initial stood for "Highways." *(Both photos: Federal Highway Administration)*

Two heads of the Federal Highway Administration who oversaw much of the Interstate construction, Bertram Tallamy (left) and Rex Whitton (right). Tallamy, who had built the New York Thruway, then the longest superhighway in the United States, served under Eisenhower. A career engineer from Missouri, Whitton served under Kennedy and Johnson. Neither man chose to drive on the Interstates. Tallamy suffered from poor eyesight; Whitton preferred the back roads.

(Federal Highway Administration)

Federal and state highway administrations were dominated by white males. When the first woman joined the Bureau of Public Roads in 1962, the story made the front page of the bureau's newspaper. *(Federal Highway Administration)*

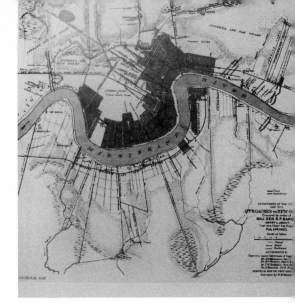

REVOLT

Transportation . . . has the power to
destroy as well as to build.
THOMAS HARRIS MACDONALD

More than anything else, the river defines New Orleans. As it reaches the city, the broad Mississippi becomes more twisted and torturous, locked in a struggle with the very land itself to keep it from emptying its mighty flood of water and silt into the Gulf of Mexico. At one strategic bend in the river that from the air resembles a crescent, Jean-Baptiste Sieur de Bienville, governor of the French colony, established the city of New Orleans in 1718. Adrien de Pauger, assistant to the French royal engineer, laid out streets and located public buildings around the Place d'Armes, a broad square near the riverfront. In time, the area became known as the French Quarter, or the Vieux Carré.

Viewed from the levee on a quiet summer day, the dark coffee-colored Mississippi seems as torpid as the languid atmosphere. Beneath the torpor, however, lurks a swift and often destructive current that surprises even the most experienced river pilot. As New Orleans stands at a mean elevation of four feet and less, the city instantly suffers the river's changes and movements. Realizing early on that they had located their city at the bottom of a great saucerlike depression, and that just a few feet beneath the surface the ground yields water, French colonists learned they had to bury their dead in sepulchres above ground. To contend with the river, French engineers built walls and a moat at the city's edge.

Over the years New Orleans became an ethnic and architectural gumbo, a hot and spicy mixture of race and style. In 1788, a quarter century after Louis XV ceded New Orleans and the Louisiana Territory to Charles III of Spain, a disastrous fire leveled about eight hundred houses and much of the city. Yet another fire in 1794 took an additional two hundred buildings. In 1801, after rebuilding many of the structures on the Vieux Carré's narrow streets in their architectural style, the Spanish returned the land to the French. With the Louisiana Purchase two years later (conveyed in a signing ceremony in the Place d'Armes), the United States acquired all the land between the Mississippi and the Rocky Mountains. In the years following the purchase, Americans settled in their own "Garden District" west of the ramparts surrounding the Vieux Carré. When the Creoles—those descended from the French—joined with General Jackson and the Americans to defeat the British at the Battle of New Orleans, the gumbo was complete. In 1856, residents of the Vieux Carré renamed the Place d'Armes "Jackson Square," and at the center erected a great bronze statue of the general, saber at his side, cocking his hat, and sitting astride his furious, rearing horse.

The river also defines the path of New Orleans's streets. For the Vieux Carré, de Pauger designed a grid of fourteen streets perpendicular to its banks. Streets outside the French Quarter tend to run perpendicular as well, following the river's course around the bend, so that they resembled the ribs of a gigantic fan. Because de Bienville had chosen such a low point on the land for his city, engineers in the late nineteenth century had to build an elaborate drainage system beneath broad avenues with wide median strips. Giant subterranean pumps empty excess water into Lake Ponchartrain to the north. These medians, which Orleanians call "neutral grounds," conveniently separate the city's various districts.

Well into the twentieth century New Orleans ranked as the largest city below the Mason-Dixon line, with a port second in tonnage only to New York's. It boasted a huge grain elevator and refineries capable of cracking half a million barrels of oil a day. Nine railroad lines served the city; fourteen steamship lines took passengers and goods around the globe. The Sugar Bowl drew crowds on the first day of the new year, while Mardi Gras drew them for a final bash before Lent. Creoles and their descendants lent a gaiety to the city throughout the year.

By 1965, however, cracks had begun to show in the city's facade. The population of the metropolitan area, which had grown steadily over the century to a high of 620,000 in 1960, was slowly ebbing, and the venerable Vieux Carré had been suffering since the 1920s. Most old Creole families had moved to houses in uptown New Orleans. Developers had quietly replaced historic buildings in the district with tall, commercial structures that increased the density of automobile and truck traffic and diminished its architectural integrity. The French Quarter had slipped into seedy decay, a place known for its tawdry bordellos, rowdy music, glittery striptease clubs, and sin. "Certain parts of the Quarter were just rock bottom slums. . . . In many places they didn't even have indoor plumbing," said Fred Guice, president of a large New Orleans real estate appraisal firm. "I've heard many a man looking down there say they ought to take a match and burn the whole damn thing down."

It was the Vieux Carré, particularly on the land between Jackson Square and the Mississippi, that became the scene of a furious battle between highway builders and citizens for the soul of one of America's most venerable cities. But the battle's importance had national significance. The revolt in New Orleans helped to define the future relationship between the highway and the city for urban areas across the nation. It forced builders, businesses, and ordinary citizens to redefine the value they placed on their society and the environment.

For as long as most can remember, the Napoleon House in the Vieux Carré has been a place where locals congregate, and where visitors come for a drink and the atmosphere of French New Orleans. So named because of the legend that Napoleon had planned to live at the house after a rescue party from the city had spirited him from his prison on St. Helena, the bar at the corner of Chartres and St. Charles streets possesses the atmosphere that typifies the French Quarter. It is little changed from the time of Napoleon: Decaying brown paint peels from its high dark ceiling; dusty and faded photographs of politicians and locals line the walls; dilapidated chairs and tables rest unsteadily on the bare wooden floor. Only the long wooden bar, the resting place for countless elbows and drinks, seems solid.

At Christmastime in 1965, Bill Borah and Dick Baumbach, two transplanted New Orleans natives, each in town for the holidays, met for a drink at the Napoleon House. In 1955, while a freshman at Tulane

University, Borah had succumbed to the Quarter's temptations ("I majored in French Quarter," he remembered), and low grades forced him into the marines. Wiser after his two years of service, he returned to New Orleans to resume his study at Tulane—and to live in the Vieux Carré. He completed his B.A. in history in 1961 and later received a degree in law. Baumbach had been Phi Beta Kappa at Tulane. After receiving his law degree there, he spent a year in Latin America on a Fulbright Fellowship.

In December 1965, Borah had returned from study at the London School of Economics for a holiday visit with his parents. Baumbach was back in New Orleans on his Christmas break from study at Columbia University's School of International Affairs. Christmas had passed, and now they were looking forward to their flights to London and New York. (Borah was particularly anxious to get back, as his girlfriend and two tickets to Sir Laurence Olivier's *Othello* awaited his arrival.) A chance conversation with the owner at the Napoleon, however, changed Borah's and Baumbach's plans and ultimately the course of their lives. They learned for the first time of the plan to build the "Vieux Carré Expressway," a 40-foot-high, 108-foot-wide elevated federal Interstate highway in front of Jackson Square.

In fact there had been a plan for an elevated expressway along the river in front of the Vieux Carré since 1946. That year the Louisiana Highway Department hired New York's Robert Moses, the one whom everyone revered as the most progressive highway planner in the nation, to address New Orleans's traffic problems. Moses' solution was to ring the city with multilaned expressways that would bring automobiles and trucks to the city's core. Vehicles must get "into and out of the very heart of the City from the east and west," said the great urban planner and builder. One highway would cross to the north of the Vieux Carré and meet with an expressway that linked the river with Lake Ponchartrain to the north and the Greater New Orleans Bridge that crossed the Mississippi. Along the riverfront, a "new route would consist of an elevated express highway over the railroad tracks to Esplanade Avenue, and thence at ground level along Elysian Fields Avenue" until it completed the circle with the highway to the north.

It was no surprise that Moses designed the highway in front of the French Quarter to rise five stories above the land. Elevated highways

Divided Highways

through and around cities were all the latest rage with futuristic thinkers. In 1922 in France, Le Corbusier had shown the way. His sketches of the "Ville Contemporaine" pictured roadways soaring over parks and high among tall skyscrapers. Popular fanciful artists followed with highways on slender stilts high above the ground as they went through or around skyscrapers at about the tenth story. Moses himself had created graceful elevated approaches to his bridges in New York. Before World War II, he built a "parkway" through a crowded section of Brooklyn on the pillars of an old elevated transit line. "When Commissioner Moses finds the surface of the earth too congested . . . he lifts the road into the air and continues it on its way," gushed an editorial writer for the *New York Times*, ignoring the darkness and blight the commissioner had created for the citizens below. "The problem was solved successfully. . . . Beginning today . . . Brooklyn reaps a new incalculable highway benefit." The idea of a highway soaring above the crowded city dwellers toiling below enchanted the master builder. The same year he solved New Orleans's traffic problems with an elevated expressway, he presented sketches to the New York City Planning Commission for three crosstown highways. Though Moses was careful to avoid the word, each one was elevated. One, the Mid-Manhattan Expressway connecting the Lincoln and Queens Midtown tunnels, featured a six-lane, 160-foot-wide highway that cut through the sides of great skyscrapers a hundred feet above New York's 30th Street.

Since the automobile represented the great achievement of the twentieth century, Moses believed engineers should build the highways that carried them above rather than below the land. At the General Motors' Futurama at the New York World's Fair, Norman Bel Geddes ended his highway in a city of the future *below* the sidewalks for pedestrians, suggesting that human beings still had some control over their technology. Moses considered it foolish to put the automobile in a tunnel, a structure he frequently dismissed as a "great tiled bathroom."

In the period following World War II, Moses stood at the height of his power. His publicity machine issued lavishly illustrated reports detailing his achievements that lent to his aura as the expert who could solve America's urban transportation problems. His ideas dominated popular thinking about planning. Newspaper editors across the country praised him for his ability to turn plans into elegant strands of concrete and asphalt that threaded their way into and above crowded cities. The automobile was the personal choice of transportation for most Americans, so the editors reasoned. It had to move as fast as the trains that Americans had once favored. If they wished to survive and prosper, cities had to accommodate the automobile just as they had once accommodated the railroad. The greater the number of highways, the greater the city. New York and Los Angeles owed much of their success to the network of highways that made them so attractive to travelers. True, highways sometimes brought distress to those who lost their houses, but the editors believed that was the nature of "progress." "Progress," so Moses said, "sometimes involves some temporary hardships." Few in New York in 1946, aside from the tens of thousands who lay in the path of one of his giant highways, questioned the thinking, and more often than not Moses had been careful to make sure that they were ones with little voice and even less political power.

Moses issued his prescription for New Orleans's progress during the first year in office for the city's reform mayor, deLessups Story Morrison. Morrison first had to attend to other items on his agenda, including slum clearance, rail modernization, and construction of a new city center. For the moment he had neither the money nor the time to build what citizens came to call the Riverfront Expressway. In 1951, he asked the prominent St. Louis planning and engineering firm Harland Bartholomew and Associates to recommend a solution for the city's traffic problems. It suggested a ground-level riverfront highway or, if necessary, Moses' scheme for an elevated roadway. Still, no one acted on these proposals. The Bureau of Public Roads did not include a line for a riverfront highway in the Yellow Book it presented to Congress in September 1955, though it did show the routes of other Interstate highways—I-10 and I-610.

Were it not for the New Orleans Chamber of Commerce's creation of the Central Area Committee, a group of the city's most powerful and influential citizens, the highway might never have been considered further. The committee was similar to dozens of others formed in cities across America in the 1950s, each with a mission of city improvement and keeping urban dwellers from moving to the suburbs. Many were disturbed that the population in the nation's largest cities was holding steady or declining, while beyond the city limits suburbs were booming with new homes and shopping malls. Increasing automobile and truck traffic, so the members of the Central Area Committee thought, was making the Central Business District of New Orleans, the "downtown" area that actually lies above Canal Street directly to the west of the

Divided Highways

Vieux Carré, unattractive to shoppers and businesspeople. Together with the city's Planning Commission, they funded studies that demonstrated why a riverfront expressway was imperative for the future of New Orleans. One engineering report citing the urgent need for "an elevated expressway of at least four (4) lanes" was typical in its conclusions.

For Fred Guice, the expressway was a matter of keeping the city and its port alive and up-to-date. His real estate appraisal offices were in downtown New Orleans. From his window he could see much of the river and the port as well as the Central Business District. He served on the Central Area Committee at the time it proposed the expressway. The Interstate would bring benefits both to the port and the Central Business District, in Guice's estimation. "Our bread and butter was always tied into the port. There would be no New Orleans if there had been no port. We had to get trucks to the ships." The Central Business District begins at Canal Street, one of the widest streets in America. Major department stores line both sides of Canal Street, while on the downriver side, behind the stores, are offices filled with professional and clerical workers. The Riverfront Expressway would bring shoppers to the foot of Canal Street.

Guice and others saw an additional benefit to the elevated expressway: traffic relief for the French Quarter. The port of New Orleans has both downriver and upriver piers with only one avenue—known as Decatur Street in the Vieux Carré—to connect them. New Orleans's spongy soil translated the vibrations of the trucks into tremors that were physically shaking the older buildings of the French Quarter apart. In the estimation of Guice and his colleagues on the Central Area Committee, diverting heavy trucks onto an elevated expressway and getting them away from the French Quarter would actually help to save it.

By 1964, with the Interstate Highway System under construction across the country, political momentum in New Orleans—and all of the political power—favored the Riverfront Expressway. The steps to making it a reality seemed relatively simple: Convince the Bureau of Public Roads to include the project in the Interstate Highway System (thereby ensuring that the federal government would pay ninety percent of its costs); hold public hearings on the specific plans; secure final federal approval; take the land; tear down everything in the highway's path; and build.

Those on the Central Area Committee knew they would have little trouble persuading the Bureau of Public Roads to make the highway into an Interstate. New Orleans had the best possible representative in Washington imaginable, the Democratic congressman from Louisiana's second district who had helped devise the Highway Trust Fund in 1956, Hale Boggs. Boggs's roots lay in the reform movement that he and his law partner, deLessups Morrison, helped to found in the late 1930s. He had grown in stature and power since he was first elected as the youngest member of the 77th Congress in 1940. Though defeated in 1942, he returned to the 80th Congress in 1947. Throughout the 1950s, he opposed all civil rights legislation and in 1956 vowed with ninety-six other southern congressmen to take "all lawful means" to resist the Supreme Court's decision in *Brown v. Board of Education of Topeka*. But in the 1960s he became more of a national presence as he took on the stature of chairman of the House Ways and Means Committee and majority whip. He closely tied himself to the policies of John Kennedy and, after 1963, of his friend Lyndon Johnson. Boggs's political positions became more liberal than those of many of his constituents, but he appeased them by delivering big government projects to New Orleans. The Riverfront Expressway was just the sort of project he liked, one that brought money and jobs to the city, and he gave it his full support. On October 13, 1964, several months after he had voted in favor of the most sweeping civil rights legislation in the history of the country, Boggs proudly announced that the Vieux Carré elevated expressway would now be designated Interstate 310, a part of the Interstate Highway System. Mayor Victor H. Schiro, who succeeded deLessups Morrison, exulted with optimism for the future of his city: "The Riverfront Expressway and its already built and building tributaries will supplement and nourish the giant skyscrapers we are constructing in New Orleans. We are entering an age of economic dynamics. The old ways in New Orleans are done with."

Schiro had good reason to gloat. Preliminary studies had pegged the cost of the 3.5 miles at $29 million. Now that it was part of the Interstate Highway System, the road would cost New Orleans just under $3 million.

Up to October 1964, the highway had few opponents outside of a small group of dedicated preservationists and the residents of the Quarter, and many of those were willing to accept a ground-level roadway. Most thought that now the expressway had taken substantial shape in drawings, it was certain to become a reality. From the east the highway would connect with Interstate 10 at Elysian Fields Avenue, a broad thoroughfare with a neutral ground that ran diagonally up to the grid of streets in the Vieux Carré. At Esplanade, the easternmost street in the French Quarter, it would rise dramatically five stories over the railroad tracks that ran along the riverbank. At Iberville, the westernmost street in the Vieux Carré, the highway dipped into a short tunnel under the "Rivergate," a projected convention center that the city was about to construct, and then rose once again to ground level and a connection with the Greater New Orleans Bridge and the Ponchartrain Expressway. Further evidence that the highway was closer to becoming a reality came a month after Hale Boggs made his announcement. The Louisiana Highway Department began construction on the tunnel part of the highway under the future "Rivergate."

Mayor Victor H. Schiro and the powers behind him in New Orleans were wrong if they thought that the Riverfront Expressway would be built without serious opposition. As often happens, city hall and the federal officials of the Bureau of Public Roads underestimated the enormous power of local and loosely knit organizations. The preservationists were a small group, on the fringes of the power structure, but they were vocal and they had a network of ties with other individuals and groups throughout the city. Many of them thought that the expressway's effect on the Vieux Carré in general and Jackson Square in particular would be devastating.

One of the most important preservationists who had earned the respect of like-minded people throughout the city, the state, and indeed the nation, was Martha Gilmore Robinson, founder and president of the Louisiana Landmarks Society. "The automobile is a Frankenstein," said Robinson. "We've got to stop somewhere." To her and others the destruction by air and noise pollution seemed almost willful. Worse still was the highway's four-story elevation. Should the expressway be constructed, it would have the effect of a giant spite wall built to keep those in Jackson Square from having any connection whatsoever with the river that flowed before them. That November and December, as builders were digging the tunnel for part of the highway, preservationists mobilized for what they felt was the soul of New Orleans.

Anyone who wondered what the impact the Riverfront Expressway might be had simply to drive over to Claiborne Avenue, a wide commercial street to the north of the Vieux Carré. There, another Interstate was taking shape. Claiborne Avenue had once been a thriving black district of the city, filled with families and small shops. Typically a black entrepreneur operated a business on the ground floor of a building fronting the avenue and lived with his family in an apartment above. Claiborne Avenue had once boasted the longest single stand of oak trees anywhere in America. Their impressive branches reached forty feet into the sky, a leafy shelter from the sun and heavy air. The shops and homes lining the avenue abounded with commerce and life. Each spring the street became the center of the black Mardi Gras. For eleven days everyone gave themselves to revelry.

There had been virtually no opposition to building Interstate 10 down Claiborne Avenue—not from the residents, who did not possess the political power to resist the demand that they yield their land for "progress"; not from preservationists, who might at least have cared for the oaks. Preservation then was a local matter, and while there were preservationists in the Vieux Carré and the Garden District, there were none on Claiborne Avenue. This was a black neighborhood that few white people entered until Interstate 10 took them through it at fifty miles per hour. Chain saws leveled the trees. A grubbing crew, as they are called, moved in with huge machines that ripped the mighty boles from the earth and placed them into trucks to be hauled away. Where forty-foot-high oaks once stood, builders were erecting a twenty-five-foot-high elevated roadway, part of Interstate 10 that crosses the nation from Jacksonville, Florida, to Santa Monica, California.

It was after the easterly segment of Interstate 10 opened in March 1968, that residents could understand the full destructive effect of this urban expressway. Trucks and automobiles speeding by second story living rooms and bedrooms filled them ceaselessly with noise and fumes. On the ground below there was little sign of either light or life. Soon businesses moved away and residents fled, if they were able, only to be replaced by crime and instability. And in the spring the black Mardi Gras moved to brighter and quieter ground. Later, even the highway planners were appalled by what they had wrought. One engineer admitted it was a "rather grotesque structure." Another reflected, "If we had it to do over again we wouldn't." Yet planners had done it before in other cities and contemplated doing it many more times in cities across the land. The Vieux Carré expressway was a different case, they contended, and anyway the road was necessary for the survival and the future growth of the city and the port.

The French Quarter *was* a different case from Claiborne Avenue, but not in the way that the planners thought. Throughout America in the

1950s and early 1960s, highway engineers found it relatively easy to place an expressway through a black neighborhood. They took their cues from Robert Moses, who each year leveled the homes of tens of thousands of blacks to make way for ever more miles of expressways around and through New York. Black citizens did not share in a city's power structure, and as a consequence lacked a sense of civic cohesiveness. New Orleans city officials had no difficulty forcing Claiborne Avenue residents from their homes and businesses and taking their land. The white community had not cared, either. After all, the highway did not impinge on their territory. The Vieux Carré would be different, however. Residents and businesspeople had already given notice that they would not be passive when they held a large protest rally at the end of January 1965. In the years since the expressway had become a serious proposal, the nature of the Vieux Carré had changed, too. Legitimate businesses had risen and were slowly displacing the corruption. The Vieux Carré Commission, established by an amendment to the Louisiana constitution in 1936 in reaction to the destructive building of the twenties, began to exercise its mandate to preserve the "quaint and distinctive character" of the area. Fewer citizens of New Orleans advocated taking a torch to the area. Most significantly, more and more residents of the Vieux Carré who had accepted the expressway at first were beginning to question and even oppose it. They had a remarkable cohesion fostered by the nature and size of their neighborhood. Narrow streets filled with apartments, houses, and shops—along with numerous bars like the Napoleon House—enabled them to exchange information moment by moment. The editor of the Quarter's newspaper, the *Vieux Carré Courier*, was fervent and articulate in his opposition to the highway.

It was about this time that Bill Borah and Dick Baumbach met for a drink at the Napoleon House. Though he had spent a lot of time in the Quarter while he was busy failing his freshman year at Tulane and had lived there when he returned from the marines, Borah was different from most of the residents. Borah's roots were firmly planted among the most influential families in the Garden District of New Orleans. Boys from the Garden District were sent to the Newman School before being packed off to boarding school. (Borah went north to the Woodbury Forest School in Virginia. "The best thing a parent could do for a boy was to get him out of New Orleans and its temptations," Borah remarked.) They returned at vacation time for debutante parties and tennis matches at the New Orleans Lawn Tennis Club, then embarked on a college career at Tulane or at institutions like the University of Virginia or Princeton. After graduation they could expect, perhaps, to marry an ex–Mardi Gras queen, travel the St. Charles trolley line to work in the Central Business District, and take their lunch at Galatoire's, the restaurant treasured by businessmen, politicians, and those with political power.

Borah grew up in a modest-sized house on Philip Street in the Garden District. He came from a family of lawyers. His grandfather had been a lawyer in New Orleans. His great-uncle, for whom he was named, had been a lawyer and a famous Republican senator from Idaho. His father, Wayne G. Borah, had served on the federal bench since the Coolidge administration, first as a district court judge, and after 1949 on the Fifth Circuit of the Court of Appeals. Well connected with New Orleans society, the judge had been named Rex, King of the Mardi Gras Carnival, one year. A good name and reputation for probity go a long way among the best of families in the Garden District, and certainly everyone considered the Borahs to possess both. Bill Borah followed the pattern of other young men of his standing, but only up to a point. After he received his law degree from Tulane, a position with one of New Orleans's dignified law firms awaited. He clerked at a firm before graduation, but decided to study at the London School of Economics.

Borah and Dick Baumbach had been friends since their days at Newman. Athletic prowess was the coin of success among the boys at Newman, and Baumbach ranked among the wealthiest. Following in the footsteps of his father, who had been an All-American football player at Tulane, Baumbach became an all-state quarterback. In the winter he played basketball. His family, too, had its place in the great web of power that controlled the city's commerce. His father was a director of the Port of New Orleans and a good friend and business partner of Clifford Favrot, a member of the Central Area Committee and a staunch supporter of the expressway. After his career at Stanford and Tulane, Baumbach went north to study international affairs at Columbia.

As students, Borah and Baumbach had often sat late into the night talking with youthful idealism of New Orleans's problems, the power interests that were neglecting them, and what they might do. The city was in the grip of those who operated in the Central Business District and seemed, in their view, to be motivated only by profit without concern for the commonweal. In 1962, the city's powerful interests had allowed the publishing magnate Samuel I. Newhouse to add the *Times-Picayune* and the *States-Item* to his conglomerate of newspapers without any protest. They seemed unconcerned about the racial relations that were deteriorating rapidly. "It was the usual stuff that students talk about," Borah remembered. If what they were hearing at the Napoleon House was true, those same powers they had so often criticized in the past were about to wreak a great civic disaster. The day after their conversation they visited the chamber of commerce to learn about the highway. It would be six lanes, a Great Wall of China blocking the Mississippi from Jackson Square. The chamber had not seriously considered any other alternatives since Robert Moses had made his report in 1946. Several days later, Borah and Baumbach talked over coffee at Café du Monde, a broad-roofed structure in the oldest part of the French Market. They had arranged to return to their universities, but the highway was interfering with their plans. After Columbia, Baumbach intended to take a degree at Harvard Business School, which would complete his preparation for a career in international affairs. A law firm in Paris had promised Borah a job when he finished at the London School of Economics. And then there were the tickets to Olivier's *Othello*. . . .

Yet Café du Monde, part of the French Market and long one of the principal attractions in the Quarter, lay in the shadow of the future elevated highway. The next time they sat over coffee and doughnuts, fumes from sixty-eight thousand trucks and automobiles would be drifting down. The roar from six lanes of vehicles forty feet above their heads would make all conversation impossible. "Is there anything we've got to do that's more important than stopping this highway?" asked Baumbach. "At that point," Borah recalls, "a stake went down." They took leaves of absence from their schools and cashed in their plane tickets.

They might just as well have dropped out of school altogether. Unlike military battles, which rarely last more than a few days, or perhaps weeks, urban highway battles—especially after the 1960s—take place over decades. Andrew Jackson took just half an hour of fierce fighting to defeat a powerful force of well-seasoned British soldiers in the battle to save New Orleans. Highway battles, when they are finally engaged, are another matter altogether. The public can demand its chance to respond to the plans; the highways affect the lives and businesses of thousands, the natural environment, the architecture and landscape, as well as the social fabric of all the neighborhoods they cross. Lawyers representing the state, the federal government, private citizens, and civic groups file suits and countersuits. Cases sometimes move from state courts to federal courts. No one yields an inch of land without a fight. Sometimes a highway battle ends in victory either for the highway builders or for their opposition. A stalemate can be as good as a victory for the opposition. There is rarely room for compromise. Moving a road from one district to another doesn't solve the problem, it merely shifts it to a new group of citizens who are apt to be just as angry about losing their homes. The only thing that lasts longer than a highway battle is the bitterness of the individuals caught in the struggle. Usually they take that to the grave.

Between the fall of 1964, when the Bureau of Public Roads announced it was adding the Vieux Carré expressway to the federal Interstate System and the Louisiana Highway Department began digging the tunnel that would pass under the Rivergate, and January 1966, when Borah and Baumbach decided to join the opposition, preservationists had tried in vain to reason with the proponents to modify the plans. Did it have to be an elevated expressway? What about a ground-level road? What about burying the road altogether in a tunnel under the Vieux Carré? What about rethinking Robert Moses' very premise that vehicles had to move into and out of the city from the east and the west? Highway experts and officials in New Orleans, Baton Rouge, and Washington rejected every question the preservationists raised.

The chamber of commerce and the Central Area Committee were employing a strategy for getting the expressway approved that had worked well for them in the past. Their powerful members controlled every commercial interest in the city. Their influence reached into the congressional delegation, the statehouse in Baton Rouge, the mayor's office, and the city council chamber. They used the media, including the morning *Times-Picayune* and the evening *States-Item* and the CBS-affiliate television station WWL, to reject the objections of the "minority" who were opposed to progress. "If they decided to take a position or support a particular project," said Borah of the chamber and its committee, "it was a slam dunk. That's the way it happened."

Beyond the powerful commercial interests in New Orleans and the enormous bureaucratic structure of the Bureau of Public Roads, small but significant signs of change were beginning to appear that gave highway opponents some hope. After meeting with a delegation from the city in July 1965, and at the urging of Martha Robinson, Secretary of the Interior Stewart Udall said that the entire Vieux Carré should be designated a National Historic Landmark. In Washington, Lady Bird Johnson's interest in roadside clutter, especially proliferating billboards and junkyards at the roadside, made highway beautification a concern for all. People began to question the impact Interstate highways were having on their lives. Proponents of the elevated expressway did not quite understand the implications of these events. Fearing that National Historic Landmark status for the Vieux Carré might jeopardize construction of their highway, the New Orleans City Council, then dominated by the chamber of commerce, rejected the designation. Though it did not enjoy legal status as an historic landmark, everyone acknowledged the Quarter's historic significance.

By 1965, some in New York City were beginning to challenge Robert Moses' abilities as master builder and urban problem solver. "Men have begun to feel that it is safe to question Robert Moses," said the New York *Post* in an editorial that signaled it would no longer be cowed by the aura of his ability and expertise. Citizens did question, too. Contrary to his bold promises, the 627 miles of expressways Moses had built across the New York landscape not only had failed to solve traffic problems, but in some cases had exacerbated them. The low-income residents whose "slums" he had cleared to make way for his roads, and whom he had warehoused in high-rise "urban renewal" apartments, had become angry at the indignities they daily suffered. The black critic and writer James Baldwin characterized urban renewal more caustically as "Negro removal." "When you operate in an overbuilt metropolis, you have to hack your way with a meat axe," said Moses in response to the new challenges. "I'm just going to keep right on building. You do the best you can to stop it."

On the same former garbage dump that served as the site of the 1939–40 New York World's Fair, Moses had raised yet another New York World's Fair for 1964–65 that proved to be a brazen commercial promotion and a financial disaster. In 1939, the fair adopted the slogan "The World of Tomorrow." For 1964, Moses proclaimed the theme to be "Peace Through Understanding," yet there seemed to be little of either. On opening day, angry blacks, many of whom had awakened in one of Moses' urban renewal projects, sought to block Moses' superhighways that encircled the fair site. The largest exhibit at the 1939 New

York World's Fair, the one that took up the greatest number of acres and boasted the largest building, had belonged to the Association of American Railroads. Visitors walked through futuristic cars of streamlined passenger trains and enjoyed a musical review by Kurt Weill. By far the most popular exhibit, however, had been Norman Bel Geddes's Futurama, the General Motors' bright promise of superhighways that would improve the quality of American life in the "World of Tomorrow."

Twenty-five years later, the world of tomorrow had arrived. Passenger railroads faced bankruptcy, subways in many cities had broken down, and trolleys had been replaced by General Motors' buses, while urban highways seemed clogged with traffic. At the 1964 New York World's Fair, visitors found no railroad exhibit and the General Motors pavilion seemed nothing more than a visionless automobile showroom. The largest structure at Moses' fair was a tawdry Ferris wheel made to look like a U.S. Royal tire. When it closed in October 1965, the New York World's Fair had racked up at least $10 million in debt.

Still, those opposed to the expressway through the Vieux Carré were at a distinct disadvantage when dealing with the officials at city hall and in Washington. The power structure in the Central Business District might listen to them respectfully, but never seriously. Publishing their opposition became difficult, too. Aside from the biweekly *Vieux Carré Courier*, they could rely on one television station, WDSU, an NBC affiliate, and the *Clarion Herald*, the weekly newspaper of the Catholic Archdiocese of New Orleans. The Bureau of Public Roads had an obligation to weigh the concerns of all citizens of the United States before reaching a decision about a particular road. It often sent a representative to attend a public meeting, even a protest meeting. But after listening, the bureau was free to act in the way it wanted. Furthermore, historical precedent was against the opposition. While the federal government might modify the specifications of an Interstate highway project—change the alignment of a roadway, for example—it had never canceled a project altogether. Once state and federal officials designated an Interstate, it was only a matter of time before it was built.

To the mounting frustration of highway opponents, those who favored the Vieux Carré expressway quickly dismissed every argument they made. Highway proponents and the staff of the Bureau of Public Roads always assumed the air of knowing what was best for New Orleans. Their public statements, which the *Times-Picayune* and the *States-Item* dutifully published, always contained the same theme: The road was essential to keep people from fleeing to the suburbs. Working together, the proponents and federal officials would transform New Orleans into a progressive and modern city, one that could compete with thriving southern cities like Houston, Atlanta, or Dallas, which were encircling their city centers with great rings of Interstate concrete. New Orleans had to keep up.

The only significant weakness in local control of the highway debate appeared in the *Times-Picayune* and its editor, George Healy. A native southerner of Irish descent, Healy was a well-respected newspaperman who had been with the *Times-Picayune* since 1926. He stood foursquare for good government and against the corruption of Huey Long and his machine, and his articles helped to send several of the Kingfish's cronies to jail. When it came to the issue of the Riverfront Expressway, however, Healy lost all perspective. If they were lucky, readers found notices and stories about highway protest meetings buried deep inside the paper. Early on in the debate, however, opponents learned just how easy it was to goad Healy into battle. In July 1965, Walter Lowrey, a Quarter resident, sent a letter to the *Washington Post* explaining the situation in New Orleans. "Local Babbits and political entrepreneurs," wrote Lowrey, "have called upon the federal government to support (to the tune of some $30 million) an elevated expressway along the Mississippi River which will shamefully desecrate the French Quarter." Stung by the charge of Babbitry, Healy reacted in an editorial, thereby bringing it to the attention of all Orleanians. The next month the *Saturday Evening Post* published a travel article that remarked that the expressway was a "noble massacre." Again, Healy fulminated against the criticism in an editorial that took the author and publication to task. From then on, highway opponents knew they could count on Healy to articulate their criticism in an editorial reply.

Within six months of their taking up the anti-expressway cause, Borah and Baumbach became convinced that there was no way they would be able to prevail in an argument controlled by the local media, so they decided to change the nature and tone of the debate in ways that would pierce the veneer of gentility so characteristic of those who held power in New Orleans. Their backgrounds ensured they would act with courtesy; the controversy over the Vieux Carré would remain a falling out among gentlemen. ("They were sharp young men, nice people, not sleaze bags . . . both class acts," Fred Guice was quick to point out.) In March 1966, after a group of architects from San Francisco equated the Riverfront Expressway with the Embarcadero Freeway, George Healy wrote an editorial in the *Times-Picayune* saying the comparison was spurious. Later he refused to print a letter one of the architects wrote in reply. Highway opponents did, however. WHY WAS THIS LETTER NOT PRINTED? asked the title on ten thousand leaflets. Borah and Baumbach enlisted some of their debutante friends to distribute them. "They would be at key intersections of the downtown, they'd be in front of key office buildings. . . . It was particularly interesting because the fathers of some of these young women wanted to build the highway. At lunch time they would have to pass their daughters handing out leaflets." Henceforth, broadsides about the expressway became a part of the noonday scene in the Central Business District.

Borah and Baumbach realized as well that they had to make the highway into a national issue. They released a steady stream of press releases to newsmagazines, monthlies, and influential architecture critics. Knowing that the national press covered the Mardi Gras parades as they passed through the Quarter, they arranged to have anti-highway banners unfurled from balconies of houses along the route. Some balconies without banners were merely draped with black crepe to announce the impending death of Jackson Square. That year signs saying STOP THE RIVERFRONT EXPRESSWAY appeared in newspapers and on television screens across the country.

Press releases, broadsides, placards, and black crepe were hardly enough—a new ally was needed. He showed himself in the person of Edgar Bloom Stern, Jr., who decided to help Borah and Baumbach move the fight to the national level. The Stern family had long been active in New Orleans business and civic life. Stern's father, Edgar Bloom Stern, had worked hard and married well. He began as a cotton merchant in New Orleans before marrying Edith Rosenwald, daughter of Julius Rosenwald, who operated Sears Roebuck. In due time he became chairman of the board of Sears Roebuck, and also began WDSU, the city's first television station. Edgar Stern also possessed a deep sense of civic duty, spreading his money frequently and liberally among universities, the orchestra, libraries, and a variety of civic organizations. Edgar Stern, Jr., followed his father's path closely, serving on the board of Sears Roebuck and on many of the same civic organizations. On his recommendation, the Stern Family Fund, a foundation created by his father, hired Borah and Baumbach in mid-1966 to study other highway protests around the country. Their work was consistent with the fund's mandate to support "systematic reform efforts that attack the root causes of problems . . . projects designed to stop or prevent government and corporate abuses."

"It was a heady time," said Borah. "Here we were, still in our twenties, with air travel cards in our pockets flying all around the country to learn what highways were doing to cities; how people were stopping them; and how we could stop the expressway in New Orleans."

In Philadelphia, Borah and Baumbach learned of highway planners' proposals for a crosstown expressway across South Street to connect Interstate 76, the Schuylkill Expressway, with Interstate 95, the Delaware Expressway. South Street lies between stately Rittenhouse Square and an African-American neighborhood. The highway would disrupt the lives of a prosperous black district and appeared in these apprehensive times to be a wall intended to divide the blacks from whites. In a plan similar to the one for Jackson Square, highway builders also called for the Delaware Expressway, the principal Interstate between Florida and Maine, to be elevated as it ran along the Delaware River, thereby preventing residents of the city's venerable Chestnut and Walnut streets access to their historic port. As was the case with the Vieux Carré, however, a group of citizens who called themselves the Committee to Preserve our National Heritage were having difficulty persuading the builders to move the roadway entirely or put it underground.

In the District of Columbia, residents were busy protesting an inner beltway that would be connected to Virginia by a new two-mile-long bridge across the Potomac. Much of the eight-lane inner beltway would run in an open trench just a half mile from the White House. As was the case in most other urban areas, the road ran through low-income African-American neighborhoods, becoming, as one black protester charged, "a white man's road through black men's bedrooms."

In Memphis, Tennessee, Borah and Baumbach found a huge swath of houses already leveled to make way for Interstate 40. State and federal officials had designed the road to pass through the city center, as well as through one of the few plots of green to be found on a map, Overton Park. Angry protesters there were arguing that engineers had deliberately taken the homes of blacks and had not considered any reasonable alternatives.

In New York City, they saw further evidence of Robert Moses' declining influence. The three great elevated crosstown expressways that would cut Manhattan Island neatly into thirds remained mired in controversy (and would never be built). They learned also of the destruction the Interstates had wrought. The great Verrazano Bridge, part of Interstate 278 that helped to encircle New York, was nearing completion. The approach on the Brooklyn side alone had wiped out more than fifteen hundred homes, including almost the entire section known as Bay Ridge.

On the waterfront in San Francisco, they saw the elevated stub of Interstate 280, the Embarcadero Freeway, which the city council had refused to fund any further. The year Borah and Baumbach visited, the council voted to reject entirely the $280 million the Bureau of Public Roads would give to complete the highway that would serve to separate San Franciscans from their bay. Rising two stories into the air, the abandoned road had become a legend for highway protesters across the nation, a concrete and steel symbol of all they might achieve.

In Boston, Borah and Baumbach found a titanic highway battle under way. In 1955, highway builders had completed the Massachusetts Turnpike from the Berkshires in the west to the outer beltway, Route 128, at the threshold of Boston in the east. The Bureau of Public Roads later designated the road as Interstate 90. In 1960, planners proposed extending the turnpike into the heart of the city, where it would connect with an inner beltway—a $500 million, eight-lane circular route running through thirteen different communities, including Cambridge, Somerville, Charlestown, the downtown area, South End, Roxbury, Brookline, and the Fenway. Known as the Inner Belt, the highway would serve as a hub for a number of roads radiating north, south, and west. In 1961, the newly elected governor of Massachusetts, John A. Volpe, announced he would extend the turnpike twelve miles into the Prudential Center, the city's flashy new urban renewal project. As the road neared completion, Bostonians could see the price they were paying for their new highway that sliced through the western ring of stable city neighborhoods only to dump thousands of cars and trucks onto two-hundred-year-old streets designed in an age of horse and carriage.

The Inner Belt, as it was known, promised to do even more damage to the thirteen communities it would affect, but because it touched so many communities, an unusual cooperative spirit grew up among residents who heretofore had had nothing to do with each other. Suddenly people from Cambridge were traveling to Roxbury or Somerville to plan a strategy to combat the highway. Had the proposed road bypassed Cambridge, say, then the people in Cambridge would probably not have cared about the welfare of the other communities. (The same had happened in New Orleans, when the residents of the Vieux Carré had not concerned themselves when Interstate 10 destroyed Claiborne Avenue.)

Borah and Baumbach learned new ways of protest, too. In Cambridge, for example, the students at MIT had set up an alarm system as elaborate as anything devised by the Civil Defense authorities. Should bulldozers move in to clear the way for highway construction, the alarms would sound, sending students into the streets to chain themselves to the equipment and the trees.

Borah and Baumbach found the America they were crisscrossing was changing, too. Americans had been shocked in May 1960 when they learned that Dwight Eisenhower, the president whom they had revered and trusted, had lied to them when denying that the air force was flying U-2 reconnaissance planes over the Soviet Union. Even the word of the president of the United States had become suspect. As the sixties progressed, many Americans seemed to have less assurance in their country's future than they had a decade before. As a great shadow fell between the promise and the reality, cynicism seemed to spread across the land. Civil rights bills promised liberty for all citizens, but violence against blacks, including the ambush and shooting of James Meredith, the first African-American graduate of the University of Mississippi, seemed to be the reality. The Supreme Court's *Brown v. Board of Education of Topeka* promised school integration, yet after a dozen years and hundreds of court orders, southern states like Alabama still openly defied the law of the land, while in the North local boards of education practiced evasion in more subtle ways. Massive urban renewal schemes of the 1950s promised to clear slums and rejuvenate the nation's cities, yet cities seemed to be slipping further into decay. Despite promises the president and his Secretary of Defense made in 1964 and 1965 that just a few more troops and bombs would force the Viet Cong and North Vietnamese into submission, the Communists seemed to be stronger than ever as they tenaciously endured the United States' bombing of North Vietnam's capital, Hanoi, and its port city of Haiphong.

On all fronts, long-held assumptions were being challenged. The technocrats who had spoken with such authority in the twenties, who had flooded into Washington beginning with Franklin Roosevelt's administration, and who had become a standard part of the federal government, suddenly found ordinary citizens asking questions and holding firm convictions about matters that formerly they would have left to "experts." For two days in 1966, demonstrators across the nation protested the war in Vietnam. Students at the University of Wisconsin took over the administration building in opposition to the military draft. Students at Amherst College and New York University walked out of their commencement ceremonies when the Secretary of Defense, Robert McNamara, rose to accept an honorary degree. That year, as Procter and Gamble began marketing Pampers, the first disposable diapers, and the Department of Interior published a list of endangered species of wildlife (including the nation's symbol, the bald eagle), many people began to question what they were doing to the environment of their nation and the planet. Often—and this was the case with the New Orleans expressway—people who raised the questions found the technocrats' answers to be wanting.

That summer the Arthur D. Little research firm published a study of all transportation planning in New Orleans that showed how thin some of the technocratic expertise could be. Underwritten by the Stern Family Fund, the study demonstrated that planning rested almost exclusively in the preserve of the Central Planning Committee and therefore served principally the special interests of the Central Business District. Furthermore, no group had considered alternative routes for the expressway since Robert Moses had presented his plan two decades earlier. To Borah, Baumbach, and Edgar Stern, the Little report carried enough weight to enable them to mount a lawsuit.

In the spring of 1966, two important events took place in Washington that in the course of time would have a profound effect on the controversy in New Orleans.

First, on the Senate floor, Pennsylvania's senior senator, the patrician Joseph Sill Clark, unleashed an attack on the highway program almost without equal in its ferocity. "It is presently being operated by barbarians," Clark said. "We ought to have some civilized understanding of just what we do to spots of historic interest and great beauty by the building of eight-lane highways through the middle of our cities." Clark knew of what he spoke: While he was mayor of Philadelphia from 1952 to 1956, planners had designed many of the roads that were later built as part of the Interstate Highway System. Foremost among them was Interstate 76, the Schuylkill Expressway. Named for the river whose path it follows, the Schuylkill Expressway was an engineering and civic disaster. More dangerous than most Interstates, commuters called it the "Surekill." Engineers added extra lanes in hopes of alleviating the daily traffic jams, but they had little effect. One planner even proposed doubling the capacity by adding a second level to the highway. Its most destructive section passed through the city's famous Fairmount Park, curtailing almost all access to the west bank of the Schuylkill River. Clark and Richardson Dilworth, his successor as mayor, intended the Schuylkill Expressway to be part of a new highway system that would bring about a renaissance in downtown Philadelphia and stem the flow of citizens to the suburbs. Yet since 1950, the city's population had decreased by 107,000 people and the exodus showed signs of increasing rather than decreasing.

Other senators followed Joseph Clark's lead. Wayne Morse of Oregon, never at a loss for inflammatory words, titled his speech "The Uglification of America." Ralph Yarborough of Texas, the state with the most miles of Interstate highways, grew concerned that a proposed Interstate might destroy San Antonio's Brackinridge Park. Yarborough used his time on the Senate floor to decry the effect of Interstates that have "cut great swaths through urban communities . . . and the intricate, closely woven texture of the city's tapestry has been demolished. . . . One of the finest ways a citizen can express his patriotism is to join the fight to save as much as possible of America the beautiful."

The second event also took place on Capitol Hill. In a special message to Congress of March 2, 1966, President Johnson proposed a consolidation and reorganization of the nation's agencies that regulated roads, ports, waterways, and air travel into a single Department of Transportation with cabinet-level status. "The country's transportation facilities respond to the needs of an earlier America," said Johnson. It was time to create "a coordinated transportation system." On April 1, 1967, the Bureau of Public Roads became a part of the Federal Highway Administration within the new department. With its $4.4 billion highway program, it ranked as the largest agency within the Department of Transportation.

In the fall of 1966 and winter of 1967, Borah, Baumbach, and Stern decided it was time to move their opposition to the Riverfront Expressway from protest to litigation. Quietly, they pursued their options with the prominent Washington attorney Louis Oberdorfer. Oberdorfer's credentials were impressive: a B.A. from Dartmouth and a law degree from Yale; clerk for Hugo Black on the Supreme Court; assistant attorney general for tax litigation in the Kennedy administration. Now a partner in the Washington law firm Wilmer, Cutler, and Pickering, Oberdorfer had a reputation for writing legal briefs that were models of thoroughness and research.

Working with Borah and Baumbach (who went to Washington to assist him), Louis Oberdorfer reviewed federal and state highway and preservation statutes to produce an ironclad legal brief that became the linchpin of the case against the Vieux Carré expressway. Thus far, highway planners in Louisiana and Washington had overlooked four sections of federal laws pertinent to the proposed expressway: The Federal-Aid Highway Act of 1962 stated that the federal highway administrator should not approve a highway project unless it is based on "a continuing, comprehensive transportation planning process." The 1966 Department of Transportation Act stated that the Secretary of Transportation could not approve a highway through a historic site unless "there is no feasible and prudent alternative." It also required that the Advisory Council on Historic Preservation must have an opportunity to comment on any highway that would have an effect on a historic site. Finally, the National Historic Preservation Act of 1966 called for the Secretary of Transportation to consider the "effect" such a highway would have on a historic site. On April 13, Oberdorfer submitted the brief in a hearing with the new federal highway administrator, Lowell K. Bridwell.

Bridwell's appointment as federal highway administrator signaled that a subtle but important shift in highway policy was taking place on the federal level. A former correspondent for the Associated Press and the Ohio *State Journal*, Bridwell joined the Scripps-Howard Washington bureau in 1958 to report on transportation issues. The most important story he covered, of course, was the progress of the Interstate Highway System and the changes it was bringing to the nation. Bridwell did not confine himself to Washington, however. He attended national and local meetings of groups like the American Road Builders Association and the American Association of State Highway Officials. As he traveled the country, he became well versed in the intricacies of finance, construction, federal and state relationships, and, as time progressed, the emerging controversies over the Interstate's incursion into urban areas. In 1964, he joined the federal government, acquiring first the bureaucratic title of "acting deputy federal highway administrator" and, later, "deputy secretary of commerce for transportation." When the Department of Transportation began in 1967, he took office as federal highway administrator. Unlike all others who had preceded him in the post, however, Lowell K. Bridwell lacked a degree or any formal training in civil engineering.

"The last thing a bureaucrat wants is to receive a memorandum like the one we produced from one of the top legal firms in the country," Borah recalled. "They knew we were playing hardball. They knew they had to take us seriously." Along with the brief, Oberdorfer presented nationally recognized architects and environmental designers to give their views on the proposed highway. "The tide has changed in America," warned one landscape architect, "people are awakening to the problem of cities and the uglification of America." Bridwell decided he had better pay a visit to New Orleans.

By the time of Bridwell's arrival in June 1967, the opponents of the Riverfront Expressway had added significant numbers to their ranks. A few months earlier, New Orleanians had learned just why highway proponents attached such importance to building an expressway through the Vieux Carré. If state highway planners had their way, the expressway would not terminate at the Greater New Orleans Bridge but would continue about five miles upriver and connect with another divided state highway, the Earhart Expressway. Plans also called for a new "uptown" bridge across the Mississippi at Napoleon Avenue, deep in a residential area above the Garden District that would lead eventually to a planned west bank expressway. Planners had decided to turn residential Napoleon Avenue into an expressway to serve the bridge. In short, highway planners and members of the Central Business District intended to turn the entire New Orleans riverfront into an expressway.

Singlehandedly the Louisiana Highway Board had transformed what heretofore had been a local community issue into one that affected the entire region around New Orleans. The proposed extension to the Vieux Carré expressway would cut through the Lower Garden District and cross the magnificent Audubon Park that served thousands of residents. Residents of these areas who had been largely indifferent to the fight in the French Quarter now understood that an expressway through the Quarter did far more than create a wall between Jackson Square and the Mississippi. The road would deny them access to the river, too, and it promised to bring untold numbers of trucks and automobiles into their neighborhoods. They realized, too, that stopping the expressway through the Quarter would kill the entire highway project.

Groups that formerly had little to do with each other formed powerful new alliances. Blacks in the Lower Garden District near the river found themselves meeting with whites about a common problem that went beyond race. Upper-income residents of the university area around Audubon Park and the Garden District discovered that their fate was intertwined with the Quarter contingent. Many of these residents joined to form a new group opposed to the highways, the Crescent Council of Civic Associations. Even the New Orleans Junior Chamber of Commerce, which had heretofore taken no interest in highways, called for a new study leading to a comprehensive transportation plan.

Citizens on both sides of the issue seemed disenchanted with city government officials, too. In the years since he had boasted about what Interstate 310 would do for New Orleans, Mayor Victor H. Schiro watched popular support for the project drift away. Orleanians watched the mayor blunder his way through the emerging controversy. In early 1965, Schiro had hired a local engineer to produce "the first complete, impartial survey of the whole situation," which prompted George Healy at the *Times-Picayune* to complain, "there's been too much conversation and too little action." When the engineer made his report after just a cursory appraisal, preservationists and other expressway opponents criticized Schiro for breaking his promise to undertake a thorough study. In January 1966, Schiro proposed a surface-level, four-lane expressway through the Vieux Carré, only to have it attacked by the Mississippi Bridge Authority, the Levee Board, and the preservationists. Failing in that effort, the mayor proposed a freeway with two decks—three lanes below ground and three on the surface. Both sides attacked the proposal as impractical.

Proof that the expressway issue had become increasingly divisive came at the contentious city council meeting of June 16, 1966. After twelve hours of debate, the council rejected by a five-to-two vote a motion to reexamine all transportation in the New Orleans metropolitan area. Council members then voted four to three to put themselves on record "in a positive manner regarding the expressway."

Such was the temper of New Orleans in June 1967, when Lowell K. Bridwell opened the public meeting on the Vieux Carré expressway. "We did not come down here with an alternative plan, but to see if alternatives can be developed," the federal highway administrator began. Would a ground-level route be feasible, Bridwell asked, if some of the railroad tracks were removed? Yes, conceded the president of the Levee Board, but all responsible commissions had recommended an elevated structure. "Why not just take it easy," the president added, "and enjoy a little of our Creole gumbo." Bridwell promised that he would make a recommendation to the Secretary of Transportation and that he would make a decision in two or three months.

Two months passed. Three. Fall passed into winter. Finally, Bridwell disclosed his decision in an interview for a magazine article entitled "Reconciling the Conflict of Highways and Cities." "A city's conflict with a highway usually means an internal conflict," said Bridwell. "It means a city has not yet thrashed out what it wants to be." New Orleans had not based its Riverfront Expressway decision on "a continuing, comprehensive transportation planning process," as called for in the Federal-Aid Highway Act of 1962. Bridwell, however, had devised his own three-part solution: Elevate the expressway except at Jackson Square, where it would dip to ground level; stabilize the levee in front of the square and move the highway fifty feet toward the river; and redevelop the riverfront with a hotel and shopping complex.

Bridwell's compromise decision made little sense. Even though Louis Oberdorfer's testimony had persuaded him that New Orleans lacked a "bona fide long-range transportation plan," as required by federal law, he decided to issue, almost ex-cathedra, a highway policy of his own devising. Rather than resolve the dispute, Bridwell's plan intensified it. Preservationists were in no mood for a settlement, either. The five percent grade on the ramps from the elevated to the ground-level portions of the expressway would create an intolerable noise of trucks gearing up and down. They had learned that highway planners wanted to build an entrance and exit for the expressway at Iberville and Bienville streets, which would connect with Interstate 10 north of the Vieux Carré. If the planners had their way, two of New Orleans's narrowest streets would become one-way channels for a stream of traffic between the two highways. The subjection of the Vieux Carré to the business and highway interests would be complete.

In the spring and summer of 1968, the national press—especially the newsweeklies—ran stories on the Riverfront Expressway. "A war that may well determine the shape of urban America," said *Newsweek* in a story the magazine titled "Fighting the Freeway." Military metaphors came to mind easily that spring and summer as America seemed to have given itself over to violence. In March, General William C. Westmoreland called for 206,000 more troops to fight in Vietnam, while that month the number of U.S. casualties exceeded those of the

Korean War. A protest march in Memphis led by the Nobel Prize winner for peace, Martin Luther King, Jr., deteriorated into a riot that left one black youth dead. King himself and Robert F. Kennedy fell victims to assassins' bullets. Student protests and riots at Columbia University closed the campus. It seemed that almost every political, civic, and intellectual institution in the United States was under attack.

Few of America's grand plans for the cities were working as well-meaning federal and local officials had intended. The United States had begun a "War on Poverty"—yet another martial metaphor—but urban decay seemed to increase. That spring, New York reported eight hundred thousand of the city's apartments to be substandard. Highways, too, represented the government, the technocracy, the establishment. Those who supported them were not to be trusted. The optimism Americans held a decade ago was but a memory.

The battle in New Orleans continued against this backdrop of unrest and failure. Following Bridwell's lead, the highway department recommended a grade-level expressway. With the support of the chamber of commerce and various agencies concerned with the river and docks, the city council endorsed the proposal four votes to three. It was December 1968, and time was running out for Bridwell and the Johnson administration. Three days before he left office, Lowell K. Bridwell approved the New Orleans Riverfront Expressway. The roadway "not only avoids interference with the aesthetic quality of the area," said Bridwell, "but will, in fact, bring new development possibilities."

The final act of the New Orleans drama appeared close at hand. The presidential election of 1968, however, introduced a *deus ex machina,* an unexpected intervention brought about by the most unlikely agent. President-elect Nixon nominated the governor of Massachusetts and former federal highway administrator John Anthony Volpe to fill the post of Secretary of Transportation.

Believing the action lay in foreign affairs, Nixon cared little about domestic matters and probably least of all about the Department of Transportation. No matter who was in charge, so the new president believed, departments like Housing and Urban Development, Commerce, and Transportation would just rumble on as they had in the past. Still, he owed John Volpe a sop. Whenever he had thought it useful during the primary campaign, he dropped the governor's name as a possible running mate. It had been a fiction, of course. Nixon wanted a vice presidential candidate who would be better able to appeal to the South, a tough and unpleasant scrapper, who would act as Nixon himself had when he served as vice president, so he passed over Volpe in favor of Spiro Agnew, governor of Maryland. Making Volpe Secretary of Transportation would assuage his feelings as well as add an Italian-American to the cabinet. The American Association of State Highway Officials had recommended him and him alone for the position. Volpe possessed still another attribute to recommend him for the job, one that the president-elect could not understand: The man actually cared about transportation matters.

Volpe's job would not be an easy one, for it was not an especially tranquil period for transportation of any kind in the United States. The Penn Central Railroad—itself a merger of two failing lines, the New York Central and the Pennsylvania—was caught in a swift stream that led to bankruptcy. Hijackers were commandeering passenger airliners at an alarming rate. Air traffic controllers were forming a union and talking about a work slowdown or even a strike. Increasingly angry and impatient citizens across the country were frustrating Interstate highway construction through contentious litigation. And in the cities and suburbs, automobiles and trucks clogged the streets and highways. Nevertheless, Volpe accepted the position with enthusiasm. On January 20, 1969, Volpe moved into the department's headquarters at 800 Independence Avenue. From his office he could see the new Department of Transportation headquarters at 400 Seventh Street. He knew the building well, for it was being erected by the John A. Volpe Construction Company.

Across America, preservationists and highway opponents went into shock at word of Volpe's appointment. Certainly nothing in Volpe's record suggested he would call for anything but more concrete. He was a contractor by trade. As commissioner of public works in Massachusetts, he inaugurated the most ambitious highway building plan in the state's history; as interim federal highway administrator, he had ensured a fast start to the construction of the Interstate Highway System; as governor, he had pushed the Massachusetts Turnpike twelve miles into the heart of Boston. Whenever Lyndon Johnson or his Secretary of Transportation, Alan Boyd, had contemplated a cutback in highway construction, Volpe issued a broadside condemning their failure to keep the construction crews going full-bore. He had been an anathema to conservationists and neighborhood preservationists. As one critic said, "John Volpe never saw a highway he didn't like." Volpe's appointment of Francis C. Turner to be federal highway administrator also gave the preservationists pause. The former secretary to the Clay committee and assistant federal highway administrator had always championed Interstate construction in urban areas.

On the afternoon of January 27, just seven days after Volpe became secretary, highway opponents took hope. Word filtered out of the Department of Transportation that he had withdrawn approval for the New Orleans project because the Advisory Council on Historic Preservation had not considered it, as required by the National Historic Preservation Act of 1966. "A ground-level expressway between Canal Street and Elysian Fields, in our opinion, will do no violence to the historic charms of the Vieux Carré," said the *Times-Picayune* editorial that advised the council to act promptly. The council did just that, but not in the way George Healy wished. The expressway, reported the council, would "have a serious effect on that quality of the district which has been described as the 'tout ensemble,' a quality of high importance." It would introduce "visible, audible, and atmospheric conditions out of keeping" with the historic district. The secretary should seek an alternate route or depress the highway. The battle was not yet over.

"Another stumbling block was thrown on the road of progress," said the president of the chamber of commerce as he himself stumbled through a thicket of metaphors. "Isn't it amazing that here in 1969," said a WWL-TV executive in an editorial, "more than four years after it was first approved—we are still conducting surveys of the proposed Riverfront Expressway." Clearly, expressway proponents had begun to sense that they were losing. A flurry of appeals ensued. Mayor Schiro and Councilman Moon Landrieu flew to Washington to see Frank Turner. The New Orleans Central Area Council hired a public relations firm for $6,000 to conduct a belated "educational" campaign promoting the virtues of the expressway.

On the afternoon of Friday, March 28, 1969, former President Dwight David Eisenhower sat propped upon pillows in a bed at Walter Reed Army Hospital in Washington. Eisenhower was now seventy-eight and had recently suffered another heart attack. "I want to go," he said to his wife, son, and grandson at his side. "God take me." With that, the former five-star general and thirty-fourth president of the United States closed his eyes and died. Five days later, on the morning of April 2, a twelve-car funeral train arrived at the platform of the old brick railroad depot in Abilene. It was from the same spot the young farm boy had started out for West Point fifty-eight years earlier. Police estimated the crowd at the burial to have been between seventy-five thousand and a hundred thousand people. Most who attended, including President Nixon and former President Johnson, came not by train but over the Interstate highways that Eisenhower had created. However, many who wanted to attend could not because they were stuck in a three-mile traffic jam on Interstate 70.

Understanding that his decision to rescind the approval of the Vieux Carré expressway had raised a storm in New Orleans, John Volpe sent his assistant secretary for urban systems and environment, James D'Orma Braman, to meet with both sides in the controversy. In one of his first acts since taking office, Volpe had created the assistant secretary's post so that someone could work full-time addressing the growing dissatisfaction of people across the nation with the highways' incursion into cities. He was beginning to question some of the rules highway engineers had cherished for years. Braman was well qualified for his position. As a former city council member and mayor of Seattle, Washington, he had listened many times to highway authorities justify the construction of Interstate 5 through the city, and he had witnessed the displacement of thousands of families and the razing of five thousand homes to make way for the highway. He knew firsthand how an Interstate could cut a city in half, destroying the stability of neighborhoods in its path.

After meeting on June 6, Braman promised a decision "in a month or two." In fact he made his recommendation to John Volpe in less than a month. On the afternoon of Monday, July 1, Bill Borah and Dick Baumbach were working in their office when a friend phoned from Washington. "Have you heard?" the caller asked Borah. "Secretary Volpe canceled the highway." Borah and Baumbach both agreed they would believe the story only when it appeared in the *Times-Picayune*. The next morning a banner headline on the paper's front page announced Volpe's decision.

Those who had supported the expressway were bitter. "We were the villains," said Guice a quarter century later. "We thought we were doing the Vieux Carré a service by getting all these heavy trucks out. . . . We weren't the bogey men they tried to portray us as being." For a time, Guice remembers, tempers flared just at the mention of the expressway. "I damn near needed a visa to get into the Vieux Carré. This was a very divisive topic." Reflecting on how they could have lost to two young men and a group of preservationists, he commented, "They were good salesmen. They had a powerhouse behind them and money was no object. We were outpoliticked." There was another reason, too, which Guice reflected on a quarter century later. He called it "the wives." "I'm sure there was more than one wife who jumped on more than one husband, who said 'Why are you doing this? I can only think of my own home.' "

Exhausted though they were, Borah and Baumbach quietly celebrated. "I think I was drunk for about a week," Borah said. Yet he emphasized the celebration had to be restrained. "We were in an armed camp," Borah said. "It didn't do to gloat. We had to get along with these people."

Having been in the trenches for so many years, freeway opponents were wary that the fight was not over. Was Volpe being honest? Was this just another tactic to slip the expressway through after the opposition quieted down? Perhaps the apprehensions were justified. For the next several years, champions of the Riverfront Expressway tried to revive the project, but to no avail. In the next two decades, some diehard advocates sought a way to slip the Riverfront Expressway into future transportation studies. Up to 1985, it appeared on master plans for the city. Today there are some who still want to raise the girders and pour the concrete.

Though he no longer wants to build the highway, nearly thirty years later, Fred Guice believes that "the traffic problem has never been solved. The Vieux Carré is still shaking apart on its foundations." Indeed, several walls, including part of the Pontalba Building, have collapsed. And, Guice says, "We've still got problems with the port."

The "Second Battle of New Orleans," some called it. Indeed, it was a battle. But the analogy ends there. Andrew Jackson fought and defeated the British at New Orleans on January 8, 1815, two weeks *after* the Treaty of Ghent ended the War of 1812. Jackson's was truly the last battle of the war. The Battle of New Orleans that took place a century and a half later represents the first victory in a much larger urban civil war that was raging across the American landscape.

Once President Eisenhower signed the Interstate highway bill on June 29, 1956, states scrambled to begin construction. Missouri was the first to begin a project in August, but neighboring Kansas was the first to complete a section of the new highway in November.

(*American Highway Users Alliance*)

Ribbon cuttings like this one, celebrating the opening of a new section of Interstate in Wisconsin, took place thousands of times, but as more and more miles of Interstate were completed, Americans seemed indifferent and sometimes even hostile to their presence.

(*State Historical Society of Wisconsin*)

When the Interstates entered the cities and disrupted the lives of thousands, citizens began to question the very purpose of the highway system and what it was doing to the nation. One of the first battles was fought in New Orleans, where highway officials wanted to erect a forty-foot-high elevated highway between the Mississippi River and Jackson Square in the city's famous French Quarter. William E. Borah (left) and Richard Baumbach (right), two young scions of the New Orleans establishment, organized protests and a legal case, eventually preventing the highway from being built.

(Courtesy of William E. Borah)

A model of the proposed elevated expressway through New Orleans.

(Courtesy of William E. Borah)

While the Borah and Baumbach coalition succeeded in stopping the Interstate through the French Quarter, New Orleans's African-American residents did not have the political power to keep an elevated section of Interstate 10 from destroying their neighborhood on Claiborne Avenue. The avenue had once boasted the longest single stand of oak trees anywhere in America. But in the early 1960s, chain saws leveled the trees and builders erected a twenty-five-foot-high elevated roadway, a part of Interstate 10, which crosses the nation from Jacksonville, Florida, to Santa Monica, California. The neighborhood was destroyed.

*(All photos courtesy of
William E. Borah)*

Across America in the 1970s and 1980s, citizens took to the streets to stop highways from destroying their neighborhoods. In many cases they were successful.

(American Highway Users Alliance)

At the same time, highway lobbyists bemoaned America's clogged expressways and argued for more roads.

(American Highway Users Alliance)

(Darius Aidala, California Department of Transportation)

At times protesters have succeeded not only in preventing the Interstates from being built but in actually tearing them down. Such was the case in San Francisco, where the building of the Embarcadero Freeway was stopped—and then completed sections of the highway were demolished. As these photographs of the San Francisco Ferry Building make clear, the results of removing the highway were dramatic.

(G. P. "Bill" Wong, Federal Highway Administration)

As Americans traveled further from home on the Interstates, they appreciated the familiarity of franchised services. Charles Kemmons Wilson of Holiday Inn and Ray Kroc of McDonald's understood this better than most. The very first franchises that reassured motorists were gasoline stations with names like Esso, Gulf, Mobil, or Cities Service. Their symbols, like the Esso logo on the pumps at a Pennsylvania Turnpike service area, assured motorists of a consistent quality.

A quarter century after the 1939 New York World's Fair proclaimed the "world of tomorrow," the automobile dominated American life. Passenger railroads faced bankruptcy, subways in many cities had broken down, and trolleys had been replaced by General Motors' buses, while urban highways seemed clogged with traffic. The largest structure at the 1964 New York World's Fair was a tawdry Ferris wheel made to look like a U.S. Royal Tire.

In 1973 the Organization of Petroleum Exporting Countries, or OPEC, imposed an embargo on oil exports to the United States. As gasoline prices soared, a succession of presidents urged conservation. Public sentiment, this cartoon suggests, sharply turned against those who threatened America's dependence on the automobile.

The landscape transformed. Breezewood, Pennsylvania, near the intersection of Interstates 70 and 76.

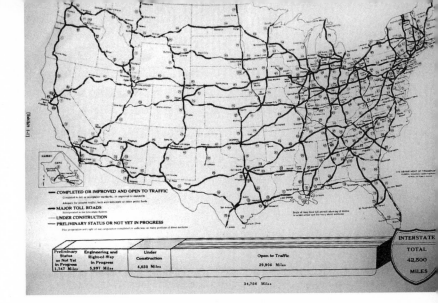

COMPLETED OR IMPROVED AND OPEN TO TRAFFIC

MAJOR TOLL ROADS

UNDER CONSTRUCTION

PRELIMINARY STATUS OR NOT YET IN PROGRESS

Preliminary Status or Not Yet in Progress 3,747 Miles	Engineering and Right-of-Way in Progress 5,997 Miles	Under Construction 4,850 Miles	Open to Traffic 29,906 Miles

34,756 Miles

INTERSTATE

TOTAL

42,500

MILES

BUSTING THE TRUST

I think that the problem about highways is [that] we permit engineers to have a profound effect upon cities and, in fact, design them.

IAN MCHARG

A Federal Highway Administration "status map" of the Interstate Highway System, March 1970. Each quarter, the federal government published the map in engineering periodicals, and occasionally in mass-circulation magazines like *Life* and the *Saturday Evening Post*, to show its progress in completing the network of superhighways. By March 1970, the status map showed nearly thirty thousand miles—three-quarters of the puzzle pieces—were in place and close to five thousand more miles were under construction. For nearly fourteen years, highway builders had been transforming thin lines that denoted "under construction" or "not yet in progress" into bold red lines signifying "open to the public." Since the Bureau of Public Roads published its first Interstate highway map in 1956, officials had added a small inset depicting "H1," "H2," and "H3," Hawaii's Interstate highways on the island of Oahu. Though the highways could not be truly "interstate," they would provide express connections to important military bases.

To be sure, some important pieces of the puzzle were missing. Interstate

80 crossed only four states without a break, and in two of those—Ohio and Indiana—highway officials had simply designated Interstate status to already constructed toll roads. There were large gaps on Interstate 90, the major northern transcontinental route. Engineers had not even made preliminary surveys on major sections of Texas's Interstate 10. Nor were any of the principal north–south routes—Interstates 5, 35, and 95—entirely complete.

Still, the status maps showed what was possible. In North Dakota, drivers could take Interstate 94 from Fargo on the Red River clear to the Montana state line in under five hours. Interstate 87 was complete from the South Bronx to the Canadian border, and drivers on Interstate 5 had a clear run from the Canadian border at Blaine, Washington, to Hornbrook, at the California state line.

From an airplane the changes the Interstate Highway System had brought to the American landscape were even more apparent, especially at interchanges. The entrances and exits usually divided the land into four quadrants, each ready for developers to transform into cash-producing real estate. By this time it was conventional wisdom among real estate speculators that an interchange on an Interstate would start a succession of events: gas stations, motels, and quick-food restaurants opened nearby. Farther away, housing developments or shopping centers took shape. The average distance between exits on the Interstates was three miles, about seven times as many exits as there were on toll roads like the Pennsylvania Turnpike or the New York Thruway. Builders and speculators who had seen the potential of land near toll roads quickly realized the federal government had given them seven times as many opportunities to become rich.

It was from airplane cockpits that two entrepreneurs, Raymond Albert Kroc and Charles Kemmons Wilson, often chose the sites for their establishments. In 1954, Kroc, a Bohemian-born milkshake-machine salesman, bought the rights to franchise a hamburger business from the McDonald brothers. Following the lead of the brothers, who had located their restaurant at the western end of Route 66 in the land of early California freeways, Kroc located his franchise adjacent to great highways, in places accessible only by automobile. In 1952, Wilson, a high school dropout, former popcorn salesman, and jukebox distributor, opened a motel named after the Bing Crosby movie *Holiday Inn* on one of the four main roads leading into Memphis, Tennessee. Though perhaps not the first to create motel and fast-food franchises, Kroc and

Divided Highways

Wilson were the first to locate them in relation to the Interstates. From the vantage point of an airplane cockpit, they could see the new patterns of American life that their establishments were helping to create. By the late 1960s a new McDonald's was opening every business day, and a new Holiday Inn every three.

Those building the highways took pride in their accomplishments. In 1970, the American Association of State Highway Officials published an eleven-page "Report on Benefits of Interstate Highways" in its quarterly magazine. The statistics were impressive and the figures precise: "The Interstate program has achieved an average 10 percent reduction in travel time between cities." Travel speed in intercity corridors increased from exactly 35.6 miles per hour to 46.4. The highways had saved $15.8 billion in accident costs. The payload weight of trucks increased from an average of two and a half to sixty tons, while at the same time shipping costs had decreased. Communities benefited as highways helped to raise land values. In Washington, D.C., "one minute less driving time from the central business district has been found to be the equivalent of $65 in the price of houses." The Interstates expanded opportunities for recreational travel. The average distance of family vacation trips increased substantially, and the more than twenty-five hundred rest areas on Interstates made that vacation travel still more enjoyable. Even Sunday attendance at the thirty-six churches located near interchanges on Interstate 495, the Beltway around Washington, D.C., had increased faster than it had at other churches farther from the highway.

The list of benefits went on: Cities had prospered because of the Interstates. Good highway planning could "generate positive community benefits." Many homeowners displaced by a new road have "taken the opportunity . . . to upgrade their properties." The report confidently predicted that "this will be even more common in the future as highway and other relocation workers learn how to evaluate and replace intangible aspects of the displaced person's environment." Not even the environmental quality need be affected by a six-lane highway carrying tens of thousands of vehicles a day. Some Interstates, the report noted, had rest areas "utilizing Indian mounds, dinosaur tracks, or other historic or natural features." No list of benefits would be complete without an enumeration of the aesthetic qualities of Interstates. "Recent advances in the design of Interstate highways not only make them appealing, minimize neighborhood social and economic disruption, but are also beneficial in reducing air and noise pollution levels," the Panglossian author noted.

Tom Lewis

"A modern, well designed elevated structure is visually pleasing, does not inhibit mobility and reduces noise levels in nearby areas."

Members of the Road Gang were speaking only to themselves. On the hard surface of the landscape, away from the abstraction of a map, the perspective from the sky, or the glowing, self-serving treatise, all was not well either on the highway or in the nation. And the Road Gang knew it.

Confrontation and reassessment became the norm in America during the 1970s. Much of the confrontation originated in the deeply held opposition to the Vietnam War. Demonstrations against the war that began in Lyndon Johnson's presidency intensified in Richard Nixon's. In May 1970, when Nixon announced he had expanded the war into Cambodia, protests erupted throughout the nation. After National Guardsmen killed four anti-war demonstrators at Kent State University, students from Maine to California closed down their colleges and took to the streets. The president characterized those at colleges and universities who opposed his policies as "bums," while his right-hand hatchet man, Vice President Spiro Agnew, compared them to "enemy soldiers." That fall, Nixon and Agnew continued their appeal to the darker angels of Americans—and further divided the nation—in one of the nastiest midterm congressional elections in America's history.

The president seemed to escalate confrontation throughout the land. Bishop Spottswood, chairman of the NAACP, said Nixon had a calculated anti-Negro policy. Black riots erupted in cities like Hartford and Atlanta, and even New Bedford, Massachusetts. In New Haven, the president of Yale professed to be skeptical that black revolutionaries could get "a fair trial anywhere in the United States." Malcontents protesting one injustice or another set off bombs in places as diverse as New York; Madison, Wisconsin; and Omaha, Nebraska. Police officers were being shot, while unprovoked police attacks on blacks and protest groups became the norm. Demonstrators in San Jose threw eggs, rocks, and bottles at the president's motorcade. Dissent even reached into Nixon's cabinet when the Secretary of Interior, Walter Hickel, said that the vice president's continued attacks on college students only served to harden their hostility and foreclose communication. Hickel's statement certainly foreclosed all communication he would have with his president. After the November midterm elections Nixon fired him.

Divided Highways

In 1970, the fissures in American culture that had first appeared in the sixties only became deeper. Nothing seemed to be working as smoothly as it had in the past, and some parts of society were falling apart. The nation's air—especially in the cities—became more and more clogged with pollution as automobiles burned 130,000 gallons of gas each minute. That year, Americans spent $131 billion for highway transportation and $75 billion for all education programs. The Penn Central Railroad filed for bankruptcy. Americans' purchasing power declined precipitously, while the jobless rate climbed. The United Automobile Workers closed General Motors for fifty-seven days, the longest and bitterest strike for the automaker in two decades. General Motors paid Ralph Nader $425,000 to settle his invasion-of-privacy suit against the corporation. To discredit Nader, whose book *Unsafe at Any Speed* had indicted the Chevrolet Corvair and General Motors, the corporation had put private detectives on his trail and sought to tempt him with prostitutes. (To their consternation, detectives could find no flaws in their dour and humorless target.) When papers published the seamy revelations, the news further tarnished the automaker's image, making Nader into a hero, and *Unsafe at Any Speed* into a best-seller.

The Road Gang felt the unrest and the reassessment, too. A generally conservative and quiet group, they were not inclined to question their government or its policies in international affairs. Why should they? Since the time of Thomas MacDonald, they regarded themselves as above political disagreements, because they had a single mission of giving Americans the highways they needed. They were builders of Interstate *and* defense highways, and active partners with those who were working to preserve the nation's security. They could not quite understand why so many were questioning and even repudiating their policies. Nevertheless, this was happening, and they saw it in the stunning defeats of two of their most ardent champions in the Congress.

On September 15, 1970, George Hyde Fallon, the congressman from Baltimore who had written the legislation creating the Interstate Highway System and who had consistently supported any request of the highway lobby, was defeated in a primary election to run for a fourteenth term in the House of Representatives. His opponent was an unsmiling, thirty-seven-year-old lawyer, Rhodes scholar, former Princeton basketball star, and classmate of Ralph Nader's, Paul Sarbanes, who gathered support from anti-war groups and environmentalists. Fallon proved an easy target. He had steadfastly supported Johnson's and

Nixon's stances on Vietnam. He had never questioned the need for a highway despite the Interstate controversies that were smoldering in Baltimore. Shortly before the election, when polls confirmed what the seasoned politician sensed, Fallon remarked, "I had thought my name would go down in history because of the Interstate bill. Now highways seem to be unpopular." After his defeat, he reflected, "I only tried to help people."

On November 3, 1970, Albert Arnold Gore, who had shepherded the act creating the Interstate Highway System through the Senate, lost his seat to William Brock, a young Republican congressman inflamed with the political tactics of Richard Nixon and the rhetoric of Spiro Agnew. Throughout the campaign, Brock portrayed the senator as pro-Communism and anti-South, pro-black and anti-prayer, pro-busing and anti-guns. Gore would leave to his son his hope to be vice president, or even president. But the Road Gang looked after their own. In January 1971, Gore left the Senate for a seat on the board of directors of the Occidental Petroleum Corporation.

The state highway officials, automobile manufacturers, and truckers who made up the Road Gang took some comfort in knowing that election defeats of representatives and senators—even those who looked favorably upon highway construction—were part of the natural selection process in Washington. As important as Fallon and Gore had been, others on the public works committees were working their way to the top and would no doubt dispense the pork—a highway for one state, a bridge for another—into the mouths of their eager colleagues.

The actions of the Secretary of Transportation, however, left the Road Gang confused and angry. John Volpe's decision to cancel the Vieux Carré expressway in 1969 had certainly shaken them. No federal highway administrator or Secretary of Transportation had ever even considered dropping an Interstate highway. Volpe had not only withdrawn the New Orleans expressway, but had allowed his successor in Massachusetts, Governor Francis Sargent, to stop construction of the Inner Belt in Boston. It was a highway that Volpe had, in effect, begun by bringing Interstate 90, the Massachusetts Turnpike, to the Prudential Center and the heart of Boston. Now the secretary's actions seemed almost anti-highway.

Just what had caused John Volpe—building contractor, former head of the Massachusetts Department of Public Works, former president of the Association of General Contractors, former member of the American

Divided Highways

Association of State Highway Officials, and former federal highway administrator—to experience such a Pauline conversion on the road to his cabinet post as Secretary of Transportation? Probably reality. No longer a builder or the head of a state public works department or a governor, Volpe had charge over all forms of transportation in the country. Politically astute, he understood the government had to try to achieve a measure of balance in its transportation policy. Roads would not solve all the transportation problems in the nation any more than railroads had earlier in the century.

One had to look no further than to a medium-sized or large city to see evidence that highways did not move large numbers of people efficiently. In the fifties and early sixties, planners like Robert Moses responded to the challenge of highway overcrowding by building a new highway or adding lanes to an existing one. New lanes would solve the problem, the planners assured everyone. Yet as soon as they were built, the roads acted as powerful magnets that attracted ever more cars and trucks. Planners found that highways designed to meet traffic needs for a decade would be clogged within a year or even a month. As subways deteriorated and trolley lines were abandoned, even more cars entered cities, causing pollution and congestion.

Better than most in the Nixon administration, Volpe understood that the country could not depend on a single form of transportation, that there would have to be highways, rail lines, trolleys, and subways in cities, and airplanes for long distances. While the nation had been putting its energies into creating a high-speed highway system, it had torn out its trolley tracks, neglected its subways, and allowed its railroads to become a national disgrace. The case of the railroads was particularly distressing. Once famous names that had been synonymous with America's financial strength—Pennsylvania, Reading, Boston and Maine, Erie Lackawanna—had died or were heading into bankruptcy. Aging and broken equipment was the norm. Demoralized conductors appeared to care little for the welfare of passengers. So bad was the track bed that train engineers frequently had to slow their engines to ten miles per hour. Passengers often watched grimly through grimy windows at automobiles whizzing along on nearby Interstate highways.

Volpe's thinking on transportation matters contrasted starkly with the opinions of Richard Nixon's inner circle, especially the head of the president's Domestic Council, John D. Ehrlichman, and his principal adviser, H. R. Haldeman. Nevertheless, Volpe prevailed, and sometimes for absurd and even farcical reasons. Though Ehrlichman had decided the administration should simply let the railroads die, especially the passenger lines, and took care to keep Volpe away from the Oval Office, the Secretary of Transportation was able to slip in one day. Within a few minutes he convinced the president to save the railway passenger system. Nixon's father had been a train conductor, said Volpe in his sentimental appeal. When he accepted his party's nomination for president, Nixon had told the Republican faithful of his boyhood in Yorba Linda. Lying in bed, he had listened to the sound of a distant train whistle, thought of his father riding the rails, and thought as well of America's future. He wouldn't want to deprive future generations of American boys that experience, would he? To Ehrlichman's annoyance, the ploy worked. On October 30, 1970, Nixon signed the administration-sponsored legislation creating a national railroad service, Amtrak.

Amtrak was all well and good, but what of the need for more highways? The highway lobby recognized that with thirty-five thousand miles of Interstates planned or under construction, the day the lucrative contracts would run out was close at hand. At the annual meeting of the American Association of State Highway Officials in the fall of 1970, senators and representatives met to discuss "The Federal-Aid Highway Program Present and Future." Everyone was edgy. The Nixon administration had held up money from the Highway Trust Fund to build the Interstates. Bridges were deteriorating at an alarming rate. Some of the state highway departments were completing their part of the Interstate program and would have to lay off employees if there wasn't a transition to a "post–Interstate program" Older, secondary roads needed modernization, and yet pressure was mounting to stop all highway construction.

To the Road Gang the solution was simple: Keep America going by modernizing and building highways. Frank Turner, Volpe's federal highway administrator, proposed a new, "son of Interstate" program to meet America's highway transportation needs in 1990. The cost: a mere $600 billion—far more than the national debt in 1972. Though well-intentioned, Turner was playing the role of Doctor Frankenstein. The monster he had helped create was now controlling him. Volpe recognized there was little to justify such expenditures. "We do not think it advisable or necessary to advance a proposal which would result in $600 billion in highway construction," he told Congress. Highways had to be controlled. They should not be the only solution to the nation's transportation problem. He had other ideas for meeting the nation's transportation needs.

As early as June 1969, the highway industry paper *Transport Topics* reported some disturbing statements the secretary had made to the Automobile Manufacturers Association: "The federal government spends as much money on highway construction in six weeks as it has put into urban transit in the last six years. . . . Unless we intend to pave the entire surface of the country—and no one wants that—we have to stop this trend. We already have one mile of highway for every square mile of land area in the U.S.A." The secretary expected that his department would propose a transit plan patterned on the "already fabulously successful Highway Trust Fund." To the editor of *Transport Topics*, it was clear that soon someone would make an attempt to break the Highway Trust Fund.

The editor was right. Since its creation in 1956 as a way of paying for the Interstate Highway System, the Highway Trust Fund often faced attempts from presidents and members of Congress to manipulate the money or divert it for other purposes, but they had only partially succeeded. Lyndon Johnson's administration had cut payments from the fund in order to hold inflation down. At the time, Governor Volpe had criticized the "hold downs." Early in 1969, the Nixon administration had ordered Secretary Volpe to cut payments from the fund. When asked by a reporter about the matter, Volpe replied, "Now I have to see the other side of the picture as well."

Though no one had ever used the trust fund for any purpose other than highway construction, the movement to do so was gaining strength. In February 1970, a report of the Joint Congressional Subcommittee on Economy in Government made abolishing the fund its prime recommendation. "The trust fund . . . throws the budget out of control," the report complained, "and effectively insulates programs from the effective congressional scrutiny which efficiency demands." As the fund was due to expire with completion of the Interstate Highway System in 1972, Volpe believed that the time was ripe for creating a "national transportation trust." But he knew, "We have a great deal of education ahead of us if we are to convince industry and Congress." Though highway lobby groups wanted Congress to extend the fund until 1985, it was clear that many senators and representatives—since they were hearing more complaints from their constituents and had witnessed the defeat of George Fallon—did not possess the same ardor for road construction as they had before.

While members of the Road Gang worried about a possible administration and congressional attempt to dilute the purpose of the Highway Trust Fund, a torrent of books appeared, enumerating the social ills that came about as a result of America's increasing reliance on highways as the solution for all transportation problems. Helen Leavitt was the first into the breach with *Superhighway—Superhoax*, a denunciation of the highway lobby and all it had wrought. Dedicating her book "to urban dwellers everywhere," Leavitt declared, "We must stop building freeways and obliging automobile traffic in areas of dense population. We must stop listening to engineers and highway planners, men who explain the effects of displacing people and services in very vague terms." In *Superhighway—Superhoax*, road builders, automobile manufacturers, and oil and rubber companies became "highwaymen," who were destroying the nation for their personal gain. One reviewer suggested that Leavitt had done to the highway "what Ralph Nader did to the automobile."

Other books, including *Dead End: The Automobile in Mass Transportation*, *The Great American Motion Sickness*, and *Autokind vs. Mankind*, swiftly followed Leavitt's. Though these attacks were hard enough for the Road Gang to bear, surely the most stinging one came in a book entitled *The Pavers and the Paved* by Ben Kelley. In addition to enumerating the numerous abuses of the Trust Fund juggernaut then moving across the nation and crushing communities in its path, Kelley included a chapter entitled "How to Halt a Highway." Designed to give citizens the political and legal skills necessary to mount an opposition, the chapter served as a manual of practical steps they could take to prevent construction: *"Avoid the Wait and See Approach"*; *"If you are attempting to discourage a highway route plan because it would destroy or desecrate a park, wildlife area, or historic site, become familiar with recent law to discourage road building in such locations"*; *"Do demand a full public hearing on the proposal"*; *"If highway officials decide against you, consider appealing to a higher authority"* were some of the methods Kelley enumerated in italics so that they might not be missed. Most disturbing to the Road Gang was the fact that the words came from an apostate. From 1967 to early 1969, Kelley had served as director of public affairs for the Federal Highway Administration. Having abandoned his faith in all that the Interstate highway program stood for, Kelley was, so the Road Gang thought, perfidiously using inside information to aid the opponents of progress, who were traitors to the American way of life.

Since the time of Thomas MacDonald, members of the highway lobby had controlled most of the information about the benefits that road building gave to America. Not only did they send speakers around the country and place favorable articles in popular publications, but they also produced a steady stream of self-serving movies that flickered across the screens of high school, church, Boy Scout, and civic auditoriums through the land. Highway engineers and the ever-formal MacDonald played in an early production supported by Ford, but they were soon replaced by a cast of Hollywood extras. Inevitably the movies began with shots of traffic jams and ended with footage of automobiles gliding smoothly over idyllic four-lane roads. In the middle scriptwriters included scenes that demonstrated the numerous ways the new highway under consideration would bring prosperity to the region and strengthen defense as well. Usually the movie's plot revolved around the coming highway and the changes it would bring to the town. The highway department announces plans for a new highway that will go through the town. Worry besets the citizens who gather at a public meeting. Wise men from the highway department patiently talk to them, carefully and courteously addressing all their fears. Tension arises when the town heavy, named "Mr. Snavely" in one production, always the xenophobic Luddite, makes a mean-spirited speech about outsiders and progress. A respected citizen, often a virtuous and marriageable local schoolteacher who possesses reason and an open mind, rises to counter the heavy. She had come to the meeting worried about the new highway and what it might do to the town, but she's been persuaded that it will bring great economic and social benefits to everyone. Others rise to say they agree. The highway is built; traffic moves freely; the town prospers in every way. Only rarely did the highway take a house, and never did a black person or a black neighborhood appear. For the highway interests, the town and its citizens were always white.

By the mid-1960s, rather than going out to watch movies about a highway's virtues, Americans were going into the streets to protest their evils. Often, in the evening they were driving home over the very highways they so deplored to watch themselves on the evening news. By the 1970s, highway opponents became as adept at using television news to their advantage as the highway lobby had been at using the movies.

By 1972, it was clear to all that the highway lobby was beginning to come apart. The National Governor's Conference, once a strong supporter of the Highway Trust Fund, passed a resolution at its annual meeting calling for the Highway Trust Fund money to flow into a general transportation fund. In an advertisement in the *New York Times*, the Mobil Oil Company suggested that perhaps "special earmarked funds are no longer the best approach" for highway funding. Most shocking of all, Henry Ford II, grandson of the man who had started it all and president of the second largest automobile and truck manufacturer, called for the Highway Trust Fund to support mass transit, or at least mass transportation research and experiments. Despite an extensive advertising campaign of its own, which included radio commercials, speakers, films, and the Federal Highway Administration's *Resource Book on the Federal-Aid Highway Program*—a loose-leaf binder packed with happy stories about the benefits of Interstate highways to America—the highway lobby was losing ground.

Still, the Highway Trust Fund remained much as it had since Congress created it in June 1956, guarded by a vigilant group of representatives and senators who fought hard whenever anyone had the temerity to suggest that the method of transportation funding be changed. Chief of the guard on the Senate side was Jennings Randolph, the courtly and portly gentleman from Randolph County, West Virginia. Randolph held a B.A. degree from West Virginia's Salem College and had worked as newspaper editor, professor of public speaking and journalism, and college dean before being elected to the House of Representatives in 1932. In a career that paralleled the rise and fall of the New Deal, Randolph had been an ardent supporter of Franklin Roosevelt. As a member of the House Public Works Committee for seven terms, he sponsored the first legislation to give federal aid to airports and had served as chairman of its subcommittee on roads. Unable to resist the Republican sweep of Congress in 1946, Randolph retreated to the offices of Capitol Airlines and the American Road Builders Association. Both the airline and the association valued Randolph as one who knew his way around the halls of Congress, one who could help them make the case for any legislation they needed. Randolph had done just that in 1956 when Congress passed the bill creating the Interstate Highway System. The death of West Virginia's senior senator in 1958 midway through his term brought Randolph back to Congress. In the special election held the next year, West Virginians chose him by a solid margin, and they reelected him in 1960 and 1966.

"He is one of us," said the president of the American Road Builders Association, when presenting Randolph with its annual award in 1966.

Indeed, the senator was. Public works were Randolph's consuming interest. He wrote articles for *Road Builder*, the official magazine of the American Road Builders Association ("Financing the Remainder of the Interstate Highway System"; "Deferment of Highway Construction? No!"), and frequently addressed conventions of the American Association of State Highway Officials. By the 1970s, Randolph had become chairman of both the Senate Public Works Committee and its Subcommittee on Roads. Possessing a quiet southern sense of decorum, Randolph had managed for years to disarm, with his reasoned courtesy, many colleagues who otherwise might have opposed highway construction.

Chief among the guards on the House side stood Representative John Carl Kluczynski, who, after George Fallon's defeat, had taken over the chairmanship of the Subcommittee on Transportation. A big man whose restaurant and catering business in Chicago seemed a fit occupation, Kluczynski had worked his way through the Chicago Democratic machine. For many years he had served in the Illinois Senate before his voters of the Fifth District elected him to the U.S. Congress in 1950. From the start of his eleven terms, he had supported highways and the trucking industry. As he rose in stature, he took delight in dispensing pork, and since 1956, he believed his primary mission in Congress was to protect the Highway Trust Fund.

Between Randolph and Kluczynski the highway lobby believed it had Congress under its control. But the tone of the debate was changing, especially in the Senate. There, newer, younger senators, men like Lowell Weicker of Connecticut, Edward Kennedy of Massachusetts, and John Tunney of California, lacking the courtly decorum of a Jennings Randolph, were bringing the language of street protest onto the floor of the Senate against highways, particularly against their incursion into cities. If there was any chance of breaking the grip of the highway lobby, it was now.

In 1972, a full three years into his tenure as Secretary of Transportation, John Volpe made his move to open the fund. It was then or never, Volpe figured. The administration realized that the cities were choking with automobile traffic while all mass transit systems were in trouble. Yet the demands on the general budget dimmed the likelihood of increasing support for mass transit. Nixon would probably be reelected in November, but Volpe knew he had so annoyed the president's "German mafia," the name he gave to Ehrlichman and Haldeman, that he would not survive in the second administration.

Volpe had already pried some money from the fund in 1970 for auto-mobile safety programs; now he proposed to Congress that the 1972 Federal-Aid Highway Act give states and cities the option of using Highway Trust Fund money for capital investment programs in mass transportation, including rail. Appropriations would begin at $1 billion for the 1974 fiscal year and increase to $2.25 billion by 1976. The federal government would pay seventy percent of the costs for mass transportation projects, while states and cities would pay the remainder. "Highway investments alone cannot cope with the pressing and severe problem that is so harmful to the effective functioning of urban areas," said Volpe; only a mix of highways and mass transit could help cities solve their traffic problems. Because his proposal would relieve congested highways and improve mass transit, too, his solution would "benefit transit and auto users alike."

The highway lobby did not buy the secretary's logic and they were ready with their own well-tried arguments and strategies. There was a new tone of urgency in their words, though. "Collectively, the state highway departments know more about the nation's highway inventory and needs than anyone else, or any other group," said the testy president of the American Association of State Highway Officials, John C. Dingwell, adding: "Why should highway users subsidize rapid transit in a dozen large cities?" The American Road Builders Association sent three executives to Capitol Hill to express its opposition. J. B. Creel of the American Automobile Association dismissed Volpe's proposal as simply a "fiscal maneuver" to make highway users bear the costs of mass transit, which was the responsibility of the general fund. The only small crack in the solid front of the highway interests appeared in the Senate testimony of D. Grant Mickle, president of a new lobby group, the Highway Users Federation for Safety and Mobility. The federation represented the thinking of about six hundred businesses, associations, and industries that had joined together in January 1970 to speak with a single, more effective voice on highway matters. Mickle recommended continuation of the Highway Trust Fund, but also suggested that up to $300 million be used to help bus companies make capital improvements. Buses were not the issue, of course, as they traveled on highways, but railroads, trolleys, and subways were.

Volpe had his supporters, too. As was expected, mayors of cities large and small backed the proposal. The United Auto Workers, the National League of Cities, the National Governors Conference, and even the American Institute of Architects all wanted Congress to open the fund for mass transit. "Mass transit has always been a poor stepchild when it comes to federal help," said Bella Abzug, the outspoken and sometimes abrasive representative from Manhattan, noting that the administration had appropriated just $900 million for it in fiscal 1972, and had proceeded to impound $300 million of that.

Such champions of the secretary's proposals were not unusual. Indeed, many had been arguing the case to break up the Highway Trust Fund for many years. This time they were joined by a new anti-highway lobby group, the Highway Action Coalition. Claiming to represent 750,000 people across America, the Highway Action Coalition was actually a loose alliance of those who supported environmental causes like the Sierra Club, Environmental Action, Friends of the Earth, and Zero Population Growth. A year earlier they had joined together with the common goal of persuading Congress to ground the supersonic transport plane, a project that Volpe and the Department of Transportation had long championed. Fresh from that victory, they reconstituted themselves as an anti-highway coalition with the single goal of "busting the trust." This time Volpe and coalition members were on the same side of the issue.

To some, the coalition's staff looked like sixties flower children who had gone to seed. Tie-dyed shirts, jeans, and sandals seemed to be the uniform for the staff of four. Mangy furniture, guitars, and grime were the most prominent features of their shabby seventh-floor offices on Dupont Circle. The contrast with their more established and wealthy adversaries could not have been more striking. Officials of the American Association of State Highway Officials and the American Road Builders Association generally dressed in dark suits and conservative ties. The road builders had built their quarters close to the new Department of Transportation building, while the highway officials preferred a gleaming building on North Capitol Street, close to the offices of the senators and representatives whom they so ardently courted.

The well-tailored lobbyists did not quite know what to make of John D. Kramer, the executive director of the Highway Action Coalition. Kramer had grown up in California, taken a B.A. at Stanford, and was on leave from his fellowship at Oxford University, where he was studying international relations. His weekly salary of $75 did not equal the daily expense allowance of most of the lobbyists whom he faced. Yet Kramer had been brash enough to suggest in December 1971 that "in maybe just two years, we can open up the Highway Trust Fund for broader purposes, like mass transit." The executive director made up for the coalition's lack of funds by tapping the growing reservoir of resentment about urban Interstates. He alerted and educated writers and newspaper editors about the coming vote on the Highway Trust Fund and they responded with stories. THE UNTOUCHABLE HIGHWAY FUND AND OUR MISGUIDED PRIORITIES, read the headline in one newspaper. The fund was nothing more than an "overgrown piggy bank," said another. Helen Leavitt weighed in with an article for the Washington *Star* in an article under the headline THE MOVE TO SHAKE LOOSE SOME OF THAT ROAD MONEY. THE HIGHWAY LOBBY AIMS TO PROVE THERE IS NO HIGHWAY LOBBY, a headline in the *Wall Street Journal* read, while another article in the *Journal* called the fund THE CONCRETE BLOC. The *Wall Street Journal* and the *Journal of Commerce* borrowed Helen Leavitt's term to describe the trust supporters: "Highwaymen."

The rhetoric the Highway Action Coalition employed was like none highway lobbyists or Congress had ever heard before. Kramer and his staff were careful not to testify before Congress themselves. Instead they used a member of their board of advisers. "We now subsidize the highways up to a 90–10 matching ratio that encourages the states to divert funds from other pressing needs to get those 10-cent dollars from the federal government," the respected labor mediator Theodore W. Kheel told the House Public Works Committee. "It is a form of addiction similar to the pusher in the schools of our nation who tries to get the kids on dope so that they will have to go out and get more money." If highways were the drug, were the engineers the pushers?

Still the highway groups were confident. True, opinion surveys suggested that the public no longer favored urban highways and newspapers had been giving them bad press. It was simply a matter of educating the people about the benefits of highways. They formed TRIP (The Road Information Program), which produced radio commercials that ended with the slogan "Your highways. You've got a lot riding on them." As their lobbyists resolutely worked offices on Capitol Hill, counsels to the Senate and House Public Works Committees crafted favorable legislation. Frank Turner, who retired as federal highway administrator in June, assisted them in drafting legislation to save the fund. Because of his experience and his encyclopedic knowledge of past legislation, Turner proved to be a formidable asset to the fund's supporters. Since 1972 was an election year, the odds against Volpe and the Highway Action Coalition succeeding in their quest to free money from the trust were great. A highway contractors organization, the Committee for Action, was doling out close to $75,000 to the deserving incumbents in checks of $1,000 to $2,500, while the Truck Operators Non-Partisan Committee offered campaign contributions to congressmen who listened to the logic of their money.

The first stroke of fortune for Volpe and those who wanted to break the trust came on the floor of the Senate. In debate on the Federal-Aid Highway Act, Senators John Sherman Cooper of Kentucky and Edmund Muskie of Maine introduced an amendment that would allow up to $800 million in highway funds to be used for public transportation, including railroads and subways. The federal-aid highway program, the senators argued, was creating severe problems of urban congestion and pollution, and suburban sprawl. States and the people in the cities should decide how the money is spent. Senator Muskie added that "the looming energy crisis" made the passage mandatory. Remarkably enough, the highway interests could muster just twenty-eight votes in opposition. The Cooper-Muskie amendment passed with forty-eight votes evenly divided between Republicans and Democrats.

The Highway Action Coalition's achievement should not be understated. It marked the first time that either house of Congress had agreed to allow the Highway Trust Fund to be used for any other purpose than highways since its creation in 1956. But the coalition had won only half the battle.

On the other battle front—the House side of the Capitol—the Public Works Committee had conducted its hearings on the legislation over thirteen days in February and March, before rejecting by a wide margin a proposal to use money from the Highway Trust Fund to finance bus lines and rail systems. The coalition expected to lose in committee, as the committee was firmly in the grasp of the fund supporters, but Kramer and his staff believed they would win a vote on the amendment in the full House. Representative Glenn M. Anderson, a Democratic member of the Public Works Committee from California, had already announced his intention to propose just such an amendment when the bill came before the House.

Highway lobbyists knew that the fight was far from over. The full House had to vote on the measure, and then if the bill passed it would go to a joint committee of senators and representatives to rectify the differences between the House and Senate versions. The highway lobbyists knew their opponents had a good chance of winning, in either the House or the joint committee. Their best chance for success lay in using a parliamentary maneuver to prevent a vote on a mass transportation amendment from ever taking place. On October 3, the House Rules Committee, which controls the flow of legislation through the House, added a special directive allowing members to raise points of order against any attempt to add mass transit funding. To circumvent the committee's decision, Congressman Anderson went to the House parliamentarian, the ultimate authority in such matters, who assured the congressman he would rule that his motion to amend the bill for mass transit funding was in order. Anderson would have no need to worry. His amendment would come to the floor. But on the morning of October 4, the parliamentarian ruled with the highway lobbyists because of the request of one of the most powerful representatives in Congress, the head of the House Ways and Means Committee, Wilbur D. Mills.

Today, people remember Wilbur Daigh Mills—if they remember him at all—for his alcoholic indiscretions with Argentine striptease dancer Fanne Foxe. (In October 1974, Mills crashed his car through a retaining wall into the Potomac River tidal basin at the Jefferson Memorial. There Mills and Miss Foxe went for an extended swim until police fished them out. The next month, Mills and Miss Foxe made a joint appearance on the stage of a Boston burlesque house.) In 1972, however, the name of Mills was synonymous with power. More often than not, newspapers identified him as "the powerful chairman of the House Ways and Means Committee" or "chairman of the powerful House Ways and Means Committee." Mills achieved his power by thoroughly understanding all the nation's tax laws and applying a firm and cordial will that forced all other members of the House Ways and Means Committee to bend to his thinking. He achieved consensus simply by grinding down the opposition. Whatever Mills decided was good enough for his conservative colleagues; his liberal colleagues did not have the votes to counteract him.

Just before the House took up the highway bill, Wilbur Mills announced that any change in the trust fund should originate with his House Ways and Means Committee, as it had written the original trust fund legislation in 1956, and it alone had the power to alter it. He would tolerate no amendment of the sort Anderson proposed to make. That Wilbur Mills took such a position was no surprise. Before entering Congress, he had served as a judge in White County, Arkansas, where he had charge of highway building. It was there that he first met the regional administrator of the Bureau of Public Roads, Francis Cutler Turner. The two men had been friends ever since and shared the same philosophy about highways.

All was not lost for those who wanted trust fund money for mass transit, however. Through a full vote of the House, they could still override the decision of the Rules Committee. But the highway forces had that angle covered as well. The next day two dozen highway lobbyists worked the hallways and corridors of the Capitol to keep key representatives in line. When the vote was taken on the procedural matter, the highway forces won by a margin of 200 to 168. The House voted its Federal-Aid Highway Act for 1972 without any funds for mass transit.

Having learned a valuable lesson, Kramer and the Highway Action Coalition figured they had a few legislative tricks up their own sleeves. In the conference committee, John Sherman Cooper became adamant that the final legislation include Highway Trust Fund money for mass transit. To split those who wanted to break the trust, representatives offered the Senators a plan to appropriate $4 billion from the general fund for mass transportation. Senator Harrison Williams from New Jersey, anxious to get any relief for the broken-down trains in his state, leaped at the plan, but John Sherman Cooper would hear nothing of it. Cooper wanted nothing less than reform of the entire system. Leaving the fund intact meant that mayors would be forced to accept highway money in addition to mass transit funds. The Interstates would still be built and would continue to devastate the cities. This negotiation was one of the last Cooper would have as a senator, and he wanted to go out with honor. Meeting after meeting of the conference committee ended in deadlock. It was now mid-October in an election year; senators and representatives were anxious to return to their states and districts for the campaign. The Gallup poll showed President Nixon leading his hapless Democratic opponent, George McGovern, by as much as thirty-four percent. Many in Congress wondered if the coming Republican landslide might sweep them from office. Finally, on October 18, the joint committee reached a decision to appropriate $3 billion from the general fund for mass transit and rushed the bill to the floor of the House.

Many were suspicious. Appropriating the money from the general fund sounded fine, but that would require more legislation. "Since the federal highway legislation does not expire until June 30, 1973," said John Anderson of Illinois, "I suggest that the better part of wisdom would be to come back in the 93rd Congress." Representative Gerald Ford of Grand Rapids, Michigan, who had opposed opening the trust fund for mass transportation ("You're going to have the floodgate opened"), opposed the compromise on the grounds that the hour was too late to begin a program of such potential magnitude. Those who wanted to crack the trust fund had one maneuver left. When it came time to vote on the bill, one raised a point of order: a quorum was not present. The speaker ordered the clerk to call the roll. Wilbur Mills rose to ask that the request be vacated. But Representative Thomas O'Neill, who was presiding over the session, said, "The Speaker does not have that authority under the Constitution." Republicans and those who favored opening the trust refused to answer the roll call. There would be no federal-aid highway legislation in 1972.

The highway lobby was furious. "LEAVE THE HIGHWAY TRUST FUND ALONE: ITS JOB IS NOT YET DONE," wrote the editor of *Better Roads*, the official magazine of the American Road Builders Association. "Now is the time for all good highway men and all other reasonable men and women who use outdated and deteriorating roads to do something about the unfortunate anti-highway attitude that exists in Congress." It was too late. Federal highway funds would soon run out. Both sides knew that the days of a dedicated trust fund were numbered. "We've used about every cent we have," lamented Douglas B. Fugate, the highway commissioner in Virginia. "Kentucky won't be able to continue any of its primary or Interstate program" said the state's highway engineer, "until Congress acts and passes a highway bill." Faced with the prospect of no funds at all, the highway interests would have to compromise.

John Volpe's premonitions about his future in the new Nixon cabinet were correct. Haldeman and Ehrlichman, who regarded the secretary as a lightweight, prevailed upon the president to get rid of him. But the second-generation Italian-American realized his dream when Nixon offered him an appointment as U.S. Ambassador to Italy. Volpe gladly accepted, happy to be free of Washington and its vicious intrigues. He would be happier still in the coming months, far removed from the ugly revelations about the Nixon administration and the vice president's and president's resignations in disgrace.

Divided Highways

No doubt his failure to crack the Highway Trust Fund and the resolve of highway lobbyists must have disappointed John Volpe. Members of the House and Senate Public Works Committees regarded him as an enemy, and members of the American Association of State Highways Officials thought him a turncoat. Yet Volpe possessed a prescience that few others had. He understood that if the highway program were to succeed, members of Congress and state and federal officials would have to make it responsive to citizen needs. More than anyone else, he realized that more highways would aggravate rather than solve urban problems and that America had to find other methods of travel than the automobile.

Happy to see Volpe leave, highway lobbyists took a small measure of hope in his replacement, Claude S. Brinegar, of Rolling Hills, California. In making Brinegar's nomination, Richard Nixon cited his Ph.D. in economics from Stanford and called him "one of the most gifted, young executives in the United States today." "He likes cars," said the president's press secretary, Ron Ziegler, after revealing that the forty-seven-year-old Brinegar was a director of the Daytona Speedway, the stock car racetrack in Florida. Highway lobbyists were more interested in the fact that Brinegar had worked for Union Oil Company for the past twenty years and was now president of its Union 76 Division. John Kramer of the Highway Action Coalition announced he was "outraged." Union Oil had been responsible for a recent oil spill ("probably the worst environmental disaster in California's history," said Kramer) that had polluted much of the coastline near Santa Barbara, had conducted running battles with environmentalists, and had worked vigorously to defeat a California ballot proposition to use gasoline tax revenues for mass transit.

Perhaps, both the Highway Action Coalition and the highway lobbyists wondered, Brinegar would bring his petroleum interests to his position on the Highway Trust Fund. Perhaps he would weaken Volpe's inflexible stand on the matter. However, two days after Nixon made the nomination, Ziegler reported that Brinegar shared the president's view that the trust fund should be used for "the continued development of mass transit." The secretary-designate, who admitted "no vast background in transportation problems" other than logging millions of air miles and "being bogged down in traffic on the Harbor freeway getting to work," set about to study national transportation problems. By February 1973, he was ready to move on the trust. "I well recognize that arguments have been made that use of the trust fund monies for non-highway projects is unfair to those [motorists] who pay taxes into the fund," the new secretary told a subcommittee of the Senate Public Works Committee. But, he argued, "the beneficiaries of improved mass transit are a broad group—including those . . . who must use hopefully less congested highways." For the fiscal year 1974, Brinegar said, Congress should vote $1.1 billion from the Highway Trust Fund for mass transit projects.

At the same Senate hearings, many of the nation's governors concurred with Brinegar. "Highways alone cannot meet the transportation needs of our cities," said Francis Sargent, who had recently stopped the Inner Belt in Boston. In early March, President Nixon told a radio audience, "I propose that our States and communities be given the right to use a designated portion of the Highway Trust Fund for capital improvements in urban public transportation, including improvements in bus and rapid rail systems." Changing the fund was one of the "top items on our national agenda," Nixon said, warning that if the nation did not act now, "our children will grow up in cities which are strangled with traffic, racked by noise, and choked by pollution." He followed the speech with a message to Congress. "Some communities now feel unduly obligated to spend Federal monies on controversial Interstate highway segments in urban areas." Opening up the Highway Trust Fund, he argued, would help resolve urban controversies over highways and allow "local governments the best solutions for their urban transportation problems." A few days later, Nixon sent Congress a message on the environment endorsing the use of the Highway Trust Fund for mass transit, "not only to reduce urban congestion but also to reduce the concentrations of pollution that are too often the result of our present methods of transportation."

Despite Nixon's support for opening the Highway Trust Fund, members of the highway lobby knew that, with the exception of one notable defection, their side still enjoyed about as much support in the 93rd Congress as it had in the 92nd. The defection was troublesome, however: Over the holidays Representative John Carl Kluczynski had a talk with Richard Daley, mayor of Chicago. The city's transit system was out of money, Daley said; the congressman had to change his position. Kluczynski agreed. "My city of Chicago has one of the finest freeway networks of any city in the world," he said in the floor debate. "The transit system is, however, in trouble. No longer can we rely on the fare box to keep the system solvent."

Divided Highways

Despite Kluczynski's new position on opening the trust, the voting was much the same as the previous year's. In the Senate, Edmund Muskie joined with Howard Baker of Tennessee in sponsoring an amendment to the Senate Public Works Bill that would give cities the choice of spending the $850 million they got each year from the Highway Trust Fund on mass transportation; Jennings Randolph weighed in with his opposition and prevailed in the committee; the amendment passed in the full Senate on March 15, by a 5-vote margin. In the House Public Works Committee, Glenn Anderson of California sponsored the same amendment to the highway bill as he had the previous year, which voted it down by a wide margin. The House Rules Committee allowed Anderson to propose his amendment on the floor, but on April 19 it lost by a 25-vote margin, 215 to 190. The highway lobby had won again.

The argument over the use of the Highway Trust Fund for urban mass transit had virtually halted Interstate construction in some states, so the House-Senate conferees who met on May 9—especially those who supported the Interstate program—felt a special pressure to reach a compromise swiftly. The conference dragged on. Day after day they reported in the standard language of the Congress, "Conferees met in executive session to resolve the differences between the Senate and House passed versions of S502 . . . but did not reach agreement." Meeting after meeting yielded the same terse statement. Meanwhile, the pressure to compromise mounted. It took the conferees fourteen meetings and two and a half months before announcing an agreement on July 27. Their agreement left the Highway Trust Fund intact for the first year, fiscal 1974, but phased in the use of the trust for mass transportation beginning in 1975. By fiscal 1976, cities were allowed to use any part of their highway funds to build rail lines and buy subway cars. Cities might also decide not to build a portion of their urban Interstate and use the money for mass transportation instead. At last, the cities, urban members of Congress, senators of populous states, and the Highway Action Coalition had busted the trust.

Despite the victory in Congress, the grim fact remained: The Highway Action Coalition had only busted the trust for the future. The building that had begun would go on. No matter how great the goodwill on the part of the parties, it is no more possible to stop a multibillion-dollar federal project creating the largest structure in the history of the world than it is to stop a speeding truck on a dime. Nowhere was this more evident than on Interstate 93 at Bailey Road in Somerville, Massachusetts.

By any measure, the Interstate 93 corridor that cuts through the Ten Hills section of Somerville ranks as one of the meanest and most disagreeable portions of highway in America. At this point the highway squats on heavy, gray concrete supports about a story above the ground. Few souls venture on foot to the land of perpetual shadow beneath the roadway, a place one person described as "Muggers Mall." Those who do, want to get out as fast as they possibly can. On the ground at the base of the graffitti-scarred supports are pieces of cars and trucks that have floated down from above: a bit of muffler or catalytic converter; a piece of chrome trim or a side mirror; and the dirt and trash that perpetually moving cars and trucks inevitably spawn.

To the seventy or so families who live immediately adjacent to the Interstate on Bailey Road, dirt and shadow are but minor problems in comparison with noise and vibration. In the 1950s, Bailey Road was home to quiet, working-class Catholic families who lived in two-story, two-family structures, usually divided into upstairs and downstairs apartments. Those survivors who still live on Bailey Road endure cars, trucks, and vans speeding about seventy feet away from their living room windows. The problem is even worse for those who occupy second-floor apartments, as their windows are level with the passing cars and trucks. To Nora Driscoll, one of the survivors who lives in a second-story apartment, the noise and vibration seem unrelenting, a ceaseless tumult of humming and shaking that spikes to a thunder of noise and rattle as trucks pass and gear down for the exit ramp to Mystic Avenue.

In the 1920s, engineers at Bell Laboratories developed the decibel scale to measure relative loudness. They found that the rustling of leaves generates a level of about ten decibels, most human conversations about thirty to forty, a vacuum cleaner about sixty-five or seventy. Like the Richter scale that measures earthquake intensity, the decibel scale is exponential. Thus, a measurement of twenty decibels represents a sound a hundred times more intense than one of ten, while a measurement of seventy decibels represents one that is ten million times more intense. Most people can tolerate about fifty-five decibels of noise without feeling uncomfortable, but they find it difficult to sleep when the noise goes above forty-five decibels. In 1976, technicians measuring the sound of automobiles and trucks as they passed Bailey Road on Interstate 93, found the noise level to be at seventy-eight decibels, which meant—after factoring in the sound insulation of the building—the noise in Nora Driscoll's living room was sixty-eight decibels, about the intensity of a loud vacuum cleaner.

After the Ten Hills section of Interstate 93 opened, most conversation and activity ceased in the front living room on Bailey Road. "We just abandoned it, retreated to the back," said Driscoll about the decibel battering she and her family endured in their living room. "But there was no escape. We couldn't talk and we couldn't sleep." Actually, the noise level was not a steady sixty-eight decibels, and that made it all the worse. At times the level would subside to fifty-five or even less, but suddenly a truck gearing down for the exit would pass the living room, rattling windows and spiking the noise to well above sixty-eight. The technicians, who benignly called these noise spikes "vehicle peaks," found that they occurred as many as 175 times an hour. Prolonged exposure to such a din leads to chronic physiological disturbances, stress, tension, and high blood pressure. Noise spikes like those delivered by passing cars and trucks on Interstate 93 alter endocrine, neurological, and cardiovascular functions.

How did human beings ever conceive of and create such a concrete monster on legs as the Interstate 93 corridor past Bailey Road? The road had been part of the proposed Inner Belt. Governor Francis Sargent had stopped the highway but not before construction had begun on Interstate 93. Sargent allowed the work to proceed.

Protests in the other areas of the city worked, but nothing seemed to help in Somerville. The mayor and city officials gave the proposal for an elevated highway their blessing before citizens had adequate time to respond. Only after the approval had been granted and the state began taking land for the highway did citizens start to comprehend what was happening to their community. With the leadership of a new mayor, the Reverend S. Lester Ralph of Christ Episcopal Church, they formed SCAT: Somerville Committee for Adequate Transportation. SCAT tried in vain to have the highway placed underground. The cost would be $110 million, federal officials told the group—three times that of an elevated section. Yes, the Somerville *Journal* agreed, "But the costs to the city, both short and long term . . . economics, health, safety, aesthetics . . . are infinitely greater."

In 1969, after Richard Nixon named John Volpe to be Secretary of Transportation, it fell to the new governor, Francis Sargent, to make the decision on the Inner Belt. The governor found himself in the middle of an enormous tug-of-war, and he was the rope. Pulling on one side were those opposed to this monstrous destroyer of property and spirit, while on the other were the powerful highway forces—the associations, contractors, consultants, government officials, oil companies, and automakers. Though Sargent had been commissioner of public works, he was an environmentalist at heart. On Cape Cod he had operated a sporting goods store, loved fishing and hunting, and had been director of maritime fisheries and commissioner of natural resources. "Four years ago, I was the commissioner of the Department of Public Works—our road building agency," said Sargent in February 1970. "Then nearly everyone was sure highways were the only answer to transportation problems for years to come. We were wrong." Eventually, Sargent decided to stop the Inner Belt. "You, your family, and your neighbors have been caught in a system that has fouled our air, ravaged our cities, choked our economy, and frustrated every one of us. . . . The old system has imprisoned us; we have become the slaves and not the master of the method we chose to meet our needs. . . . Shall we build more expressways through cities? Shall we forge chains to shackle us to the mistakes of the past? No." But it was too late for Somerville.

The Ten Hills section of the Interstate 93 corridor had opened in 1972. Even as it was being constructed, people realized the irreparable damage the federal and state bureaucracy was inflicting upon the lives of those living on Bailey Avenue. By 1975, the Federal Highway Administration and the Massachusetts Department of Public Works had hired a group of planning, architecture, and acoustical consultants to examine the problems. In the cool language such consultants use, they reported:

- The highway is completely out of scale with the urban zone through which it passes.
- There is a great deal of "wasteland" associated with the right-of-way, and extensive visual voids.
- Highway-related building materials are limited and visually monotonous.
- Fences, barriers, and other highway-related structures have a significant negative visual impact.
- Noise, fumes, and litter from the highway corridor have a major negative impact on the adjacent residential areas.

These problems—not the vast amount of money spent to build and maintain the road itself—were the true costs of urban highway construction.

The Somerville section of Interstate 93 is a grim and barren monument to an older way of thinking about highway building—the thinking of decent and scrupulous men like Frank Turner and Rex Whitton, engineers who carefully followed the rules given them, and who believed those rules were right for the nation. It is a monument to malign builders like Robert Moses who, by his own admission, went at cities with a meat axe. It is a monument to the Highway Trust Fund.

NEW RULES

*As new and greater road-systems are added
year by year they are more splendidly built.
I foresee that road will soon be architecture
too . . . great architecture.*

FRANK LLOYD WRIGHT

 If you're looking at a map, the roads surrounding the cities of Dallas and Forth Worth suggest a large barbell. An Interstate rings each city while two other Interstates connect them in a straight east-west line. These highways serve the same purpose for cars and trucks as a railroad roundhouse. Drivers can get on the Interstates and turn in any direction they wish. The roads connect them not only to places in Texas but to anywhere in the nation.

You can find the same roundhouse pattern in city after city of the South and Midwest. The Department of Defense wanted roads on the periphery of cities, and engineers had been only too happy to oblige them. In the process they transformed the landscape. Atlanta, Indianapolis, Columbus, Cincinnati, St. Louis, Houston, San Antonio, Minneapolis—they all rely on the giant automobile roundhouse for their travel and communication. The old central arteries of the urban landscape—Washington and Meridian streets in Indianapolis, for example, or Bankhead and Northside in Atlanta—gradually yielded to belt highways around the city core.

Francis Cutler Turner, the federal highway administrator responsible for building so many of the Interstates, had grown up in Fort Worth, where his father had worked on the railroad. The Turner house, close by the tracks, had no electricity or plumbing (the family used a "necessary" in the backyard), and only a pump near the kitchen door. While supervising the construction of the Alaskan Highway during World War II, Turner received a letter from his brother and sister inviting him to help purchase a new house for his parents. "Of course I said yes," Turner remembered, "and paid my share." When he returned to Fort Worth after the war, the house had been built and his parents had moved. Turner's mother greeted him at the front door: " 'This is the house I hope to die in,' she told me. I replied I hoped that wouldn't be anytime soon." Turner visited his parents many times over the years, but none was more momentous than a visit in the early 1970s when he was federal highway administrator. On this trip he was confirming what maps in Washington had already told him: Interstate 35 through Fort Worth would take his parents' house. "When I arrived, I saw the stake for the centerline in front of the living room window." Turner's mother greeted him at the door, asking, "Frank, can't you do anything?" "I can but I won't," Turner replied. "You'll just have to move." Turner would never compromise the Interstate Highway System, not even for his parents.

The story illustrates more than Frank Turner's probity. Across the country engineers had proven their ability to choose routes and build highways. But it was not enough. For all the technocratic expertise that enabled them to build the perfect highway and move automobiles and trucks efficiently, the engineers had been indifferent to human ecology, how the structures they were creating had changed the fundamental relationships between humans and their environment. (The very term, ecology, which Americans had not used much since Thoreau, came into vogue in the 1970s.) Ironically, the Interstate highway program had inspired citizens to take a greater interest in their ecology, a subject they had cared little for until they saw the potential negative side to their reliance on technology. Maps of some cities, especially those in the East, show that the circles of highway are broken in places. Those breaks mark the places where American citizens stopped the highways and changed the rules.

. . .

After President Nixon signed the Federal-Aid Highway Act of 1973, the new rules began to catch up with the reality of the times. Up to the 1970s, engineers built the highways along the least expensive right-of-way—usually through lower-class or black neighborhoods, a public park, or along a riverfront—so that they could get as many miles as possible for the government's dollars. They also built them to handle large volumes of traffic so that they could cite the low cost of the highway in relation to the number of cars and trucks it served each day. After 1973, however, planners, politicians, engineers, federal and state highway officials, and citizens worked with a very different set of assumptions and guidelines. No longer could planners decide the location of a highway and engineers design and construct it at will, barely consulting with those whose lives they affected. The New Orleans battle, the various highway revolts across the country, the Interstate projects stalled by litigation, the opening of the Highway Trust Fund for mass transit, and the loss of the highway lobby's hold over Congress and the public had shaken the confidence of engineers and federal highway officials.

All decent people, the engineers and planners of the Federal Highway Administration had been stunned by the opposition to their program that had grown up over the past decade. They had thought their sole job was to build highways. After all, they had studied highway construction in their university courses, and they had taken jobs that called upon them to use their training. By 1973, however, they had come to realize that, more than mere builders, they were powerful agents of social change. They—and many others—had seriously misjudged the temper of the country. Moreover, they realized, they did not know what they should be doing. In an attempt to understand what was going on, officials in the Federal Highway Administration commissioned and published dozens of studies on beautification, environment, commuting, bus lanes, road design, and urban transportation planning.

The federal officials acted the only way they understood, with a full bureaucratic press of studies and publications. Over the previous decade, Congress had passed a series of laws, which administrators had followed, but not as strictly as they might. The 1969 National Environmental Policy Act called for a full study of the environmental implications of a proposed highway; and the 1970 Federal-Aid Highway Act directed the Secretary of Transportation to create guidelines that would assure a full consideration of the social, economic, and environmental effects of a federally funded highway. In February 1974, a national committee of federal officials responded with a "Nationwide Action Plan." From now on, a "Pre-Construction Branch" in the Federal Highway Administration would weigh the social, economic, and environmental effects of a proposed highway as well as *the alternative of not building the project.*" It was dramatic proof of just how far highway administrators had come in their thinking.

In accordance with a federal relocation assistance act that Congress passed in 1970, the Highway Administration published a list of friendly guidelines in 1977, *Your Rights and Benefits as a Highway Displacee.* A simple line drawing on the green cover showed the happy, white, nuclear family, smiles on their faces, suitcases in hand, walking confidently away from their house and heading into the future. It was "one of the unfortunate, but unavoidable consequences of a modern highway program in a progressive nation" to displace a "small percentage of the population" for a greater good. The law provided reimbursement of moving costs, the pamphlet assured anxious readers. Owners could elect to receive their moving expenses and the comparable cost of a replacement house. Those displaced would have the right of appeal, and there would be relocation counselors and a variety of support services to help families grow accustomed to their new surroundings. In fact, this change in attitude was long overdue. In the past, people had been forced out of their houses often without adequate reimbursement or without substitute housing that they might afford.

The question of citizen participation in highway location decisions had long exasperated federal administrators and supporters of the Interstate program. In the words of John Kluczynski, citizens who opposed an Interstate were nothing more than "people with big mouths running around the country making loud noises and doing all they can to distort the truth." As long as they had the backing of Congress, particularly those on the Public Works Committees, highway administrators did not feel it necessary to consult any more than they did. Some federal engineers, including the ones overseeing the construction of the beltway around Washington, thought it their actual duty to ignore the public and opposed consulting with them about planning. Only with great reluctance did these engineers hold public hearings.

The friendlier Federal Highway Administration realized how such arrogance had ill-served the Interstate program. In 1973, it convened a panel discussion on the subject of community involvement in planning and design and, following that, hired two consulting firms—Arthur D.

Divided Highways

Little and Justin Gray Associates—to find "how citizens can be involved most effectively." The "fundamental ingredient" of successful transportation planning, said the consultants in their two-volume report, was an "open planning process." Highway planners should include the public early on, not with plans in hand, but with the question of even the need for a highway. And always, stressed the consultants, highway officials should be careful to maintain a dialogue. The study merely acknowledged the clear and present reality: Highways were no longer "the exclusive province of professional planners." Citizens with very different perspectives and values had an interest that was often greater than that of the planners, and should be allowed to influence the decision.

The flow of studies continued: on the assessment and mitigation of the impact of highways on the ecology ("the direct relevance of ecology to highway engineering"); on auto traffic in urban neighborhoods ("heavy traffic leads to much less social interaction and activity on the street"); on highway noise ("the number of highway vehicles has become so large and the people live so much closer to the sources of noise that vehicular traffic noise is a major concern"). The Federal Highway Administration looked at everything in its desperate effort to understand the changes in the nation, which, in many cases, it had wrought. Surely one of the odder studies commissioned by the Federal Highway Administration was one in 1971 concerning the travel patterns and problems of ten thousand white high school males from suburban Boston. The Harvard researcher who conducted the study chose whites because he knew he could not include enough blacks to make a valid sample, and males because "mixing the sexes seemed likely to inhibit participants' comments . . . and males would have more freedom as to when, where, and how they travel." Those who bothered to wade through the 610-page report learned the startling fact that all teenagers wanted to drive their own cars. Teenagers with licenses and wheels made an average of 5.6 car trips per day. Those who owned their cars spent $15.40 a week on their travel; those who borrowed the family car spent $4. Other findings were disturbing, but hardly news to their parents: No one wanted to take a bus or a train. Many reported that even if it were free and convenient, they would not take public transportation. Even teens without licenses preferred to walk. Public transportation restricted their independence and anonymity. In this respect the teenagers' attitudes mirrored their parents'.

The Harvard researcher had hit upon two of the unintended

consequences of federal highway and housing policies that had prevailed over the past quarter century. Americans had wanted to leave the cities, and the highway system offered them a subsidized way of having houses, land, and space in suburban subdivisions. As long as everyone could drive and had a car, the system worked well. But those without a license—children, teenagers under sixteen, the old and infirm—found themselves completely dependent on someone who did. Such dependence led to the second unintended consequence: the virtual entrapment of wives and mothers as chauffeur slaves. As about sixty percent of married women did not work outside their homes in 1970, it naturally devolved upon them to shepherd their children to games, friends' houses, parties, lessons, and shopping.

As the number of Interstates increased in the 1960s, another quiet change was taking place in America that most of the public knew little about. Gradually the country was growing dependent on oil. Since World War II, when Americans had to endure fuel rationing, gasoline had been plentiful and cheap. Americans had steadily increased their consumption of gasoline from 55 billion gallons in 1956 to 115 billion gallons in 1973. As long as the nation was able to produce most of the oil used to make the gasoline, prices remained steady. American production reached a peak of 11.3 million barrels a day in 1970, but then slowly declined. Producers could not keep pace with the increasing consumption. Taking to the new Interstate roads at higher and higher speeds, motorists continued to burn more fuel, which forced the United States to rely increasingly on oil from Venezuela and the Middle East to meet the demand. By 1973, the United States was importing thirty-six percent of the oil it used for its cars and trucks, about 6 million barrels a day. Supplies became tighter than at any time since World War II. When he was President, Eisenhower had imposed a quota of 2 million barrels a day on foreign oil, to keep it from flooding the market. Faced with the problem not of a surplus but of apportioning the available oil, Richard Nixon had to abolish the quotas. Inevitably, the prices began to rise. Americans had been used to paying about 30 cents a gallon in 1964; by the end of 1973, they were paying close to a dollar. As a State Department officer who studied oil production for the Nixon administration wrote in *Foreign Affairs*, "This time the Wolf is here."

In the late fall of 1973, the wolf began to knock. Prior to that time,

Divided Highways

few Americans knew or cared about the Organization of Petroleum Exporting Countries, or OPEC. Soon it would become the most famous acronym in America, the subject of countless newspaper stories and dinner table conversations. The Arab states had formed OPEC in 1960 with the thought that if it controlled the flow of oil to the West, it would be able to raise the price. As long as the United States could produce enough oil to supply most of its needs and, in time of international crisis, the needs of its allies, the organization's power remained an impuissant dream of Arab potentates. But on October 6, 1973, when Egypt and Syria attacked Israel on the holiest of Jewish holidays, Yom Kippur, OPEC at last had the chance it had long dreamed of to use oil supplies as a weapon. At the same time Israel was reeling from the surprise Egyptian and Syrian attacks, OPEC members were meeting in Vienna to discuss raising the price of petroleum that American companies extracted from their oil fields. Now the war enabled OPEC to dictate the price increase: seventy percent. Later in the month, the cartel placed an outright embargo on shipments of oil to the United States. The cost jumped from $3 a barrel in October to $11.65 in December. By mid-December, buyers were bidding $17 for a barrel of Iranian crude.

Normally, when a commodity becomes precious, the natural laws of economics take over: People conserve, which lessens the demand and forces the producer to lower the price. If sugar or coffee became scarce, as they had briefly after World War II, people cut back their consumption. In the case of oil, however, America's highways made conservation difficult if not impossible. The roads had so changed the way people travel that most had no option but to drive. To many, mass transit was something quaint that existed only in larger, older cities, places where few wished to live.

Across the land, people went into a panic. Gasoline was not a commodity but an entitlement. It was as necessary to sustain life in America as water or air. Gasoline prices jumped from 37 cents for a gallon of regular in April to over 90 cents a gallon in December. More shocking than even the price increase was the shortage. Stations posted $5 limits on purchases—if they had gas to sell. Television newscasts showed lines of cars coiled around filling stations, and motorists fighting over spaces in the lines. Talk of rationing began to be heard among members of Congress and the administration. That April, before the embargo, John Ehrlichman greeted the idea of oil conservation with a dismissive sneer: "Conservation is not the Republican ethic." That November, after the embargo, Richard Nixon told the citizens of the nation in a television address that conservation was the new American ethic. Americans must turn down their thermostats, form car pools, and use mass transportation, which they had long neglected. Later, the president imposed Daylight Savings Time to conserve electricity. To conserve gasoline, he lowered the speed limit on the Interstate Highway System to fifty-five miles per hour. By December, the federal energy chief, William Simon, asked Americans to limit their gasoline purchases to ten gallons a week. After five months, OPEC nations ended their embargo and the gas began to flow again—but at a higher price than ever.

Motorists were angry. Naturally they took their aggressions to the Interstates. The gas shortage was bad enough, but the call to conservation and the lowering of the speed limits seemed even worse. On December 3, about fifty Pennsylvania drivers staged a protest on Interstate 80 that closed a fifteen-mile section of the highway through the Pocono Mountains. Six truckers blocked the eastbound lane of Interstate 84 near the New York state line. About thirty truckers in Brighton, Colorado, refused to move their rigs in protest of the high cost of diesel fuel, fuel shortages, and the fifty-five-mile-per-hour speed limit. Other drivers followed suit in Iowa, Illinois, Michigan, Nevada, Nebraska, Connecticut, and Delaware. In New Jersey, the governor had to call on the National Guard to remove blockading trucks. The truckers complained that higher fuel prices and lower speed limits were threatening their profits.

Nevertheless, for the first time since World War II, Americans actually reduced their use of gasoline in 1974. Conservation only diminished the flow of dollars into the Highway Trust Fund, for when gas sales went down, tax revenues lagged. In times of abundance, government statisticians could expect the revenues to increase by about five percent annually; now they were decreasing at about two and a half percent. One government expert estimated that in 1975, the fund would decrease by $400 million. The consequence of conservation trickled down to the states, too, as gasoline taxes supplied 40 cents of every dollar they spent on highway programs.

For decades, Americans had learned that theirs was the land of expansion and abundance. They had a moral duty to work and move with efficiency. Railroads had increased the pace of nineteenth-century America "by getting rid of all avoidable obstructions on the road," as Ralph Waldo Emerson said, and "leaving nothing to be conquered but pure space." The railroad had yielded to the highway in the twentieth century, especially the Interstate, and afforded Americans freedom as well as speed. The speed limit on the Interstates was 65 or 70, but the high number posted on automobile speedometers was usually 110 or 120, or sometimes 140. Even the highest number on the speedometer of the lowly Volkswagen read 100. Now, because of the schemes of a few despots from desert lands few Americans could find on a map, they were told to go no more than 55, if they had the gas to go at all.

These global events underscored how much Americans relied on their highways, particularly the growing network of Interstates. By 1973, Americans could find few if any goods—televisions and microwave ovens, refrigerators and stoves, chairs and tables—in their houses that had not traveled over the Interstate to reach them. Americans were so used to traveling by automobile that it was difficult for them to consider any other way. The Federal Highway Administration studied the impact of the gasoline shortage on urban travelers in Chicago and found that people chose to drive rather than use public transportation, and "carpooling was almost ignored." Those questioned ignored the suggestions to carpool because, the report found, they did not wish to forsake "the comfort, convenience, independence, and freedom of action" that the automobile afforded. At Christmas, in 1973, twelve percent of the populace traveled by planes to their holiday destination, seven percent by train, four percent by bus, and seventy-seven percent by private car.

The gasoline shortage and energy "crisis" compounded the country's general malaise. Abroad, the Nixon administration was pursuing a policy of "Vietnamization" of the war that had dragged on far longer than anyone cared to admit. Despite all the cheery talk from Washington, most realized that Americans were dying for a cause that few could understand, and, what was worse for the nation's psyche, the American side was losing. At home, Spiro Agnew had resigned from the office of vice president in disgrace after investigators discovered he had extorted money for state contracts when he was governor of Maryland. His successor, the minority leader of the House of Representatives, seemed to most Americans to be a cheerful and earnest lightweight whom Lyndon Johnson once described as being unable to walk and chew gum at the same time. Even more disturbing for most were the revelations of the Watergate investigations in progress. At the same time the energy crisis was unfolding, Nixon fired the special prosecutor who had been investigating him. Now the new vice president, Gerald Ford, a person whom everyone seemed to like but few seemed to respect and no one had elected to the office, stood only an impeachment and conviction away from the presidency. These events were shaking the foundations of American faith: military supremacy, progress and prosperity, faith in the probity of the president and vice president, and faith in the future.

How to break the American dependence on automobiles, trucks, and gasoline for transportation? Nothing seemed to work either for Nixon or his successor, Gerald Ford. Nixon imposed controls on the price that companies could charge for domestic oil, rushed approval of an eight-hundred-mile pipeline to carry oil from the north slope of Alaska to the port of Valdez on the southern coast, and proposed a grand scheme to make the United States self-reliant by 1980, "Project Independence." Ford set about to improve the efficiency of automobiles from their dismal average of thirteen miles per gallon. Talk abounded about synthetic fuels, gasohol, and how someday car engines would run on hydrogen molecules magically extracted from water. Ford's successor, Jimmy Carter, borrowed a phrase from the philosopher William James to call the energy crisis the "moral equivalent of war."

Little seemed to go as planned. In January 1979, the revolution in Iran sparked talk of another gasoline shortage, which in turn sparked another panic. No driver felt secure without a full tank, and it always seemed as though everyone had decided to fill his or her car at the same time. Once again, automobiles coiled around gasoline stations, more fights ensued among angry drivers, even murder. "I ask you to drive 15 miles a week fewer than you do now," said President Carter in a speech to the nation that only heightened the anxiety. "At least once a week take the bus, go by car pool—or, if you work close to home, walk." Once again, Americans were being denied the substance that made their life possible. No sooner had the panic and gas lines eased than a band of Iranians stormed the U.S. Embassy, taking eighty Americans hostage.

Naturally, the public looked for scapegoats: Unquestionably the Arab sheiks were public enemy number one, but the American executives of oil companies ran a close second. When average earnings of the ten largest oil companies rose over fifty percent in 1973, many Americans blamed their troubles on a conspiracy of oil barons. It was clear, so the thinking went, that they had conspired to fix the prices artificially high. In public hearings, senators outbid each other to denounce the executives. Henry F. Jackson, senator from the state of Washington, declared the profits to be "obscene."

Divided Highways

The shortage renewed the interest in mass transportation. Since 1969, when John Volpe became Secretary of Transportation, the Federal Highway Administration had been encouraging people to use buses and commuter trains. It prodded cities to designate special "HOV" (high-occupancy vehicle) lanes on suburban and urban Interstates, and promoted other schemes like "Dial A Ride." Except in large cities, however, mass transit for commuting was doomed to failure.

Much of the failure came about because large cities, particularly older cities in the East, were in serious trouble. Lured by the siren call of suburbia, whites had long since abandoned their urban apartments and left the task of maintaining an older infrastructure to minorities. In the space of a generation, Americans had become wholly dependent on the automobile to connect them with commerce and culture. Parents relied on their cars for their employment, their food, even a trip to the library. Children needed their parents or a school bus for their education, their shopping, and their recreation.

Since the 1950s, businesses, too, had followed people in their exodus to the country. New York, the city of corporate headquarters through the first half of the century, is a good example. General Foods left for suburban White Plains in 1954; a decade later, IBM left for a more distant suburb, Armonk, north of the city; then Olin to Stamford, Connecticut, and Union Carbide to Danbury—about thirty-eight major corporations over two decades had fled the city. Often corporations arranged to build a connecting road between their new headquarters and the Interstate. Soon Connecticut had its own problems with massive congestion, as new cities came to the country—except at night, when the headquarters closed and the workers left for their suburban houses and the CEO for his country estate.

It was the country estate that often decided the move. Of thirty-eight corporations that abandoned the city for the country, the astute urban anthropologist William H. Whyte found "thirty-one moved to a place close to the top man's home." The distance from the CEO's home to company headquarters averaged eight miles. It was as though these chief executive officers who had no love for the city were waiting for the highways to improve so they could then move their offices closer to their homes. Everyone else had to follow along. But, Whyte also found, not everyone moved with the corporation. When Union Carbide went to

Danbury, twelve hundred of the thirty-two hundred employees located in New York refused to rusticate themselves. That meant twelve hundred jobs opened up, and corporate personnel offices looked to people living in the suburbs to fill them. Many of the jobs were taken by suburban women, a well-educated group who wanted to work.

There are even more fundamental reasons why mass transportation does not succeed: It coordinates people's movement through both time and space in ways that Americans find to be repellent. Train and bus schedules are not flexible; car schedules are. Trains and buses are not convenient; cars are. Trains and buses demand that one ride with someone else; cars allow one to drive alone. For the past two decades, Americans had been told that privacy was an essential freedom. How can one maintain privacy sitting next to someone else?

There were exceptions, of course. Older cities like New York and Boston operated subway systems that helped to take the strain off the highways. Many cities in the East had commuter train service that regularly transported thousands to work annually. But as men like Robert Moses had held control of most of the transportation dollars, which they put into road construction, both the railroads and subways had been allowed to decline. Equipment was broken or worn out, service was inefficient and often delayed. Such neglect had taken its toll, too. Ridership was down on most lines, as commuters had more or less given up on the service. Now officials were urging those same commuters to go back to the lines that had been neglected for decades.

Many commuters would have nothing to do with the new ethic. They asked why drive the car to a lot in order to take public transportation, when one can drive to one's destination alone for just a little more effort? There seemed to be a fundamental hypocrisy to those who wanted to get Americans to abandon their cars for mass transit, for more often than not they drove about (or were driven) in their own private cars. "Many people advocate mass transit for the other person," Eric Sevareid wryly commented on CBS television, "so they themselves will be able to enjoy riding on congestion-free expressways."

Despite the nation's increasing reliance on its highways, especially the Interstates, most Americans in the 1980s seemed indifferent and even hostile to their presence. Cynicism about the nation's achievements came naturally to many, and the greatest engineered structure in the world was not spared. Even though Interstates were vital to the lives Americans led—the way they worked, the goods they consumed, and the places where they lived and played—the superhighways represented little more than miles of blandness. "Thanks to the interstate highway system," America's most famous road traveler, Charles Kuralt, remarked acerbically, "it is now possible to cross the country from coast to coast without seeing anything." Though in many cases the highways were engineering feats that made Americans' way of living possible, most people took them for granted.

There had been a time when Americans reveled in their achievements of great civil engineering projects, when Walt Whitman had sung of the "strong light works of engineers." In 1825, four former presidents of the United States—John Adams, Jefferson, Madison, and Monroe—joined John Quincy Adams in New York City to celebrate the opening of the Erie Canal. On that occasion Governor DeWitt Clinton, the canal's great champion, poured a keg of water he had brought from Lake Erie into the Atlantic Ocean. In 1883, President Chester A. Arthur spoke at the opening of the Great East River Bridge connecting the cities of Brooklyn and New York. Speakers called the structure, whose 159-foot-tall towers dominated the cities, the river, and the skyline, an "astounding exhibition of the power of man to change the face of nature" and a testament to the "moral qualities of the human soul." In 1913, President Woodrow Wilson had pressed a button in the White House to light the Woolworth Building. One speaker at the dedication proclaimed the nickel dime tower, then the tallest in the world, to be a "cathedral of commerce." In 1936, President Franklin Delano Roosevelt addressed the Third World Power Conference in Washington, D.C., on the importance of engineering in solving the nation's social problems. At the conclusion of his speech, he pressed a button that stirred the turbines in the Boulder Dam to "creative activity." "Boulder Dam," said the president as his right index finger came down, "I call you to life!"

Only one president presided over the opening of a section of the Interstate highway. On Thursday, November 14, 1963, John Kennedy flew to the Mason-Dixon line between Delaware and Maryland to cut a blue and gray ribbon across Interstate 95, the principal north-south highway between Maine and Florida. To Kennedy the occasion symbolized the "partnership between the Federal Government and the States . . . the effort we have made to achieve the most modern interstate highway system in the world."

Tom Lewis

In comparison with other technological accomplishments of the time, the Interstate highways seemed distinctly ordinary. Despite the engineering feats that went into it, for mile after mile it did nothing but lie on the ground. In 1957, the year the Interstate program really got under way, the first nuclear electric power plant opened in Shippingport, Pennsylvania, moving some to predict that electricity would soon be free for everyone. Operators of the *Nautilus*, the first nuclear-powered submarine, reported that it had used 8.3 pounds of uranium in its first sixty thousand miles of undersea travel. Three air force pilots flew their jets from London to Los Angeles in fourteen hours, five minutes, and the Boeing Company was designing its 707, the first commercial jet plane to be built in the United States. Americans fixed their imaginations not so much on the earth as the heavens, as space exploration and intercontinental rocketry came into prominence. That year Bernard Lovell completed the world's largest radio telescope at Jodrell Bank, England, in time to track the Russians' *Sputnik 1*, the first artificial satellite, a 184-pound sphere that was orbiting the earth every ninety minutes. Russia successfully tested an intercontinental ballistic missile, while the United States was developing its own rockets, the Redstone and the Vanguard. Was the United States vulnerable to attack? Americans wanted to know. Could the Russians obliterate American cities with nuclear bombs delivered by ICBMs launched from Eastern Europe or Moscow?

But Americans' obsession with the space program waned after Neil Armstrong stepped on the moon. By 1974, astronauts had made six lunar landings, spending a total of nearly two weeks gathering rocks, riding around in a sophisticated electric dune buggy, planting American flags, and playing golf. Television networks curtailed their coverage of the rocket launches and moon landings as viewers seemed no longer interested. If Americans were inured to feats of rocketry, why would they care about a new superhighway? The commonplace had become boring to a culture that demanded ever greater technological achievements.

If highway construction seemed more ordinary than most engineering projects, that's because it was. Much of the building of the Interstate demanded little ongoing engineering imagination. Since the days of the Pennsylvania Turnpike, engineers had known they could build roads that would allow cars and trucks to travel fast safely. (Gone were the days of the genteel forty-five-mile-per-hour speed limit that Robert Moses imposed on his parkways.) Beginning with the Pennsylvania Turnpike construction in 1940, engineers had standardized highway construction—mile after mile of divided roadway with lanes twelve feet wide; ten-foot breakdown lanes; curves and grades that allowed for speeds of seventy miles per hour. The Bureau of Public Roads and the American Association of State Highway Officials issued specifications for construction that left little leeway for interpretation. Engineers simply applied the rules to the task at hand, be it Interstate 10 through Santa Monica, California, or Interstate 94 through Dickinson, North Dakota. They simply repeated the tasks in small increments of usually five, ten, twenty, or thirty miles many times over: surveying, walking the line, grading the land, laying the substrate, laying the asphalt or concrete, painting the lines, erecting the signs, holding the ribbon-cutting ceremony, and moving on.

Despite its uniformity, there are numerous sections of the Interstate Highway System that do represent extraordinary engineering. Almost always, too, these achievements involved massive amounts of materials and a small army of workers. Outside Washington, D.C., where Interstate 395 passes by the Pentagon, engineers spent $51.5 million constructing one mile of highway known as the "Mixing Bowl." To construct that one mile, workers moved 1.5 million cubic yards of earth; poured 68,000 cubic yards of concrete; and erected 17 million tons of steel, much of it in 19 bridges. When they finished in 1971, they had created 28 highway lanes on 3 different levels of roadway.

Surely one of the greatest structural accomplishments in the entire Interstate system took place on Interstate 70 in the middle of Colorado. The borders of Colorado form a perfect rectangle about four hundred by three hundred miles, a surveyor's convenience, that does not consider any natural features of the land. The great natural feature the Rockies runs through the center of the state to form a ten-thousand- to fourteen-thousand-foot barrier separating east from west. Denver and Colorado Springs developed on the eastern side of the mountain range, and Glenwood Springs and Grand Junction on the western. Cross-state travel was difficult in the summer and impossible in the winter. It was not until 1928 that Denver, the state capital, became a part of the transcontinental railroad. Automobile travelers took winding roads through one of nineteen mountain passes with colorful names like Wolf Creek,

Slumgullion, Rabbit Ears, and Muddy. Airline companies had started service in Colorado in the 1920s, but without pressurized cabins planes could not fly over the mountains. Denver had flights to Cheyenne and Albuquerque and points east, but none west. Towns on the western slope, like Breckenridge and Dillon, were economically isolated as well, for few from Denver would make the perilous drive through the mountains. "Colorado was more like two states independent of each other," said one Coloradan. "There were months and months during the winters when you didn't go to Steamboat Springs on the highway; you didn't go to Grand Junction; you didn't go any place on the Western Slope."

Because of the difficulties they anticipated in crossing the Rockies, officials with the Bureau of Public Roads had stopped Interstate 70 at Denver. The great east-west Interstates 10, 40, 80, and 90 avoided the formidable heights one encountered in Colorado. It was not until 1957 that they decided to extend the highway from Denver to Interstate 15 at Cove Fort, Utah. Their plan was to follow the Loveland Pass and, close to the summit at 11,158 feet, tunnel through the Continental Divide. A tunnel at such a height had never been attempted before. The person in charge of construction would be a man who held no degrees in civil engineering and had just one year of education beyond high school, Charles Shumate.

Shumate was a man of outspoken opinions that even in the contentious 1970s made some around him cringe. Yet no one ever doubted his professional competence. Born in 1904, Shumate grew up on a farm in Illinois and, after graduation from high school, went to the University of Illinois. "But I ran out of money, after a year," he said. His family moved to Colorado, and, at age twenty, Shumate took a job with the state highway department as a chainman, the one who assisted surveyors in measuring distances. "Ninety dollars a month and my Ford for wheels," he remembered a half century later. "Lowest form of engineering help in the world." But he advanced swiftly through a succession of posts—instrument man, project engineer, resident engineer, then chief administrative engineer of the maintenance division. Then, in 1954, after the state legislature exempted Shumate from the law that said he had to be a graduate engineer, Governor Love appointed him state highway engineer.

The design contract for the "Straight Creek Tunnel," as the Continental Divide tunnel was called, was awarded in February 1966. Everyone agreed it would be a formidable job. In 1947 and 1956, the state highway department proposed tunnels, but could not interest contractors to make any serious bids to build them. Now, with the Interstate extending to Cove Fort, its construction was imperative. The tunnel would be huge. Shumate likened the task to "putting a five-story building through a mountain." As building a tunnel at that altitude and that length for automobiles and trucks had never been attempted, there were numerous questions for which only testing and experience would provide answers.

Engineers decided early on to build *two* tunnels or bores through the mountain, one for eastbound traffic, the other for west. Their plan was simple in outline: They would begin by making a smaller-diameter "pioneer bore." From the geologic information they gathered in the bore, they would then proceed to drill a large bore for traffic. Once they had opened the first tunnel, they would enlarge the pioneer bore, making it into the second tunnel. At either end, motorists would enter a gigantic portal before heading into the proper tunnel. While the plan looked easy, the details ensured its difficulty.

Though Shumate and his engineers knew in general that an increase in altitude meant an increase in carbon monoxide emissions, they had little specific data. They decided to conduct a variety of tests to determine how great a problem carbon monoxide would be at this height, and to help them plan a ventilation system for the tunnel. By monitoring the performance of forty vehicles of various ages and sizes, driven by a variety of drivers, the engineers were able to establish how great the ventilation fans should be—six fans at each end capable of delivering 1.6 million cubic feet of fresh air per minute. The air would enter the tunnel at the level of the roadway and leave through exhaust ducts in the ceiling. The three-story-high ventilation buildings at the entrances would each have a floor space of 47,000 square feet. The exhaust duct alone would have an area of 225 square feet.

Questions about carbon monoxide paled in comparison with those about geology. The information gleaned from the pilot bore would help geologists and engineers determine how much steel reinforcement they needed to prevent a cave-in. They learned that the bedrock was seventy-five percent granite and twenty-five percent metamorphic gneiss and schist. Considering the rock composition as well as the numerous faults and sheer zones that they encountered, they guessed where they would need minimum, intermediate, and maximum support. But it was merely a guess as to what they would find when they made their first bore. As one of the geologists said to Shumate, "Charlie, you've got to remember, we can't see into that mountain any further than you."

While they were drilling the pilot bore, geologists realized that water would be a major problem. After recording water flowing from the tunnel opening at a rate of three hundred gallons per minute during spring runoff, the engineers designed a drainage system capable of handling five hundred gallons a minute.

"We had done everything that was humanly possible [to anticipate the problems]" Shumate reflected, but it was not enough. "We came up with a design and everything looked fine until we got there—in the big hole. Then it started giving way. There's a place up there now—there's six and a half feet of reinforced concrete out there to keep it from pushing in."

But Shumate's battle went on. It took about six thousand people working a total of 4.9 million hours over five years to complete the first bore. Three men lost their lives. In 1969, with the opening of the first bore still several years away, Governor John Love asked the legislature to name the tunnel in honor of the president who had signed the Interstate legislation. When he opened the first bore of the Eisenhower Tunnel in March 1973, he called it "possibly the most effective answer to tying east and west Colorado together and opening the way West." The second bore did not open for six and a half more years, in December 1979. It had taken thirteen years and nine months to complete the Eisenhower Tunnel—longer than it took to build the Brooklyn Bridge. In the end, the tunnel cost $125 million, about two and a half times the original estimate. But everyone acknowledged that it was a masterful engineering triumph. When the second bore was completed, Charles Shumate decided to retire: "I told many people that one of those in a lifetime is enough."

In November 1970, the Colorado State Highway Department offered Mr. Jamet P. Bonnema a job as an engineering technician in the Straight Creek Tunnel. The job involved gathering and analyzing data from various monitoring stations within the tunnel. Bonnema, who was an honors graduate from the University of Colorado and had worked as an engineering aide at Boeing in Seattle, scored very high on the department's application test. When Janet P. Bonnema called on the Highway Department to claim her job, officials were stunned to learn that through the department's clerical mistake they had hired not a man but a woman. She could not work in the tunnel, she was told. A long-standing belief among tunnel workers held that if a woman should enter a tunnel while it was under construction, it was doomed to collapse and men would lose their lives. "Some years ago I took my wife into a tunnel," said one of the officials, "and the next day we had a man get killed." The department offered Bonnema a drafting job instead. She took it, but then filed a class-action suit demanding $100,000 and the right to work in the tunnel. "She was a brilliant gal," Shumate remembered. "She caused me a lot of misery."

Shumate and the highway department refused to relent. "We just didn't go for it." Already far behind schedule and with the project well over budget, Shumate was unwilling to challenge the men and their superstition. A tunnel was no place for a woman. The men there used foul language. A woman would not be equal to the task. "You put one woman in there with a hundred other men," went the specious chivalric argument of the time, "you've got to have the same toilet facilities for her as you do for all the rest of them." The arguments made little sense to Bonnema, who drove a motorcycle, was an accomplished rock climber, and was used to hitchhiking in parts of the world where there were no toilet facilities. She could do the job. Her suit never went to trial. In November 1972, the citizens of Colorado ratified the Equal Rights Amendment to the Constitution, and the state officials quickly settled out of court for $6,750 and gave Bonnema the right to work beneath the ground. "The District Judge called me one night at home," Shumate remembered. "'For Christ's sake,'" said the judge, "'why don't you send her in there.' And that's what we did."

On November 9, 1972, Janet Bonnema walked into the tunnel for the first time, and sixty men walked out in protest. Daryl B. Benz went to the locker room where the men dressed and turned in his badge, boots, hard hat, and slicker. "They had a woman in the tunnel, and I will not work there," he told a reporter. "It's a jinx. I've seen too many die after a woman was in a tunnel." Benz never returned to the site; but the rest did, and the tunnel did not collapse.

Taking other signals from the temper of the times, the Federal Highway Administration expanded Lady Bird Johnson's concept of highway beautification. Starting in 1969, the administration gave design awards for superior highways. By the mid-seventies, good design counted for more than an efficient roadway. Now, environmental considerations became paramount. To be sure, sometimes the engineers' acquiescence to the demands of environmentalists came grudgingly, and often after a prolonged battle that usually included litigation, but the fact remains that the engineers did listen.

Interstate 66 in Virginia is a good example of how the Federal Highway Administration finally responded after prolonged battles. The four-lane highway begins at Interstate 81 at Middletown in the west and proceeds east for seventy-five miles across the top of Virginia, crosses the Potomac River on the Theodore Roosevelt Bridge, and ends at a city street in the District of Columbia near the Watergate Hotel. Planners had something different in mind when they first proposed the highway. The section through Arlington was to be eight lanes; it was to cross the Potomac into the District of Columbia farther north, on a bridge to be erected over Three Sisters Island; and, most importantly, it would connect with the proposed Inner Beltway. Environmentalists changed the designers' plans. As opposition to the original plans grew, the engineers played highway triage. They scuttled the Three Sisters Bridge. The Inner Belt followed. Only Interstate 66 remained in their plans. It fell to William T. Coleman, the African-American lawyer and coauthor of the brief to the Supreme Court in *Brown v. Board of Education of Topeka*, whom Gerald Ford had appointed Secretary of Transportation, to determine what should be done with the highway. Coleman decided for the Interstate, but with numerous environmental restrictions: He cut the number of lanes from eight to four and called for noise barriers to be erected beside the roadway as it passed through Arlington. There would be abundant landscaping, and a hiking and biking trail near the right-of-way. To encourage mass transportation, the highway had room in the median for the light-rail Washington Metro. To encourage car pools, he called for it to be closed to all but high-occupancy vehicles during rush hours.

By the mid-1980s, the Federal Highway Administration seemed more inclined than ever to embrace the notions that small is beautiful and less is more. Through the White Mountains in New Hampshire, Interstate 93 becomes a parkway for ten miles. The problems began as soon as designers issued their plans for a four-lane highway beneath the symbol of New Hampshire, the Old Man of the Mountain, the great granite outcrop overlooking Franconia Notch. Would blasting for the highway bring down the face? Would vibrations from passing cars and trucks do the same? What of the destructive force of pounding an Interstate through one of the more fragile spots in America? After much debate, engineers came up with a plan for a three-lane—and sometimes two-lane—parkway in the early Robert Moses tradition, complete with wooden barriers, stone bridge supports, and a severely restricted speed limit of forty-five miles per hour. For these ten miles of landscape, strict Interstate rules were forgotten.

Indifference. Scorn. Embarrassment. Such were the attitudes of many in the country in the 1980s as the construction of the Interstate Highway System was coming to a close. Many accepted the highways as a part of contemporary life and thought little about them, except, on occasion, to complain that they were overcrowded or falling apart. Others, especially environmentalists and those who lived in urban areas, considered the Interstates destructive forces that had played havoc on the ecology and community. Still others, especially some engineers and officials in the Federal Highway Administration and the federal Department of Transportation, seemed embarrassed by all that they had achieved.

Surely, there was no more telling indicator of their embarrassment than the opening of the last section of Interstate 80 in Salt Lake City, Utah, on August 22, 1986. The five miles signified the completion of the first transcontinental Interstate highway, thirty years and fifty-five days after Dwight Eisenhower had signed the bill that had made it possible. Many who commented on the occasion compared it with another great feat in the history of transportation that took place 117 years earlier about seventy-five miles from Interstate 80: the driving of the golden spike at Promontory, Utah, to complete the nation's first transcontinental railroad. Curiously, though, few of any prominence wanted to celebrate this landmark of federal and state cooperation. The governor of Utah, Norman R. Bangerter, did not attend. Nor did Elizabeth Dole, Secretary of Transportation. Nor did Ray Barnhart, head of the Federal Highway Administration. It was not politically expedient to do so. The lieutenant governor and the head of the local region of the Federal Highway Administration were the best anyone could muster for the occasion.

Though politicians and Americans in general tried to ignore the Interstates, they used them. American drivers had taken to the highways in ever-increasing numbers. By 1986, builders had completed ninety-seven percent of the system. True, there were still key sections that remained to be built—Interstate 287 around metropolitan New York, a small section of Interstate 90 in Idaho, Interstate 105 the Century Freeway in Los Angeles, among them—but the concrete and asphalt serpent had coiled its way across the nation. Even though it accounted for about one percent of the nation's highways, by 1986 the system carried about twenty percent of the nation's traffic and fifty percent of all its trucks.

In many cases, there was no other option for travel but the Interstates and the tangle of roads that fed them. Long ago, trolleys had been sent to the dump. Long-distance and commuter railroads were declining. Commuting distances increased and communities scattered as builders in the suburbs—and indeed many zoning boards—had decided that every house needed at least a half-acre of land around it. Through their representatives in Congress and with the generous assistance of the engineers, public officials, manufacturers, and truckers who make up the highway lobby, the American people had shaped the Interstate Highway System. Now the Interstates were shaping them.

CONTINENTAL DRIFT

Las Vegas is not a good town for psychedelic drugs. Reality itself is too twisted.

HUNTER S. THOMPSON

The city of Las Vegas, Nevada, on Interstate 15. Interstate 15 begins in the center of San Diego and traverses Nevada, Utah, and Idaho, before ending 1,435 miles later at Sweetgrass, Montana, on the Canadian border. Along the way the route touches major cities, including Las Vegas; Salt Lake City; Pocatello, Idaho; and Great Falls, Montana. With a population increase of fifty-seven percent between 1980 and 1990, Las Vegas ranks with the fastest-growing cities in the nation. But there are places on Interstate 15 that rank with the most inhospitable territory in the United States. And there are places that are nearly deserted: Baker, California, home of the world's tallest thermometer; ZZYZX Road in the Mojave Desert; the Valley of Fire in Nevada; the Virgin River in Arizona; the Juab Valley in Utah; the Monida pass in Idaho; and Wolf Creek in Montana. "In the United States," Gertrude Stein once observed, "there is more space where nobody is than where anybody is."

Like other superhighways, Interstate 15 functions as a great spinal column that gives commercial life and cohesion to everyone and

everything on either side. People and businesses place their lives in rela-
tion to the highway. ("We're about three miles east of 15 on high-
way 21." "Victorville is situated . . . just north of the San Bernadino
Mountains, at the edge of the Mojave Desert. Interstate 15 and State
Highway 1 intersect near the heart of the city.") Burghers of local cham-
bers of commerce use the highway as a magnet to lure businesses: "Helig-
Meyers Selects Hesperia," reads the press release from the California city.
"The agreement . . . calls for development of a 456,000 sq. ft. building at
Interstate 15." "Park and Ride" lots dot the exits in San Diego.

By 1990, the desolate inhospitable stretch of Interstate 15 northeast
of Las Vegas had become one of the great highways for UFO sightings.
("When I was sixteen, I saw my first alien spacecraft on the side of Interstate 15," says a veteran witness to many landings.) Other travelers had
come to regard the desert portions of I-15, the space where nobody is,
as a vast dumping ground, a place to discard possessions and people no
longer needed. Just off the roadway lie old refrigerators, cars, clothing,
mattresses, those possessions the culture does not know quite what to
do with when they have served their purpose. Highway patrols—and
sometimes startled motorists—find human remains, for those in Los
Angeles or Las Vegas with an unwanted body on their hands regard
Interstate 15 as the road of choice for disposal. There, in the unrelenting
sun and wind, the flotsam of American culture waits silently to be consumed by sand.

LAS VEGAS—THE AMERICAN WAY TO PLAY! reads the sign on
the Santa Monica Freeway, Interstate 10. Las Vegas! the electrified oasis
in the desert, Bugsy Segal's paradise. To get there, head east on I-10 and
then, at Mira Loma, take I-15 north. Hundreds of thousands do just that
each year, and some never leave. As the California economy went sour
in the 1980s and early 1990s, men, women, and children packed up
their cars and trucks and headed north on Interstate 15. Many never
returned. By 1993, four of every ten people applying for a driver's
license in Clark County, Nevada (home to Las Vegas), came from California. The transplanted Californians, lured by cheap housing, cheap
energy from nearby Hoover Dam, adequate schools, and virtually segregated living, helped to make Las Vegas a boomtown in 1990. The 1990
census counted over 741,000 people in the Las Vegas area. In 1990, an
average of 75 people arrived each *day*. The workforce in Las Vegas numbered about 371,000 people. Of those, 277,000 drove to work alone;
57,000 went in a car pool; 7,500 took public transportation; and 13,500

walked. (The rest listed their transportation as "other.") In Las Vegas, almost twice as many people walked to work as took the bus.

The seventy-five who arrived in Las Vegas each day were really just the variation of a long-running theme in American life. When many of our grandparents and great-grandparents got off the boat at Ellis Island in the first decade of this century, they could have traveled much of the East Coast on a slow but functioning trolley and train system. Some did just that. The grandparents of tomorrow arrive not by boat but by plane, and usually at an airport in New York or Los Angeles. From there, they must take a bus or a car on the Interstate to get anywhere. Once they get somewhere, they know they can move again by car or bus over an Interstate.

Americans depend on the automobile, and the Interstates have hastened that dependence. Many Americans are not happy about this fact of contemporary life, and some would even say we made a pact with the devil when we embraced the automobile as a way of life. The Interstates are conduits of noise and pollution, conformity and blandness. They take us everywhere and nowhere. They have become the roads we love to hate, but we cannot imagine our world without them. Such is the case in Las Vegas and around the nation.

In 1990, Las Vegas was into its third decade of extraordinary expansion. Between 1970 and 1980, the metropolitan Las Vegas area ranked among the leaders of the nation with a population growth of 69.5 percent; in the next decade, it again led the nation, with 57 percent growth. Las Vegas was an extreme example of what was happening throughout the South and West. Between 1980 and 1990, all the fastest-growing metropolitan areas—Dallas–Fort Worth; Phoenix; Orlando; Austin; Tucson; Lakeland–Winter Haven, Florida; and McCallen–Edenberg–Mission, Texas—were in the South and West. Conversely, all the metropolitan regions that lost population were in the Northeast and Midwest, places like New York, Philadelphia, St. Louis, and Buffalo. By 1990, the economic energy of the nation had moved from the railroad to the highway, and the highways were opening up new regions in the South and West for development.

Demographers like to determine the "population center" of the United States, that fictional fulcrum on which the nation and all the people on it would balance perfectly—provided, of course, the land were flat and every man, woman, and child stood still and weighed the same amount. Each decade, after statisticians digest the census reports, they fix on one precise spot on one property in the Midwest and declare it to be the fulcrum of the nation on the national census day, which significantly is April Fool's. Inevitably, after the news gets out, reporters arrive on the scene to interview the owner, who often does not quite understand what the fuss is about or the significance of being at the center. Local officials regard the news as free publicity and frequently hold a parade and erect a sign on the highway proclaiming their town's importance to the nation. They all enjoy their fifteen minutes of fame. More than just an interesting exercise, however, the demographers' finding shows how the American people are shifting across the landscape. The center always moves west, and usually—though not always—slightly south. In 1950, it stood at the 38th latitude and the 89th longitude, 8 miles north-northwest of Olney, in Richland County, Illinois. Forty years later, the population center had crossed the Mississippi into the 37th latitude and the 91st longitude, 9.7 miles southwest of Steelville, in Crawford County, Missouri. In four decades the population center had moved 195 miles west and 65 miles south.

If the population was moving west and south, it was also moving to the suburbs. As it did, the suburbs became population extensions of the city, and more and more a part of the metropolis. In the fifties and sixties the suburbs had often been an appendage to the host city on which they relied for jobs and culture. By 1990, the suburb had metamorphosed into something more, often an urban area in its own right. The case of Phoenix was typical. Between 1980 and 1990, it grew by twenty-four percent, while its outlying suburbs increased by forty. The same held true for Albuquerque, Dallas, Atlanta, and many other cities with suburbs. Suburbs of the past often grew into strip cities, some with a hundred thousand or more people, lined up along the Interstates. By 1990, about seventy-seven percent of Americans lived in metropolitan areas, and most of the new metropolitan areas were in the South and West.

By 1990, nearly three of every four workers drove to their jobs alone, while the number riding in car pools and the percentage riding on mass transit declined. On every business day the average American took 22.3 minutes to drive an average of 10.9 miles to work. The year 1990 was one of firsts for car ownership: For the first time ever, the number of households without a vehicle slipped below ten percent; nearly thirty-three percent of American households had one vehicle; forty percent owned two; and nearly twenty percent owned three or more. Even in New York City, hardly an environment hospitable to cars, two thousand households reported owning at least three cars, trucks, or vans. America had just about completed the shift to the automobile and the highway.

One might think Americans would resent their dependence upon a single means of transportation, and their having to spend forty-five minutes each day commuting. Serious and intelligent critics of the Interstate Highway System like Andreas Duany often make the point that America gives us the illusion of freedom while actually tying us to our automobiles: "Our standard of living, statistically, is very high. . . . Our quality of life, however, is not," said Duany, making the comparison with Italy and France. "The Frenchman or the Italian might have smaller square footage and perhaps one car per family, but they have an awful lot of free time, because they don't spend their free time commuting—you know, commutes are very short, or walkable. . . . So they have an awful lot of free time and in my opinion, quality of life is measured by having free time, and having the funds to do something with that free time. And, the kind of compact planning that you have in Europe both liberates that time and funds for your leisure pursuits." By contrast, the American system commits one to commuting. It is also true that those with higher incomes usually live farther from their work and therefore have longer commutes.

Duany's arguments—and the arguments of others against the procrustean commute that many endure each day—makes good sense. But it assumes that Americans could have been trained to do something else. It also ignores the fact that American commuters seem to enjoy rather than endure their circumstance. "We've been told over and over that driving a car just to get from one place to another is a form of mental hibernation," wrote Jack Smith, a columnist for the *Los Angeles Times*, in 1971. But, Smith continued, "the only time most of us have for reflection is behind the wheel." Readers concurred. One anthropologist wrote to say that "Freeways and freeway driving are a popular devil. And the Freeways during the traffic crunches are the devil, certainly. But there are glorious times. Those times of privacy and contemplation, of separateness and selfness when one can be truly alone and thoughtful."

"Mass transportation is doomed to failure in North America," Marshall McLuhan prophesied in 1965, "because a person's car is the only place where he can be alone and think." Surely intellectual privacy accounted in part for the declining percentage of commuters who rode in car pools, buses, or trains, but there were other reasons people enjoyed their cars. Anyone who stands at the side of a really congested highway, say Interstate 405 in Los Angeles, will see drivers engaged in myriad activities—filing nails, talking on cellular telephones, grooming, picking noses, shaving, watching television, dressing, undressing, or reading. Only occasionally do drivers show signs of anger.

If the Interstates make privacy possible, they also foster something else that many Americans desire: isolation. Those no longer clustered in cities often revel in the fact that they have the space of at least a building lot between themselves and their neighbors. One Las Vegas resident, a consultant recently migrated from California, cited the high wall surrounding his property. "Now nobody knows who I am or what I do, and I like it that way. I don't want to know my neighbors, and I don't want them to know me. I want to be left alone to do what I please." For some, the shared experience of a community is a negative quality.

Despite the wealth of activities that can take place during Interstate driving, the roads have remained the safest in the nation and the envy of every other nation. Most accidents are singular affairs. A moment's inattention at sixty-five or seventy miles an hour can send a car flying off the roadway with serious consequences.

Since the first Interstates of 1956, engineers have worked constantly to make them safer. At least some of the credit for these improvements should go to an obscure television repairman from the Bronx, whose consistent criticism of safety on the Interstates made complaining into a high art form. In the 1960s, Joseph Linko began asking questions about the highways. Lane barriers tended to do more damage to vehicles than they should. Engineers mounted signs on solid supports rather than ones that would break on impact. Linko wanted to know why. What about sand barrels? What about median barriers? Linko wanted them and he wanted them now. "What Linko does," said the *Washington Post*, "is nag, nag, nag." The nagging did not stop at the Federal Highway Administration, either. Members of Congress and their staffs, and the Insurance Institute for Highway Safety, all heard from Linko. In 1971, he closed his television repair shop and went to Washington to continue his nagging. His speciality, said Linko, was "the stupidity of engineers and construction crews who just don't think about what they're doing."

Divided Highways

As a result of Linko's complaints and the efforts of the Federal Highway Administration, the Interstates became much more forgiving highways. Road designers included clear zones, places with no obstructions where a car, were it to leave the road, would have room to stop without hitting an obstruction. They designed highway hardware—light poles, sign poles, and the like—to break on impact. They created guardrails that would slow a car or truck and guide it to a stop. Those objects that could not be moved, like bridge abutments, the engineers shielded with elaborate plastic barriers that repel a car or truck on impact.

When they do occur, however, accidents on the Interstates are often spectacular and often deadly. In just an instant a dozen people perished on Interstate 75 near Calhoun, Tennessee. Stretching from Sault Ste. Marie, Michigan, to Fort Lauderdale, Florida, Interstate 75 is one of the main north-south highways east of the Mississippi. Near cities like Detroit, Cincinnati, and Atlanta, the road is clogged each morning and evening with commuter traffic. The road past Calhoun, a small town about forty miles northeast of Chattanooga, is busy but not overcrowded, which means that about twenty-eight thousand vehicles traveling at about sixty miles an hour pass by each day. Indeed, the safety of the Interstate depends on swift movement, which is why most of the highways have a minimum speed limit as well as a maximum. Stopped cars and trucks on the highway act like a derelict ship that is a danger to all other vessels. There are times, of course, when vehicles must stop. Such was the case about nine A.M. on December 11, 1991, on a level stretch crossing the Hiwassee River when a sudden fog enshrouded the highway.

Fog ranks among the most terrifying dangers for motorists on any road, and takes about eight hundred lives a year, but on the Interstates, where traffic moves swiftly, it can be especially lethal. Coastal regions of the country, especially in the Northeast and Northwest, frequently experience fog thick enough to ground airplanes with sophisticated navigation instruments, yet cars and trucks rarely stop. Calhoun experiences between thirty and forty-five foggy days a year, but the fog that engulfed Interstate 75 on December 11 was sudden and thick. One person described it "like someone throwing a sheet over you." Within seconds, ninety-nine cars, buses, vans, and trucks all traveling about sixty-five miles per hour collided, leaving fifty hurt and twelve dead.

To Jerry Nye of the Bradley County Sheriff's Department, "It sounded like the end of the world. They were bringing in helicopters from Knoxville, Chattanooga, everywhere; we were hearing ambulances running constantly along the Interstate; I really didn't realize how bad it was until I saw some people still trapped in vehicles burning, wedged between trucks in positions where nobody could get them out."

Among those trapped was Donald Albrecht. He, his wife, Nancy, and their teenage son had been traveling the Interstates for six years as self-proclaimed missionaries, preaching the gospel at truck stops and rest areas to anyone who would listen, and earning money by selling jewelry they made from rocks and gems they had found along the wayside. On impact, the Albrechts' converted bus was engulfed in flames. Nancy and her son escaped. Donald remained trapped. "I could hear my husband saying, 'Somebody help me!' And I looked around and he had managed to get half of his body out the window and there were some men there trying to pull him out and they couldn't get him out and the flames got worse and finally they quit. And I was laying there and I was screaming, 'Somebody please help him,' and they kept saying, 'He's gone, lady, he's gone,' and I got up and walked over to where he was and tried to pull him out, but I couldn't do it, and this man just kept saying, 'He's gone, lady; he's gone.' "

Such accidents, though rare, are indelible, and always make for a dramatic newspaper photograph of a tangled steel snake stretching along the highway. Often taken from the vantage point of the air, the photograph conveys the enormity of what has happened. On the ground, as the poet Peter Sears has written,

A crowd moves in
to autograph their eyes.

But such photographs give a false impression of the highway's safety. On the entire Interstate Highway System in 1990, just 4,941 people lost their lives. The number is especially low when one considers that cars, trucks, and buses traveled 479 billion miles on the Interstates. The death rate per 100 million vehicle miles was 1.03.

The building of the Interstates complemented the extensions of freedom and independence that were taking place across the nation. In no case were these extensions more apparent than with black Americans and women.

From the 1920s to well into the 1950s, as the automobile brought them more mobility, African-Americans encountered hostilities at the hands of whites. The automobile brought new opportunities for violence, as James Baldwin captured in his short story "Sonny's Blues": "The car was full of white men," we learn from the narrator's mother. "They was all drunk, and when they seen your father's brother they let out a great whoop and holler and they aimed the car straight at him. . . . And the car kept on going and ain't stopped until this day."

Courtland Milloy, a writer for the *Washington Post*, remembered his own experiences as a young boy in the late 1950s riding in the backseat of his father's Buick Special "on the long drive to grandma's house." On the evening before such trips, his mother would fry chicken and boil eggs. It was 1958, and the trip though through Louisiana, Mississippi, and Arkansas was hell. With every request from Milloy and his sisters to stop so that they might relieve themselves, his father became more tense and seemed to speed up: "Those back roads were simply too dangerous for parents to let their little black children out to pee." Overnight accommodations posed an even greater problem. African-Americans had to plot their trips from town to town with the stealth of a scout, so that they wouldn't get caught on the road without anyone to take them in. As Milloy remembered, "So many black travelers were just not making it to their destinations."

Even in the North, where they faced fewer overt hostilities, African-Americans often found it difficult to get accommodations. Enterprising individuals created guidebooks to help African-Americans in their travels. The guides went by various names: *The Negro Motorist Green Book*; *The Traveler's Guide: Hotels, Apartments, Rooms, Meals, Garage Accomodations, Etc. for Colored Travelers*; the *Afro Travel Guide*; the *Go Guide*; and the *Travel Guide*. Even the U.S. Travel Bureau (a New Deal agency) published *Negro Hotels and Guest Houses* in 1941. Subtitled *Authentic Guidance for ALL Peoples*, the *Travel Guide* offered "Vacation & Recreation Without Humiliation." *The Traveler's Guide*, published by the National Association for the Advancement of Colored People, claimed to be the oldest, having begun in 1929.

Among the most successful of the travel guides for blacks was *The Negro Motorist Green Book*, begun by a New York City mailman,

Tom Lewis

Victor H. Green, in 1936. Green modeled his book on Jewish publications, which had "long published information about places that are restricted," and "numerous publications that give gentile whites all kinds of information." The first issue of what soon came to be called the *Green Book* was a mere ten pages and listed only New York establishments that would cater to blacks. Buoyed by his success, Green increased the guide's listings to cover the rest of the United States. In the 1940s, a marketing division of Esso Standard Oil Company known as the "race group" endorsed the *Green Book*, because it enabled Esso customers "to go further with less anxiety."

Through the fifties and well into the sixties, African-Americans bought the *Green Book* and other guides. But just being on the highway could be a frightening experience. In the summer of 1960, Irene Staple's parents drove her to Anniston, Alabama, to give her a look at their roots and to teach her a lesson in the present-day life in the Deep South. "By the time we got to Raleigh-Durham in North Carolina there was a tension in the air," Staple remembered. "By the time we got to Alabama I was hysterical." The Shell Oil Company had provided the family with detailed route maps and a list of all the Shell service stations along the route. When the family returned to New York, Staple's father returned his credit card to the company. Shell stations in the South had refused to serve him because he was black.

"There will be a day sometime in the near future when this guide will not have to be published," Victor Green wrote in 1948. "That is when we as a race will have equal opportunities and privileges in the United States. It will be a great day for us to suspend publication for then we can go wherever we please without embarrassment." The day did not come until President Johnson signed the Civil Rights Act of 1964, and even then, of course, African-Americans often experienced difficulty when traveling.

Integration was coming whether or not there were Interstates, of course, but the Interstate gave a boost to integration. Once you were on the Interstate, you could be anywhere; an Interstate in the Deep South felt much like an Interstate in the North. One assumed there was a measure of protection on the roads, as thin a veneer as that protection might be. And the accommodations at interchanges came at a time when the new civil rights bill was passed. At last, African-Americans enjoyed the right to move where and when they wanted. By 1987, Courtland

Divided Highways

Milloy could write, "Today, I'm happy to be riding in comfort with my dad along a road where we both feel free."

In 1966, *The Negro Motorist Green Book* published its last edition.

Like African-Americans, women also profited from the new opportunities for mobility and safety on the Interstate highways. From the start, women had relished the possibilities that the automobile afforded. After cruising around England in the back of her chauffeured French-made model, the American writer Edith Wharton wrote in 1904, "The motor-car has restored the romance of travel. . . . It has given us back the wonder, the adventure, and the novelty which enlivened the way of our posting grandparents." Back in America, many women were not content to be driven about but took to driving on their own. Some drove fast. In the summer of 1905, a woman won two auto races at Cape May, New Jersey. When the state of New Jersey began issuing driver's licenses the following year, a hundred women applied. In 1907, Mary D. Post published an account of her six-thousand-mile trip through the Northeast, *A Woman Summers in a Motor Car*. Some followed the path of Alice Huyler Ramsey, the first woman to drive across the country in 1909. (Ramsey had piloted her forest-green Maxwell by following telephone poles after she observed that "the ones with the more wires went to the larger town.") Ramsey had enjoyed the novelty and adventure of driving herself and her three female passengers across the continent, as well as the fact that the Maxwell Automobile Company, seeing the commercial potential of the venture, had sponsored the trip. Suffragettes often drove automobiles in protest parades to publicize their cause. In 1915, Sarah Bard Field, Frances Joliffe, and two Swedish women drove from San Francisco to Washington, D.C., to deliver their petition for voting rights personally to President Woodrow Wilson.

By the 1920s, after the states ratified the Nineteenth Amendment, and as the automobile took its place as a democratic and convenient machine, women saw it as a vehicle of emancipation. It helped to end the loneliness of farm women, as now they could get out of their houses and go to town to do their errands. To the consternation of some social critics, those women who were privileged to have access to automobiles used them to explore new territory. "Thrill-seeking flappers found new possibilities for fun in the driver's seat as well as the back seat," one commentator wrote. "Rural women forged new ways of combining domesticity and sociability."

Over the years, however, the automobile became synonymous with other "labor-saving devices" like the automatic washer and the dishwasher. The cover illustration of a 1957 *Saturday Evening Post* suggests how women—particularly those who lived in the suburbs—used their cars: A harried-looking young wife in a dressing gown arrives at the train station, leaps from her late-model car, and runs to the train waving her husband's briefcase. Other *Post* covers of the period show mothers ferrying children in the family car. Advertisements stress women at the wheel of cars with power steering, "big car room," and "compact car economy and handling." Detroit's advertising made it clear that people in the suburbs needed a car that would suit the needs of the one-car suburban family, a car that a man would enjoy on weekend drives and that his wife would be able to drive on her myriad shopping errands and chauffeuring excursions during the week. And in fact, at suburban train stations all over, wives drove in the family car to meet the 6:17 from the city every night, then patiently shifted to the passenger's seat to let the "breadwinner" assume his rightful place behind the wheel.

When automobile makers wanted to show the nuclear family on an outing, Father invariably drove the car. The images over Dinah Shore's singing "See the USA in your Chevrolet" usually showed the man piloting his family across the country in a station wagon. Clearly, care of the family was man's work. Of course, muscle cars like the Corvette were high-testosterone territory and always had a man behind the wheel. When they wanted to show youth at play in their advertisements, however, car companies placed a fun-loving young woman behind the wheel. "Where there's Youth and Fun there's Pontiac" reads the caption on the advertisement that shows a woman with her male companion beside her in the passenger seat, as their happy friends greet their arrival at a skating party. Father had responsibility; daughter had fun; mother was a drudge.

Beginning in the 1960s, women used the car and a reliable highway system for different sorts of adventures than the ones Alice Huyler Ramsey and the suffragettes experienced, and for different sorts of activities than those of their mothers in the fifties. Virginia Scharff has observed that the Interstates enabled young women "to get away from their parents in order to get away with all the behaviors that we've dubbed the 'sexual revolution.'" In another way that few would have dreamed of in 1956, the builders of the Interstates were helping to forge a new social order, in which women as well as men were able to leave home. In this new world Janis Joplin would record a song about hitchhiking across the country, and Huck Finn, Walt Whitman, Woody Guthrie, and Jack Kerouac would eventually have to share the road with Thelma and Louise.

The difference was one that was deeper than the sexual revolution. Barbara Smith catches it in her poem "Desert":

> On I-80 I set the cruise control on 65
> the air on max and head into the desert
> alone
> so different from 1954.
> Dad drove the desert
> arm resting on wide open window sill
> Mom with one leg half out the other window
> three kids stuck to each other
> shirtless on a mattress in the back seat . . .

Now the car is air-conditioned; Smith is alone.

For all the talk of extension of mobility, increased safety, and ways the Interstates have changed how we work, there are harmful and adverse aspects of the system that some would contend outweigh the good.

By the mid-1970s, engineers finally recognized noise as a significant by-product of an Interstate. Nearly all of us say we do not like noise, but different people have different tolerances. The standard seems to vary between countries. The Department of Housing and Urban Development maintains that fifty-five decibels—about the sound of an electric mixer—to be tolerable; while Canada's housing authority maintains that living rooms should not have a sound level above forty decibels.

The noise is everywhere, engineers like to say, and it is continually changing. Sounds seem to become louder when they travel through humid air. Vegetation helps to filter traffic noise, so noise becomes louder in the winter when the foliage falls. The sources of highway noise change, too. Tires, road surface, and the type of vehicle traveling all generate different amounts of noise.

Over the years, the federal government has passed a number of laws intended to curb highway noise: The 1969 National Environmental Policy Act obligated the government to evaluate and mitigate highway noise; the 1970 Federal-Aid Highway Act called for noise standards; and the 1972 Noise Control Act gave the federal Environmental Protection Agency the authority to establish noise regulations. Regulations, especially on truck noise, have been strengthened, but still the number of noise spikes from a busy highway is serious.

Noise from traffic on Interstate 787 around Albany, New York, was so bad that city officials had to close a low-income housing project about fifty feet away from the road. In 1993, after contractors completed New Jersey Interstate 287, a new highway designed to relieve traffic around New York City, state highway officials began to receive complaints. Anthony DiOrio lives on Linden Lane, a cul-de-sac in a hilly and wooded section of the town of Franklin Lakes. Every ten minutes, an average of fifty-five tractor-trailers pass seventy feet from his house. As the Interstate is on a hill, they often have to gear up or down as they pass. When the state engineers took readings at the DiOrio property, they found the decibel level inside the house to range between seventy-nine and eighty-two. "It's worse on Sunday nights and Monday mornings, DiOrio said, "when the trucks get going after a weekend."

There are few ways to deal with noise that will please everyone. Noise barriers, made of wood, metal, concrete blocks, or bricks, usually dampen the sounds, but only by about ten decibels, and they create steep canyons for motorists. Since they are the only option other than closing an offending highway, states with irate homeowners have adopted them with enthusiasm. "I think noise walls are a realization that highways have negative impacts," said Ken Krulkemeyer, a highway engineer from Boston. "If we're going to have highways, then noise walls are something that really ought to be a part and parcel of designing them so that they can fit into what is otherwise an environment that cannot tolerate the level of noise that highways make." By 1992, forty of the fifty states agreed with Krulkemeyer's assessment. They had erected 640 miles of noise barriers along their highways at a cost of nearly $686 million.

Critics of the Interstates have focused on the isolation they promote: Historian George Kennan reminds us that in fourteenth-century England, Geoffrey Chaucer recounted the tales pilgrims told each other on their way to the shrine of Thomas à Becket in Canterbury. Before their journey the pilgrims had not known each other, but today they live on as some of the great characters of literature. "In the twentieth century," Kennan laments, "one can travel hundreds of miles on an Interstate without speaking to another soul. Surely there has never been a lonelier means of moving great masses of people about than an Interstate highway." Lewis Mumford, who deplored the Interstate Highway System and all that it had done to change America's landscape and culture, once called it "a rootless, aimless, profoundly disharmonious environment that replaced the indigenous one."

Kennan and Mumford and countless others make valid points about an essential feature—and failure—of the Interstates. Kennan suggests that as we drive about locked in our motorized capsules, with all the amenities of a sophisticated private home—heat and air-conditioning, light and sound, and general comfort, we are alone and away from any human intercourse. No words pass between ourselves and our fellow travelers. We are distant from one another. The individual is made to count for less. Mumford suggests that beneath the comfortable familiarity of this built environment lurks a disturbing alienation and loneliness. There was a time when roads connected with the towns—and even the cities. Each place the road took us to had its own distinctive countless coffee shops, diners, and small restaurants that beckoned to us along the way. Even the curious and vulgar commercial flotsam and jetsam along the highway—a coffee shop shaped like a coffeepot, a chicken restaurant like a chicken, a doughnut shop like a doughnut, a motel in the West shaped like a tepee—represented individuals talking to other individuals. Today, standardization in our highways and in the way we purchase our food and even our gas produces efficiency; but efficiency produces impersonality, loneliness, and alienation.

Many critics point to the matter of anti-social acts and crime. With the increased mobility and anonymity that the Interstates afford, our highways have become, for some, broad avenues for misbehavior and misdeeds; this, too, is a part of the change Interstates have brought. Like the Interstates themselves, the crimes seem bigger than they did a few years ago. The stories that appear in serious newspapers like the *Washington Post* and the *New York Times* make for sensational reading: Police in North Platte, Nebraska, seize a trailer on Interstate 80 headed for New York from California with $40 million worth of cocaine. Police in Seminole County, Florida, arrest a woman for murdering her boyfriend, chopping him up, and tossing the pieces from her car as she takes a ride down Interstate 95. On Interstate 295, Jacksonville, Florida, police hide in trees in an attempt to catch juveniles shooting from overpasses onto cars below. On Interstate 95 in Miami, authorities cut down the trees so that robbers preying on passing vehicles will have no place to hide. In Port Washington, Ohio, two men murder a woman, steal a car, and head to Interstate 70 for a week of murder and mayhem, killing people and taking their cars along the way. In Kingdom City, Missouri, population 112, just off Interstate 70, people enjoy the economic benefits that the nearby highway has brought to their town but worry that serial killers—including the two from Ohio—might make it their stop of choice. In Virginia, police call Interstate 95 the Iron Road because of the number of guns they find in automobiles. In Maryland, they call the same highway Cocaine Alley because of the amount of drugs they intercept. On Interstate 580 in California, police have posted signs forbidding sexual acts at the rest stops. "When you live near the Interstate," says a resident of a bordering town, "you ought to be on your guard."

To be sure, criminals, too, use the technology available to them, be it the Thompson submachine gun favored by mobsters in the 1920s, the Ford V-8 favored by Bonnie and Clyde in the 1930s, or the Interstates today. The roads offer the best way to dump bodies, run drugs, and move from town to town on a binge of rape, murder, and theft.

The alienation can be the stuff of comedy, too. In *L.A. Story,* Steve Martin whips his pistol from the glove compartment of his car while driving on the freeway. It is spring and it is time to shoot other drivers who cut you off. Soon others whip out their revolvers and start firing. It is difficult to imagine such an act occurring on a city street; instead it must take place between fast-moving cars. Of course, crazed people on occasion shoot up city streets, railroad trains, and even airplanes. Authorities usually judge them to be insane and send them off to a psychiatric ward. But generally when we are walking, we can shout at those who cut us off, or avoid people who walk into us. Traveling on the Interstate in the splendid isolation of a car, a rude gesture or a shot from a gun seems the only way to communicate.

Still, Americans seek to communicate from their automobiles in more benign ways, while at the same time maintaining their distance. Many equip their vehicles with cellular telephones, some even with fax machines. In Miami and Los Angeles, freeway dating services have grown up. For a fee, the service (with a suggestive name like "Drive Me

Wild") assigns a number to a car. Those interested in the driver—or the car?—may call the service and arrange an assignation. For these lonely drivers the surface becomes the reality.

The Interstate promotes speed of communication at the expense of grace. On the highways we must move fast, and we cannot tolerate anyone in our way, much less someone who cuts us off and impedes our passage to new and better things.

Most critics of the Interstate Highway System point to the roads' intrusion into and destruction of American cities. "They are wonderful, but they should have stopped at the outer limits of the city," said Bill Borah, who helped stop the Interstate in New Orleans. Yet even the smoothness and sleekness of the Interstates in the countryside has come under attack. The cultural critic Theodor Adorno has written about what he calls the "shortcoming of the American landscape." It comes not from the "absence of historical memories," as some would have it, but because "it bears no traces of the human hand." This applies, says Adorno, above all to the roads:

> They are always inserted directly into the landscape, and the more impressively smooth and broad they are, the more unrelated and violent the gleaming traces appear against its wild, overgrown surroundings. They are expressionless. . . .
>
> It is as if no one had ever passed their hand over the landscape's hair. It is uncomforted and comfortless. And it is perceived in a corresponding way. For what the hurrying eye has merely seen from the car it cannot retain, and the vanishing landscape leaves no more traces than it bears upon itself.

We may attribute Adorno's complaints to the need for speed and uniformity. As we move faster, we demand wide spaces for travel. Our progress cannot be impeded by the unfamiliar—unfamiliar road markings, signs, lane widths—so through our engineers who serve our desires, we have opted for the familiar. Those were our desires in the 1950s, and they remain the desires of most today. For them we have created what the geographer Joni Seager has called "a conduit of national blandness," roads without "real places . . . only blurry landscapes."

No matter how many benefits it might bring, and no matter how benign it might appear to be, technology always has a downside. Gutenberg's movable type for the printing press put a lot of scribes out of work; Chester Carlson's Xerox machine put the manufacturers of carbon paper on the unemployment lines—and between Gutenberg and Carlson we have put a whole lot of forests to the saw. The Interstates' progress has been more gradual than movable type or the copier, but the Interstates have brought a revolution nonetheless.

THE GREATEST OF IMPROVEMENTS

Good roads, canals and navigable rivers by diminishing the expense of carriage, put the remote parts of the country more nearly upon the level with those in the neighborhood of the town. They are upon that account the greatest of improvements.

ADAM SMITH

Those who live in Saratoga Springs know Route 50 as the road to the malls. From this vantage point one sees not the malls but the parasitic enterprises that attach themselves alongside the edges of the great host, the indoor shopping mall—fast-food restaurants, a cheap steak house, gasoline stations, and the automobile shopping plaza that sells five car brands. These are the icons of the new American corporate Eden—as Gertrude Stein might have put it, a land where there is no there there.

It had not always been that way. This part of the country is known as Wilton. The land had been fields, sometimes plowed and sometimes left fallow, then home to the rare Karner blue butterfly. In 1960, when the population of Saratoga Springs numbered eighteen thousand, engineers walked the center line of Interstate 87, which came to be called the Adirondack Northway. Planners decided to give Saratoga Springs three interchanges with the Northway, Route 50 being the northernmost junction. In 1968, the State of New York made the section of Route 50 from Saratoga Springs to Exit 15 into a four-lane divided highway.

Following the established pattern across the country, it would be only a matter of time before developers turned those fields into a shopping mall.

Interstate 87 is not an interstate at all, but an *intra*state. It begins in a forbidding tangle of connecting roads at Interstate 278 in the Bronx and proceeds up the Hudson River, as part of the New York Thruway. At Albany, the thruway heads west as Interstate 90, while Interstate 87 continues through the great Adirondack Park, before ending 346 miles north of the Bronx at Champlain, the desolate customs and immigration outpost at the Canadian border. The highway travels through the past: Plattsburgh, once home to the Cold War bombers of the Strategic Air Command; Fort Ticonderoga and Lake Champlain, the route of British General Burgoyne in the American Revolution; Bolton Landing on Lake George, where President Eisenhower's Interstate highway program was first proposed; Glens Falls, once one of the wealthiest communities in the nation; and Saratoga Springs.

Geology and greed had conspired to make Saratoga Springs famous in the nineteenth century. Geology, which appeared on the surface of the earth as mineral springs, came first. As the glaciers receded following the Pleistocene epoch, they revealed what geologists call "Lake Albany," a plain of sand, shale, and sandstone. Later, Precambrian rocks were thrust through the Lake Albany sand plain along two fault lines, and allowed numerous carbonated mineral springs to make their way to the surface. For more than a century, people came to Saratoga to take the waters.

After the Civil War, greed joined with geology. Ostensibly the efficacious waters still drew visitors to Saratoga Springs, but horse racing, prostitution, and the promise of easy riches from gambling tables held them. At the turn of the century, Karl Baedeker reported in his guidebook of the United States that the village's hotels could accommodate twenty thousand visitors. The United States and Grand Union hotels ranked with the largest in the world. The Grand Union, a huge Victorian pile that took up nearly a full square block, boasted a 275-foot dining room and offered two thousand beds starting at $5 a night. The United States followed close behind with 917 rooms, a "Large Interior Court . . . Beautiful Shade Trees," and "Sparkling Fountains." Each July and August, Saratoga Springs' population of thirteen thousand people quadrupled with visitors.

In the nineteenth century, most arrived by train. The Boston & Maine

Railroad brought passengers from New England. The Delaware & Hudson, a line that ran from Albany to Montreal and connected with the New York Central, ran a "Saratoga Special" that left Grand Central terminal in New York every afternoon and arrived at the spa in time for dinner.

Shortly after the turn of the century, the mode of travel to Saratoga Springs began to change. In 1906, forty-eight drivers steered their Pierces, Pope-Hartfords, Packards, Marmons, Oldsmobiles, and other automobiles into the village on an automobile tour through New York and New England. Four years later, one of the local newspapers, the *Saratogian*, boasted in a *Visitors' and Automobilists' Guide Book* that the six state roads entering Saratoga Springs made it the "automobiling center of the east" and "the mecca of every automobile tourist."

A photograph of Broadway, the main thoroughfare through the town, in midsummer 1917 shows some automobiles and many carriages and wagons along the elm-lined street; in a postcard photograph of 1927, no horses or wagons are to be seen. The *Directory of Saratoga Springs* in 1927 lists sixty-five businesses related to the automobile, including nine car dealers, fourteen garages, and three filling stations. And Saratoga Springs' commissioner of public safety had installed the city's first traffic light, at Broadway and Lake Avenue by city hall.

In 1926, Broadway became part of Thomas Harris MacDonald's federal-aid highway system and was designated U.S. Route 9. The route began in northern Manhattan (as it does today), passed through old river towns like Dobbs Ferry, Peekskill, Poughkeepsie, Hyde Park, and Hudson, before crossing to Albany on the west side of the river and proceeding north to Saratoga Springs, Glens Falls, Lake George, the eastern shore of Lake Champlain, Plattsburgh and Rouses Point at the Canadian border. This simple but profound change meant that Saratoga Springs was part of a larger web of federal "interstate" routes that connected the village of 13,000 with the nation of 117 million.

By 1960, when Exit 15 on Interstate 87 was planned, Saratoga Springs was facing hard times. The federal government had embarrassed the state into closing the gambling casinos. Over the years the number of summer visitors who came to partake of the mineral springs gradually diminished. On Broadway, the United States and Grand Union hotels were but a memory—the former to be replaced by a mercifully short-lived hamburger chain called the Red Barn, and the latter by the Grand Union Supermarket and seediest of fifties-style strip malls. The majestic elms died. Most of the other buildings had vacant storefronts, and those that did not had inferior shops.

In 1970, the Pyramid Corporation, an aptly named enterprise, announced it would build Saratoga Springs' first enclosed shopping mall at Route 50, which locals called the "arterial," and the Northway. The development boom began. Soon, stores along Broadway announced that they would be moving to the new mall. The commercial stampede was on, and many predicted that Saratoga Springs would go the way of other small towns and cities that the Northway bypassed. The oracles had good reason for their prophesies. South of the city at Exit 2 of the Northway, Colonie Center, a large two-story indoor shopping mall, had opened with a Macy's at one end and a Sears at the other, and like two big hens, Macy's and Sears gave shelter to about seventy little stores in between. It drew shoppers out of Albany, eventually making Central Avenue, Albany's main shopping thoroughfare, into a derelict district. North of the city at Exit 18, Glens Falls offered some downtown stores, one shopping mall, and another under construction. Saratogians were already leaving the city to take advantage of the cosmopolitan shops just thirty minutes away.

Saratoga Springs seemed to be following a familiar pattern: first the Interstate; then the housing developments clustered close to the highway's exits, home to new suburbanites from the grittier cities of Albany, Troy, and Schenectady; then a shopping center.

Of course, the enclosed shopping mall predates the Interstate Highway System by many years. Many of the early enclosed, climate-controlled shopping malls were designed by Austrian émigré Victor Gruen, who in 1947 created Southdale Center outside of Edina, Minnesota. Gruen's design was in response to the suburbs that were steadily creeping out from the center of Minneapolis. Being something of an idealist, he saw the virtues of a small community. Main street to Gruen was not Sinclair Lewis's *Main Street*, the novel about the mythical Gopher Prairie, Minnesota. Lewis's heroine, Carol Kennicott, might have found Gopher Prairie seething with provincialism, prejudice, and smugness, but at least there was a main street. The new extensions of the city had denied even that. Building on European models, Gruen wanted his structure to include the elements of town life that suburban developments had squandered: the town hall, the police department, a post office, places to sit and chat, a library—all the amenities of a town center. Gruen wanted to restore the main street.

It did not work out quite the way Gruen had envisioned. Ever conscious of their profits, developers included lots of shops and a few places to sit, but little else. By 1956, indoor shopping malls had taken hold; the new highways simply added millions of new acres where speculators might build them. Eventually, Gruen rued the day he'd had the idea, for "fast buck promoters and speculators" had turned his idea of enclosed shopping malls into nothing "more than selling machines." The selling machines gained momentum in the fifties and sixties and took over much of consumer America in the seventies and eighties. It was only natural that they would do so. The enclosed mall gave people the illusion of control in their shopping that they sought in their cars and highways. It offered consumers a predictable climate, predictable background noises, and always predictable stores.

Inside the shopping malls, between the great anchor stores, the JC Penneys, the Nordstroms, the Lord & Taylors, and the Macy's, nestled smaller franchise stores—Radio Shack, Bed & Bath, Walden, B. Dalton, Friendly's. Outside along the roads, franchising crept across the landscape with the Interstates and the malls. Given the success of Raymond Albert Kroc and Charles Kemmons Wilson, it was only natural that McDonald's and Holiday Inn soon had competitors: Burger King, Taco Bell, Ponderosa, Ramada Inn, Wendy's, and Econo Lodge, and dozens of others. The imitators provided intense competition. "This is rat eat rat," said the hamburger magnate Kroc, speaking of the competition, "the American way of survival of the fittest."

In fact, competition among franchises had been a part of the American landscape since the beginning of the century. The first business franchises were actually gasoline stations with names like Esso, Gulf, Mobil, or Cities Service. Commissioning plans from architects and designers like Frank Lloyd Wright, Walter Dorwin Teague, and Norman Bel Geddes, the companies standardized the packaging of their product. Service stations had the same architecture. The symbols were familiar, bold, and unique—an orange disk, a flying horse, a dinosaur. Color schemes became standard at each station; even the uniforms the workers wore were standard. Motorists found it all reassuring.

The first franchiser to create restaurants that appealed to the mobile

American was Howard Buster Johnson, who in 1930 opened his first small restaurant in the town of Woburn, Massachusetts, outside Boston. Its quick success encouraged Johnson to branch out to neighboring towns. By the mid-thirties there were thirty-five "Howard Johnsons"; at the start of World War II, there were more than a hundred. Johnson housed each in a white New England cape-style building, which he made especially distinctive by adding a bright orange tile roof and a white cupola.

Travelers found reassurance in familiarity. When the Pennsylvania Turnpike began, the commissioners invited Johnson to operate its restaurants and Esso to provide gasoline. In keeping with the turnpike's architectural themes, which mimicked those of the Pennsylvania Dutch country, the commissioners took care to build a stone house for the restaurant and a stone barn for the filling station. Motorists liked the idea so much that many families actually made special trips on the turnpike for their Sunday lunch.

Everything is sterile and bland in such franchise establishments as Holiday Inn and McDonald's, so the criticism went. "The [motel room] was immaculate," John Steinbeck complained in his narrative of a cross-country trip he took with his dog, *Travels with Charley*. "Everything was done in plastics—the floors, the curtains, table tops of stainless burnless plastics, lamp shades of plastic. I went to the restaurant run in conjunction. It was plastic too." McDonald's came in for the most abuse. The restaurant chain was the butt of jokes across the nation. It represented the worst of America, the "reductive kitchen for a classless culture," as novelist Tom Robbins put it, "that hasn't time to dally on its way to the next rainbow's end."

Despite the jokes and remarks about blandness that they endured, Kroc and Wilson and a host of imitators understood the nation better than many of their critics, and they carefully catered to its desires. In the beginning, at least, Kroc placed his franchises along the fringes of cities; customers could reach the nearest McDonald's only by car, or by a perilous walk alongside a service road to an Interstate—a place designers made to be intentionally inhospitable to pedestrians. Careful to make his restaurants inaccessible to those on foot—by the 1960s, it was certainly suspect and even un-American to consider walking anywhere—Kroc also took care to connect his product with positive American values. A flagpole graced the front lawn of almost every one of his sites, and that, too, was intentional. Old Glory flew throughout the tempests of the sixties and seventies, but Kroc avoided controversy whenever possible.

Divided Highways

Once a manager in Ohio phoned McDonald's home office to say that anti-war protesters were converging on his site for a demonstration at the flag-pole. Headquarters told him to have a delivery truck knock the pole over. The demonstrators left in frustration.

Motorists liked the product precisely because they were often traveling in unfamiliar territory. No matter where they were, they knew they could take refuge and sustenance under the flamboyant golden arches or behind the outrageous sign announcing a Holiday Inn. Yes, the food and the beds were predictable, but they were also safe. McDonald's customers knew they would not succumb to bad meat or bad milk or be treated to watery Cokes. Holiday Inn patrons knew that the bed linen and the bathroom would be clean and the mattress firm. And both Holiday Inn and McDonald's catered to speed and modernity. Holiday Inns offered quick checkout. At McDonald's, motorists knew they could eat and run, and after the restaurant introduced "drive-thru" windows, they could run and eat.

The only thing to rival the sameness of the commercial enterprises along the edge of the Interstates was the sameness of the highways themselves. As the states received ninety percent of the money to build these highways from the federal government, they had to conform to federal standards in much the same way that a restaurant or motel franchise must meet the standards of its parent company. This simple fact in effect makes the Interstate Highway System the largest franchise in America. McDonald's and Holiday Inn might be big, but the Interstates are bigger.

With few exceptions, franchising along the sides of the Interstates destroyed the individual establishments along secondary roads. Exit 15 at Saratoga Springs is a good example. Interstate 87 north parallels the federal-aid highway Route 9. In the forties and fifties, seven small motor courts, cabins, and motels lined Route 9 between Saratoga Springs and Glens Falls—establishments with typical names like Lonesome Pines Cabins and Balsam Lodge. Small hamburger and ice-cream stands beckoned to the hungry. Today, none of the motels or cabins remain; the hamburger stands are gone. Some have been converted to other uses, but most are abandoned and derelict, quiet reminders of an earlier period of mobility and individuality.

While franchising—the McDonald's and Holiday Inns, Taco Bells and Ramada Inns—stands out among the most important changes to American life that the Interstates have helped to bring about, another equally significant change has also taken place: America depends on trucks as never before. Industry statistics, which show among other things that shipping goods by truck increased 257 percent between 1955 and 1990, tell a part of the story. Through its Interstate Highway System, the U.S. government had created great commercial channels for the shipping of goods, so the growth of the trucking industry was no great surprise.

The surprise came, however, with the way other industries made use of trucks. In the 1920s, the railroads thought of the trucks as a way of feeding goods to their freight lines for long distance shipping. They purchased trucking companies and went so far as to sponsor "good roads" trains that traveled the country promoting the advantages of an improved highway system. Over the years the trucking industry grew, and it was no accident that Lucius Clay chose Dave Beck, head of the Teamsters Union, to be a member of the President's Advisory Committee on Highways. Railroads were falling behind.

Certainly by the 1960s the effects of the trucking industry began to be felt. Industries moved from multistory buildings on crowded streets in downtown locations to single-story buildings on wide roads in suburban areas, and almost always near an Interstate. During the 1970s, it became possible to ship goods four hundred and five hundred miles overnight and by truck. By far the most important change for the trucking industry took place in the 1970s, when industries in the United States began adopting a sophisticated and complex Japanese system of production known as "Just in Time."

Just in Time meant an end to the plant inventories of old. In the 1950s, automobile plants, for example, would keep huge stockpiles of the components for cars—engines, batteries, seats, radios, bumpers, and the like—that workers drew from to assemble a car. If a plant saw a strike of one of its suppliers—say a transmission company—on the horizon, it would increase its stock in hopes of evading the shortage. The practice was inefficient. Inventories were subject to theft and damage, and tied up space and large amounts of money. Today, automobile companies rely on parts suppliers to ship their goods to their assembly plants continuously. At any hour of the day, trucks laden with transmissions leave the plant where they were manufactured on a trip over the Interstates to the assembly lines where they will become part of a car. Often truckers make a delivery to a work in progress.

The system is extraordinarily complex and fragile, but it is also remarkably efficient. Computers and global positioning systems often keep track of the materials from the time they leave the manufacturing plants to the time they arrive at the assembly lines. Manufacturers have turned the highway system into a vast rolling and fluid warehouse, made their operation more efficient, and cut their costs. More often than not it is a strike that demonstrates the fragility of the system. In 1996, the General Motors alternator plant went on strike. Within several days, assembly lines in General Motors plants began to shut down. In ten days, the entire General Motors operation had ground to a halt. Sometimes an Interstate can affect fragility of Just in Time: If part of the road network shuts down, as happened in the Los Angeles earthquake in 1994 and the floods in the Midwest in 1993, manufacturing plants across America can close because their warehouses are on the road.

By 1970, it was apparent that the Interstates would carry more trucks than anyone had anticipated—about fifty percent of all truck traffic now traveled on the superhighways. As an eighteen-wheel semi carries as much as 73,280 pounds of cargo, even the best-engineered highways were taxed by such heavy loads. The effects on the Interstates were dramatic. By the end of the 1970s, it was not unusual for politicians and local luminaries to be cutting ribbons to open a section of Interstate at one end of the country, while engineers and construction workers were struggling to rebuild older sections of the highway at the other end. The Interstates were shaking apart.

Usually the Interstates that took the greatest abuse were in the East and Far West, where the truck traffic was heaviest and the superhighways were generally the oldest. Magazines and newspapers began publishing lists of the "worst superhighways." "I-287, in New York State from Tappan Zee Bridge to White Plains," read a typical early entry in 1979, "surface consists of little more than aggregate and steel." In 1992, *Overdrive*, the "Magazine for the American Trucker," found Pennsylvania had the worst highways overall. Sections of Pennsylvania's Interstate 80 and the Pennsylvania Turnpike tied for the title of the worst highway in the United States. Engineers were frustrated; over the preceding eight years they had spent half a billion dollars rebuilding 310 miles of Interstate 80. In surveys of this sort, New York City's Interstate 95, the Cross Bronx Expressway, usually takes top honors among truckers for being the single worst highway in the nation. Said one critic, "It's more like a logging road sprinkled with chunks of asphalt." Despite their complaints about the condition of the Interstates, and despite the damage the highways are doing to their equipment, truckers have steadfastly opposed any increase in the fuel tax to help pay for the cost of reconstruction.

While some highways were crumbling under the weight of trucks and their loads, others were disintegrating because of poor maintenance. This was especially true in the case of bridges. On June 28, 1983, a one-hundred-foot-long section of the northbound deck of Connecticut's Mianus River Bridge on Interstate 95 collapsed, taking the drivers of two cars and a truck to their deaths. Investigators found poor maintenance and inspection, and possibly poor design, to have been the causes. The state of Connecticut had just a dozen engineers, working in two-person teams, to inspect 3,425 bridges. Poor maintenance had allowed for the deterioration of crucial pins and hangers that held the section in place. Some questioned whether or not the particular design of the bridge—a common design of the 1950s that allowed for cheaper construction—made it more liable to collapse. As the facts came out, the public grew alarmed. If it had been a common practice to construct Interstate bridges in this manner, could such a disaster happen on other highways, or perhaps even on the Interstate they traveled every day? Bridge inspectors in other states found similar problems. Some said that as many as half of the nation's bridges were in danger of collapsing either because of poor maintenance or because they were not equal to the stresses of modern traffic.

As horrible as the failure in Connecticut had been, it did not equal the collapse of another bridge that occurred on Interstate 90, the New York Thruway, four years later. On Sunday morning, April 5, 1987, the center span of the 550-foot bridge over the Schoharie Creek collapsed without warning. Witnesses heard "an eerie groan" as the span fell, taking an eastbound tractor-trailer and a car with it. Within minutes, three more cars plunged 80 feet into the creek. In all, ten people perished. Again, investigators found the cause to have been improper structural inspections, but they also found a case of basic engineering hubris.

When designing the bridge in the early 1950s, engineers had failed to consider the dark history of the Schoharie Creek, the largest tributary of the Mohawk River. The creek can be deceptive. For most of the year the Schoharie is a minor stream that carries little water on its eighty-three-mile journey from its source in the Catskill Mountains to the Mohawk River. But the source of the stream is high, about four thousand feet above sea level, and in the springtime, especially after a hard winter, a swift torrent can build as the water plunges toward the river. Everyone nearby respects the creek. Local historians tell of two other bridges that were swept away in spring floods. Sheriffs know just where to recover bodies of people who from time to time are swept up in the Schoharie's currents. Curiously, the highway engineers chose to ignore the history and hydrology of the creek. Instead of designing the structure with piers well away from the creek's path supporting a longer span between them, they placed two of the four supporting piers in the creekbed. Later, they disregarded an engineering report that warned of ice jams and severe flooding, and the danger they posed to the bridge. The foundations for the two piers would restrict the swift currents that could undermine and perhaps destroy them. To prevent that damage to the foundations, the designers called for rip rap—large stones or blocks of concrete—to be placed at the base of the piers to serve as an abutment against the swift currents. Residents did not think that was enough. "Everyone knows it's a bear," said a local engineer. "No one who knew the stream could ever expect to tame it."

Bridge inspections over the years had been haphazard and often cursory. Despite federal regulations and the fact that the Thruway Authority had to replace missing rip rap in 1981, no one had ever conducted an underwater inspection of the foundations. The most recent inspection before the collapse had been especially ludicrous. A thruway worker who was not an engineer checked the piers from an embankment 280 feet away, then from a catwalk 70 feet above the stream.

The day before the collapse, hydrologists measuring the current rated the flow of the Schoharie Creek at sixty-five thousand cubic feet per second—fifteen thousand cubic feet per second faster than the average flow over Niagara Falls. (So intense was the current that the following day it carried the fallen span eighty feet downstream.) Alarmed by the rising water, the local sheriff had taken the precaution of closing all bridges over the creek, except the one on the thruway, over which he had no authority.

Interstate 90 across New York is just the latest in transportation links that have helped to bind the state together economically. Governor DeWitt Clinton had pushed for the construction of the Erie Canal in 1825. The canal declined after Cornelius Vanderbilt ran the tracks of his New York Central Railroad parallel to the waterway in the 1850s. Thomas Harris MacDonald and the Bureau of Public Roads had designated a highway parallel to the canal and railroad to be federal-aid Route 20. In the 1950s, the railroad declined after Bertram Tallamy built the New York Thruway along the same route. For more than three decades the thruway had formed the primary connection between western and eastern New York. With the collapse of the thruway bridge over the Schoharie Creek, that connection was severed.

It was not until June that the thruway authorities were able to devise a way to cross the Schoharie, by making a temporary detour through a farmer's property and commandeering and reinforcing a local bridge. Because of the collapse, the thruway lost over $7 million in toll receipts. In the meantime, the collapse had a devastating effect on local economies. The disaster showed dramatically how much New York State relied on trucking for its goods. The detour routes barred tandem trailers, which also increased shipping costs. The greatest effect was upon manufacturing plants along the route that required Just in Time shipments for their production lines.

"Every politician likes to open a highway," said one caustic engineer, "but few wish to vote the money or have the will to maintain it." The Interstate Highway System has been expensive to build, but also expensive to maintain. As the older portions of the system, especially those in the East, have given way to the ceaseless attack of trucks and automobiles, few have wanted to spend the money for repairs. When the Interstates begin to crumble elsewhere, in wealthy cities like Houston or Dallas or Atlanta, will officials have the money and the will to restore the highways that have helped to make those cities prosper?

By 1985, transportation studies began to note something new that was happening in America. Since the beginning of urban Interstate planning, planners had been concerned with the peak commuting hours between the cities and the suburbs. In the early eighties, however, they began to note a new trend: Peak commuting in many instances was not between the suburb and the city, but between the suburb and the suburb. Urban traffic problems were migrating to the suburbs. The age of the "edge city" had arrived.

These new centers of living and commerce may be found near any large American city. The edge city has housing developments, shopping centers, and corporate parks, and they line up like beads on a string alongside the Interstates that surround major cities. In Atlanta, Georgia, four edge cities, accessible only by cars, have grown adjacent to Interstates 285, 75, and 85.

Where do edge cities come from? "They grew," says Joel Garreau, the writer who coined the term, "because certain phenomena came together: Computers started to be used for communication. The Interstates were nearly finished. And women, intelligent and well-educated women, living in the suburbs, were entering the workforce. Corporations saw that they had good communications, excellent transportation, and a fine labor pool outside the city—and all in a convenient location." Garreau believes Americans wanted to work in one place, live in another, and play in a third. The coming of the Interstates and the individual transportation system made it all possible.

Of course, an edge city is not a city at all, but an extension of the suburb. Many who live there appreciate that they are left alone in splendid isolation among pleasant, faceless buildings. The edge city offers shopping, hotel accommodations, workout gyms, cosmetology parlors, and a sense of security, but it lacks the culture, jostling, interrelationships, and serendipitous contact that comes from walking down a city street. Indeed, nobody walks outside the enclosed shopping mall. Those who escaped to the suburbs and edge cities in order to avoid urban congestion and crowds made a bad mistake. Congestion has followed them.

The job opportunities and housing that edge cities offer have actually reversed in a small measure the movement of African-Americans from the South to the North. Again, events have converged to make this possible, especially the Civil Rights Act of 1964 and the Voting Rights Act of 1965. In Atlanta, Georgia, for example, integrated housing and employment have enticed African-Americans south to form a new black middle class in a state where only recently a popular elected governor kept an axe handle at the ready to beat them. Typically, these new arrivals from the North do not join other African-Americans in central Atlanta, an area long abandoned by whites, but they take a condominium in one of the edge cities near the Perimeter Road, Interstate 285. During the 1980s, the percentage of African-Americans living in the South actually increased. Like almost every city, Atlanta now has more jobs in its edge cities than it does downtown. Between 1980 and 1990, the city actually decreased in population, while metropolitan Atlanta increased.

No matter what the designers do, the cars and trucks keep coming. Add another lane and they will fill it. The very highways that promise to reduce congestion only create more. In Walnut Creek, California, an edge city on Interstate 680 outside San Francisco, transportation officials spent $310 million rebuilding a single interchange on the highway, yet it did little to ease the traffic. Traffic engineers have even coined a term for the phenomenon: "induced demand." A new or improved highway attracts motorists the way a flame attracts moths. Said one frustrated civil engineer, "It's as if we hadn't learned anything in the last fifty years."

Over the years, census enumerators have tracked America's ever-growing dependence on the automobile and the highway. By 1990, there were 115 million workers in the United States age sixteen and older. Fully 99.8 million of those workers rode a car, motorcycle, or truck to work; 6 million used public transit; 5 million walked or rode a bike. The remaining 4.2 million used other means or worked at home. More than ever, Americans depend on their automobiles for survival. Most love their independence, for behind the wheel they can dream, as Maria Wyeth did in Joan Didion's *Play It as It Lays*:

> Once she was on the freeway and had maneuvered her way to a fast lane she turned on the radio at high volume and she drove. She drove the San Diego to the Harbor up to the Hollywood, the Hollywood to the Golden State, the Santa Monica, the Santa Ana, the Pasadena, the Ventura. She drove it as a riverman runs a river, every day more attuned to its currents, its deceptions, and just as a riverman feels the pull of the rapids in the lull between sleeping and waking, so Maria lay at night in the still of Beverly Hills and saw the great signs roar overhead at seventy miles an hour, Normandie 1/4 Vermont 3/4 Harbor Fwy 1.

Didion has given expression to a culture enamored with the automobile, which, with the Interstate, has the potential to liberate us from the routine of our daily lives. Never mind that most of our trips on the Interstate are only to work or to a shopping mall. We know they can take us across the nation.

Yet at the same time that we wish to perpetuate our automobile culture, we also wish to make our highways more compatible with our land. In our cities we now seek to bury the highways and return the land above to the people. The soaring roadway over the city, the highway along the waterfront—once the dream of engineers, planners, and right-

Divided Highways

minded citizens—we now regard as a curse upon civic life. In Seattle, a city that builders tore apart in order to create a network of super-highways and access roads, engineers have now put sections of Interstate 5 underground and covered them with public parks they call "Lids." In Hartford, Connecticut, they are doing the same thing to Interstate 91 along the Connecticut River. The most dramatic example is the "Central Artery," Interstate 93, in Boston. In the early fifties, before the Interstate program began, engineers and many Bostonians regarded the idea of the Central Artery as one of the greatest transportation projects ever. No longer would traffic clog two-hundred-year-old city streets; instead it would soar above the land on a great skyway. The Central Artery did not turn out quite the way planners had envisioned. Soon after its opening in 1954, citizens found that the highway left much of the landscape in shadowy blight. The value of land nearby declined and businesses moved out. Four decades later, highway builders are busy at the "big dig," burying the road in a tunnel and returning the land to the city. Highway officials admit to the project costing $10 billion for 7.5 miles of highway; many believe the final cost will be closer to $20 billion.

Federal and state highway engineers have proven they can build Interstate highways that are less harmful to the environment: Interstate 70 through the Glenwood Canyon in Colorado, a highway that engineers, after much prodding from environmentalists, introduced into the landscape with a minimum of damage to the setting; Interstate 15 through Virgin River Gorge in Arizona, a highway that actually enhances the natural beauty of the area; Interstate 75 at the Everglades Parkway, which features a special underpass for panthers; the Sunshine Sky Way Bridge on Interstate 275 across Tampa Bay, which ranks as one of the most spectacularly beautiful bridges to have been built in this century. Yet most of these projects have cost tens, and even hundreds of millions of dollars more in order to make them fit into the landscape. How much money are Americans willing to pay in order to indulge their desire for such a transportation system?

"Desire" is the key word, for the Interstates reflect our desires more than we care to believe. We value speed, and space, and privacy. As much as we might dislike them, we cannot escape the fact that the Interstates are a central feature of the contradictory and yet extraordinary landscape of present-day built America. In the fifties and early sixties, they reflected the spare brutalist aesthetics so often expressed in concrete. We could do everything and we could do it to excess. Our

Interstate highways emphasized the conquest of engineering. Like our cars, whose fins could not be too high and whose gas mileage could not be too low, they made a statement with adolescent vigor: "Look at me, there's nothing I can't do; no place I can't go." It was a time when we valued speed and efficiency and allowed them to take precedence over natural beauty. We took little care in the way we imposed the roads on the landscape. The Interstates were a concrete snapshot of ourselves and what we valued at a time when we fervently believed there was nothing beyond our reach.

"O public road," wrote Walt Whitman in oft-quoted lines, "You express me better than I can express myself." In building the Interstate Highway System, the American people expressed themselves in all of their glory, all of their virtues, and not a few of their vices. The highways show our grace and vision, but they also reveal, at times, our impetuousness and our shortsightedness. They represent the height of American technology. They suggest all our dreams for what America might become—one nation, indivisible, bound for all time by concrete and asphalt strands. As so often happens, the dream played out differently over the four decades it took to build the Interstates, and we learned that the very roads that we thought would unite us have sometimes actually divided us. Over the decades, the Interstates have reflected our shifting attitudes about technology, landscape, community, race relations, and the quality of our lives. Indeed, as our image of ourselves has changed from the one we had in 1956, so have our highways. In this way the Interstates have revealed our dreams and realities better than any of us could have predicted.

In 1991, Congress passed the Intermodal Surface Transportation Act, which mandated that planners take an integrated approach to all forms of transportation, from bicycles to airplanes. No longer would America seek to meet its desire for mobility only with highways. Congress also declared a new name for the roads that had occupied the energy of the nation for nearly four decades: the Dwight D. Eisenhower System of Interstate and Defense Highways. The age of building the largest engineered structure in the world was over.

Sources and Notes

I have based this book on original documents, interviews, legal briefs, congressional testimony and debates, and published materials. To save space in the source notes that follow, I have used the following abbreviations:

COLLEGE PARK   Documents pertaining to the Bureau of Public Roads and the Federal Highway Administration at the National Archives in College Park, Maryland.

DDEL   Papers located in the Dwight David Eisenhower Library, Abilene, Kansas.

FDRL   Papers located in the Franklin Delano Roosevelt Library, Hyde Park, New York.

FHWAL   Library at the Federal Highway Administration building, Washington, D.C.

MACDONALD   Thomas Harris MacDonald's papers at Texas A&M University, College Station, Texas.

Sources and Notes

WEINGROFF   Richard Weingroff of the Federal Highway Administration, Washington, D.C., has amassed an extraordinary collection of papers pertaining to the history of the Interstate Highway System and of highways in general

Readers should note that the papers located in COLLEGE PARK and MACDONALD collections have not been cataloged in any systematic way. The help of an archivist will be especially valuable when working in either of these collections. The COLLEGE PARK collection is vast. Untold treasures about the Bureau of Public Roads and the Interstate Highway System, only hinted at in this volume, await scholars who do research there.

Unless I have noted otherwise, the statistics in this work come from information in the U.S. Census reports; *Historical Statistics of the United States: Colonial Times to 1970*, published by the Bureau of the Census; *Statistical Abstracts*; and annual issues of the *World Almanac*. I have not made specific citations to these books unless I felt it absolutely necessary.

Bibliographic information about the books and periodicals referred to in the sources may be found following this section.

Chapter 1: THE CHIEF

3   *Leo J. Beachy*   Information about Leo J. Beachy comes from Maxine Beachy Broadwater's *My Camera Lens Does Not Lie: Photographic Works, Writings, and History of Leo Beachy* and from an interview with Maxine Beachy. Leo Beachy lived from 1874 to 1927. During his lifetime he recorded much of the daily life of Grantsville, Maryland, and those who passed on the National Road nearby, on thousands of glass plate negatives. About twenty-five hundred survive.

4   *"restless temper"*   de Tocqueville wrote in his diary on June 7, 1831, "A restless temper seems to me one of the distinctive traits of this people. . . . We have been told that the same man has often tried ten estates. He has appeared successively as merchant, lawyer, doctor, minister of the gospel. He has lived in twenty different places and nowhere found ties to detain him. Cited in George Wilson Pierson's *Tocqueville in America*, p. 77.

4   *Route 40*   Information about Route 40 comes from George R. Stewart's *U.S. 40: Cross Section of the United States of America;* and from Thomas R. and Geraldine R. Vale's *U.S. 40 Today*.

5   *Thomas Harris MacDonald*   There is no adequate biography or even a decent biographical sketch of Thomas Harris MacDonald. For my portrait I have relied

Sources and Notes

upon the MACDONALD papers; interviews with MacDonald's daughter, Margaret Oberlin; the MacDonald family papers in Mrs. Oberlin's possession; the WEINGROFF papers; the Bureau of Public Roads papers at COLLEGE PARK; MacDonald's speeches and articles in the Department of Transportation Library; a taped interview with Theodore Holmes conducted in April 1971 at the Federal Highway Administration; William E. Lind's "Thomas H. Mac-Donald: A Study of the Career of an Engineer Administrator and His Influence on Public Roads in the United States, 1919–1953," a master's thesis written at American University in 1965; and Bruce Seely's *Building the American Highway System: Engineers as Policy Makers*. The last is a thorough examination of the Bureau of Public Roads under MacDonald, and has proven to be invaluable.

5   *"in Mr. MacDonald's presence"*   Theodore Holmes interview.

5   *"Mr. MacDonald" or "Chief"*   Theodore Holmes interview; Oberlin interview.

5   *despite its exotic labeling*   Miss Alice Underwood of Montezuma kindly provided information about the town and Poweshiek County. See also Federal Writers' Project, *Iowa: A Guide to the Hawkeye State*.

6   *As a boy*   MacDonald had two brothers, Ross and Charles, and two sisters, Jean and Florence. His brother Ross served as Poweshiek County treasurer for many years.

7   *"other scientific and classical studies"*   Information about Iowa State comes from annual catalogs. Source of academic record: MACDONALD.

7   *Albert Augustus Pope*   Information about Pope comes from Charles E. Pratt, "American Bicycling and Its Founder," *Outing*, Vol. 18, July 1889, pp. 342–349; and John Lacy, "When Hartford Was Center of U.S. Bicycle Industry," Hartford *Courant*, March 14, 1995.

7   *"American roads are among the worst"*   See Charles E. Pratt, "American Bicycling and its Founder," pp. 342–349. See also the *Dictionary of American Biography*.

8   *"Next to the education of the child"*   MacDonald often made such statements. This is quoted from "A Nation's Highways," a talk he delivered to the Second Pan American Highway Congress at Cordoba, Argentina, September 9, 1929. FHWAL.

9   *either fraudulent or ignorant*   Information about MacDonald's work in Iowa comes from an article in the Montezuma *Republican* of 1919 announcing his intention to become chief of the federal Bureau of Public Roads.

Sources and Notes

9   *"a straighter man"*   Montezuma *Republican*, 1919. The writer added: "In many cases he has stood between taxpayer and the contractor, who endeavored to hold up the various communities. Mr. MacDonald would not have to work today, had he been of the crooked sort. Men of lesser ability and lesser conscious [*sic*] have passed along the road of wealth."

10   *a full-fledged highway commission*   MacDonald's salary had increased to $4,200 by the time he left Iowa.

10   *salary of $6,000*   Macdonald never made a great deal of money in his position. He officially began work on May 3, 1919, at a salary of $6,000. He received a $500 raise in 1925, 1926, and 1927. A $1,000 promotion in 1928 brought his salary to $8,500. In 1935 it was raised to $9,000; and again, in 1943, to $10,000. Pay adjustments in 1948 and 1949 brought his salary to $15,000, where it remained until his resignation in 1953 MACDONALD.

10   *"a steady going man"*   Undated editorial from the Des Moines *Capital* in the MacDonald family papers.

11   *"the shells of a big gun"*   Quoted from a paper delivered by MacDonald's assistant, H. S. Fairbanks. FHWAL.

12   *"the qualities of manliness"*   Quoted from "Our Highways and the Burden They Must Carry," *Public Roads: A Journal of Highway Research*, Vol. 1, June 1918: pp. 4–29. See also Bruce Seely, *Building the American Highway System,* p. 76.

12   *"gigantic business"*   MacDonald's speech to the 5th Annual Meeting of AASHO, December 8, 1919. FHWAL.

12   *only after a thorough study*   See *Public Roads: A Journal of Highway Research*, January 1920.

13   *"This is an All-American job"*   See Bruce Seely, *Building the American Highway System*, pp. 71–80.

14   *technocrats*   The Oxford English Dictionary credits the first use of the word "technocracy" to W. H. Smyth, who coined the term in a 1919 issue of *Industrial Management*. "Technocrat" did not become current until 1932.

15   *the best shapes, colors, lettering, and placement*   AASHO published its first *Uniform Manual for Highway Signs* in 1927.

Sources and Notes

16 *By the end of 1921* Source: *Public Roads: A Journal of Highway Research*, November 1923.

17 *The machines that MacDonald* Sources for this section include the *Dictionary of American Biography*. Analysis of the cost of moving earth is found in COL-LEGE PARK.

18 *in its 1921 Federal-Aid Highway Act* In addition to giving $75 million a year, it obligated the states to pay an equal amount and required them to pay for maintenance and repairs.

18 *They were, he said, "interstate"* "The Urgent Necessity for Uniform Traffic Laws and Public Safety Devices." Speech to the 10th Annual Meeting of the American Association of State Highway Officials, November 1924. FHWAL.

19 *federal shields emblazoned with route numbers* See "Nation and States Want Better Roads," *New York Times*, March 1, 1925.

21 *As recently as 1915* All the statistics in this section come from the *World Almanac* for 1936. I am also grateful to Alan Wheelock for the information about railroads.

22 B. & M. WOULD DROP 1,000 MILES *New York Times*, December 20, 1924. Information about the elimination of grade crossings may be found in the National Archives.

22 *"There is no form of improvement more necessary"* Tom Berry, governor of South Dakota, sent this wire to the president on May 23, 1933. FDRL; of 129. Similar telegrams came from other governors.

24 *pleased to meet "Mr. Hitler"* Oberlin interview.

Chapter 2: MASTERING NATURE

26 *Robert Moses was the master builder* Anyone who writes about Robert Moses owes a great debt of gratitude to Robert A. Caro for his monumental biography *The Power Broker: Robert Moses and the Fall of New York*. I have referred to it continually throughout this chapter, but I have also consulted Eugene Lewis, *Public Entrepreneurship: Toward a Theory of Bureaucratic Political Power: The Organizational Lives of Hyman Rickover, J. Edgar Hoover, and Robert Moses*; Cleveland Rodgers, *Robert Moses, Builder for Democracy*; Joel Schwartz, *The New York Approach: Robert Moses, Urban Liberals, and Redevelopment of the Inner*

Sources and Notes

City; and Robert Moses, *Public Works: a Dangerous Trade*. These books have also been valuable.

27   *On the north shore lay the "Gold Coast"*   See *The Power Broker*, especially chapter 9, "A Dream."

28   *like none other in the world*   *Good Roads* magazine, October 1908, reported on the construction of the Long Island Motor Parkway, pp. 317–322. A. R. Pardington, general manager of the Long Island Motor Parkway, told about the lampblack at the first annual Good Roads and Legislative Convention, called by the American Automobile Association, in Buffalo, New York, July 1908. His remarks were quoted in the *Proceedings*, pp. 125–127. Additional information for this section came from Robert Miller's "Long Island Motor Parkway: Prelude to Robert Moses," in Joan P. Krieg, ed., *Robert Moses: Single-Minded Genius*, pp. 151–158.

30   *"The day of the automobile"*   Nursing his hay fever, Vanderbilt was unable to attend the ceremonies, but sent a message. It was printed in the July 1908 issue of *Good Roads* magazine, p. 225. The Long Island Motor Parkway began at Rocky Hill Road in Queens and followed a course east through farmland and adjacent to a spur line of the New York Central Railroad. The designers were careful to avoid towns and built-up areas like Mineola, Hicksville, Farmingdale, and Bethpage.

30   *"healthful recreation"*   Quoted from *Year Book of the American Automobile Association*, 1907, p. 21.

30   *"Reliability Tours"*   Information about the Glidden Tours comes from the American Automobile Association Library, Heathrow, Florida. Material for Glidden came from the University of Lowell library, Lowell, Massachusetts. Everywhere they went, Charles and Lucy Glidden stopped for photographs. The rotund Charles usually dressed in a white suit and pith helmet, stern-looking Lucy in a practical gray duster always at his side. Often the couple posed with local monarchs and potentates or with a local attraction like the Eiffel Tower or Nelson's Column at Trafalgar Square in the background.

31   *The automobile owed its exclusivity*   Much of the information in this paragraph comes from Peter J. Hughill's excellent paper *The Elite, the Automobile, and the Good Roads Movement in New York: The Development and Transformation of a Technological Complex, 1904–1913*, pp. 4–5. The paper was part of Syracuse University Department of Geography's "Discussion paper" series, no. 70, March 1981.

31 *"Automobilists are a picture of arrogance"* This oft-quoted statement first appeared in "Motorists Don't Make Socialists, They Say," *New York Times*, March 4, 1906.

32 *Farmers attached steel wheels* Much of the information about the Model T. came from Floyd Clymer's *Henry's Wonderful Model T.*, especially pp. 23 and 29. The person on the cross-country trip in the fashionable European car was Emily Post. See also Emily Post, *By Motor to the Golden Gate*, p. 139.

33 *The Fords went by because* Mass production made the Ford Motor Company wealthy, too. Net income jumped from $13 million in 1912 to $27 million the next year, and reached a high point of nearly $76 million in 1921. Statistics on Ford's net earnings appear in Allan Nevins, *Ford: The Times, the Man, the Company*, Appendix VI, p. 647. I also consulted *Ford Sales Bulletin* ("Issued every Saturday by the Sales Department of the Ford Motor Company, Detroit, in the Interests of the Selling Force of Ford"), found in MACDONALD.

33 *"Cars, cars, fast, fast!"* Le Corbusier, *Urbanisme*, 1924. Translated as *The City of the Future*.

34 *"Why on earth do you need"* Quoted from Robert S. Lynd and Helen Merrell Lynd, *Middletown: A Study in Contemporary American Culture*, p. 252.

34 *"To George F. Babbitt"* *Babbitt*, p. 24.

38 *a consummate work of art* Mumford wrote about the Taconic Parkway: "Not every highway, it is true, runs through country that offers such superb opportunities to an imaginative highway builder as this does; but then not every engineer rises to his opportunities as the planners of this highway did, routing the well-separated roads along the ridgeways, following the contours, and thus, by this single stratagem, both avoiding towns and villages and opening up great views across country, enhanced by lavish planting of flowering bushes along the borders." *The Highway and the City*, pp. 234–246. See also the article Mumford wrote with Benton MacKaye, "Townless Highways for the Motorist: A Proposal for the Automobile Age," *Harper's Monthly*, Vol. 163, 1931, pp. 347–356; and Benton MacKay's "The Townless Highway," *New Republic*, March 12, 1930, pp. 93–95.

38 *"a real parkway"* Quoted from Bruce Radde, *The Meritt Parkway*, p. 15.

38 *"fantastic farm where ashes grow"* *The Great Gatsby*, p. 23.

42 *"Looming ahead is a 1960 Motorway"* Quoted from the "Text of Script for Sound Chair Tour of General Motors Highways and Horizons Exhibit at

Sources and Notes

the New York World's Fair," found in MACDONALD. For my description and discussion of the Futurama, I am indebted to Roland Marchand's "The Designers go to the Fair II: Norman Bel Geddes, The General Motors 'Futurama,' and the Visit to the Factory Transformed" (*Design Issues*, Vol. 8, No. 2, Spring 1992, pp. 23–40). Marchand's article contains the essence of much of what I have said about Teague. It is also the source of my observation that the "Futurama" presented Fair visitors with a way of life.

43   *"We enter a new era"*   Bel Geddes's absurd schemes were so elaborate that one can dare to mention him in the same breath as Leonardo da Vinci and Gyro Gearloose. For a stage version of Dante's *Divine Comedy* he proposed creating a special five-thousand-seat theater with space for a two-hundred-member orchestra and a six-hundred-member chorus. Bel Geddes calculated everything he did for the effect it would produce upon his audience. For many years friends visited his house every Wednesday evening to compete in a huge war game of his invention that involved two mythical countries. The guests would decide the nations' destiny with many divisions and ships on a sixteen-foot-long table. When one player—an admiral—lost eight ships under his command, Bel Geddes had him court-martialed. Humiliated, the officer never returned. For a while in the thirties he kept in a New York apartment over two thousand snakes and lizards, which he liked to film in the throes of mating. At Christmastime and at birthdays he often gave friends pregnant rabbits. Even his name was a design: He appropriated the "Bel" from his first wife, Helen Bel Sneider.

43   *"Just as surely"*   Quoted from Bel Geddes's *Horizons*, p. 23.

43   *which they named the "Airflow"*   See Jeffrey L. Meikle, *Twentieth Century Limited*, pp. 201–209, 145–150.

43   *"bunk"*   *Twentieth Century Limited*, p. 208.

43   *the designer took little notice*   For Bel Geddes, the Futurama was simply the beginning. He proposed to General Motors that the exhibit be flown about the nation in a dirigible, which would drop his vision of the future on selected cities in America. The less visionary General Motors executives would hear nothing of it. Regarding the Futurama as little more than an amusing and successful $8 million marketing strategy, they thought the dirigible scheme preposterous. The Futurama would end with the Fair, in October 1940.

44   *"A modern highway system"*   *Magic Motorways*, p. 288.

Sources and Notes

44   *"Every highway intersection"*   *Magic Motorways*, p. 82. See also pp. 83, 98–99.

44   *"residential, commercial and industrial"*   The "Text of Script for Sound Chair Tour of General Motors Highways and Horizons Exhibit at the New York World's Fair." I have also borrowed freely for the language of this paragraph from Alfred P. Sloan's "A Description of the General Motors Highways and Horizons Exhibit at the New York World's Fair and a Discussion of the Theme of the Exhibit as Reported to Stockholders on June 10, 1939" found in MACDONALD.

45   *"one of the most depression-proof"*   See *Middletown in Transition: A Study in Cultural Conflicts*, p. 266.

45   *"owns some kind of an auto"*   *Middletown Revisited*, p. 453.

Chapter 3: THE DREAMWAY

47   *"the cynosure of all eyes"*   Quoted from a speech by Jones entitled "Pennsylvania's Dream Road: A Milestone of Progress." For this chapter I have relied upon documents found in MACDONALD, COLLEGE PARK, FDRL, WEINGROFF, the Pennsylvania Turnpike Commission's archives in Harrisburg, and a variety of secondary sources, including Phil Patton's *The Open Road*; Charles M. Noble, "Design Features—Pennsylvania Turnpike," *Civil Engineering*, July 1940, pp. 437–440; Thomas D. Larson, "Pennsylvania and the Interstate System," *Transportation Quarterly*, Vol. 41, No. 2, April 1987, pp. 117–132; and monthly issues of the *Turnpike News*, published while the highway was under construction.

49   *"overseas road and bridge"*   "Memorandum for the Secretary of the Interior," May 30, 1936, FDRL.

50   *"If you remember"*   "Memorandum for the Secretary of the Interior," February 10, 1936, FDRL.

50   *six years later, Alice Huyler Ramsey*   See Alice Huyler Ramsey's account of her journey, *Veil, Duster and Tire Iron*.

50   *"The highways of America"*   Quoted from Drake Hokanson, *The Lincoln Highway: Main Street Across America*, p. 7. See also Philip Langdon, "Westward on the Old Lincoln Highway," *American Heritage*, April 1995, pp. 49–60; *The Complete Official Road Guide of The Lincoln Highway*, 1919 and 1924; and Fisher's obituary in the *New York Times*, July 16, 1939.

Sources and Notes

50 *"Let's build it"* Drake Hokanson, *The Lincoln Highway: Main Street Across America*, p. 6.

51 *and the Dixie* See *Fabulous Hoosier*, the biography of Fisher written by his former wife.

51 *"High speed highway from the Atlantic to the Pacific"* Harold Ickes, speech of 1933, FDRL.

51 *"Imagine this Super-Highway"* Edward Snodgrass, Jr., "A Trans-Continental Super Highway Needed," November 1934, FDRL.

52 *"Undoubtedly, decentralization"* Quoted from letter of Henry Wallace to Roosevelt, October 5, 1934, FDRL.

52 *"discussed with congressional advisers"* *Washington Post*, February 15, 1935.

54 *fill Moses' coffers as well* Whenever someone suggested providing a lane for public transportation—a railroad trestle beside a parkway or over a bridge—Moses ignored them.

56 *George Washington, to bury the General's remains* From a Church of England prayerbook, the lieutenant colonel read the funeral service by torchlight. Fearing that the Indians might desecrate Braddock's body, he ordered it placed in a deep trench in the middle of his road, and then directed the retreating horses, wagons, and footmen to tamp down the earth so that no mark of the grave remained. The spot was soon forgotten, and Braddock's road swiftly reverted to a trace through the dense forest.

56 *Thomas Jefferson, built a "National Road"* See Phil Patton's *The Open Road*, pp. 25–28, 29, 53–54.

57 *railroad competition often turned savage* A good account of the history of the South Penn railroad may be found in William H. Shink's *Vanderbilt's Folly: A History of the Pennsylvania Turnpike*.

58 *appointed Walter Adelbert Jones of Pittsburgh* Information about Jones comes from FDRL, the Pennsylvania Turnpike Commission archives, and his obituary in the *New York Times*, September 4, 1943.

59 *"the only time you'll hold on to a million dollars"* Undated article in the Carlisle *Sentinel*, and interview with Edna Eberly Thrush in the Pennsylvania Turnpike Commission archives.

Sources and Notes

60 *fell upon the shoulders of Samuel Marshall*   Information about Marshall comes from the *Turnpike News* and his obituary in the *New York Times*, November 26, 1943.

60 *"You were there when something"*   Interview with Jesse Aycock, July 1, 1992. Pennsylvania Turnpike Commission archives.

63 *The company suppressed all stories*   Interview with C. Ralph Seasley, July 1994. Seasley worked in the Blue Hill and Kittatinny Mountain tunnels.

64 *three and a half miles a day*   Memorandum in COLLEGE PARK.

64 *From his office at the Bureau of Public Roads*   See the various memoranda in the COLLEGE PARK archives.

66 *"Imagine a great road"*   *New York Times*, August 27, 1940.

66 *"I never thought I could drive"*   Washington *News*, August 28, 1940.

66 *"This road is absolutely extraordinary"*   *New York Times*, August 27, 1940.

67 *"a magnificent accomplishment"*   MacDonald's remarks, which were dated July 30, 1940, are found in COLLEGE PARK.

68 *"I expect you are wondering"*   Walter Jones to Jesse H. Jones, September 17, 1942, FDRL.

68 *"Jones says that he felt"*   Moses' letter, dated August 21, 1940, is in COLLEGE PARK.

69 *"by present and future main arteries"*   *New York Times*, February 1, 1940; "Memorandum for the President," May 24, 1940, FDRL.

Chapter 4: THE GI AND THE GENERAL

71 *On the fringes*   David Halberstam, *The Fifties*, p. 142. Information about Levitt, Levittown, and the suburbs comes from Halberstam; newspaper and magazine articles; Barbara M. Kelly, *Expanding the American Dream: Building and Rebuilding Levittown*; John Thomas Liell, *Levittown: a Study in Community Planning and Development*; and especially Kenneth T. Jackson, *Crabgrass Frontier: The Suburbanization of the United States*. Jackson's chapter "The Baby Boom and the Age of the Subdivision" has been very helpful for this study.

Sources and Notes

73   *not members of a subversive organization*   "Injunction sought to Stop City from Requiring Tenant Oaths," *New York Times*, January 30, 1953, p. 12.

73   *"men of moderate means"*   Whitman, *I Sit and Look Out*, New York, 1932, p. 145. Cited in Jackson, *Crabgrass Frontier*, p. 28.

74   *"that the American people do not intend"*   Quoted from Doris Kearns Goodwin, *No Ordinary Time*, p. 513.

76   *"No man who owns his own house"*   William J. Levitt, 1948; quoted in Jackson, *Crabgrass Frontier*, p. 231, among other places.

76   *"The same man does the same thing"*   Alfred Levitt, quoted from "Levitt's Progress," *Fortune*, 1952, p. 152.

77   called his development *"Island Trees"*   Quoted from "Levitt's Progress," p. 155.

77   *"universally and exclusively inhabited"*   Quoted from Stephen E. Ambrose, *Eisenhower: The President*, p. 535.

78   *"The longer we wait"*   See Barbara M. Kelly, *Expanding the American Dream: Building and Rebuilding Levittown*.

78   *No dwelling shall be used"*   "FHA Can't Prevent Negro Housing Ban," *New York Times*, March 19, 1949, page 2. See also Gwendolyn Wright, *Building the Dream: A Social History of Housing in America*, pp. 247 ff.

78   *"We can solve a housing problem"*   Widely quoted. See, for example, Jackson, *Crabgrass Frontier*, p. 241.

79   *Owners could erect no fences*   Information from an interview with Mrs. Thomas P. O'Neill, a former Levittown, Pennsylvania, resident.

79   *"almost as much of a nightmare"*   *The Highway and the City*, p. 228.

81   *The models were sleek*   Automobile pictures, prices, and features may be found in John Gunnell's *Standard Catalog on American Cars, 1946–1975*.

82   *"The county now has"*   Quoted from Harry S. Bronson, "Change to Metropolitan Area Poses New Problems," *Better Roads*, October 1954, p. 21.

82   *"we are not keeping step"*   E. L. Schmidt, "Financial Problem Is Most Baffling

Sources and Notes

One of All," *Better Roads*, November 1954, p. 17. See also "Neglected Roads Taking Auto Toll," *New York Times*, January 30, 1953, p. 23.

85   *Nor was there poetry*   Information about the railroad situation in the 1950s comes from a variety of sources, including the *New York Times*, August 2, 1954, and information provided by Alan Wheelock.

85   *"liberal on human issues"*   Quoted in Ambrose, *Eisenhower: The President*, pp. 114–115 and 157–158.

86   *"The Potential Use of Toll Road"*   Bureau of Public Roads papers in COLLEGE PARK.

87   *depended on the services of an average of eight engineers*   General John S. Bragdon found that in 1956 it took eight engineers per million dollars of roadwork. Bragdon papers, Eisenhower Library, memo of May 9, 1956.

88   *"That's about all the pens"*   "Eisenhower Signs Highway Aid Bill," *New York Times*, May 7, 1954, p. 25. Speech of Senator Francis Case to the annual meeting of the American Association of State Highway Officials, November 1957. Quoted in *American Highways*, January 1958.

89   *"Large crops of wheat"*   Karl Baedeker, *The United States*, p. 457.

89   *"It was definitely"*   Eisenhower, *At Ease: Stories I Tell to Friends*, p. 68. John F. Stover, *American Railroads*, pp. 93–94.

90   *"partly for a lark"*   Much of the information for the army's 1919 cross-country trip comes from Eisenhower's *At Ease*, pp. 155 ff, as well as his "History Lesson in Travel for Eisenhower Grandchildren and Others," found at the end of the book on pages 385–387.

90   *"We have enjoyed the blessings"*   *The Encyclopedia of the Third Reich*, Vol. 1, pp. 57–58.

91   *a single 8½-by-11-inch page*   The organization charts may be found in COLLEGE PARK.

92   *"activate coordinated efforts"*   Quoted in *American Highways*, January 1953.

92   *By train*   The story of MacDonald's dismissal was told to me by Lee Mertz and confirmed by Frank Turner.

Sources and Notes

Chapter 5: A GRAND PLAN

95   *visionary designer, Pierre Charles L'Enfant*   Information for this section comes
      from Richard W. Stephenson's *"A Plan Whol[l]y New": Pierre Charles L'Enfant's
      Plan of the City of Washington*, especially pp. 32–34 and 48–50; John W. Reps,
      Washington on View: The Nation's Capital since 1790, pp. 10–23 and 108.

96   *"spacious avenues that begin"*   Dickens published his observations of Wash-
      ington in *American Notes*, p. 169.

98   *"a more effective"*   Quoted from Stephen E. Ambrose, *Eisenhower:
      1890–1952*, p. 482.

99   *"dramatic plan"*   Memorandum in DDEL.

99   *His father, Thomas Coleman du Pont*   Information about Thomas Coleman du
      Pont comes from John B. Rae, "Coleman du Pont and his Road," *Delaware
      History*, Vol. 16, Spring/Summer 1975, pp. 171–183. See also Leonard
      Moseley, *Blood Relations*, pp. 227–228, 262, 334.

99   *"a paved United States"*   National Highways Association documents in FDRL
      and COLLEGE PARK.

100   *His appointment . . . had been buried deep*   *New York Times*, March 18, 1953.
      On April 1, 1953, the *New York Times* also reported that du Pont had been
      sworn in as commissioner of the Bureau of Public Roads.

101   *It was du Pont's rationale*   *Washington Evening Star*, May 21, 1962.

101   *John Stewart Bragdon*   Information about Bragdon and his actions may be
      found in the Bragdon papers, DDEL.

103   *"the Federal Constitution must be obeyed"*   Jackson's letter to Van Buren is
      quoted in Robert V. Remini's *Andrew Jackson and the Course of American
      Freedom, 1822–1832*, p. 256.

104   *"[a] grand plan"*   Quoted from the *New York Times*, July 13, 1954. and
      Robert L. Bryan and Lawrence H. Larsen, *The Eisenhower Administration: A
      Documentary History*, pp. 537–538. Eisenhower was right. The population
      reached 203,225,000 in 1970.

104   *"electrifying effect"*   Memorandum from Highway Consultant Robinson New-
      comb to the Council of Economic Advisers, August 24, 1954; Bragdon
      Papers, DDEL; *The Eisenhower Administration, 1953–1961, A Documentary His-*

tory, pp. 539–540; Gary Schwartz, "Urban Freeways and the Interstate System," *Southern California Law Review*, Vol. 49, No. 406, p. 428. Schwartz's article is superb and I have drawn on it frequently while writing this chapter.

105 *"That is one crowd"* Ambrose, *Eisenhower: The President*, p. 250.

106 *"eight millionaires and a plumber"* Cited frequently in books about twentieth-century America or Eisenhower. See, for example, Samuel Eliot Morison, *The Oxford History of the American People*, p. 1082.

107 *"What's good for General Motors"* Actually, Wilson never said it. At his Senate confirmation hearings, Wilson was asked about a possible conflict of interest if he did not divest himself of his GM stock. Wilson replied, "For years I thought that what was good for the country is good for General Motors and vice versa." Taking a cue from the last two words, the press chose to reverse the statement. Editorial writers across the nation viewed the rewritten quotation as proof positive that America was in the grip of businessmen.

108 *list of 185 "target areas"* Gerald R. Gallagher, "Roads—Key to Survival?" *American Road Builder*, January 1958. See also Ambrose, *Eisenhower the President*, p. 294.

108 *"on a route that had suffered"* Quoted in Jay Dugan, "Highways in the National Defense," *Freedom of the American Road*, p. 18.

109 *Francis Cutler Turner* Information about Turner comes from interviews and Stephen B. Goddard's *Getting There: the Epic Struggle between Road and Rail in the American Century*, p. 53.

109 *was just 65 cents* Information about Clay's work, including mess bills, comes from the Clay papers at the DDEL.

111 *"Crozet Super Highway Commission"* Clay papers, DDEL.

112 *"views on financing a highway program"* Clay memorandum to six bankers and brokers, December 6, 1954, Clay papers, DDEL.

112 *"a capital asset"* See *A Ten-Year National Highway Program: A Report to the President*, January 1955, "Summary of Conclusions and Recommendations," p. v.

113 *"There has never been"* *American Highways*, March 1955.

113 *"There was much"* Bragdon papers, DDEL.

Sources and Notes

113 *"I am inclined"*   See Bragdon papers, DDEL; and Eisenhower, *Public Papers: 1955*, No. 39, pp. 279–280.

114 *Harry Flood Byrd*   This section draws upon John M. Martin's "Proposed Federal Highway Legislation in 1955: A Case Study in the Legislative Process," *Georgetown Law Journal*, Vol. 44, 1956.

114 *The administration's bill never*   The quiet end for the administration's bill came in May, when the Senate voted it down as a substitute motion, 31 to 60. The lone Democrat to support the measure was the junior senator from Massachusetts, John F. Kennedy.

114 *"Provide sufficient funds"*   Bragdon papers, DDEL.

116 *George Hyde Fallon*   *Baltimore Sun*, March 21, 1980. George H. Fallon's one moment of prominence in the national consciousness came in 1953, when he was shot in the leg—"in a delicate place," as one colleague put it—by a group of Puerto Ricans who decided to make their case for nationalism on the floor of the House with guns. Even then he was quickly forgotten.

117 *Fallon's fervor for highway construction*   Curiously, Fallon disliked driving himself and would take the train whenever possible.

117 *and created a highway trust fund*   The principal feature of Fallon's bill was its methods of funding. Normally the House Ways and Means Committee determines what taxes to levy to fund legislation, but as Fallon said when introducing his bill, "We did not have a normal situation."

118 *"Road Gang"*   The Road Gang was secretive about its membership and activities for the most part, which was odd because what it did was so predictable.

118 *Typical of the views*   Henry W. Osborne memorandum to General Bragdon and Colonel Meek, November 17, 1955. Bragdon papers, DDEL.

119 *"Legislation to provide"*   Eisenhower, *Public Papers: 1956*, No. 1, p. 18.

120 *"While there may be some portions"*   *Congressional Record*, 84th Congress, Second Session, p. 6379.

120 *"Yellow Book"*   FHWAL.

123 *"When the American"*   Mumford, *Highway and the City*, p. 234.

123 *"simply because we Americans"* Quoted from the Ford Motor Company's *Freedom of the American Road*, p. 1.

123 *"We have seen"* *Freedom of the American Road*, p. 8.

Chapter 6: THE GREAT PUZZLE

125 *to dedicate the first eight miles* Long ago I learned that writers play a dangerous game when they declare something to have been the "first," and the ribbon-cutting on Interstate 70 in Kansas bears out that lesson. Kansas was the first to open a paved section of the Interstate Highway System, but its neighbor Missouri was first to let a contract to build a section of the Interstate when the state highway department signed a contract on August 2, 1956. Pennsylvania also can legitimately make a claim for being first, as a part of the original Pennsylvania Turnpike became Interstate 76.

126 *"straight shot" between Topeka* The article was entitled "Formal Dedication for US-40 Segment," Topeka *State Journal*, Wednesday, November 14, 1956.

128 *constructed on new right-of-way* *American Highways*, July 1957.

129 *John Anthony Volpe* Much of the information about Volpe comes from the papers found in WEINGROFF.

131 *"We must think big"* *American Highways,* January 1957.

131 *twenty-two thousand men and sixty-two women* These numbers have been drawn from *Statistical Abstract of the United States* for 1957 and census reports. The number of women and blacks in civil engineering has never been significant. A study by the National Science Foundation found that in 1982 there were 159,708 engineers. Of those, 2,673 were female and 2,210 black, 83 black women, 259 Asian women, 55 other. Source: The 1982 Postcensal Survey of Scientists and Engineers. National Science Foundation Surveys of Science Resource Series, NSF 84-330.

132 *"We don't stress the fact"* Letter from Richard H. Schmelzer to Edward H. Dion, January 28, 1958. Source: Rensselaer Polytechnic Institute Archives.

132 *The case of Walter T. Daniels* Information about Daniels was provided by the Moorland-Spingarn Research Center at Howard University.

132 *"The man we honor today"* *American Highways*, January 1961. The man being honored was Rex Whitton.

133   *Of greater importance than*   In 1930 a civil engineering student at the Rensselaer took sixty-one courses, of which six (three in English, two in a modern language, and one in physical training) were outside the sciences and technology. By 1950 the number of courses had shrunk to sixty, of which eight were "nontechnical" electives, physical training, or English. The "nontechnical" electives were the institution's weak attempt to broaden its students' outlook, but the students themselves considered these few courses in the humanities and social sciences to be of little consequence.

133   *"Anything that wasn't engineering"*   Interview with Frank Griggs, 1996.

134   *"steel design, concrete design"*   Interview with John H. Shafer, AASHTO archives.

135   *"I had surveying"*   Interview with Ellis L. Armstrong, AASHTO archives.

135   *"Civils were building it"*   Interview with Frank Griggs, 1996.

136   *"We tended to consider"*   Interview with Ellis L. Armstrong, AASHTO archives.

136   *"all known" safety features*   "U.S. Sets Standards for New Highways," *New York Times*, July 22, 1956.

136   *three-color federal "shield"*   *New York Times*, September 27, 1957; and *American Highways*, October 1957.

137   *colors for the large exit signs*   Sources include the *New York Times*, January 27, 1958; Interview with Ellis L. Armstrong, AASHTO archives; and my own interview with Armstrong, 1996.

138   *"Insolent Chariots"*   The term comes from John Keats's book of the same name. Actually it was the Chrysler Company that was first enamored of the streamlined airplane design, especially after the Douglas DC-2. In 1934, Chrysler introduced the aerodynamic "Airflow" model, which featured built-in headlamps (most cars still had them mounted on the fenders), slanted radiator and windshield, and a smoothly inclined rear end that had a low drag coefficient. However advanced its engineering, the car's shape proved far too radical in a world of sit-up-straight automobiles and sales proved to be dismal. So strange was the front grille that Chrysler offered an attachable nose with more conventional lines before withdrawing its marketing mistake in 1937. The Airflow did point to the future, however. By 1941, Ford and General Motors had gradually introduced many of its design features into their models.

Sources and Notes

141   *"Most of them"*   Interview with Ellis L. Armstrong, AASHTO archives.

143   *Bertram Tallamy told Congress*   Bragdon papers, DDEL.

143   *"wage a relentless battle"*   Bragdon papers, DDEL.

144   *"The present economy"*   Bragdon papers, DDEL.

144   *"Our great highway programs"*   Bragdon papers, DDEL.

145   *In the spring of 1959*   Stephen E. Ambrose puts the date as July 1959 when Eisenhower became aware that Interstates were being constructed in cities. But he was well aware of the problem before that. See *Eisenhower: The President*, p. 547; and John Stewart Bragdon's memorandum of June 17, 1959, DDEL. Other sources for this section on Bragdon are "The Bragdon Committee," an undated paper by Lee Mertz; and Gary T. Schwartz, "Urban Freeways and the Interstate System," *Southern California Law Review*, Vol. 49 (March 1976), pp. 406–513.

146   *"routing the Interstate"*   Bragdon papers, DDEL.

146   *"Reexamine policies"*   Bragdon papers, DDEL.

147   *"in danger of becoming"*   Bragdon papers, DDEL.

148   *"The 1944 interregional"*   Bragdon papers, DDEL.

149   *General Bragdon's philosophy*   Bragdon papers, DDEL.

150   *would "cut the heart" out of*   Scherer's remarks are reported in *Congressional Quarterly Weekly*, p. 1416, October 16, 1959. Chavez's appear in *Congressional Quarterly Weekly*, p. 179, January 29, 1960.

151   *Tallamy brought only the Yellow Book*   This story was recounted by Lee Mertz in "The Bragdon Committee." Mertz confirmed it in a conversation with me in 1992.

151   *Eisenhower nominated his old West Point*   Eisenhower's nomination of April 25 was not met with universal acclaim. One senator accused the president of loading federal aviation agencies with too many retired military. Such men, said one senator, "lack the mental orientation to take on these civilian regulatory jobs, and run those agencies as they should be run." Another called the Federal Aviation Agency a "little Pentagon." But a majority of the

Senate thought otherwise, confirming Bragdon with a vote of 73 to 18. Perhaps relieved to move him out the White House and his role as chief critic for the Interstate Highway System, Dennis Chavez and Albert Gore voted with the majority. Bragdon's term expired on the last day of December 1960. He lived in an angry retirement, writing a tirade against the bureaucracy of the federal government, which no one would publish. See Bragdon papers, DDEL; and *Congressional Quarterly Weekly*, July 1, 1960, pp. 1129 and 1172.

152 *"In the councils of government"* See Stephen E. Ambrose, *Eisenhower: The President*, p. 614.

Chapter 7: LINES OF DESIRE

157 *announcement of the "fancy highway"* Sunday *World Herald*, Omaha, January 5, 1964.

157 *"Platte Valley Platter"* The "Farm Wife" was actually Eleanor Seberger. She used to write regularly for the North Platte *Telegraph Bulletin*. This column is dated October 1, 1963.

158 *"Those were real contentious days"* Interview with Merle Kingsbury, 1985, quoted in George E. Koster, "A Story of Highway Development in Nebraska," p. 67, an undated paper in WEINGROFF.

158 *Kennedy appointed Rex Marion Whitton* Most of the information about Whitton comes from papers found in WEINGROFF. See also St. Louis *Post-Dispatch*, January 8, 1961; July 7, 1963; and December 18, 1966. See also the St. Louis *Globe Democrat*, November 28, 1964; *Constructor*, February 1966; and the Kansas City *Star*, January 6, 1967.

159 *In 1951 . . . reached the top* Whitton was fortunate, too, to grow with the department. When he began, Missouri had about 200 highway employees overseeing 400 miles of state roads, of which about 150 miles were paved. When he went to Washington, the state had about 32,000 miles of road, of which more than 7,200 were paved.

161 *"monument to our system"* WEINGROFF.

161 *Whitton took his case to his friends* American Highways, April 1963.

162 *"Problems and challenges"* WEINGROFF.

162 *Gas-saving cars accounted*   "Small Cars in the Traffic Stream," *American Highways*, July 1959.

164 *a Democratic judge named Harry Truman*   David McCullough writes of Truman's judgeships in *Truman*, pp. 160–180, and his first automobile, pp. 92–94. In 1925, Truman sold memberships in the Kansas City Automobile Club, clearing $5,000 in commissions in a single year.

165 *"Well, you decision makers"*   Interview with Ellis L. Armstrong, AASHTO archives.

166 *"I had a boy"*   *New York Times*, December 7, 1960. See also the *New York Times*, October 13 and 14, 1959; March 20, May 12, November 29, and December 9, 10, 11, and 14, 1960; January 6, January 13, and June 4, 1961; and May 5, 1963. Also see *Congressional Record* for 1960, pp. 11322–11328, 11512–11514, 18775–11782; for 1961, pp. 11159–11165, 15290–15296, 20847–20850; and for 1962, pp. 10504–10509.

167 *"Great Highway Robbery"*   The half-hour investigative documentary hosted by David Brinkley appeared on NBC on October 1, 1962.

167 *The facts often differed*   See "Analysis of David Brinkley's Television Program of October 1, 1962 Entitled 'The Great Highway Robbery,' Prepared by the Bureau of Public Roads, U.S. Department of Commerce" in WEINGROFF.

168 *"The Interstate program"*   "New Roads and Urban Chaos," *Reporter*, April 14, 1960, p. 13.

169 *"billboard alley"*   *New York Times*, March 11, 1958.

169 *"I am against those billboards"*   WEINGROFF.

170 *"the nuclear option"*   *Going Places*, March/April 1988, pp. 13–17.

171 *"Thanks to the miles"*   Fletcher Knebel in *Peter's Quotations*.

171 *"yet we live in a land"*   *The Quiet Crisis*, p. viii.

171 *"I look forward to an America"*   Kennedy, *Public Papers: 1963*, No. 439, p. 817.

172 *"In the final analysis"*   The Circular Memorandum, dated March 1, 1963, was published in *American Highways*, April 1963.

Sources and Notes

172 *"How can one best fight"*   Quoted from a 1966 film clip, ABC archives.

172 *"A highway is more than a ribbon"*   Quoted from a 1966 film clip, ABC archives.

173 *"I look forward eagerly"*   *American Highways*, January 1963.

174 INTERSTATES A BOON TO IOWA   These positive and negative comments are quoted from newspaper articles found in WEINGROFF.

Chapter 8: REVOLT

179 *More than anything else*   For the opening of this chapter I have relied upon the New Orleans section of the Federal Writers Project, *Louisiana* volume; personal knowledge; and Richard O. Baumbach, Jr., and William E. Borah, *The Second Battle of New Orleans*.

181 *"Certain parts of the Quarter"*   Interview with Fred Guice, 1996.

181 *Bill Borah and Dick Baumbach, two transplanted*   Much of the information in this chapter comes from two days of interviews with William E. Borah in 1996; personal observations; *The Second Battle of New Orleans*; and discussions with my editor, Wendy Wolf.

182 *Along the riverfront, a "new route"*   Robert Moses, "Arterial Plan for Orleans," November 1, 1946. Moses' plans also called for two parking garages in the Vieux Carré, one for 465 automobiles, the other for 230.

183 *"The problem was solved"*   *The Power Broker*, p. 520

183 *"great tiled bathroom"*   See *The Power Broker*, chapter 29, for Moses' opposition to tunnels.

185 *"Our bread and butter"*   Interview with Fred Guice, 1996.

186 *"The Riverfront Expressway and its"*   *The Second Battle of New Orleans*, p. 49.

187 *The automobile is a Frankenstein"*   *The Second Battle of New Orleans*, p. 38.

188 *rather grotesque structure"*   Interview with William E. Borah.

189 *"quaint and distinctive character"*   *The Second Battle of New Orleans*, p. 52.

Sources and Notes

189 *It was about this time that* Interview with William E. Borah.

193 *"Men have begun"* Editorial in WEINGROFF.

194 *a tawdry Ferris wheel made to look* I am indebted to Alan Wheelock for this observation.

195 *"Local Babbits"* *The Second Battle of New Orleans*, p. 65.

195 *"noble massacre"* *The Second Battle of New Orleans*, p. 66.

195 *Healy fulminated* A year later, Healy wrote an editorial about a wire service story concerning the president of the American Institute of Architects. The president cited the Riverfront Expressway as an example of "roadbuilders ploughing through cities blindly . . . with disastrous results." Accusing the president of "incoherence," Healy advised him to be quiet "until he gets his facts and his philosophy straighter." Once again, Healy managed to make a minor story into a major one.

197 *"a white man's road"* Interstate 66 file in WEINGROFF.

197 *In Memphis, Tennessee, Borah* Overton Park file in WEINGROFF.

198 *Interstate 280, the Embarcadero Freeway* Embarcadero Freeway file in WEIN-GROFF.

198 *outer beltway, Route 128* Personal interviews with residents of Somerville, Massachusetts, and Justin Gray.

199 *students at MIT had set up* Interview with William E. Borah.

200 *"It is presently being operated"* *The Second Battle of New Orleans*, p. 102.

201 *"The country's transportation"* Johnson, *Public Papers: 1966*, No. 98, pp. 247–263. See also No. 240, p. 547.

203 *"The tide has changed"* *The Second Battle of New Orleans*, p. 138.

204 *"there's been too much conversation"* *The Second Battle of New Orleans*, p. 140.

204 *"We did not come down"* *The Second Battle of New Orleans*, p. 152.

205 *"A war that may"* *The Second Battle of New Orleans*, p. 164.

Sources and Notes

207 *recommended him and him alone*   Benjamin A. Kelley, *The Pavers and the Paved*, p. 82.

208 *"Another stumbling block"*   *The Second Battle of New Orleans*, p. 178.

208 *"I want to go"*   Stephen E. Ambrose, *Eisenhower: The President*, p. 675.

209 *a three-mile traffic jam*   "Ike-Mamie Buried Here," Abilene *Reflector-Chronicle*, memorial edition, n.d.

209 *razing of five thousand homes*   The figure comes from testimony Robert Durham gave to the Senate Subcommittee on Public Roads in 1968. Cited in Helen Leavitt, *Superhighway—Superhoax*, p. 194.

209 *"We were the villains"*   Interview with Fred Guice, 1996.

Chapter 9: BUSTING THE TRUST

211 *Hawaii's Interstate highways*   In the Federal-Aid Highway Act of 1959, Congress ordered the Commerce Department to study and report on the advisability of extending the Interstate Highway System to Hawaii and Alaska. On January 13, 1960, the Department recommended that fifty miles of Interstates be built in Hawaii, but said that "neither the present conditions nor anticipated further developments during the next 15 to 20 years warrant the designation of any Interstate mileage in Alaska."

212 *Raymond Albert Kroc*   Information about Kroc and Wilson comes from Phil Patton's *The Open Road* and author interviews with McDonald's managers.

214 *compared them to "enemy soldiers"*   *New York Times*, April 28, 1970.

214 *"a fair trial"*   *New York Times*, April 25, 1970. See also Nora Sayre's *Sixties Going on Seventies*, pp. 161–165.

215 *$131 billion for highway*   Helen Leavitt, *Washington Evening Star*, March 5, 1972.

215 *General Motors paid Ralph Nader*   *New York Times*, August 14, 1970. See also Tom Wicker's column on General Motors and Nader, *New York Times*, August 16, 1970. Nader's book *Unsafe at Any Speed: The Designed-in Dangers of the American Automobile* was published in 1965.

Sources and Notes

216   *"I had thought my name"*   *New York Times*, September 15, 1970.

218   *To Ehrlichman's annoyance*   See Dan Rather and Gary Paul Gates, *The Palace Guard*, pp. 190–192 and 37–38. Ehrlichman writes in his memoir, *Witness to Power*, p. 107, that "within a year" Volpe "had totally lost Nixon's confidence."

219   *"The federal government spends"*   *Transport Topics*, June 30, 1969, WEINGROFF.

219   *"Now I have to see"*   Benjamin A. Kelley, *The Pavers and the Paved*, p. 85.

219   *"The trust fund . . . throws"*   *Transport Topics*, February 23, 1970, WEINGROFF.

219   *"We have a great deal of education"*   *Engineering News Record*, May 14, 1970.

220   *Other books, including*   Ronald A. Buel, *Dead End: The Automobile in Mass Transportation*; John Burby, *The Great American Motion Sickness: Or, Why You Can't Get There From Here*; and Kenneth R. Schneider, *Autokind vs. Mankind*.

220   *"How to Halt a Highway"*   See *The Pavers and the Paved*, chapter 6, pp. 127–150.

222   *"special earmarked funds"*   *New York Times*, January 8, 1972. See also *Baltimore Sun*, January 15, 1973.

222   *Henry Ford II*   *New York Times*, January 16, 1972. Bernard Markwell, executive director of the Gulf Oil Corporation, endorsed a proposal to allow state highway money to be used for mass transit. *Business Week*, December 11, 1971.

222   *Jennings Randolph, the courtly*   Sources for Randolph include *Superhighway—Superhoax* and *Congressional Quarterly*.

222   *"He is one of us"*   *Superhighway—Superhoax*, pp. 132–133. See also *Washington Post*, April 16, 1973.

223   *"German mafia"*   *The Palace Guard*, p. 192.

224   *"Highway investments alone"*   WEINGROFF.

224   *"Collectively, the state"*   WEINGROFF.

224   *"fiscal maneuver" to make*   WEINGROFF.

Sources and Notes

225 *"Mass transit has"* WEINGROFF.

225 *Highway Action Coalition* See *New York Times*, October 24, 1972.

225–226 *"in maybe just two years"* WEINGROFF.

226 THE UNTOUCHABLE HIGHWAY FUND Item marked only as *Courier-Journal*, November 13, 1971, WEINGROFF.

226 THE MOVE TO SHAKE *Washington Evening-Star*, March 6, 1972.

226 THE HIGHWAY LOBBY AIMS *Wall Street Journal*, February 17, 1972.

226 THE CONCRETE BLOC *Wall Street Journal*, March 17, 1972.

226 *"Highwaymen"* *Journal of Commerce*, May 24, 1972.

226 *"We now subsidize"* WEINGROFF.

226 *"Your highways"* Quoted in "The Highway Lobby Aims to Prove There Is No Highway Lobby," *Wall Street Journal*, February 17, 1972.

227 *close to $75,000* *Wall Street Journal*, October 10, 1972. The actual figure was $74,400.

227 *"the looming energy crisis"* WEINGROFF.

228 *dancer Fanne Foxe* "Foxe" also billed herself as the "Argentine Firecracker." In her private life she was known as Mrs. Annabell Batrtistella. See *New York Times*, October 10 and 18, 1974. Though he won reelection handily in November 1974, Democrats stripped the House Ways and Means Committee—and Mills—of much of its power. He resigned the chairmanship before the end of the year. The humbled Mills apologized to his constituents for his behavior, underwent treatment for alcoholism, joined Alcoholics Anonymous, and gave public lectures on the dangers of alcohol.

229 *The two men had been friends* Information about Mills and Turner comes from interviews with Frank Turner.

229 *thirty-four percent* The poll taken on August 26 and 27 showed Nixon leading McGovern 64 to 30 percent; in the poll conducted between September 22 and 25, Nixon led 61 to 33 percent. In the most recent poll, which Gallup conducted between September 29 and October 9, and published on October 16, McGovern had slashed Nixon's lead by one percentage point, 60 to 34 per-

cent. On October 16, the Harris Survey published a poll that showed voters favored a Democratic Congress 48 to 39 percent.

229–230   *"Since the federal highway"*   *Congressional Quarterly*, October 14, 1972.

230   *"You're going to have"*   *Congressional Quarterly*, October 14, 1972.

230   *"The Speaker does not"*   *New York Times*, October 19, 1972, See also *Congressional Quarterly*, October 14, 1972.

230   *"LEAVE THE HIGHWAY TRUST"*   *Better Roads*, December 1972.

230   *"We've used about every cent"*   *Wall Street Journal*, October 23, 1972.

231   *"one of the most gifted"*   Quoted from a press release issued by the White House on December 11, 1972.

231   *"probably the worst"*   *New York Times*, December 24, 1972. See also *New York Times*, December 8, 1972.

231   *"the continued development"*   *New York Times*, December 10, 1972.

231   *"I well recognize"*   *Los Angeles Times*, February 8, 1973.

232   *"Highways alone cannot"*   Washington *Evening Star-News*, February 16, 1973.

232   *"I propose that our States"*   Richard Nixon radio address on community development, March 4, 1973; Message to Congress, March 8, 1973.

232   *"not only to reduce"*   Washington *Evening Star-News*, February 20, 1973.

232   *"My city of Chicago"*   See also Washington *Evening Star-News*, March 5, 1973; and *Baltimore Sun*, March 20, 1973.

233   *"Conferees met"*   See, for example, *Congressional Record*, May 12, 1973.

233   *Highway Action Coalition had only busted the trust*   After busting the trust, John Kramer left the Highway Action Coalition, not to continue his doctoral studies at Oxford, but to head the Office of Policy and Planning at the Illinois Department of Transportation. In 1977, Illinois Governor James Thompson appointed Kramer to be the state's secretary of transportation. He succeeded a past president of the American Association of State Highway and Transportation Officials.

Sources and Notes

234 *Ten Hills section*   Information for this section comes from an interview with Nora Driscoll and documents provided by her and Justin Gray.

235 *"We just abandoned it"*   Interview with Nora Driscoll.

235 *they formed SCAT*   Driscoll documents.

236 *"Four years ago"*   Videotape of Frances Sargent from the Massachusetts Department of Public Works.

236 *The highway is completely*   Noise Abatement Basic Design Report and Project Summary, prepared for Massachusetts Department of Public Works, March 1976, p. 13.

Chapter 10: NEW RULES

240 *Francis Cutler Turner*   Source of this story and quotations that follow is from an interview with Turner. See also Patton, *The Open Road*, p. 149.

242 *"the alternative of not"*   See *Action Plan for Consideration of Social, Economic & Environmental Effects*, U.S. Department of Transportation, Federal Highway Administration, Washington, D.C., 1976.

242 *Your Rights and Benefits*   *Your Rights and Benefits as a Highway Displacee Under the Federal Relocation Assistance Program*, U.S. Department of Transportation, Federal Highway Administration, Washington, D.C., 1977.

243 *"how citizens can be"*   *Effective Citizen Participation in Transportation Planning*, U.S. Department of Transportation, Federal Highway Administration, Washington, D.C., 1976, 2 vols.

243 *"The direct relevance"*   *Highways and Ecology: Impact Assessment and Mitigation*, prepared for the Federal Highway Administration, Springfield, VA: National Technical Information Service, March 1978, p. ii.

243 *"heavy traffic leads"*   *Liveable Urban Streets: Managing Traffic in Urban Neighborhoods*, Federal Highway Administration, Washington, D.C., 1976, p. xvi.

243 *"the number of highway vehicles"*   *Transportation Noise and Control*, Department of Transportation, Washington, D.C., p. 10.

243 *"mixing the sexes seemed"*   Douglas B. Gurin, *Travel Patterns and Problems of Suburban High School Males: Exploratory Study of the Physical Mobility of Popula-*

Sources and Notes

tion Subgroup, with Recommendations, U.S. Department of Transportation, Federal Highway Administration, Office of Program and Policy Planning, Socio-Economic Studies Division, Washington, D.C., 1974, pp. 81–82 and 352.

244 *"This Time the Wolf"* Daniel Yergin, *The Prize: The Epic Quest for Oil, Money, and Power*, p. 591.

245 *"Conservation is not"* *The Prize: The Epic Quest for Oil, Money, and Power*, p. 591.

246 *Motorists were angry* New York Times, December 4, 1973; and WEIN-GROFF.

246 *Conservation only diminished* See "Highway and the Petroleum Problem—4 Reports," FHWA Bulletin, October 2, 1975. The statistics in this paragraph come from Joseph Ullman's report "The Anticipated Effects of the Gasoline Shortage on the Federal Highway Trust Fund," pp. 9–10; and James W. March's "Highway Financing as Affected by the Petroleum Shortage and Inflation," p. 5.

246 *"by getting rid of all"* Ralph Waldo Emerson, "Manners," *Essays*, Second Series, 1844.

247 *"carpooling was almost ignored"* Quoted from Robert L. Peskin, Joseph L. Schofer, and Peter R. Stopher, *The Immediate Impact of Gasoline Shortages on Urban Travel Behavior*, Federal Highway Administration Final Report, April 1975.

248 *"Project Independence"* Nixon spoke on November 7, 1973. Even though his advisers told him "the goal of energy independence by 1980 was impossible," the president persisted in holding out such a hope to the American people. See *The Prize: The Epic Quest for Oil, Money, and Power*, pp. 617–618.

248 *"moral equivalent of war"* Quoted from Carter, *Public Papers: 1977*, p. 656. Actually, Carter borrowed the phrase from his energy secretary, James Schlesinger, who in turn had borrowed it from William James. See Yergin, *The Prize: The Epic Quest for Oil, Money, and Power*, pp. 662–663.

248 *"I ask you to drive"* Carter, *Public Papers: 1979*, p. 803.

249 *"thirty-one moved to a place"* William H. Whyte, *City: Rediscovering the Center* pp. 287–288. Whyte's chapter "The Corporate Exodus" contains the figures that I repeat in this section.

Sources and Notes

250   *"Many people advocate"*   Quoted in *Peter's Quotations.*

251   *"Thanks to the interstate"*   Quoted from *On the Road with Charles Kuralt*, p. 17.

251   *"strong light works of engineers"*   Walt Whitman, "Passage to India."

251   *"astounding exhibition of the power"*   Quoted by David McCullough in *The Great Bridge: The Epic Story of the Building of the Brooklyn Bridge*, p. 533.

251   *"cathedral of commerce"*   Samuel Parkes Cadman, quoted in *The Cathedral of Commerce*, a promotional brochure published in commemoration of the opening of the Woolworth Building. The words "nickel dime tower" are not mine, of course, but come from Hart Crane's *The Bridge.*

251   *Boulder Dam to "create activity"*   *Papers and Addresses of Franklin D. Roosevelt*, Vol. 5, p. 355.

251   *"partnership between the Federal Government"*   Kennedy, *Public Papers, January 1 to November 22, 1963*, p. 854. See also *New York Times*, November 15, 1963; and archival film from CBS and NBC.

252   *viewers seemed no longer interested*   In 1970, when Apollo 13 encountered life-threatening difficulties on its journey to the moon, television networks pre-empted their daytime programming to present coverage of the drama taking place in space. Many viewers, however, were not happy and phoned the networks to complain about the interruption of soap operas and reruns of programs like *I Love Lucy.*

253   *highway known as the "Mixing Bowl"*   Douglas Fugate, "Unscrambling the Mixing Bowl," *American Highways*, October 1970.

254   *Charles Shumate*   Though environmentalists later derisively called him "Blacktop Charlie," Shumate was a thoroughly decent individual. Information about him comes from his 1989 interview with the American Association of State Highway and Transportation Officials; author's interview with Ellis Armstrong; "Presentation of the 1970 Thomas H. MacDonald Award to Chas. E. Shumate," *American Highways*, January 1971; and Shumate's article "Colorado Straight Creek Tunnel I-70," *American Highways*, October 1969.

254   *"But I ran out"*   Shumate, AASHTO interview.

255   *"putting a five-story building"*   "Colorado Straight Creek Tunnel I-70," *American Highways*, October 1969.

Sources and Notes

256 *"We had done everything"* Shumate, AASHTO interview.

256 *"possibly the most effective"* WEINGROFF.

256 *"I told many people"* Shumate, AASHTO interview.

256 *Mr. Jamet P. Bonnema* See *Life*, December 8, 1972.

257 *"Some years ago"* *Washington Post*, November 10, 1972.

257 *"She was a brilliant gal"* Shumate, AASHTO interview.

257 *"You put one woman in"* *New York Times*, November 10, 1972.

257 *"The District Judge"* Shumate, AASHTO interview.

257 *"They had a woman"* *Life*, December 8, 1972.

258 *Interstate 66 in Virginia* See correspondence and plans for the highway in COLLEGE PARK. Typical of the opposition was this December 1973 letter from a Falls Church resident: *"One* mature tree is the equivalent of *10* room air conditioners running *20* hours a day. The estimates of trees to be destroyed should Route I-66 be built range from 20,000 to 80,000!! . . . Concrete and automobile exhaust ruin our environment. Public transportation is our only hope." See also I-66 file in WEINGROFF.

258 *Interstate 93* See I-93 file in WEINGROFF.

259 *Interstate 80* "Dedication Interstate 80," a ceremony program found in WEINGROFF. Though the regional administrator said, "This will go down in history," there was little fanfare about the opening in the newspapers. See *Deseret News*, August 23, 1986. On August 19, several days before the opening, the Ogden, Utah, *Standard-Examiner* published an editorial cartoon depicting a jam of automobiles waiting to enter the new highway. The caption read, "Ladies and Gentlemen, Start your traffic congestion."

Chapter 11: CONTINENTAL DRIFT

261 *"In the United States"* *Gertrude Stein's America*, p. 79.

262 *"Helig-Meyers Selects Hesperia"* Press release, City of Hesperia, California, October 17, 1996.

Sources and Notes

262 *"When I was sixteen"* From a letter found on the Internet UFO Bulletin board.

263 *determine the "population center"* Information about the population center comes from the *World Almanac*.

265 *"Our standard of living"* Interview with Andreas Duany, 1996.

265 *"We've been told over and over"* See *Los Angeles Times*, November 11, 1971, Section IV, p. 1; and December 23, 1971, Section IV, p. 1.

265 *"Freeways and freeway driving"* See *Los Angeles Times*, December 23, 1971, Section IV, p. 1.

266 *"Now nobody knows"* Private interview, November 1996.

266 *"What Linko does"* *Washington Post*, February 26, 1972.

267 *"It sounded like the end"* National Public Radio broadcast on "All Things Considered," February 1992.

268 *"A crowd moves in"* Peter Sears, "Accident," anthologized in Kurt Brown's *Drive, They Said: Poems About Americans and Their Cars*, p. 181.

269 *"The car was full of white men"* James Baldwin, "Sonny's Blues," in *Going to Meet the Man*, p. 117.

269 *"on the long drive"* Courtland Milloy, Jr., "Black Highways: Thirty Years Ago in the South, We Didn't Dare Stop," *Washington Post*, June 21, 1987.

269 *The Negro Motorist* These guidebooks are rare. I found *The Negro Motorist Green Book*, along with *The Traveler's Guide: Hotels, Apartments, Rooms, Meals, Garage Accommodations, Etc. for Colored Travelers*, the *Afro Travel Guide*, the *Go Guide*, and the *Travel Guide*, in the Schomberg Collection at the New York Public Library. A copy of *Negro Hotels and Guest Houses* is located in the Library of Congress.

270 *"long published information"* *The Negro Motorist Green Book*, 1948, p. 1.

270 *"to go further"* *The Negro Motorist Green Book*, 1948, p. 11.

270 *"By the time we got"* Interview with Irene Staple, 1997.

270 *"There will be a day"* *The Negro Motorist Green Book*, 1948, p. 1.

Sources and Notes

271 *"Today, I'm happy to be"* Courtland Milloy, Jr., "Black Highways: Thirty Years Ago in the South, We Didn't Dare Stop," *Washington Post*, June 21, 1987.

271 *"The motor-car has restored"* Edith Wharton, *A Motor Flight Through France*, p. 1. See Virginia Scharff, *Taking the Wheel: Women and the Coming of the Motor Age*, p. 24.

271 *"the ones with the more wires"* Alice Huyler Ramsey, *Veil, Duster and Tire Iron*, p. 79.

271 *In 1915, Sarah Bard Field* Cited from Virginia Scharff, *Taking the Wheel: Women and the Coming of the Motor Age*, p. 86.

271 *"Thrill-seeking flappers"* Virginia Scharff, *Taking the Wheel: Women and the Coming of the Motor Age*, p. 163.

272 *"big car room"* Quoted from automobile advertisements found in 1957 issues of the *Saturday Evening Post*.

272 *"to get away from their parents"* Virginia Scharff, letter to Larry Hott, Florentine Films, February 3, 1993.

273 *"On I-80"* Barbara Smith, "I-80," in Kurt Brown's anthology *Drive, They Said: Poems About Americans and Their Cars*, p. 34.

274 *"It's worse on Sunday nights"* Author's interview with Anthony DiOrio, February 1997.

274 *"I think noise walls"* Interview with Ken Krulkemeyer, Florentine Films.

275 *"In the twentieth century"* Quoted from George F. Kennan's *Around the Cragged Hill: A Personal and Political Philosophy*, p. 162. Kennan indicts all of the automobile's bad qualities—"the enemy of community generally . . . wasteful of material, energy, and space . . . a major polluter" (pp. 161–162). He titled the chapter in which he made these remarks "The Addictions."

275 *"a rootless, aimless"* Lewis Mumford, *The Highway and the City*, p. 179.

275 *The stories that appear* The crime stories that follow have been culled from files in WEINGROFF as well as additional contemporary newspaper materials.

276 *"When you live near"* Albany *Times Union*, September 18, 1994.

Sources and Notes

276–277   *"Drive Me Wild"*   WEINGROFF.

277   *"They are wonderful"*   Interview with William E. Borah, January 1997.

277   *"a conduit of national blandness"*   Letter to Larry Hott, Florentine Films, January 23, 1993.

Chapter 12: THE GREATEST OF IMPROVEMENTS

280   *the village's hotels could accommodate*   See the 1899 edition of Karl Baedeker's *The United States*, p. 198.

280   *"Large Interior Court"*   Quoted from an advertisement in the *Visitors' and Automobilists' Guide Book of Saratoga Springs New York*, n.p.

281   *"automobiling center of the east"*   Quoted from the *Visitors' and Automobilists' Guide Book of Saratoga Springs New York*, p. 70.

283   *"fast buck promoters"*   See William S. Kowinski, *The Malling of America: An Inside Look at the Great Consumer Paradise.*

283   *Raymond Albert Kroc and Charles Kemmons Wilson*   See Patton, *The Open Road*, pp. 197–200.

284   *Howard Buster Johnson*   See "Ho Jo Rest," *Fortune*, September 1940, p. 84 ff., and Patton, *The Open Road*, pp. 195–197.

284   *"The [motel room] was immaculate"*   *Travels with Charlie*, p. 45.

284   *"reductive kitchen"*   *Esquire*, December 1983.

287   *In 1996, the General Motors*   The strike, which was a major labor story in 1996, began on March 4 when 3,200 workers walked off their jobs assembling brakes in Dayton, Ohio. Because the factory supplied brakes to GM plants across the country, as well as Mexico and Canada, the number of workers idled grew by the hour. By March 11, some 58,000 GM workers in 30 plants were idle. The next day, the number jumped to 83,000. By March 21, the day the parties settled, over 177,000 workers were idle and General Motors had lost over a billion dollars in pretax profits. Other layoffs occurred at 1,600 companies that supplied General Motors with parts. See *New York Times*, March 12, 13, and 22, 1996.

287   *"I-287, in New York"*   WEINGROFF.

Sources and Notes

288 *Mianus River Bridge* See James D. Cooper and Eric Munley, "Bridge Research: Leading the Way to the Future," *Public Roads*, Summer 1995, pp. 23–27; and WEINGROFF.

288 *As horrible as the failure* I owe a great debt for the facts about Schoharie Creek to a student paper by Mercedes Kulick submitted in a course on the Interstate Highway System that I taught at Skidmore College.

289 *"Everyone knows it's a bear"* Interview with Frank Griggs, 1996.

290 *"Every politician likes"* WEINGROFF.

290 *In the early eighties* See Wilbur S. Smith, "Current Highway Transportation Interests," *Transportation Quarterly,* Vol. 15, No. 2, pp. 131–141.

290 *The age of the "edge city"* I have relied on Joel Garreau's excellent book *Edge City* for most of this section.

291 *"They grew"* Interview with Joel Garreau, Florentine Films, 1996.

291 *African-Americans in central Atlanta* For more on the black middle class in Atlanta, see *Edge Cities*, pp. 144–178, which is the source of my paragraph.

292 *"induced demand"* *New York Times*, June 2, 1996.

292 *"It's as if we"* David Bernstein, professor of civil engineering at Princeton University, quoted in *New York Times*, June 2, 1996.

292 *"Once she was on the freeway"* *Play It as It Lays*, p.17.

293 *"big dig"* Information about the big dig comes from the Massachusetts Transportation Library in Boston; and WEINGROFF.

Selected Bibliography

← ·— ·—·—·—·—·—·—·—·—·—·—

ARCHITECTURE AND ENGINEERING

Andrews, J. C. *The Well-Built Elephant: a Tribute to American Eccentricity*. New York: Congdon & Weed, 1984.

Banham, Reyner. *Los Angeles: The Architecture of Four Ecologies*. New York: Harper & Row, 1971.

————. *Megastructure: Urban Futures of the Recent Past*. New York: Harper & Row, 1976.

Bel Geddes, Norman. *Horizons*. Little, Brown, 1923.

Broadwater, Maxine Beachy. *My Camera Lens Does Not Lie: Photographic Works, Writings, and History of Leo Beachy*. Grantsville, Maryland: Sincell Publishing, 1996.

Brodsley, David. *L.A. Freeway: An Appreciative Essay*. Berkeley: University of California Press, 1981.

Greenough, Horatio. *Form and Function*. Berkeley: University of California Press, 1947.

Holl, Steven. *Edge of a City*. New York: Princeton Architectural Press, 1991.

Le Corbusier. *Urbanisme*. 1924. Translated as *The City of Tomorrow*. New York: Dover, 1987.

Selected Bibliography

Stephenson, Richard W. *"A Plan Whol[l]y New"*: Pierre Charles L'Enfant's Plan of the City of Washington. Washington, DC: Library of Congress, 1933.

Stewart, George R. *U.S. 40: Cross Section of the United States of America*. Boston: Houghton Mifflin, 1953.

Stofflet, Mary. *California Cityscapes*. New York: Universe, 1991.

Tunnard, Chistopher, and Pushkarev, Boris. *Man-Made America: Chaos or Control*. New Haven, CT: Yale University Press, 1963.

Twentieth Century Engineering. New York: Museum of Modern Art, 1964.

Vale, Thomas R., and Geraldine R. Vale. *U.S. 40 Today*. Madison: University of Wisconsin Press, 1983.

Wright, Frank Lloyd. *Collected Writings*. Vol. 2. New York: Rizzoli, 1992.

AUTOMOBILE CULTURE

Clymer, Floyd. *Henry's Wonderful Model T*. New York: Bonanza Books, 1955.

Donovan, Frank. *Wheels for a Nation*. New York, Thomas Y. Crowell, 1965.

Finch, Christopher. *Highways to Heaven: The Autobiography of America*. New York: HarperCollins, 1992.

Flink, James J. *The Automobile Age*. Cambridge, MA: MIT Press, 1988.

Gunnell, John. *Standard Catalog on American Cars, 1946–1975*. Iola, WI: Krause, 1995.

Jennings, Jan. *Roadside America: The Automobile in Design and Culture*. Ames: Iowa State University Press, 1990.

Laas, William. *Freedom of the American Road*. Ford Motor Company, 1956.

Pettifer, Julian, and Nigel Turner. *Automania: Man and the Motor Car*. Boston: Little, Brown, 1984.

Rae, John B. *The Road and the Car in American Life*. Cambridge, MA: MIT Press, 1971.

Sears, Stephen W. *The American Heritage History of the Automobile in America*. New York: Simon & Schuster, 1977.

COMMENTARY AND CRITICISM

Blake, Peter. *God's Own Junkyard: The Planned Deterioration of America's Landscape*. New York: Holt, Rinehart and Winston, 1964.

Brodsley, David. *L.A. Freeway: An Appreciative Essay*. Berkeley: University of California Press, 1981.

Buel, Ronald A. *Dead End: The Automobile in Mass Transportation*. Englewood Cliffs, NJ: Prentice-Hall, 1972.

Burby, John. *The Great American Motion Sickness: Or, Why You Can't Get There From Here*. Boston: Little, Brown, 1971.

Garreau, Joel. *Edge City: Life on the New Frontier*. New York: Doubleday, 1991.

Graham, David. *Only in America*. New York: Knopf, 1991.

Selected Bibliography

Jakle, John A., and David Wilson. *Derelict Landscapes*. Savage, MD: Rowman & Littlefield, 1992.

Jones, Peter C. *The Changing Face of America*. New York: Prentice-Hall, 1991.

Keats, John. *The Crack in the Picture Window*. Cambridge, MA: Riverside Press, 1956.

————. *The Insolent Chariots*. Philadelphia: Lippincott, 1958.

Kelley, Benjamin A. *The Pavers and the Paved*. New York: Donald W. Brown, 1971.

Leavitt, Helen. *Superhighway—Superhoax*. Garden City, NY: Doubleday, 1970.

McShane, Clay, *Down the Asphalt Path: The Automobile and the American City*. New York: Columbia University Press, 1994.

Marx, Leo. *The Machine in the Garden: Technology and the Pastoral in America*. New York: Oxford University Press, 1964.

Moses, Robert. *Public Works: A Dangerous Trade*. New York: McGraw-Hill, 1970.

Mumford, Lewis, *The Highway and the City*. New York: Harcourt Brace Jovanovitch, 1963.

Nader, Ralph. *Unsafe at Any Speed: The Designed-in Dangers of the American Automobile*. New York: Grossman, 1965.

Patton, Phil. *The Open Road: A Celebration of the American Highway*. New York: Simon & Schuster, 1986.

Schneider, Kenneth R. *Autokind vs Mankind*. New York: Norton, 1971.

Scientific American. Cities. New York: Knopf, 1965.

Thompson, George F., ed. *Landscape in America*. Austin: University of Texas Press, 1995.

Udall, Stuart L. *The Quiet Crisis*. New York: Holt, Rinehart and Winston, 1963.

Whyte, William H. *City: Rediscovering the Center*. New York: Doubleday, 1988.

————. *The Last Landscape*. New York: Doubleday, 1968

HISTORY AND BIOGRAPHY

Ambrose, Stephen E. *Eisenhower: The President*. New York: Simon & Schuster, 1984.

American Association of State Highway Officials. *Public Roads of the Past: Historic American Highways*. Washington, DC: American Association of State Highway Officials, 1953.

————. *Public Roads of the Past: 3500 B.C. to 1800 A.D.* Washington, DC: American Association of State Highway Officials, 1953.

American Association of State Highway and Transportation Officials. *AASHTO 1914–1989: Moving America into the Future*. Washington, DC: American Association of State Highway and Transportation Officials, 1990.

————. *The States and the Interstates: Research on the Planning, Design and Construction of the Interstate and Defense Highway System*. Washington, DC: American Association of State Highway and Transportation Officials, 1991.

Selected Bibliography

Banham, Reyner. *Megastructure: Urban Futures of the Recent Past*. New York: Harper & Row, 1976.

Baumbach, Richard O., Jr., and William E. Borah. *The Second Battle of New Orleans*. Tuscaloosa: University of Alabama Press, 1981.

Belasco, Warren James. *Americans on the Road: From Autocamp to Motel, 1910–1945*. Cambridge, MA: MIT Press, 1981

Bryan, Robert L. and Lawrence H. Larsen. *The Eisenhower Administration: A Documentary History*. New York: Random House, 1971.

Caro, Robert A. *The Power Broker: Robert Moses and the Fall of New York*. New York: Knopf, 1974.

Carter, Jimmy. *Public Papers of the Presidents of the United States*. Vol. 1, January 20 to June 24, 1977. Washington, DC: Government Printing Office, 1978.

Columbia Broadcasting System. *Fifty Years on Wheels: A Broadcast Commemorating the 50th Anniversary of the Automobile Industry in America*. New York: Columbia Broadcasting System, 1946.

Dictionary of American Biography. Dumas Malone, ed. New York: Scribner's, 1928–37.

Dunbar, Seymour. *A History of Travel in America*. New York: Tudor, 1937.

Ehrlichman, John. *Witness to Power*. New York: Simon & Schuster, 1982.

Eisenhower, Dwight D. *At Ease: Stories I Tell to Friends*. New York: Doubleday, 1967.

Foster, Mark S. *From Streetcar to Superhighway: American City Planners and Urban Transportation, 1900–1940*. Philadelphia: Temple University Press, 1981.

Gillespie, Hugh M. *A Century of Progress: The History of Hot Mix Asphalt*. N.p.: National Asphalt Pavement Association, 1992.

Gitlin, Todd. *The Sixties: Years of Hope, Days of Rage*. New York: Bantam, 1987.

Goddard, Stephen B. *Getting There: the Epic Struggle Between Road and Rail in the American Century*. New York: Basic Books, 1994.

Goodwin, Doris Kearns. *No Ordinary Time*. New York: Simon & Schuster, 1994.

Halberstam, David. *The Fifties*. New York: Villard Books, 1993.

Hokanson, Drake. *The Lincoln Highway: Main Street Across America*. Iowa City: University of Iowa Press, 1988.

Huggins, Eleanor, and John Olmsted. *Adventures on & off Interstate 80*. Palo Alto, CA: Tioga, 1985.

Jackson, Kenneth T. *Crabgrass Frontier: The Suburbanization of the United States*. New York: Oxford University Press, 1985.

Kelly, Barbara M. *Expanding the American Dream: Building and Rebuilding Levittown*. Albany: State University of New York Press, 1993.

Kennan, George F. *Around the Cragged Hill: A Personal and Political Philosophy*. New York: Norton, 1993.

Kennedy, John F. *Public Papers of the Presidents of the United States, January 1, to November 22, 1963*. Washington, DC: Government Printing Office, 1964.

Selected Bibliography

Krieg, Joan P., ed. *Robert Moses: Single-Minded Genius*. Interlaken, NY: Heart of the Lakes, 1989.

Labatut, Jean, and Wheaton J. Lane, eds. *Highways and Our National Life*. Princeton, NJ: Princeton University Press, 1950.

Lewis, Eugene. *Public Entrepreneurship: Toward a Theory of Bureaucratic Political Power: The Organizational Lives of Hyman Rickover, J. Edgar Hoover, and Robert Moses*. Bloomington: Indiana University Press, 1980.

Liell, John Thomas. "Levittown: A Study in Community Planning and Development." Ph.D. diss., Yale University, 1952.

Lincoln Highway Association. *The Complete Official Road Guide of the Lincoln Highway*. Detroit: privately printed, 1919.

Lind, William E. "Thomas H. MacDonald: A Study of the Career of an Engineer Administrator and His Influence on Public Roads in the United States, 1919–1953." Master's thesis, American University, 1965.

Lynd, Robert S. *Middletown in Transition: A Study in Cultural Conflicts*. New York: Harcourt, Brace 1937.

Lynd, Robert S., and Helen Merrell Lynd. *Middletown: A Study in Contemporary American Culture*. New York: Harcourt, Brace, 1929.

McCullough, David. *The Great Bridge: The Epic Story of the Building of the Brooklyn Bridge*. New York: Simon & Schuster, 1972.

————. *Truman*. New York: Simon & Schuster, 1992.

Meikle, Jeffrey L. *Twentieth Century Limited*. Philadelphia: Temple University Press, 1979.

Morison, Samuel Eliot. *The Oxford History of the American People*. New York: Oxford University Press, 1965.

Moseley, Leonard. *Blood Relations*. New York: Atheneum, 1980.

Mumford, Lewis. *The City in History*. New York, Harcourt, Brace & World, 1961.

Nevins, Allan. *Ford: The Times, the Man, the Company*. New York: Charles Scribners' Sons, 1954.

Newlon, Howard, Jr., and Nathaniel Mason Pawlett. *Backsights*. N.p.: Virginia Department of Highways & Transportation, n.d.

Pierson, George Wilson. *Tocqueville in America*. Gloucester, MA: Peter Smith, 1969.

Radde, Bruce. *The Meritt Parkway*. New Haven and London: Yale University Press, 1993.

Rae, John B. *The American Automobile Industry*. Boston: Twayne, 1984.

Rather, Dan, and Gary Paul Gates. *The Palace Guard*. New York: Harper & Row, 1974.

Remini, Robert V. *Andrew Jackson and the Course of American Freedom, 1822–1832*. New York: Harper & Row, 1981.

Reps, John W. *Washington on View: The Nation's Capital Since 1790*. Chapel Hill and London: University of North Carolina Press, 1991.

Rodgers, Cleveland. *Robert Moses, Builder for Democracy*. New York: Holt, 1952.

Selected Bibliography

Roosevelt, Franklin D. *Papers and Addresses of Franklin D. Roosevelt*. Vol. 5. New York: Random House, 1938.

Rosengrant, Susan, and David Lampe. *Route 128: Lessons from Boston's High-Tech Community*. New York: Basic Books, 1992.

Sayre, Nora. *Sixties Going on Seventies*. New York: Arbor House, 1973.

Scharff, Virginia. *Taking the Wheel: Women and the Coming of the Motor Age*. New York: Free Press, 1991.

Schwartz, Joel. *The New York Approach: Robert Moses, Urban Liberals, and Redevelopment of the Inner City*. Columbus: Ohio State University Press, 1993.

Seely, Bruce E. *Building the American Highway System: Engineers as Policy Makers*. Philadelphia: Temple University Press, 1987.

Shink, William H. *Vanderbilt's Folly: A History of the Pennsylvania Turnpike*. York, PA: American Canal and Transportation Center, 1973.

Small, Kenneth A., Clifford Winston, and Carol A. Evans. *Road Work: A New Highway Pricing and Investment Policy*. Washington, DC: Brookings Institution, 1989.

Stover, John F. *American Railroads*. Chicago and London: University of Chicago Press, 1961.

Taylor, George Rogers. *The Transportation Revolution, 1815–1860*. New York: Harper & Row, 1951.

Wright, Gwendolyn. *Building the Dream: A Social History of Housing in America*. Cambridge, MA: MIT Press, 1983.

Yergin, Daniel. *The Prize: The Epic Quest for Oil, Money, and Power*. New York: Simon & Schuster, 1991.

LITERATURE

Baldwin, James. *Going to Meet the Man*. New York: Dial Press, 1965.

Berger, K. T. *Where the Road and the Sky Collide: America Through the Eyes of Its Drivers*. New York: Henry Holt, 1993.

Brown, Kurt, ed. *Drive, They Said: Poems About Americans and Their Cars*. Minneapolis, MN: Milkweed Editions, 1994.

Dettlebach, Cynthia Golomb. *In the Driver's Seat: The Automobile in American Literature and Popular Culture*. Westport, CT: Greenwood Press, 1976.

Didion, Joan. *Play It as It Lays*. New York: Farrar, Straus & Giroux, 1970.

Fitzgerald, F. Scott. *The Great Gatsby*. New York: Scribner's, 1925.

Harrison, Gilbert., ed. *Gertrude Stein's America*. New York: Liveright, 1974.

Kerouac, Jack. *On the Road*. New York: Signet, 1957.

Lewis, Sinclair. *Babbitt*. New York: Harcourt Brace, 1922.

Stein, Gertrude. *The Geographical History of America, or, The Relation of Human Nature to the Human Mind*. New York: Random House, 1936.

———. *Lectures in America*. New York: Random House, 1935.

Steinbeck, John. *Travels with Charley in Search of America*. New York: Bantam, 1963.

Whitman, Walt. *Complete Poetry and Selected Prose*. Boston: Houghton Mifflin, 1959.

Selected Bibliography

TRAVEL

American Automobile Association. *Year Book, 1907*. New York: American Automobile Association, 1907.

The Automobile Green Book. Indianapolis, IN: Scarborough Motor Guide, 1923.

Automobile Legal Association. *The ALA Green Book*. Boston: Automobile Legal Association, 1966.

Baedeker, Karl. *The United States with an Excursion into Mexico*. New York: Charles Scribner's Sons, 1899.

Federal Writers' Project. *Iowa: A Guide to the Hawkeye State*. New York: Hastings House, 1949.

Kost, Mary Lu. *Milepost I-80*. Sacramento, CA: Milepost, 1993.

Kuralt, Charles. *On the Road with Charles Kuralt*. New York: Putnam, 1985.

The Next Exit. Franklin, NC: Next Exit, 1992.

Post, Emily. *By Motor to the Golden Gate*. New York: D. Appleton, 1916.

Ramsey, Alice Huyler. *Veil, Duster and Tire Iron*. Covina, CA: privately printed, 1961.

Saratogian (newspaper). *Visitors' and Automobilists' Guide Book of Saratoga Springs New York*. Saratoga Springs, NY: *Saratogian*, 1910.

Tocqueville, Alexis, Count de. *Journey to America*. Translated by George Lawrence, edited by J. P. Mayer. London: Faber and Faber, 1959.

Wharton, Edith. *A Motor Flight Through France*. New York: Charles Scribner's Sons, 1908.

Acknowledgments

It is a happy task to discharge at least some of the many debts I accumulated while writing this book.

At the beginning of this project I received sage advice from Lizzie Grossman of Sterling Lord, Literistic, who urged me to take up this project and who has given me generous encouragement along the way.

I owe a special debt to Wendy Wolf, my editor. Wendy knew when and how to ask just the right questions and helped me more than anyone else to shape this book in a way that would make it accessible to readers. I trust her counsel, value her friendship, and am ever grateful for her forbearance, which at times has passed all understanding.

I am especially grateful to Nelly Bly and Kate Griggs at Viking for their help with the production of this manuscript.

As I started my book, I began work on a documentary film about the subject with Larry Hott of Florentine Films. Larry has been a part of this project from the beginning, and he has helped me in countless ways. We have spent many hours discussing the role the Interstates have played in the transformation of American life, and I have profited

Acknowledgments

especially from his shrewd understanding of the landscape and the environment. In my own research for this book, I have used the transcripts of interviews Larry conducted with dozens of people, and occasionally have incorporated their comments into my manuscript. Others at Florentine Films have also helped me. They include Diane Garey, our editor; Allen Moore, the cameraman; and Joan E. Kane and Susan Orlosky, researchers.

Larry Hott and I were fortunate to assemble a first-rate group of highway scholars, architects, engineers, historians, and social scientists to advise us, and I have drawn freely from their observations in writing this book. They include Alan Altshuler, Ed Blakeley, Thomas Colbert, William Cronon, David Dillon, Susan Douglas, Joel Garreau, William Garrison, Willard Gatewood, Jonathan Gifford, Neil Goldschmidt, Jose Gomez-Ibanez, Michelle Grijalva, Richard Immerman, Steven Izenour, Ulrich Keller, Char Miller, Howard Newlon, Lisa Newton, Ellen-Jane Pader, Phil Patton, Mark Rose, Sandra Rosenbloom, Virginia Scharff, Denise Scott Brown, Joni Seager, Bruce Seely, Chuck Turner, Robert Venturi, Martin Wachs, and Bernard Weisberger. I want to thank particularly Frank E. Griggs, an engineer and a humanist, who helped me to better understand the profession of civil engineering in the 1950s.

I am especially grateful to Richard Weingroff of the Federal Highway Administration. He is a selfless and dedicated employee, an extraordinary repository of knowledge about the Interstates and highway history, and he has freely helped me with his time and expertise.

Alan Wheelock of Skidmore College and his wife, Renate, have read various drafts of this manuscript, made intelligent criticisms, provided useful quotations, and shared books and photographs from their private collection of American culture.

I owe a great debt to others who have generously assisted me: Ellis Armstrong, former head of the Bureau of Public Roads; William E. Borah, Fred Guice, and John Nicklaus of New Orleans; Margaret Oberlin of Orlando, Florida; William D. Hickman, American Highway Users Alliance; Francis Turner, former Federal Highway administrator; the late Lee Mertz, former employee of the Federal Highway Administration who was writing a history of the Interstate system at the time of his death and who freely shared his information with me; Charles E. Blue, public information officer, National Academy of Engineering; Steven A. Ronning, noise specialist, Federal Highway Administration; Kyung Kyu Lim and David J. Hensing, American Association of

Acknowledgments

State Highway and Transportation Officials; John Puglia, Roadway Express Company; Tamara Robinson of public television station WNET; Phyllis Geller, Noel Gunther, Sharon Rockefeller, and David Thompson of public television station WETA; William Buzenberg, former vice president for news, National Public Radio; Mary Beth Kirchner and Robert Rand, independent radio producers; Jim Daugherty and Joseph Herring of the National Endowment for the Humanities; Dr. William C. Young of Poplar Bluff, Missouri; Nora Driscoll, Justin Gray, and Jean Riesman of Boston; Sheafe Satterthwaite of Williams College; and Robert and Peggy Boyers, Ralph Ciancio, Hunt Conard, John Danison, Robert D. Foulke, Stephen Otrembiak, Phyllis Roth, and the late Philip J. West of Skidmore College.

I would not have been able to write this book without the help of numerous librarians and archivists. I want to thank particularly Marilyn Scheffer and Shirley E. Webb, interlibrary loan specialists at the Scribner Library, Skidmore College; Lee Dalzell, head of reference, and Peter Giordano, head of government documents librarians, Williams College Library; The University of Lowell Library; Verne W. Newton, director, Franklin Delano Roosevelt Library; the reference staff of the Federal Highways Administration Library in Washington; David Pfeiffer, Federal Records Center, College Park, Maryland; the Texas A&M Archives, College Station, Texas; the Eisenhower Library, Abilene, Kansas; the New York State Library; the Moorland-Spingarn Research Center, Howard University; and the American Automobile Association library, Heathrow, Florida.

Some very fine research assistants, including Kate Barrett, Jane Baldwin, Molly Conway, Miriam Johnson, Colin Lewis, Molly McGrann and Johanna Schwartz, have helped me by cataloging tens of thousands of documents and by working in libraries to answer hundreds of questions.

My greatest debt, of course, is to my wife, Jill, steadfast companion, astute critic, wise editor, and patient listener—always.

Index

Abilene, Kansas, 89, 118, 126
Abzug, Bella, 225
Adams, John, 251
Adams, John Quincey, 251
Adams, Sherman, 99, 101, 105
Adorno, Theodor, 277
Advisory Council on Historic Preservation, 208
African-Americans
  attacks on black motorists, 36
  and automobiles, 35
  automobile travel on modern roads, 269
  communities displaced by Interstates, 186–89, 197, 199
  and discrimination, 36, 269–71
  and discrimination in suburbia, 78–79
  engineers, 132
  form automobile club, 36
  travel guides for, 269–71
  urban renewal and, 193
The Afro Travel Guide, 269
Agnew, Spiro, 207, 214, 216, 247
Albrecht, Donald, 268
Albrecht, Nancy, 268
Allegheny Mountains, 3, 48, 55, 56
Allis-Chalmers, 87, 106
American Association of Highway Builders of the North Atlantic States, 13
American Association of State Highway Officials (AASHO), 92, 121, 148, 160, 161, 162, 202, 223
  connection with Bureau of Public Roads, 110
  construction standards for Interstates, 136
  discussion of federal-aid highway program, 218–19
  and female members, 132
  helps define standards, 15, 18,
  highway construction specifications, 253
  and Interstate signs, 137–38

  lobbies for road improvement, 19, 110
  1956 convention, 127–29
  numbering of Interstates, 136–37
  opposes move to open Highway Trust Fund, 224, 225
  recommends Volpe as Secretary of Transportation
    angered at his actions, 231
  reports on benefits of Interstates, 213–14
  support of Interstates, 144
  and test road, 137–38
  works with MacDonald, 13, 23–24
American Association of Township Officials, 111
American Automobile Association, 13, 36, 99, 110, 111
  Blue Book, 34–35, 36
  opposes highway bill, 117
  opposes opening Highway Trust Fund, 224
  support of Interstates, 144
American Concrete Paving Association, 110
American Highways, 126
American Institute of Architects, 225
American Institute of Public Opinion, 41
American Petroleum Institute, 111, 138
American Public Works Association, 110
American Road Builders Association, 110, 202,
  connections with Jennings Randolph, 222–23
  opposes opening Highway Trust Fund, 224, 225
  support of Interstates, 144
  works with MacDonald, 13
American Truckers Association, 110, 117
Amherst College, 171, 200
Ammann, Othmar, 40
Amtrak, 218
Anderson, Glenn M., 229, 233
Anderson, John, 230

343

Index

Index

Index

Index

Index

IBM, 249
Ickes, Harold, 49,
  as head of Public Works Administration, 59
  proposal for superhighways, 51
Indiana Turnpike, 69
Insurance Institute for Highway Safety, 266
Interagency Committee, 105
Intermodal Surface Transportation Act, 294
International Brotherhood of Teamsters, 106
Interstate Commerce Commission, 85
Interstate 5, 137, 157, 212
Interstate 10, 137, 253, 254
  route through black area of New Orleans,
    186–89, 199
Interstate 15, 140–42, 157, 254, 261–62
Interstate 25, 157
Interstate 29, 121
Interstate 35, 157, 240
Interstate 40, 197, 254
Interstate 66, 258
Interstate 70, 126, 209, 253–56, 276, 293
Interstate 75, 156
  fog on, 267–68, 293
Interstate 76, 197, 200–201
Interstate 80, 138, 155–58, 173–74, 212, 254
  crime on, 275
  drivers block, 246
  opening shunned, 259
Interstate 81, 152
Interstate 87, 137, 212, 279–81, 285
Interstate 90, 121, 137, 254, 260
Interstate 93, 234–36, 258–59
Interstate 94, 212, 253
Interstate 95, 156, 197, 251
  condition of, 287–88
  crime on, 276
Interstate 105, 260
Interstate 180, 157
Interstate 215, 142
Interstate 229, 121
Interstate 275, 293
Interstate 278, 198
Interstate 280, 153, 198
Interstate 285, 291
Interstate 287, 260, 274, 287
Interstate 295, 276
Interstate 310, 186
Interstate 380, 157
Interstate 395, construction of, 253
Interstate 405, 266
Interstate 490, 134
Interstate 495, 213
Interstate 580, 276

Interstate 590, 134
Interstate 680, 292
Interstate 787, 274
Interstate H1, H2, H3 (Hawaii), 211
Interstate Highway System, 88
  compared with other engineering feats,
    250–52
  construction to 1960, 125–53
  construction 1960–1968, 155–75
  cost, 143
  creation, 97–123
  crime on, 275–76
  deterioration of, 287–89
  franchising and, 282–85
  fraud and, 163–68
  highway beautification and, 168–69,
    171–73
  noise on, 234–37, 273–74
  opposition to, 197–99
  safety of, 266–68
  speed limit lowered, 247
  standardization of, 253
  trucking and, 286–87
  use of nuclear explosions to construct,
    170–71
Island Trees, *see* Levittown
Island Trees Tribune, 77
Iowa State College of Agriculture and
  Mechanic Arts, 6–8

Jacks Mountain (Pennsylvania), 55
Jackson, Andrew, 103, 180, 191, 210
Jackson, Henry F., 248
Jackson, Horatio Nelson, 21, 50
James, Arthur, 67
James, William, 248
Jefferson Highway, 51
Jefferson, Thomas, 56, 95, 103, 251
John A. Volpe Construction Company, 129,
  130, 207
Johns Manville, 40
Johnson, Howard, 284
Johnson, Lady Bird, 172–73, 257
Johnson, Lyndon B., 172–73, 186, 206,
  207, 209, 215, 247, 270
  cuts payments from Highway Trust Fund,
    219
Joliffe, Frances, 271
Jones, Walter Adelbert, 47, 64, 66
  appointed head of Turnpike Commission,
    58
  at ground breaking for Pennsylvania
    Turnpike, 59

Index

Index

Index

Index

Index

Index